Renewal

Praise for *Renewal: Remaking America's Schools for the Twenty-First Century*

"*Renewal* tells some important stories about district transformation. Harold Kwalwasser captures the best of the Quality Excellence of Baldrige, good common sense, and the energy and drive he knows it takes to lead system change around student performance. There are important lessons here." —**Anne Bryant**, executive director, National School Boards Association

"In his thought-provoking and thorough new book *Renewal*, Hal Kwalwasser explains the multiple forces that form the backdrop of twenty-first-century public education. By doing that, he has succeeded in weaving together those complex factors into a clear and concise picture of where we now stand, coupled with solid suggestions for the future. With specific anecdotal testimonies from successful practitioners, this is a good handbook for incumbent school district leaders, and should be required reading for all aspiring leaders." —**C. Fred Bateman**, executive director, Urban Superintendents Association of America

"Kwalwasser provides an insightful and thought-provoking overview of American education. His journey across our nation to find answers to the challenges we face in transforming public education opens the door to courageous conversations. This book moves between history and action, and calls upon citizens to be well-informed and engaged in a movement to achieve educational excellence in the twenty-first century." —**Maria G. Ott**, superintendent of schools, Rowland Unified School District, and former deputy superintendent, Los Angeles Unified School Disctrict

Renewal

Remaking America's Schools for the Twenty-First Century

Harold Kwalwasser

ROWMAN & LITTLEFIELD EDUCATION
A division of
ROWMAN & LITTLEFIELD PUBLISHERS, INC.
Lanham • New York • Toronto • Plymouth, UK

KH

Published by Rowman & Littlefield Education
A division of Rowman & Littlefield Publishers, Inc.
A wholly owned subsidiary of The Rowman & Littlefield Publishing Group, Inc.
4501 Forbes Boulevard, Suite 200, Lanham, Maryland 20706
www.rowman.com

10 Thornbury Road, Plymouth PL6 7PP, United Kingdom

British Library Cataloguing in Publication Information Available

Library of Congress Cataloging-in-Publication Data Available

ISBN 978-1-61048-687-3 (cloth : alk. paper)—ISBN 978-1-61048-688-0 (pbk. : alk. paper)—ISBN 978-1-61048-689-7 (electronic)

☉™ The paper used in this publication meets the minimum requirements of American National Standard for Information Sciences Permanence of Paper for Printed Library Materials, ANSI/NISO Z39.48-1992.

Printed in the United States of America

3 / 15 / 13

While doing research for this book, I met Glenny Soto. She was the receptionist at the Best Western in Fall River, Massachusetts, when I checked in. The place was quiet, except for two pretty little girls who were playing in the lounge at the front of the hotel.

I asked Glenny if they were her children. She gave me one of those smiles only a mother can give. So I said, "Do your kids go to school here in Fall River?" She nodded. The next question was obvious: "So how are the schools?"

The answer is the reason for this book: "I am so proud of my girls. They are so bright. The older one was reading at the second grade level when she was in kindergarten. But I don't like the schools. She is now in second grade and still reading at second grade level. I don't know what to do. . . ."

This book is for you, Glenny, and every frustrated parent like you.

Contents

Preface   ix

Introduction   xiii

Part I: The Basics of School Reform   **1**

1   Management Theory 101   3

2   Human Relations 101   9

3   Politics 101   15

Part II: Leaders   **21**

4   Superintendents   23

5   Principals   43

Part III: Teachers   **67**

6   A Brave New World   69

7   Keeping—and Working with—Those You Have   73

8   Training New (and More) Teachers Inside the System   83

9   The Rest of Your Life—Good Teachers Can Always Get Better: The Professional Learning Community   95

10   Training New (and More) Teachers: Working the Pipeline into the Classroom   105

11   Creating More Alternative Training and Certification Programs   111

12   What Is a Good Teacher?: Evaluation in a Professional World   119

13   Tenure   133

14   Motivating Teachers: Is Pay the Be-All and End-All?   141

15   The Coleman Report Effect on Motivation: Do Teachers Have Low Expectations of Poor Kids?   159

16   The Special Challenge of Hard-to-Staff Schools   163

Part IV: Customers   **175**

17   Do Not Lose Sight of the Student   177

18 Seeing Every Child for Who They Are, Not Who We
    Assume Them to Be—Replacing One Curriculum Taught
    One Way   187

19 Ending a System Designed to Lose Track of Kids—Paying
    Attention to Real Students, Not to the Assumptions We
    Make about Them   195

20 Assessing Students: Never Letting Them Fall Too Far
    Behind   209

21 Parents: One Half of a Confused Partnership   221

22 Parents: Long-Ignored Customers and Owners   239

**Part V: The Template: The Things High-Performing Schools
Have in Common**   **245**

23 Six Beliefs   247

24 Eight Practices   253

25 A Case Study in What It Takes to Fail   261

26 The Things Not Done   265

**Part VI: Beyond the School District: The Role of the States and
Federal Government**   **269**

27 The Role of the States   271

28 The Role of the Federal Government   275

Postscript: The Future of the American Public School System   **281**

29 The Education System We Need—the System of Schools We
    Want   283

Acknowledgments   293

Appendix I: The Blueprint for Action—an Outline of What We
    Need to Do   295

Appendix II: A Proposed School "Disclosure Document"   305

Index   315

About the Author   325

Preface

I used to be the general counsel of the Los Angeles Unified School District. I took the job because the superintendent who hired me, former Colorado governor Roy Romer, was committed to thorough reform of a highly dysfunctional district. We did not succeed.

I also used to be a political consultant. Given that background, our failure particularly troubled me because one important cause was the lack of widespread popular support for what we wanted to do. People had voted for reform but then did nothing to help us. What could bother a political consultant more?

But that was not the end of my frustration. For many years, when a lawyer in private practice, I tried big antitrust cases in court. A key question many times was why some enterprises would succeed and others inevitably fail. To prove such points required building up extensive expertise in management theory. When I arrived at the school district, I found the same knowledge was a great background for understanding how to reform a school district. No one else seemed to care.

There were lots of steps we should have taken, but no one (other than Romer and a few allies) was talking about them inside the district or in the periodic elections for the school board. Everyone professed to want better schools, but the candidates were not specifying what they would do, and no one else was even demanding they come up with the details. So although voters thought they were supporting change, they really had no idea whether their candidates were likely to make things better—or not.

As the national focus on school reform grew in 2007–2008, all of the problems I saw in Los Angeles seemed to be reappearing on a national scale. There was not a broad-based movement that would support reform, and the issues being discussed were not the ones likely to yield positive change. I knew how legislation got made from my stints as a senior staffer in both the California State Senate and the United States Senate. I sensed what was coming, and it was not good.

It was time for me to write a book. The result, which you are now reading, is intended to do more than just encourage you—whether you are a political leader, educator, parent, or taxpayer—to participate. It is intended to get you to promote the things that matter.

How do we know what those things are? There are hundreds of schools around the country that are high performing or transforming. They show what matters and prove it can be done.

This book reports on what those ideas and strategies are. Starting in December 2008, I began a sixteen-state road trip that eventually took me to forty public school districts, charters, private, and parochial schools.[1]

Most of the stops were in places that had distinguished themselves, either by being high-performing districts or by having transformed themselves from mediocre institutions into significantly improving ones. For example, my first two stops were in Plano, Texas, and Overland Park, Kansas (the Blue Valley School District), both suburban districts that set a standard for what a well-organized, high-performing school system should look like.

From there, I went on to investigate all the big cities in the Northeast, from Boston to Washington, as well as some of the smaller or suburban schools that cluster around them, such as Lawrence, Massachusetts; Great Neck, New York; and Montgomery County, Maryland. And there were other big cities: Chicago, Miami-Dade, Fort Lauderdale-Broward, San Diego, New Orleans, Milwaukee, Cleveland, Denver, Minneapolis, and, of course, Los Angeles.

But I also visited others that one might not consider. There were the winners and finalists for the Broad Prize, which goes to the most improved urban school district in America. Among those were Brownsville, Texas, and the Aldine District in North Houston, which won in 2008 and 2009 respectively. And while in Texas, I spent time in Freeport and Lake Jackson, whose Brazosport district won high praise for its extraordinary turnaround in the 1990s when it was recognized by the Educational Research Service as the first school district in the United States to have eliminated achievement gaps between African American, Hispanic, white, and low-socioeconomic students. I went to Pearl River, New York, a small town in Rockland County that won the National Institute of Standards and Technology's Baldrige Award in 2001 for excellence in public education. Then there was Iredell County, North Carolina, which won the same award in 2008. From there, I drove about sixty miles to Watauga County, a small rural district that has consistently been one of the highest performers in the state.

On top of that, there were visits to charters, like KIPP and Green Dot, which have received wide recognition; prominent parochial schools; and even Phillips Andover, one of the best-known private boarding schools in the country. Its headmaster for many years was Ted Sizer, an education theorist whose ideas appear throughout this book.

The story of what they have done should give you three things that are extraordinarily valuable in renewing our schools. First is context. How does some particular idea fit into the larger picture of change? Second are the details. What should we actually do? And third, and most importantly, confidence that it can be done—because it has been done in all sorts of places that have all manner of challenges all over the United States.

NOTE

1. The forty schools and districts are Aldine Independent School District (Houston, TX); Baltimore City, MD; Blue Valley School District (Overland Park, KS); Boston, MA; Brazosport Independent School District (Freeport/Lake Jackson, TX); Broward Co., FL; Brownsville Independent School District (Brownsville, TX); Chicago, IL; Cleveland, OH; Denver, CO; Duval Co., FL; Fairfax Co., VA; Fall River, MA; Great Neck, NY; Green Dot Charter Schools (Los Angeles, CA); Harlem Children's Zone (New York, NY); State of Hawaii; Iredell Co., NC; Knowledge is Power Program (KIPP) Charter Schools (San Francisco, CA); Lawrence, MA; Long Beach, CA; Los Angeles, CA; Miami-Dade Co., FL; Milwaukee, WI; Minneapolis, MN; Montgomery Co., MD; New Britain, CT; New York City, NY: Pearl River; NY; Philadelphia, PA; Phillips Andover Academy (Andover, MA); Plano Independent School District (Plano, TX); Portsmouth, VA; Prince George's Co., MD; Recovery School District (New Orleans, LA); Rochester, NY; Roslyn, NY; St. Ignatius Loyal Academy (Baltimore, MD); San Diego, CA; Servite High School (Anaheim, CA); Strategic Learning Initiatives Charter Schools (Chicago, IL); Watauga Co., NC.

Introduction

For most of the twentieth century, American public education was an exercise in mass production. From the way teachers were trained, to the contracts by which they were employed, to how kids were instructed, the system reflected many of the same attitudes and operations of a car plant. It was neither flexible nor innovative. It could educate some kids, but not all, and even then, there was a question about whether those who were capable of learning in the environment really were getting everything they could from their education.

Starting in the 1950s and 1960s, things began to change. The combination of the civil rights movement and the decline of American manufacturing, which had historically offered good jobs and good wages to those who did not have a great education, suddenly created a demand that *every child* had a right, indeed a need, for quality instruction. The fact that many of them were minorities, ethnically or linguistically, or had learning disabilities, or were just plain poor, did not matter. This country recognized that, both morally and economically, a better-educated America was an absolute necessity.

Mass-production education cannot fulfill that promise. Education that will reach every child has to be professional and artisanal. That is, teachers have to learn and apply a widely accepted body of knowledge about both content and methods of instruction. But in so doing, they have to act as if they were craftspeople, turning the raw material of each five-year-old's mind and body into an accomplished seventeen-year-old high school graduate who has been motivated to use his or her individual talents and interests to grow into an empowered young adult.

The great challenge of American education in the twenty-first century is how to move from the old vision to the new one.

* * *

The high-performing or transforming schools discussed in the book have taken great steps to meet the promise of educating every child. While the details of their strategies have varied at times, they all share one thing in common: they did not simply change one thing or even ten. They changed entire systems, from restructuring the role of the central office to how they trained teachers and delivered instruction. And they pushed, sometimes successfully, for changes in state or federal policies that could

make their task easier. As daunting as that sounds, their high performance or profound improvement demonstrates it is possible.

As you read how they met their goals, keep in mind the challenge of
systemic change:

- There are no silver bullets and no demons. No one-shot fixes. If you
  do not understand that all the moving parts in the system work
  together, something vital will inevitably not get done.
- There are some subjects, like "pay for performance" and tenure,
  which would occupy little space if we were discussing solely what
  works in the forty districts and schools. They turn out to be minor
  issues in the context of changing virtually all of the working elements of our education system. But in the current political climate,
  they are major. Without understanding how they fit in the larger
  picture, you will inevitably be caught blind-sided somewhere in the
  debate.
- Describing what systemic change should look like is one thing.
  Explaining how we get there—or stay there—is something else entirely. Without a firm understanding of the challenges in changing
  people's attitudes or overturning decades of public policy, no
  movement can hope to succeed.

There is one other caution to keep in mind: There is a temptation when
discussing public policy to think that we can dictate the details of excellence in rules written in Washington or some state capital. That is the
same mind-set as the old mass-production version of education, where
superintendents and central office administrators so lacked trust in the
capabilities of principals and teachers that they thought the right answer
was to dictate everything to the field.

Just as that vision at the school level should now be deemed out-
moded, so should its clone in the larger world of public policy be viewed
as "so last century." One cannot write all the rules for system change into
legislation. The policies that will work are those that get the right people
into the right kind of organizations, empowered to use their discretion
well to make good decisions.

The same is true for accountability. The best accountability system
does not rely on the state or federal governments, which are distant from
the scene, but on parents and taxpayers who are closest to a school. They
are most likely to see a school's work immediately and to best understand its impact on kids. Whatever rules legislators do write should focus
on fostering local participation and local accountability.

Whether you are one of those making decisions or someone holding
them accountable for their judgment, this book will hopefully empower
you to make a meaningful contribution to such an important and challenging task.

Part I

The Basics of School Reform

ONE

Management Theory 101

Downtown Brownsville, Texas, has an otherworldly feel. Nestled in a crook in the Rio Grande near where it empties into the Gulf of Mexico, the narrow streets are filled with stores selling cheap merchandise to Mexicans or to the poor from the local Hispanic community, which is often just a few years removed from the other side of the border. It is not a place that gives you the feeling that something special is happening in the local schools. You would be wrong. In 2008, Brownsville won the Broad Prize for having the most improved urban school district in America.

The great gulf between good districts and bad ones is not about race or income. If anyone harbors the notion that a majority white district is necessarily "good," and that a majority minority one is self-evidently "bad," that person simply does not know the state of education in this country ten years into the twenty-first century.

The differences in American school districts are less about the wealth of the community or the color of the students they serve than about how they organize and manage the instruction they provide. Brownsville may not look like Beverly Hills, but in a head-to-head comparison of how well they are both run, I'd be willing to put my money on the south Texas entry.

THE FOUR QUESTIONS

What, then, is the key to that organization and management?

All enterprises in the twenty-first century, including manufacturers and service industries, strive for innovation and flexibility that will best meet consumer needs. As economist Gary Hamel described it in his book

The Future of Management,[1] that pushes them toward a flattened hierarchy, with few layers of bosses and more empowered workers, where decisions are made close to the shop or the customer.

It is a prescription that fits perfectly for the crisis we face in education. For over one hundred years, we have treated elementary and secondary education as assembly line, mass production—one curriculum, taught one way, by one teacher, with little variation. Almost twenty years ago, when we decreed that every child can learn, that kind of one-size-fits-all mass production was out—although we may not have realized it at the time.

The goal of educating every child committed schools to not losing sight of any "customer." The techniques of mass production could not do that. On the contrary, decentralizing power to the schools and empowering teachers to tailor education to the distinct needs of students is precisely the best way to guarantee we can educate every child.

It is the key strategy in high-performing school systems internationally,[2] and it is fundamental to the high-performing districts I visited on my road trip around America.

How do we get there? We start by recognizing that education is a service. It faces the same challenges as any service enterprise whose goal is to build in innovation and excellence that will serve every customer. They are captured in four questions:

- How do you recruit, train, and motivate good leaders (such as superintendents and principals)?
- How do you recruit, train, and motivate good service providers (such as teachers)?
- How do you "not lose sight of the customer" (in this case, students and parents)?
- How do you continuously improve, testing whether what you are doing is working and whether you are adapting successfully to the world around you?

The first two questions are fundamental to any service business. All it has to sell are the skills of its workers. That means it needs the right people, trained well, and properly motivated to do their jobs. Experts have long said "teacher quality," is key, but so is the quality of the administrators who lead them.

The third question may be even more important because it goes to the heart of whether any business survives. If that business loses sight of its customers' needs, those customers are not going to be happy. In mass-production education, losing sight of customers was not a sometime thing. It was the inevitable result of a rigid, top-down system where, one could justifiably say, "only the strong survive." The only reason that the schools persisted was that they were geographic monopolies. Ignoring kids or parents did not matter because most people had nowhere else to go.

However, the monopoly also created the opposite problem. Most service businesses try to find a niche, a particular group of customers that they can serve better than anyone else. It gives them a competitive edge and does not stretch them beyond their expertise.

Not public schools. They had to serve everyone. Even the best staff would have found that challenging, and nothing about most schools or their staffs was that flexible and innovative. The only option was to dumb down instruction in order to meet an obligation no reasonable business would assume.

The largest parts of this book flesh out these issues in answer to the first three of the questions; there are sections on leaders, teachers, and students and their parents.

There is, however, no separate section for our fourth question—how to keep getting better. Rather, almost every discussion in the book revisits this idea because continuous improvement is fundamental to virtually any aspect of the professional and artisanal vision of schooling.

CONTINUOUS IMPROVEMENT—TOTAL QUALITY MANAGEMENT

Starting in the early 1980s, American business leaders discovered W. Edwards Deming and his game-changing idea—total quality management (TQM). TQM emphasizes that enterprises need to focus on cooperation, teamwork, customer satisfaction, and continuous improvement.[3] All of these ideas are alien to much of twentieth-century mass production, certainly education mass production. The adoption of any one of them would have a substantial effect on traditional public schools. The adoption of all of them, especially the dual commitments to data-driven decision making and continuous improvement, has had an extraordinary impact in the relatively few districts where it has happened.

TQM requires there be agreement on a vision and a determination of a set of benchmarks to assess the realization of the vision. It demands a willingness to admit failure if the benchmarks come up short, and it encourages innovation to identify what else might work better.

If students are not learning, continuous improvement pushes administrators and teachers to figure out how to improve the results.[4] Not just once, but over and over. It has to be, after all, continuous. Any idea of a silver bullet is out, and the old "one lesson plan forever" way of teaching finished.[5]

The move to data-driven decision making and continuous improvement in education began in the late 1980s, not long after businesses discovered its value. A few districts decided to implement all of Deming's TQM philosophy, and others adopted at least some form of disciplined continuous improvement. Eventually, the federal government and some thirty-six state governments began formally to encourage the process by creating awards for exemplary performance using TQM or similar strategies. The federal government's is called the Baldrige Award, named for former commerce secretary Malcolm Baldrige. Several of the districts I visited are Baldrige winners, and others have been finalists in the Baldrige competition.[6] Almost all of the districts and several of the charters I saw had adopted a form of TQM or at least a disciplined version of continuous improvement. And that, in turn, has affected virtually everything they have subsequently done. It is why you won't see one section on continuous improvement; you will simply see its role over and over again in every part of the book.

KEEPING THE STUDENT-TEACHER TRANSACTION IN FOCUS

Before moving on, there is one other piece of Management 101 to think about while reading this book: *Everything must be evaluated in terms of how it relates to the transaction between the student and teacher (or perhaps computer).*

For example, merely creating a charter school does not guarantee a good result. That will happen only if the charter adopts practices that actually improve instruction. When we realize that, we can understand why charter test scores in most surveys are not materially better than those of public schools. In almost all states, charters have to comply with far fewer state mandates than traditional public schools, and some will use that freedom well when it comes to restructuring the classroom. But some won't. Merely being a charter guarantees nothing.

So whatever change is discussed in the following chapters, think about how it affects that teacher-student transaction.

That is not all you should keep in mind when thinking about students and teachers—and how they relate to one another. Both bring attitudes and expectations, which I am going to call "headspace," into the classroom. It is as important as the mechanics of instruction. If teachers do not believe students can learn, or if students do not believe in themselves, we are not going to see the results for which we yearn.

Headspace is a problem often given no more than lip service by those who think about renewing our schools. Just because you can't see it doesn't mean it is not there. Headspace is at least half the battle. It deserves at least half the attention.

NOTES

1. Gary Hamel, *The Future of Management* (Boston, MA: Harvard Business School Press, 2007).

2. Organization for Economic Cooperation and Development, *Strong Performers and Successful Reformers in Education: Lessons from PISA for the United States* (Paris: Organization for Economic Cooperation and Development, 2010), 243.

3. Colleen A. Capper and Michael T. Jamison, "Let the Buyer Beware: Total Quality Management and Educational Research and Practice," *Educational Researcher* 22, no. 8 (Nov. 1993): 25–30, 25.

4. National Working Group on Funding Student Learning, *Funding Student Learning* (School Finance Redesign Project, Center on Reinventing Public Education, University of Washington, Bothell, WA, October 2008), 13.

5. In 2010, the National Conference of State Legislatures was still complaining that federal policy was too compliance oriented, rather than being focused on achievement and results. National Conference of State Legislatures, *Education at a Crossroads: A New Path for Federal and State Education Policy* (Denver, CO: Organization for Economic Cooperation and Development, 2010), 19.

6. Michael J. Schmoker and Richard B. Wilson, *Total Quality Education: Profiles of Schools That Demonstrate the Power of Deming's Management Principles* (Bloomington, IN: Phi Delta Kappa Educational Foundation, 1993).

TWO

Human Relations 101

The problem in public education is not the students. It is the adults.

Reform is not about changing kids. For better or worse, we cannot find the stork and send them back for better, more educable, more focused models. We have what we have.

What we change are adults. We change their attitudes. We change their training. We change their motivations. If nothing else works, we can change them.

That is messy. We cannot simply order reform and expect it to happen. Getting people to change their behavior, let alone how they see the world, cannot be accomplished by fiat. It is largely about art and nuance and little about science and precision.

It is why this book *cannot* simply be about what new policy we need to write in Washington. It is more complicated—and more frustrating—than that. It is why it is so important that any book on building good schools spend a great deal of time explaining how to put in place the right people, who, district by district and school by school, can make good things happen.

INDUSTRIAL VERSUS PROFESSIONAL

The problem is wonderfully illustrated by the conflicting views both school management and the teachers' unions have about whether teachers are industrial workers or professionals.

Education leaders in the early twentieth century saw teachers as industrial-style workers. Schools needed vast numbers of instructors in order to build and operate a system that was rapidly expanding to serve millions of children. The early Progressives believed that the best way to assure quality in a modestly educated teacher workforce that included large numbers of women and minorities was to create the school equivalent of the assembly line. That meant closely directing what teachers taught and how they taught it.

The industrial model of teaching in turn determined the nature of onsite management. The principals were not to be collaborators with their faculties but managers, assuring the workers followed directions. It was top-down, often arrogant, sometimes arbitrary, rarely collegial. And it inspired exactly what it was set up to defeat: lack of transparency, cronyism, and favoritism.

Teachers did not, at least in their own minds, think of themselves the same way management did. However undereducated teachers may have been in the eyes of school leaders, they had more education than most. It was a social distinction they wanted recognized.

But their objections were not just social. They were real and practical—and the reasons for the objections justifiably made teachers feel more like professionals than autoworkers.

Teachers had to apply districts' top-down, mass-production strategies in the classroom. They realized that such central office directives often needed to be modified—if not ignored—in order to be workable. Not every child and not every classroom's dynamics were the same. (The semi-disconnect between what the central office dictates and what winds up happening in the class has been given a name—"loose coupling.")

However, they could not bargain or strike over these directives, so they accommodated to them, which meant that they retreated to their classroom to work out what to do with the "boss's orders" when facing real kids. It reinforced the desire for teacher autonomy. It probably squelched collaboration, which, by its very nature, would have made any decision to ignore the directives far more visible to principals and superintendents.[1] It all stoked a sense of isolation and alienation, but it was better than the alternative. And it continues to this day in too many schools.[2]

The Story of Fred Bateman

The seeming schizophrenia surrounding teachers' roles in schools is nicely illustrated by Fred Bateman, the executive director of the Urban Superintendents Association, who started out in the early 1960s as a teacher in Lynchburg, Virginia. The Lynchburg School Board provided precise and detailed curriculum and lesson plans to its teachers. Each was expected to be teaching the same thing at the same time throughout the school year. It was the industrial view.

The district had a supervisor who regularly visited schools to make sure its program was being closely followed. However, at least at Bateman's school, she would not park in front when she came to visit; she parked behind the school and hoped that by entering through a back door, she could surprise the teachers.

Bateman and his colleagues, however, were on to her. They were not following the district's curriculum and lesson plans. They saw themselves as capable professionals who should adapt the district's program to the needs and interests of their students. Of course, there was the problem of what to do about the surprise inspections.

It turned out that not all the teachers' classrooms were on the main floor, facing the front of the building. The shop class was in the basement and had windows facing out the back of the building. The shop teacher had a good view of where the inspector parked. Whenever she visited, he would quickly send an alert upstairs to his fellow faculty members. They would promptly move to where they should be on the specified curriculum. The inspector would come, observe, and leave—none the wiser. They, of course, would revert to what they thought they should be doing after she left.

So Bateman's management had one view of life; the teachers had another. It's an arrangement repeated all over the country.

Will the Real Supporter of Twenty-First-Century Education Please Stand Up?

Notwithstanding these feelings of professionalism, when the locals of the two large national teachers' unions, the American Federation of Teachers (AFT) and the National Education Association (NEA), began collective bargaining in the 1960s, they responded to management's industrial vision with an industrial vision of their own. Leo Casey, who is a vice president of the United Federation of Teachers in New York and often a spokesperson for the current AFT president, Randi Weingarten, has written that the union took as its template "the contracts of the progressive industrial unions of the era, such as Walter Reuther's United Auto Workers." [3]

That set a trend. For the past almost fifty years, teacher contracts have looked "industrial," whatever teachers say about being "professional." The agreements have faithfully continued the single salary schedule, where all teachers earn the same amount—except for additional sums based on advanced education work and years of service. The single salary schedule long antedated collective bargaining, but it fit the union's industrial strategy. So did seniority and "bumping," where more senior workers could "bump" junior ones in the event of a cutback in employment. Tenure also existed long before collective bargaining, but it too fit the industrial mold. And teachers' required hours at school were closely specified, even though teachers worked many more in the quiet of their own homes.

The contracts did not look much like an agreement with professionals. There was no agreed-upon body of knowledge. Licensure was a weak sieve, and the unions had nothing to do with its administration anyway. Nor did they discipline members or even assume any obligation for the failure of one of their colleagues to exercise some minimal level of competence. That was all left to the administration. In fact, hard-core unionists specifically objected to any such idea as breaching "worker solidarity."

And, like industrial unions, the tone of the contracts was adversarial. Unions were not there to collaborate with management; they were there to oppose it.

In 1985, in the face of mounting criticism of the public schools unions, Albert Shanker, president of the AFT and a long-standing proponent of innovation,[4] called for a "second revolution" in collective bargaining, which would have brought teachers back in many ways to a professional vision of teaching. He proposed changing the union's positions on several key issues, including protecting incompetent teachers, teacher standards and certification, merit pay, and school choice.[5] He also advocated creation of meaningful standards for curriculum and student achievement, which led to the National Board for Professional Teaching Standards (NBPTS).

Unfortunately, his call went largely unheeded for over two decades by those who followed him as leaders at the AFT and NEA. They paid lip service to many of his ideas, but did little.

Management, on the other hand, was moving. They began, sometimes slowly and often haphazardly, to abandon the vision of mass-production education. Instead, they started to build a school model that attempted to work with every child. That led management to want teachers who would do more than teach the same set of lesson plans year after year. Where the new vision has fully evolved (as we shall discuss later), teachers are in fact being asked to do what is effectively a new and different job. It is more demanding, more complicated, more intense. It is, in other words, more professional.

While the NEA has maintained its hostility to most reform ideas since then, the AFT's Weingarten has tried to find a way forward that accommodates some management demands. She has support from an increasingly large number of younger teachers and from a few AFT and NEA locals that have banded together in an organization called Teachers Union Reform Network (TURN).

But she faces a real challenge, especially with her older members.[6] They remember the initial union-organizing fights, still value the union, and remain focused on the things that animated them in the first place: traditional issues of pay, job protections, and teacher autonomy.[7] And they are wedded to some degree to the job they trained for, knew, and had worked at for years.

Unfortunately, if all of that leaves your head reeling, it is still more complicated. Under pressure to get quick results or because of a distrust of teachers' effectiveness, some superintendents associated with reform and professionalization have reverted to top-down control and a heavily scripted curriculum, much like their predecessors of fifty years ago. Although they may think of themselves as still in the vanguard of reform, they are contradicting their own message. When that happens, the unions may not be on the side of the *status quo*. They may actually wind up back on the side of professionalization.

If there is any "truth" worth remembering here, it is that outside observers are probably well advised to be cautious in picking sides. Go back to the advice in Management 101 and figure out what is going to have a positive effect on the student-teacher transaction.

NOTES

1. Katherine C. Boles and Vivian Troen, "Mamas Don't Let Your Babies Grow Up to Be Teachers," in *Recruiting, Retaining, and Supporting Highly Qualified Teachers*, ed. Caroline Chauncey (Cambridge, MA: Harvard Education Press, 2005), 19.

2. Cheryl L. Kirkpatrick, "'I Love My Job, but I'm Not a Martyr': How Schools' Professional Cultures Influence Engagement among Second-Stage Teachers," American Educational Research Association, papers presented at San Diego, CA, April 13–17, 2009, 37 (retrieved from www.gse.harvard.edu/-ngt on May 18, 2009); David Kauffman, "Curriculum Prescription and Curriculum Constraint: Second-Year Teachers' Perceptions," *NGT Working Paper*, Project on the Next Generation of Teachers, Cambridge, MA, May 2005 (retrieved from www.gse.harvard.edu/-ngt).

3. Leo Casey, "The Educational Value of Democratic Voice," in *Collective Bargaining in Education: Negotiating Change in Today's Schools*, ed. Jane Hannaway and Andrew Rotherham (Cambridge, MA: Harvard University Press, 2006), 186–87.

4. For example, in 1971, in response to growing dissatisfaction with the New York City schools, he agreed to the insertion of an accountability clause in the collective bargaining agreement. The *New York Times* reported: "Mr. Shanker said the accountability system would 'provide the greatest protection teachers have ever known.' Successful teachers would be protected against unfair criticisms by providing proof of their effectiveness, he explained, and for those teachers who are not effective, the system would indicate the additional training they need to improve." *New York Times*, "A Way to Measure the Job Done by Schools," Feb. 14, 1971, 16.

5. *Education Week*, "Tensions of the Shanker Era: A Speech That Shook the Field," March 26, 1997 (retrieved from www.edweek.org/ew/articles/1997/03/26/26toch.h16.html?tkn=OLPFds7ArF732VOqUyUx1BTyXVJD97AAC&print=1 on July 7, 2009); Fred Hechinger, "About Education: A Warning from Albert Shanker," *New York Times*, March 20, 1984 (retrieved from www.nytimes.com.1984/03/20/science/about-education-a warning-from-albert-shanker.html?&on July 7, 2009); Richard D. Kahlenberg, *The History of Collective Bargaining among Teachers*, in *Collective Bargaining in Education*, ed. Jane Hathaway and Andrew J. Rotherham (Cambridge, MA: Harbard Educatio NPress, 2006), 20–21.

6. Andrew J. Rotherham and Richard Whitmire, "Making the Grade," *New Republic*, March 18, 2009 (retrieved from www.tnr.com/politics/story.html?id_82f9ab6f-32c0--46aa-8c27-37cb23e99acc on July 1, 2009).

7. Susan Moore Johnson, Morgaen L. Donaldson, Mindy Sick Munger, John P. Papay, and Emily Kalejs Qazilbash, "Leading the Local: Teacher Union Presidents Speak on Change, Challenges," *Education Sector Reports*, June 2007, 3.

THREE

Politics 101

Public schools are governed by state and federal law. The right laws make the renewal of our schools easier. The wrong laws make it nigh impossible. Here is a perfect example of the problem:

MONEY MAY BE THE SALVATION; THEN AGAIN, IT MAY BE THE ROOT OF ALL EVIL

The 1960s' "white flight" left many inner cities heavily poor and minority. Suddenly it was apparent that the old way of funding schools through property taxes left some districts with a depleted tax base and far less money per student than other, wealthier suburban enclaves. The United States Supreme Court rejected the argument that such funding violated the Constitution's Equal Protection Clause,[1] but many state courts adopted the reasoning and ordered their legislatures to remedy the problem.[2]

In response, these states assumed a much larger role in local school funding. The combination of state and federal funding has actually given at least some urban districts more than their suburban counterparts, so that the conception that they are inevitably "poorer" may simply not be true. Here are some examples:

Annual Per Student Spending (2007–2008)

California	Michigan
Oakland (urban)—$10,036	Detroit (urban)—$12,016
San Ramon Valley (suburban)—$8,434	Troy (suburban)—$10,960

15

Georgia	**Missouri**
Atlanta (urban)—$13,516	St. Louis (urban)—$14,353
Cobb (suburban)—$9,428	Rockwood (suburban)—$8,263[3]

(That does not mean that all problems of equalization are solved. When equalizing funding still seemed to leave minority schools with inadequate support, the next legal effort, begun in the late 1980s, focused on the "adequacy" of the amount of money being offered. It has not yielded the same results as the equalization suits, and, although an interesting story, not relevant here.)

While equalization was undoubtedly a worthy objective, it has come at a cost that in some ways is so significant that it inhibits the very reform that it was trying to promote.

Equalization required rejiggering school finance, so that in most states, a majority of the funds for all districts, and especially for districts with large numbers of the poor, no longer comes from local taxes. Instead of being based on property values, these districts now rely on the proceeds of state sales, income, or capital gains taxes, and the beneficence of the state legislature. For example, in California, only 27.85 percent of Oakland's revenue in 2004–2005 came from local sources, while San Ramon's was 69.5 percent local. In Missouri, 39.3 percent of St. Louis's money was local, but 72.6 percent of Rockwood's was.[4]

But a dollar is not just a dollar in the school business. A state dollar and a local dollar are very different when it comes to running a good school.

Stability of funding matters. State revenues often swing wildly because the states (with the exception of Vermont) are required to balance their budgets. Unless they are willing to increase taxes during economic downturns (a highly unpopular thing to do in recessions), they have less money for schools—or anything else. And instead of settling on a budget in March, they may go back and forth into the summer wrestling with the politics of who gets what.

In 2009 and 2010, the states were thrown a lifeline by the Obama administration, which provided $40 billion the first year and $10 billion the second in emergency funding to avoid teacher layoffs.[5] However, that support will not continue in 2011, reminding everyone just how unstable state funding can be.

That instability does not hit everyone equally. Until the recession of 2009–2010, local taxes were a stable revenue source. Property values did not dip much; on the contrary they had experienced a relatively steady rise over the decades. When downturns attack state budgets, districts that still rely on local property taxes have much less difficulty adjusting. They simply lose less. And they care about it less, allowing them to move forward without waiting for the legislature to sort things out.

Meanwhile, urban districts are unsure about the amount of money they have to spend. As we shall see when we discuss the problems of hard-to-staff schools, hard-pressed urban districts have a raft of challenges in filling positions promptly. One of them is uncertainty about how much money they will have for the coming year. And that restrains them from hiring, or at least forces them to hire at a slower pace than districts whose funding is based on local property taxes.

Similarly, as the 2009–2010 crisis has shown, these same districts are the ones more likely to fire teachers or at least hand out warnings about termination, either of which is terribly demoralizing. And either of which gives every teacher substantial motivation to move to a district not burdened by such ups and downs.

That is not the only frustration instability causes. One year, when the state is flush, the superintendent asks the staff to make plans for some new reform initiative. They do, with great enthusiasm. But by the time the plan is ready to go, the state's finances are in trouble. Everything is shelved, and the only concern is about hanging on. It is demoralizing.

The other great advantage to the local dollars is that they are unrestricted. Districts can make their own decisions about how to use the money. Some state money comes the same way; it goes to a district's general fund.

But the federal government has always required its education money to be used for specific purposes, and many states have over the years increasingly done the same thing. It is called "categorical" funding, and when trying to renew a school, or even to maintain an already high-performing one, managing how to deal with such strings is a major preoccupation.

There is a long catalog of evils attached to categorical funding. The money appropriated often does not cover the cost of what is required. A particularly irksome statute is the Individuals with Disabilities Education Act (IDEA), a law originally passed in 1975 to help those with learning disabilities, which you will read about at several points in the book. The federal government has a long list of requirements, but it has never funded more than 17 percent of the cost—despite promises to cover 40 percent.

The categoricals also layer one on top of the other. They can be contradictory, and old ones rarely are repealed. Few are ever checked for their effectiveness. For example, a California program provides money to fix up school bathrooms, and while the auditors do check to see if the money was spent on restroom maintenance, no one tries to assess if the bathrooms really became any cleaner.[6]

In a district trying to be inventive and flexible, categorical funding can be a problem, unless there is money specifically available to support the innovation at hand. When I spoke to superintendents about categoricals, they rolled their eyes. They could work with them, but it vastly complicated their jobs and made principals into bureaucrats rather than innovators. I understood. When I was LA's general counsel, I had one lawyer assigned almost full-time to find ways to keep us "just this side of the line" with categorical funding.

The amount of money tied up in categorical funding has grown into a significant share of all nonlocal support. All federal money is categorical. In states, it varies. In California, for example, there are approximately eighty categorical programs that account for over one-third of the state's spending on public education.[7] The resulting funding structure is so complex one *Los Angeles Times* columnist called it "[not] merely inefficient and ineffective, it's insane."[8]

AUTHORITY, RESPONSIBILITY, AND FUNDING AND THEIR IMPACT ON POLITICAL PARTICIPATION

The "money" story is a perfect introduction to two problems with which any effort at renewal will have to grapple constantly.

Organizations that are vibrant and thriving are more likely to have responsibility, authority, and funding all focused in the same place. That used to be the way it was in all school districts. They funded themselves from local property taxes, which they set. They wrote most of their own rules. And when they failed, it was fair to attribute responsibility to the school board and superintendent.

That is not true anymore. Over the past fifty years, the state and federal governments have taken to writing all sorts of laws dealing with schools, some of which are the strings in categorical programs, some of which are not. And, as I just described, funding has moved away from local districts as well.

Nonetheless, when a school gets bad test scores, the school, the district, and the school board get all the blame. This separation of responsibility, authority, and funding has inevitably driven up political grandstanding and driven down public participation in school districts. Parents are still active in schools, but few see the benefit of closely watching what happens when the board meets. All the action seems to have gone elsewhere. If one wants to do something, the state capitol seems like a more logical place to go.

That is a tragedy because it often leaves district politics and therefore decisions dominated by narrow interest groups, to the likely detriment of the students the district is supposed to serve.

Having said that, state and federal policy are important, even in a world where responsibility, authority, and funding are better aligned. No discussion of renewal can focus exclusively on districts. The great challenge is building a political action agenda at the state and federal level that actually has some likelihood of bringing about real improvements all the way down at the level of the student-teacher interaction. That requires understanding the process well enough to set the right priorities and resist cheap, if seductive, sloganeering.

At the end of this book in appendix I is a proposed action plan for changing schools. Some of it is focused on districts, and some parts address state and federal reform. It summarizes what you will have read and should make you as comfortable in the corridors of Congress as in the halls of your neighborhood elementary school. You will now know what is necessary for quality education and what is required to get there. Your job is to act.

NOTES

1. *San Antonio Independent School District v. Rodriguez*, 411 U.S. 1 (1973).

2. See, for example, *Serrano v. Priest*, 487 P.2d 1241 (1971) (California); *Robinson v. Cahill*, 303 A.2d 273 (1973) (New Jersey).

3. U.S. Census Bureau, *School Finances* (Washington, DC: Government Printing Office, 2010), table 17—Per Pupil Amounts for Current Spending of Public Elementary-Secondary School Systems with Enrollments of 10,000 or More 2007–08.

4. U.S. Census Bureau, *School Finances*, table 17.

5. *Education Week*, "Quality Counts," Jan. 13, 2011, 13; Sara Mead, Anand Vaishnav, William Porter, and Andrew J. Rotherham, *Conflicting Missions and Unclear Results: Lessons from the Education Stimulus Funds* (Washington, DC: Bellwether Education Partners, 2010), 7; *Education Week*, "Obama Signs Bill Aimed at Saving Teachers' Jobs," Aug. 10, 2010 (retrieved from www.edweek.org.ew.articles.2010/08/10/01jobs.h30.html on Nov. 23, 2011); *Los Angeles Times*, "More than 1,000 L.A. Unified Workers Lose Their Jobs," Dec. 1, 2010 (retrieved from http://articles.latimes.com/2010/dec/01/ocal/la-me-1201-lausd-layoffs-20101201 on Dec. 7, 2011).

6. California requires that every restroom in a K–12 school be fully operational and stocked at all times with toilet paper, soap, and paper towels or hand driers. If not, the district is ineligible for state deferred maintenance fund matching apportionments. However, the program does not set up any inspection system. California Education Code Section 35292.5.

7. *EdSource*, "School Finance 2007–08," Palo Alto, CA, Dec. 2007, 2.

8. Michael Hiltzik, "State's School Funding Process Is Failing," *Los Angeles Times*, Nov. 19, 2009 (retrieved from www.latimes.com/business/la-fi-hiltzik19-2009 nov19,0,5135920.column on Nov. 20, 2009).

Part II

Leaders

Let's begin with Question One: How does a district recruit, train, and motivate its leaders?

We talk a great deal about teacher quality being central to a good education—as if superintendents and principals do not matter. Wrong. A district's leaders set the tone. They are the ones who maintain the standards that ensure high performance, or they drive reform.

We want independent-minded, hardworking people who understand education, management, and politics from top to bottom. Mass production did not require such people; in fact, they would have probably been distrusted in the mass-production era. But if we want to move beyond that era into a time of high-performing, flexible, innovative enterprises, we have to move beyond mass production–style leaders.[1]

NOTE

1. Kenneth Leithwood, Karen Seashore Louis, Stephen Anderson, and Kyla Wahlstrom, *How Leadership Influences Student Learning* (Minneapolis: University of Minnesota Press/University of Toronto Press, 2010).

FOUR

Superintendents

Reform efforts may fail even with a good superintendent—but they cannot succeed without one. Without the right leader, even a good district can go sour. A great superintendent is key.

Finding that person is the most important choice a school board member—or mayor[1] —will likely ever face. And that decision will require a lot of hard thinking and discussion.

The conversation cannot be limited to the board members themselves. Anyone in the community interested in education has to participate. So here is another set of four questions that will help decide not only who is right for the job, but also define what the job is that the new superintendent is supposed to do.

The first three guide the selection process:

- What is the situation on the ground that the new superintendent will face?
- *What do we want the new superintendent to do in the existing situation?*
- What skills and traits should the new superintendent have in order to do that job well?

Finally, just as important as the role of the superintendent will be the role of the school board or the mayor who does the hiring. So we end with a fourth, important question:

- What are the responsibilities and the role of the board or the mayor?

23

WHAT IS THE SITUATION ON THE GROUND?

The role the new superintendent will play varies from district to district. However, that role will be effective only if there is broad agreement about it. Are parents expecting a reformer or someone who will retain the status quo, and are their views shared by the board? And does the superintendent concur in what the board wants her to do once in office?

In districts that are already high performing, the new superintendent is going to be expected to understand and perpetuate their successful operating strategies and culture. Sounds logical and simple enough, but it isn't. On the one hand, the new superintendent may not understand why the district has been successful, with the result that she abandons one or more key elements of the formula for success. That is precisely what happened in the Brazosport district after Gerald Anderson left in 2000. The new superintendent was persuaded to reduce the frequency of student assessment, and, over time, the achievement gap, which Anderson had closed, reappeared. The lesson to the board: If you want the new superintendent to follow the path of the last one, make that clear up front.

On the other hand, the satisfaction with the status quo may lead to undervaluing the need for innovation. The new superintendent cannot be a slavish adherent to "how we do things here." Places like Blue Valley and Plano have demonstrated that continuous improvement and adaptation is as important for them as it is for a turnaround situation. The lesson to the board: Don't suggest adhering to the old ways is necessarily good. The bridge between these two contradictory lessons: See if the new superintendent is a believer in continuous improvement, so that, while she is open to changes in the status quo, she won't approve any unless they are tested thoroughly first.

When a turnaround is required, the first question is: How far along are things when the new superintendent is hired? In some lucky districts, like Pearl River in 1989 and Brazosport in 1991, the boards did not just decide they wanted reform. They went further by deciding to adopt TQM (total quality management). That meant the new superintendent did not have to invent the broad vision, but he did have to adhere to it. The lesson: This hire is risky unless the new superintendent understands, and willingly agrees with, the board plan. The phrase "fully informed consent" comes to mind.

Most places are not as lucky as Pearl River. Boards may know they want change, but they do not know what it looks like. Here the burden falls entirely on the new superintendent. He or she has to come up with the plan and sell it to the board, the teachers, and an often-impatient community. It is the most common scenario, and the one that has played out in most large cities, like New York, Chicago, Philadelphia, and Los

Angeles. The lesson here: The new superintendent is going to have to be a superb politician as well as a savvy administrator. She is not just the designer of the plan, she will also have to be its chief advocate.

(Then there is the case where the board has not looked for a reformer but gotten one anyway. When Terry Holliday arrived in Iredell County, North Carolina, he found a modest district with no great outcry for thoroughgoing change. To his great credit, he was not willing to tolerate mediocrity and convinced his board that they should—and could—improve. The lesson to be drawn: Sometimes it is enough for a board to be open-minded and wise enough to see a good thing when it is presented to them. Their reward was that Iredell County won the Baldrige Award in 2008.)

Then there is one other scenario. It is the one that spells trouble even before the new superintendent sets foot in his office. In San Diego in 1998, and Fall River, Massachusetts, in 2005, a narrow majority of the school board decided to press ahead with reform, over the objections of the reluctant minority. No superintendent with an ounce of common sense should accept that offer. Many of the major mistakes of school reform happen when someone decides, unwisely, to take on that challenge, in spite of a deep division on the board.

Fall River is a good cautionary tale. After four years on the job, Nick Fischer was not renewed as superintendent. But later that year (2009), the high school achievement scores showed that Fischer had done a good job and was starting to raise district performance. He had also reduced the dropout rate more that year than any other district in the state. Based on the objective data, he should have remained.

But Fischer was an outsider and therefore vulnerable to all the complaints about not doing things "the way they had always been done around here." The district had historically functioned as a local employment agency, so many of the old-time teachers and principals were good friends of the mayor. They did not welcome the pressure of the new accountability system, a fundamental part of Fischer's reform strategy, and they complained about the changes. The mayor then put pressure on the board. A single board member changed his vote on renewing Fischer's contract, and a 4–3 split in his favor became a 3–4 split against him.

There are two important lessons here. First, if the board and mayor are not ready to stick with the superintendent, *don't even bother to start down the path to reform*. Without a clear understanding of everyone's roles, and without a commitment to longevity and solidarity, nothing is going to happen.[2]

Second, local culture and local history will have a great deal to do with whether school reform succeeds. The new superintendent needs to be sensitive to the politics of the district and able to navigate its currents. Otherwise, like Fischer, he or she will get the boot, even after real success.

The Cycle of Failure and the Blame Game

In high-performing districts, there is a sense that the board, the teachers, and the community are all on the same page. Over time, success has created trust. A new superintendent may well be found among the current district administration, because everyone shares a basic vision of success.

None of that is true when there has been a cycle of repeated failure. New York, Los Angeles, Philadelphia, and Washington, DC, have all gone through multiple attempts at reform. Again and again, after much-heralded planning and many meetings, *nothing happened*. Any internal candidates for superintendent are likely eliminated because they carry the taint of the last failure. Worse, people become dismissive of all the promises—perhaps recalling the old joke that insanity is doing the same thing over and over again, but expecting a different result.

The new superintendent will have to demonstrate why, *this time*, things are going to be different. One of the challenges will be to get everyone past the old "blame game."

The *educational blame game* goes like this:

School administration: We tried reform before, but you refused to cooperate (or just fell down on the job).
Teachers: No, you disrespected us (or just made a hash of managing the program), so we pushed back.

In three districts I visited—Brazosport, Iredell County, and Pearl River—the new leadership was able to present a vision for improvement without anyone—not the community, the press, nor district officials—suggesting that the teachers or others had failed. The new superintendents were well aware that many principals and teachers would not be equal to the challenge, but they were careful *not* to begin the dialogue by suggesting, "It's all your fault."

Then there is the *diverse constituency blame game*. It goes something like this:

Group A: All these so-called reforms are just handouts for _____ [fill in the blank: African Americans, Hispanics, the business community, voucher schools].
Group B: No, *you people* are just trying to hold on to _____ [money, jobs, political power].

Neither side trusts the other side's claims. And in this climate, no one can hear a call for improving student achievement as, well, a call for improving student achievement. There is always more than enough blame to go around, and everyone is spoiling for a grudge fight. People are stuck in a "zero-sum game,"[3] and there is no "win-win" scenario to get everyone on the same side.

Wilfredo Laboy, who was the first Hispanic superintendent in Lawrence,[4] understood how to navigate through the problem. The district is now 70 percent Hispanic; however, around 25 percent of the city, as well as the power structure, remains white. He told me that when he was hired he was emphatic about who he was and what he was going to do: "I told them that I did not want to be hired because I was Hispanic. I told them I wanted to be hired because I was going to be a great superintendent who happened to be Hispanic."

Here is where parents and taxpayers have an important role in the reform process. If they are sucked into some version of the blame game, which means that they have taken their eyes off the prize of higher student achievement in favor of revisiting old wars, then reform is going to fail. Reform requires a coalition. Coalitions can never withstand the blame game. Never.

Likewise, superintendents have to understand that feeding the blame game rarely advances their cause in the long run, as we shall see later in the book. And boards, who are the most likely culprits in stirring up old antagonisms, just need to remember they have told the superintendent their goal is reform. They need to keep their eyes on that prize—as they promised.

All of which means that if the blame game is in full swing, everyone who wants successful reform has to shut it down. Parents, taxpayers, and the superintendent all have to say that student achievement is more important than old antagonisms, and then they have to take the hardest step: heeding their own advice.

Now that we understand where the district stands, it is possible to figure out what the superintendent must do and what kind of person we need to do it.

WHAT DOES A SUCCESSFUL SUPERINTENDENT NEED TO DO?

While some of the specific tasks in front of a turnaround superintendent may be different from those facing the leader of a high-performing district, the jobs' overall requirements are really much the same. The difference is that the difficulty and intensity of meeting those requirements in one situation may be far different from what a superintendent will face in the other.

The elements of any superintendent's job are simple enough to list:

- Build trust and confidence.
- Communicate a strong vision.
- Be a great role model.
- Build a strong leadership team.

- Be an education leader, an entrepreneurial manager, and a capable political actor.

Easy to say—but difficult to do. Let's look at the job description in more detail.

Building Trust and Confidence

Building trust and confidence is the most fundamental job of a superintendent. She has to win over the board, the teachers, and the community. Unfortunately, the strategy for each one is different, depending, of course, on the "situation on the ground."

The Board

The superintendents affirmed over and over again that they succeeded because they had the support of their boards or mayor—even when that was not the popular position. Chris Steinhauser in Long Beach spoke about board support in almost lyrical terms, calling it "the cornerstone" of the district's success. Doris Kurtz in New Britain emphasized how important it was to keep the board from reflecting the underlying racial and economic divisions of the city, with its large immigrant population and shrinking, but still powerful, middle class. Her mission was to educate everybody. Her board supported her, and, most importantly, they did not let the old divisions split them into opposing camps.

Building the trust of the school board requires an immense commitment of time. There must be group meetings, one-on-one meetings, and probably some informal socializing. *Every* superintendent said the same thing. Keeping the board on track is a full-time job in itself. Actually getting to run the district is like the prize in the Cracker Jacks box.

There is also a more formal and more visible aspect of trust building. It begins with a basic tool of good organizational management—*a written plan*. Almost all the superintendents had quickly developed a plan showing how they were going to move forward over a multiyear period. (In some cases, the district had already written a plan. The new superintendents decided to adopt as much of that plan as they could—a wise move in building trust.)

Plans were not just for transformational districts. Any district that had adopted TQM had to have one. TQM requires agreement on a vision, benchmarks to assess progress, a list of priorities, and a description of a way forward. No one can assemble all that without preparing a plan. However, even for districts I visited that had not adopted TQM plans, they all had at least some quantifiable goals and clear benchmarks that allowed the board and the superintendent to explain progress (or lack of it) to each other and to the community. More importantly, these plans served as a reminder for both the board and the superintendent that all their efforts had to be in the service of student achievement.

The Teachers

Having the support of the board is critical when it comes to the second object of trust building: teachers. I heard from several transformational superintendents—Wilfredo Laboy, Tom Payzant (San Diego and Boston), and Gerald Anderson—that their resistant teachers and staff comforted themselves with the idea that "this too shall pass." The board needs to send the same message as the superintendent: This program is *not* going to disappear, so get with it or get out.

Once the superintendent has people's attention, she can then get down to the more difficult challenge: getting buy-in. Her message has to be delivered with skill and nuance. On the one hand, there has to be enough criticism to justify abandoning old, comfortable ways of doing things. However, if it is over-the-top, the superintendent falls into the education blame game trap.

That destroys the second part of the message: convincing the teachers that a new approach will make a positive difference and asking them to pull together in a common, noble effort to do better. Without some sense of being part of a gratifying, larger-than-self solution, teachers may be unwilling to help.[5] But if they think they have been unfairly blamed for past failure, the appeal will not work. If nothing else, they will not feel like joining a team led by someone who does not believe in them.

The Community

In order to build trust, the superintendent has to sell three main messages:

- "I care about the kids and the community."
- "I have the right judgment to run the district."
- "I have a plan that will make things better."

As in all politics, these ideas must be framed in terms that are *understandable* and *acceptable* to the intended audience. And they have to be communicated quickly, or the superintendent will find her opponents have defined her in a less flattering way.

Depending on the size and the character of the district, this job is a challenge.

Smaller Districts

The successful superintendents in smaller districts (like Portsmouth, Iredell County, or New Britain) did not rely heavily on media (frequently because small towns or suburbs did not have much) and built rapport directly. Often they had been interviewed by a group of community leaders during the selection process, but that did not seem to help much in building an image with their constituents. So starting on the day they arrived, they had to reach out. They worked at connecting with social and community networks. They held open houses and visited schools.

By making personal appeals in small-scale events, these superintendents could frame the message, emphasizing the benefits of change and reducing anxiety about a new way of doing things. Even when they went to the media, there were only a few reporters and editors dealing with education. They could sit down one-on-one and develop rapport, which paid off when the story came out pretty much the way *they* wanted to tell it.

Some of the superintendents used the Internet, though most were not fully comfortable with blogs or social-networking formats like Facebook. My sense is that most people, for now at least, still prefer to take the measure of a superintendent through face-to-face meetings, and superintendents feel the same way. Over time that may change, but, until it does, it operates to a new superintendent's advantage.[6]

Urban Districts

The job is far more challenging in large urban areas.

One potential source of conflict in major cities is often a muscular union. One study suggests that urban locals' militancy results from the rough-and-tumble political environment, which is considerably more confrontational than in suburban or rural districts.[7] Suffice it to say, for whatever reason, the big-city unions happen to be dominated by people who have an industrial view of teaching and labor relations. Their job is not to accommodate to management, but to confront it. While I hardly can claim my visits were an exhaustive survey, none of the suburban or rural superintendents described their union leaders (if they even had a union) the same way the big-city folks did.

The unions are not just militant; they know how to turn their attitude into big news. The press is always happy to report on finger pointing, and the unions have mastered the skill. That leads to more sniping than on a tough day in Afghanistan.

Moreover, big districts are often diverse. The various communities are likely to know little about each other, providing fertile ground for the constituency blame game: "He got his, so where is *mine?*" Organized protests get front-page photos; somebody screaming at a community meeting makes for a great TV clip.

Political agendas are also involved. School boards, after all, are often stepping-stones to higher political office—and press coverage is essential in big cities for moving up that ladder. As we all know, negative messages get more coverage than positive ones. Playing on community distrust or grievance has long been a staple of American politics. And in education, unfortunately, the last fifty years of race and class issues have created a scenario for playing every kind of card.

In the face of all that, a big-city superintendent cannot employ the same strategy as in a small town. It is difficult or impossible to get to enough places, and talk to enough people, to create the same comfort level. Michelle Rhee in Washington, DC, had a policy of being willing to talk to anyone, and several members of her staff told me they were in awe of her stamina in going to meeting after meeting. However, that still only amounted to a small percentage of the DC community.

And Washington has only around 600,000 residents. Joel Klein in New York, Arne Duncan in Chicago, and Roy Romer in Los Angeles could never spend enough time on this kind of local stumping.

So in a big city district, there's no realistic alternative to trying to use the media. But using the major urban media to get your message out is a two-edged sword. You run the risk that the coverage will make you more enemies than friends. After all, the media thrive on controversy, which the unions (and perhaps others) are happy to provide. So in the name of "balanced reporting," every story will devote some space to detractors who are eager to explain why this new face and all these new ideas are *not* what the district needs.

And now the question becomes, whom does audience trust? Is it going to be the new superintendent whom they have never seen before? Or is it going to be that wonderful teacher they have known forever?

The teachers are likely to start out ahead. People are inclined to trust teachers; after all, they have entrusted their children to them. The unions understand that. Their institutional advertising (like those TV spots with a teacher telling the viewer how much she is devoted to her students) has worked to build on that trust over many decades.

Michelle Rhee's tenure in Washington is a good demonstration of the problem. She quickly began criticizing teachers, and their union pushed back. While the white community did not put much store in what it had to say, the attacks had a damaging impact in large parts of the African American community, where teachers continued to be respected.

Notwithstanding Rhee's extraordinary efforts at meeting people, she was sucked into both the education and community blame games and never won the support of the people she was most trying to help. She wound up resigning upon the defeat of the mayor who had appointed her, even though test scores were rising and there were signs she had begun to turn the school district around.

The lesson learned from Rhee's case is straightforward. A new superintendent with new ideas has to build trust before being attacked and undermined by someone the community already knows and believes. The best news for a new superintendent may be that the union or others have lost that trust. But if they have not, trust building in the early stages of a superintendency is not an occasional thing. It may be the only thing that counts in the long run.

Communicating a Strong Vision

When the district works well, whether turnaround or high performing, the superintendent and school board have a shared *vision* of where they want to go.

In most of the districts I visited, that took the form of a commitment that every child can learn and every teacher can contribute. A good example of the connection between vision and action is Plano. As a way of assisting the growing number of poor Hispanic students—concentrated in one area of the mostly well-off district—Superintendent Doug Otto built on Plano's commitment to a well-rounded education for all its students to encourage parent-teacher organizations in the wealthier half of the district to partner with schools in the lower-income sections. Plano is on a well-defined journey to universal achievement, which the staff and community are called to join.

A Great Role Model

All superintendents must be good role models for the vision and the plan they propose.[8] That is no easy feat. Superintendents have traditionally favored "top-down" governance, and when transforming things, the pressure to move things forward tempts them to keep doing what they have always done—even in already high-performing districts.

That is *not* what you want in your new superintendent. You are asking him to build an organization that relies on a vision of professionalism based on *collaboration* and *empowerment*. The new leadership needs to embody this collaborative approach—not just talk about it.[9]

There is one other aspect of being a role model that is worth mentioning. Great districts are "no excuses" places. There are no acceptable rationalizations for students failing to achieve. If the superintendent becomes defensive about the district's performance, or even about his or her own performance, it simply does not square with the "no excuses" ethos. Being a great role model for reform means that those rationalizations are out.

Builder of a Strong Leadership Team

Carl Cohn, who was superintendent in Long Beach before he went to San Diego, understands team building. Some of the people he hired as senior staff members in Long Beach were only in their twenties and early thirties. That ruffled people's feathers—he told me with a broad smile— but it also demonstrated to everyone what he was all about. Unlike many superintendents, he was willing to skip over senior staff members in order to find people who had demonstrated the leadership skills he wanted. A candidate's ability mattered to him; position on the organizational chart did not.

The other part of the superintendent's job is to ensure the team members connect with each other and with her.[10] That is contrary to the old days in districts, which have always had more independent-minded, petty fiefdoms than medieval Europe. It is particularly important in the twenty-first-century district, where the dispersal of leadership in a flattened hierarchy could make the fiefdoms problem worse, not better.

An Education Leader, an Entrepreneurial Manager, and a Capable Political Actor

A good candidate for superintendent needs an understanding of the educational, managerial, and political requirements of the job.

We have already focused on the political dimension of leadership, but being an education leader is equally important. However, at the level of superintendent, the candidate may not need a full understanding on the day he walks in the door—although he certainly needs to demonstrate the ability to learn. Joel Klein, for example, had no education administration experience when he arrived in New York, but by the time he left in 2010, he was a leader in driving much of the education reform movement in America. Some people may disagree with his views, but no one can credibly argue that he has not mastered an understanding of education policy issues.

Another critical skill is being a good manager. The Long Beach school district performs considerably better than nearby Los Angeles—while spending significantly less money per student. There is no dispute: Long Beach manages its money better. (See chapter 27.) On top of that, in many areas, budgets continue to seesaw with fluctuating tax revenues. A key task for any superintendent will be managing to squeeze the maximum results from limited resources. The facility to manage that kind of budget mess is not simply a helpful skill; it is an essential one.

BUILD CONSENSUS? MAYBE NOT.

There is one thing missing from the list that often surfaces in discussions about hiring superintendents. The Council of Chief State School Officers' *Interstate School Leaders Licensure Consortium: Standards for School Leaders* and many job notices for new superintendents suggest a leader should build "consensus." When trying to transform a district, consensus is not what one is looking for.

Because change gurus emphasize that in order to achieve lasting reform people need to be won over to change rather than ordered to do it, [11]
there is a sense that a good, reforming superintendent has to build consensus.

On the contrary, consensus in a district that needs transformation is
impossible and anyone promising to seek it unsuitable. In other words,
the goal is still to get buy-in (rather than simply commanding people to
do things), but the strategy is to move ahead before having it in hand.
Creating a tipping point is key to bringing over the naysayers. [12] That was
Jerry Weast's strategy in Montgomery County. He built data analysis
tools, created time for sharing best practices, and made people behave as
if every child could master the content. As he got results, he got con-
verts. [13]

Consensus should not be confused with respecting teachers and
working hard to win their hearts and minds. Nor is it the same as listening to them, which is absolutely critical. It is just that in this process of
change, a superintendent has to act to make teachers believers. Waiting
for consensus before moving things forward is like *Waiting for Godot*. It
never comes.

THE SKILLS AND TRAITS OF A SUCCESSFUL SUPERINTENDENT

Once we know what a good superintendent should do, we need to turn
our attention to the kind of person who can get it done. Describing what
makes someone a successful leader is like closing your eyes and putting
your arms around the leg of an elephant (or the trunk) and then describing the whole animal based on what you feel. Recognizing that, I approach the subject with some humility. However, after hours of speaking
with dozens of successful superintendents, it became apparent they almost all shared a number of important qualities: [14]

Independence

The transformational superintendents who rose through the teaching
ranks were especially fascinating; they had one distinctive characteristic
in common: they had first transformed themselves. [15] None of them had
been taught about TQM or continuous improvement in teachers college.
They studied it much later, decided it worked, and became true believers.
When you listen to them explain what they do, you are impressed by
their sincerity. They are the perfect people to convince others it is time for
something new.

Intellectual Curiosity

The adoption of TQM or continuous improvement, often against pre-vailing orthodox wisdom, shows the superintendents are the antithesis of rigid. Their intellectual curiosity is perfect for continuous improvement, which only works when managed by people who take pleasure in iden-tifying a problem, thinking it through, and fixing it.[16]

Awareness

Quality superintendents have a way of acknowledging problems without ever seeing them as an excuse. Moreover, they convey a sense that a district without challenges to fix would not be any fun for them to run. And they are confident that they can get the district staff to feel the same way.[17]

Commitment to Others before Self

Opting for TQM or continuous improvement puts much greater pres-sure on superintendents (and everyone else in the district) than the old way of doing things. It shows a real commitment to others before self.

Self-Confidence

Bringing an entirely new management strategy to districts shows self-confidence, both in their ideas and in their ability to change the existing culture. It also reflects an inherent optimism. These traits are important in any school district, no matter how well it is run.

Discipline

Except in large urban districts like New York, getting things done means doing a lot of the work themselves. A good example is New Brit-ain's Doris Kurtz, who took on teaching the principals' academy herself.

Leadership — Persuasiveness and Organizational Ability

A reform strategy that pushes from the top down to get bottom-up leadership is an exercise in restraint and nuance. It is weirdly oxymoronic to be ordering people to be more assertive. So if superintendents are successful, it is because at some level they have mastered both pushing people to take control, and then, having mobilized them, letting go when they do. There is a Zen-like quality here that is real art.

Grit

The superintendents all emphasized to me how they had to press on, even when significant numbers of teachers and administrators resisted, and even when parents and others in the community were opposed. Whether or not initial attempts at change succeeded, magnifying the doubts and the resistance, they kept pushing.[18] That takes old-fashioned grit.

Focus

Finally, all the superintendents stuck fanatically to their message about improving achievement for all students. By relentlessly focusing on that core goal of student achievement and then getting actual improvements, each of these leaders gradually gained enough trust in the community to prevent any lingering doubt from derailing reform.[19] *They refused to be distracted*—no mean feat in a highly charged political environment.

Outsider versus Insider

Should superintendents be drawn solely from the ranks of school administrators? Recent evidence says "no." Roy Romer is the former governor of Colorado; Joel Klein, a former assistant attorney general; Paul Vallas (the superintendent in New Orleans, who previously also served in Philadelphia and Chicago) and Arne Duncan (Chicago), mayoral assistants; Michelle Rhee, the chief executive of a nonprofit, albeit one focused on education. While not everyone believes these individuals have done great jobs as superintendents, they certainly were as good as their educator colleagues, and some clearly would say a lot better.

There are skills that you want in a superintendent, such as being a good manager, which may be developed as well, or better, outside the world of education. The details of instruction can be left to *good* trusted aides—the important job for the superintendent is in being able to identify who those people are and giving them space and opportunity to do what they do best.

The Value of "Level 5" Leadership: Does It Help to Be Self-Effacing?

The other issue is temperament. Management guru Jim Collins has observed that most organizations benefit from what he calls "Level 5" leadership. Level 5 leaders are humble, self-effacing, diligent and resolute, and really good at their jobs. They are the people best able to transform workplace cultures, he says, because they spotlight the organization rather than their own contribution.[20]

Collins assigns Levels 1 to 3 to people who are good individual workers or managers—but not chief executives. Level 4s may be seen as "effective" leaders, but they are the "show horses"—that is, highly regarded executives who focus attention on themselves rather than on their organization. They get great results while in office, but those improvements are not sustained after they leave. They have persuaded people to change "for them," not for the organization or the mission.

Most of the educators I interviewed were believers in the value of self-effacing, low-key, plow-horse leadership. So do several prominent academics who are expert in school leadership.[21] In an era of high-decibel politics, a low-key approach may not seem to be the way to accomplish anything, but one should not confuse a lack of noise with a lack of action.

As is clear from the discussion about building trust in the community, anyone who can remain low-key and keep the focus on the district and its mission is perhaps the ideal person to hire. They do exist; Tom Payzant seems to have avoided celebrity status in Boston. Adrian Walker, a *Boston Globe* columnist who covered Payzant, told me that the superintendent's determined, low-key style was Payzant's foremost advantage; he did not demonize the union or even suggest he was leading a crusade. It was more matter-of-fact and focused on the elements of reform. His low-key style kept him from frittering away any goodwill (or having it taken from him) before he had built up his own local support.

Level 4s may still be able to achieve change, but its sustainability is questionable. More likely, that change simply becomes harder. Enemies become more numerous. Boards and mayors are pushed to weigh in. Longevity is harder to come by. The critical mass of believing principals and teachers may be more elusive.

THE ROLE OF THE BOARD

Every successful school district I visited had a board or mayor who followed three rules when dealing with their superintendent:

Ensure Longevity

Tom Payzant, Boston's superintendent for eleven years, was the first well-known reform superintendent I interviewed. I began with a simple question: "What was the most fundamental part of your reform strategy?" I expected to hear an answer like "hiring good teachers." The answer came back in one word: "Longevity."

After Payzant, I asked virtually every superintendent about "longevity." Everyone emphatically agreed. Doug Otto in Plano has been there fourteen years, and there have been only four superintendents in the eighty-plus-year history of the district. Gerald Anderson stayed ten years in Brazosport. McKinsey & Co., the well-known management consultants, did a recent study of successful turnarounds in other countries and concluded it takes *at least six years* to get any positive results in test scores.[22] Contrast that with the fact that the average tenure of a superintendent is under four years.[23]

As we shall see when we discuss the Miami-Dade "Zone" experiment, demanding too much, too soon, simply gets a district too little.

No Micromanagement

A second important injunction to a board facing all sorts of pressures from teachers, parents, and whoever else weighs in on all manner of issues, from large to small: Do not micromanage.

Consider the Los Angeles Unified School District's six-year relationship with Roy Romer. Unlike many of the districts that have made real improvements over the years, the superintendent's reform proposals were regularly pushed aside in favor of debates over excruciating details of everyday management. Longevity does not mean much if it merely sets the stage for doing the same bad thing over and over again and hoping for a different result.

Experts in school governance, such as John Carver,[24] tirelessly advocate *active but limited supervision*, but they are often ignored in practice.[25] That is a tragedy. In every high-performing district I visited that still has a directly elected school board, the board plays just such an active, but limited, role.

Focus on the Big Picture

Boards have limited time, and the public and media are willing to pay limited attention. A board that is dealing with too many little things is not going to engage in the big discussions about goals, objectives, and money. It is another "zero-sum" game, where they can do one or the other, but not both.

The superintendent's time is limited as well—and the time spent explaining to board members each contract or personnel decision takes away from the time needed to manage the district. Even more than low pay or accountability, political games are what drive superintendents from their jobs.[26]

Here is one important aspect of mayoral control vs. board control: Mayors have enough to do without immersing themselves in the details or dirty work of reform. They may talk about schools broadly as part of their agenda, but they happily shun the day-to-day responsibility.[27]

Boards see the world differently. It is all they have to do. Micromanagement is their catnip. It is why all the superintendents with boards, especially those that transformed districts, said the same thing: No matter how supportive the boards were in the end, it took constant care and feeding to get them there.

WHAT WE NEED TO DO

- Superintendents and boards need to have a clear agreement on what the superintendent is supposed to do. Neither the board nor parents and taxpayers should move forward unless most people are united on that one vision. And everyone has to understand that extensive reform takes time, so that if they are not prepared to live with a superintendent for many years, they need to reconsider whether they are ready to undertake real reform.
- Reformers need to demand that boards (and mayors) follow the rules. No micromanaging. A focus on the big-picture issues of mission and budget. And, especially in a reform-minded district, committing to a superintendent for a long time because reform does not happen overnight.
- Reformers also need to demand that the new superintendent have the right traits for the job. Being an insider may be a good thing in a high-performing district, but not in a transforming one. Same with consensus building.
- Most importantly, as members of the community, reformers have an even bigger role. If there is a history of blame games, then whether or not those blame games continue to play out and disrupt reform is the responsibility of every taxpayer and educator in the district. Us.
- And if the superintendent fails to understand the importance of building trust in the community, then make him understand. And help him out. If one is in the Lions Club, ask that the superintendent be invited to speak at the next meeting. Or write a letter to the editor in support of her plan.
- Above all, if you believe in the reform agenda, make clear to the naysayers that, so far as you are concerned, this new world is not going to pass. On the contrary, you are going to do everything in your power to make it stay.

NOTES

1. Everything in this chapter applies equally to the mayor, if that's who is hiring the superintendent. So the word "board" usually means "board or mayor."

2. Alan Bersin's stint as superintendent in San Diego is similar. A lawyer and former U.S. attorney, he was hired in 1998 with the backing of the city's business community on a 3–2 board vote, following a bitter 1996 strike. Bersin had an aggressive reform agenda that he pushed through over his seven-year tenure. However, his support always teetered on the 3–2 split, and the union, which opposed him from the beginning, never reconciled itself to his program. For an extensive discussion of his time in office, see Frederick M. Hess, ed., *Urban School Reform, Lessons from San Diego* (Cambridge, MA: Harvard Education Press, 2006).

3. In game theory, a "zero-sum" game is one in which any gain to player A is offset by an equal loss to player B. By definition, there is no possible outcome that represents a "win" for both players.

4. Laboy was removed in May 2010 based on charges of financial irregularities. The charges, while serious, do not cast doubt on the success of Laboy's instructional reform strategy, so I have decided to continue to use Lawrence as an example of reform.

5. Michael Fullan, *Turnaround Leadership* (San Francisco: Jossey-Bass, 2004), 44.

6. Mark J. Stock, "Superintendent Blogging," *Phi Delta Kappan* 66, no. 7 (August 2009): 10–16; Neil A. Rochelle, "To Blog or Not to Blog?" *Phi Delta Kappan* 66, no. 7 (August 2009): 17–19.

7. Karen Seashore Louis, Kenneth Leithwood, Kyla L. Wahlstrom, and Stephen E. Anderson, *Investing the Links to Improved Student Learning* (Minneapolis: University of Minnesota Press/University of Toronto Press, 2010), 97.

8. Sharon D. Kruse and Karen Seashore Louis, *Building Strong School Cultures* (Thousand Oaks, CA: AASA/Corwin Press, 2009), 49.

9. Daniel Goleman, Richard Boyatzis, and Annie McKee, *Primal Leadership: Learning to Lead with Emotional Intelligence* (Boston, MA: Harvard Business School Press, 2004), 53–69.

10. *McKinsey Quarterly*, "How Centered Leaders Achieve Extraordinary Results" (2010) (retrieved from www.mckinseyquarterly.com/article_print.aspx?L2=18&L3=31&ar=2678 on Oct. 6, 2010).

11. Michael Fullan, *Leading in a Culture of Change* (San Francisco: Jossey-Bass, 2001), *passim*.

12. Jeff Nelsen and Bob Hill, "The Tipping Point in School Culture," *The School Administrator*, April 2009, 22.

13. Stacey M. Childress, "Six Lessons for Pursuing Excellence and Equity at Scale," *Phi Delta Kappan* 91, no. 3 (Nov. 2009): 13–18, 17.

14. Daniel Goleman's pioneering work on behavior provides great insight into successful interpersonal relationships. He has characterized six types of leadership: coercive, authoritative, affiliative (leader creates harmony and builds bonds), democratic, pacesetting, and coaching. (Daniel Goleman, "Leadership That Gets Results," *Harvard Business Review*, March–April 2000, 78–90). As useful as those categories are, the superintendents I visited did not rely solely on any one of them. Their styles reflected multiple strategies, plus personal histories that created unique perspectives.

15. New Leaders for New Schools has published its criteria for selecting new trainees. Although I arrived at my list prior to reading NLNS, the two lists share many of the same traits. For NLNS's list, see www.nlns.org/Criteria.jsp.

16. Jim Collins, *Good to Great* (New York: Basic Books, 2003), 65–87.

17. Richard Boyatzis and Annie McKee, *Resonant Leadership* (Boston, MA: Harvard Business School Press, 2005).

18. Michael Fullan notes that these "implementation dips" often occur, and that good leaders know that change is a process and that they have to focus on both teachers' emotional stress and need for enough training to do the job right. Fullan, *Leading in a Culture of Change*, 40–41.

19. Ninety-two percent of superintendents believe sticking to a few core goals is key to being a good administrator. Steve Farkas, Jean Johnson, Ann Duffett, and Tony Foleno, *Trying to Stay Ahead of the Game* (New York: Public Agenda, 2001), 11.

20. Collins, *Good to Great*, 17–40.

21. Fullan, *Leading in a Culture of Change*, 1–3; Kruse and Louis, *Building Strong School Cultures*, 11.

22. Mona Mourshed, Chinezi Chijioke, Michael Barber, and McKinsey & Co., *How the World's Most Improved School Systems Keep Getting Better* (New York: McKinsey & Co., 2010), 23, ex. 5.

23. Council on Great City Schools, *Urban School Superintendents: Characteristics, Tenure, and Salary: Seventh Survey Report, Urban Indicator* (Washington, DC: Council on

Great City Schools, 2010), 2 (superintendents' tenure among 65 largest districts averages 3.64 years).

24. John Carver and Miriam Mayhew Carver, *Basic Principles of Policy Governance* (San Francisco: Jossey-Bass, 1996); Gene Royer, *School Board Leadership 2000* (Houston, TX: Brockton Publishing Co., 1996)

25. In one survey, 65 percent of superintendents surveyed agreed somewhat or strongly with the proposition that "too many school boards would rather hire a superintendent they can control rather than someone with a strong track record and proven leadership skills." Farkas et al., *Trying to Stay Ahead of the Game*, 42.

26. Farkas et al., *Trying to Stay Ahead of the Game*, 8–9.

27. Jeffrey R. Henig and Wilbur C. Rich, eds., *Mayors in the Middle* (Princeton, NJ: Princeton University Press, 2004).

FIVE

Principals

Every successful superintendent with whom I spoke said the same thing: Behind every great school is a great principal. Ninety-nine percent of superintendents agree.[1] The effectiveness of the principal makes or breaks a school.[2]

Doris Kurtz framed it almost like a military campaign: Success is achieved building by building, not district by district. The central office can talk about change, but only the principal can make it happen. The culture in which teachers operate is set—not by the state or the district—but by the school where they work. *That is the principal's world.* Whatever rules and requirements flow from Washington, the state capitol, or the district office, those rules will have impact only if the principal gives them life.[3]

The greatest single limitation on reform may be whether a district has enough qualified principals to carry it out.

GOOD PRINCIPALS ARE IN SHORT SUPPLY

David Stuckwisch, the superintendent in Portsmouth, Virginia, summed up who was a good principal in the old, mass-production world: "You were doing okay if you won your athletic games, kept the place clean, the band was good, and the kids who wanted to go to college got there."

Secretary of Education Arne Duncan had an even pithier assessment: He told me that too many administrators in the old days were "low caliber."

My interviewees had a favorite pejorative label for old-style administrators—"managers." Their image was a bureaucratic paper-pusher with a yen for detail, a predilection for rigidity, and an aversion to vision. It was the industrial, mass-production model, and for these superintendents, it was the antithesis of what they were trying to achieve.

The chart shown in table 5.1 roughly outlines the differences between the old-style principals too many schools have and the twenty-first-century type they need.[4]

The next several sections describe moving current and new administrators from the middle column to the one on the right. It comes with a caution: The process is not going to be easy.

WORKING WITH THE PRINCIPALS YOU HAVE

Many school leaders, especially in struggling districts, do not fall within the chart's description of a twenty-first-century principal. What should the new superintendent do?

Almost all the successful superintendents I talked with chose the same initial strategy: They would work with the principals who were already in place in the schools.[5] Faced with a lack of capable replacements, they limited firings at first to the few who were obviously totally incapable of ever adapting to the new world.

For the rest, the superintendents adopted a threefold strategy that looks much like what is already being done in high-performing districts: (1) push decision making down to the school level at least to the extent the principal could handle the new authority; (2) give each principal appropriate training and support to succeed; and (3) make each principal accountable for the school's performance.

For some principals, the strategy was liberating.

When Gerald Anderson became superintendent in Brazosport, Velasco Elementary School was the poorest performing school in the district. It had a relatively new principal named Sam Williams. Williams shared with me his perspective on the school's problems: He found that the teachers tended to self-pity. The kids were bored because the teaching was rote. There was not enough time for learning, and classroom management was a big issue.

Williams had in fact begun working on changing things, even before Anderson's arrival. He raised the expectations of teachers, parents, and students; he assigned teachers to the areas they could teach well; and he instituted a plan to support struggling students. So now, with Anderson's arrival—and with the district newly committed to closing the achievement gap—he had official sanction for everything he was already trying to do.

However, entrepreneurial self-starters like Sam Williams are a rarity. What then?

Table 5.1.   Old-Style versus Twenty-First-Century Principals: Traits Compared

	Old-Style Principal	Twenty-First-Century Principal
Vision	Lets the central office define the purpose of the school and goals of education. No distinct, personal vision or mission for the school.	Has a long-term vision for the school that organizes all activity; a defined mission galvanizes faculty and other staff. Vision includes the "all children can learn" approach. Sets high expectations and standards and models them for others.
Approach with staff	Autocratic, top-down style toward teachers and other staff. Not open. Not comfortable sharing power. Not focused on working with teachers. Distant. Not well schooled in education leadership.[1]	Collaborative, respects teachers and other staff. Promotes culture of continuous learning; encourages teachers to work together and with the principal. Honest. Not afraid to share power and actively contributes to collaborations. Strong human relations skills. *In reform districts*: understands tensions and distress inherent in change.[2]
Professional support for staff	Not interested in professional development based on needs at school site.	Insists on high-quality instruction. Stresses support for new teachers and professional development for faculty based on actual needs. Builds schedule to facilitate collaboration.
Administrative tools	Focuses on moving paper, passing out directives.	Focuses on finding solutions to problems. Likes to set goals and achieve them. Comfortable with continuous improvement.
Use of data	Not comfortable using data to drive decision making.	Uses data for decision making; comfortable and creative with information technology.
Approach to budget	Not trained in developing and managing a budget.	Well schooled in such management issues as budgets and planning.
Approach to union	Sees union, if there is one, as a hostile organization to be confronted.	Understands value of good labor relations and reaches out to union to find common ground.

Approach to parents	Resists parental involvement in school activities, does not emphasize parent outreach.	Reaches out to parents and welcomes involvement across racial or class differences. Not defensive.
Approach to students	Distant from students.	Likes the kids, knows their names.

[1] In a 2001 survey, only 34 percent of superintendents thought their principals knew how to delegate authority, only 33 percent were happy with the way principals involved teachers in decision making, and only 25 percent believed they were good at motivating and inspiring staff. Steve Farkas, Jean Johnson, Ann Duffett, and Tony Foleno, *Trying to Stay Ahead of the Game* (New York: Public Agenda, 2001), 23–24.

[2] Dale Ballou and Michael Podgursky, "What Makes a Good Principal? How Teachers Assess the Performance of Principals," *Economics of Education Review* 14, no. 3 (1995): 243–52, 244, 245; Sharon D. Kruse and Karen Seashore Louis, *Building Strong School Cultures* (Thousand Oaks, CA: AASA/Corwin Press, 2009), 28.

Define the Job

Most of the superintendents assigned their principals, as their first task, to focus on developing *goals* for the school. Raising test scores was always one goal, but there were others. Principals identified things like adding college-level advanced placement courses, improving teacher retention, and building up better after-school programs that supported learning. The superintendents also pushed principals' personal goals, especially those who needed help with new skills (such as data-driven decision making or facilitating teacher collaboration). The key was to keep the district's goals constantly centered on student achievement, so that principals could see a connection between their own work and the larger effort.

As a second focus, every one of the superintendents emphasized the need for continuous improvement. For principals who are used to the mass-production style, the very idea of continuous improvement is daunting. It requires confronting reality, thinking up solutions, and getting people to do things differently. Joel Klein said he wants his principals to be "the building's CEO," and Jack Dale in Fairfax County talked about always striving "to do better in order to be the best." The principals' comfort level with continuous improvement was often the "acid test" of whether they would succeed.

Train People

Training principals is not a one-time thing. Even in good school districts, training goes on throughout a career. And in transforming districts, incumbent principals need *a great deal of training*—just as a new principal would. When Nick Fischer arrived in Fall River, he found that most principals had no idea about what kids needed to know in order to be able to read.

But who will provide the training and coaching for the principals? Often the lack of teaching and coaching resources is a major obstacle in trying to improve schools. In a small district, an energetic superintendent may even decide to conduct much of the training personally, as Doris Kurtz did in New Britain.[6]

Provide a Conducive Work Environment

The third requirement for a principal to be able to do the job is to be given the necessary resources, as well as the authority to make decisions about them.

Resources: UCLA professor William Ouchi has argued strongly for giving principals virtually complete budget authority.[7] Nonetheless, no district I visited totally follows Ouchi's advice. (Charter schools are different and reflect Ouchi's model. They get a lump sum based on a per capita formula to spend as they see fit.)

Most high-performing districts give principals full control over only a specified portion of their funding. In Long Beach—which has an established culture and well-trained administrators—principals control a full 70 percent of their budgets. In Montgomery County, the central office provides about $2,000 per capita as an annual supplement for schools with large numbers of students on the free or reduced lunch program and lets the principals decide how that supplement is spent. In Chicago and New York, a select number of trusted principals are given greater-than-usual control over their budgets, depending on that level of trust. Alternatively, superintendents told me they are open to principals' requests for more money, giving them some influence over budgeting, if not actual authority. They worried about principals' lack of budgetary expertise, one of the many failings of graduate school training we will discuss shortly.

Hiring: Many of the reform districts I visited had given principals an unusual degree of influence over hiring staff.[8] Tom Payzant explained why: If a principal is going to be held accountable for an outcome that depends heavily on the quality of teacher performance, it is only fair to give her the opportunity to *select* those teachers (perhaps with input from the faculty).

Authority over teacher hiring has definite limits—most of which are the result of historic labor practices. These contractual limitations, which exist even in districts without collective bargaining agreements, include seniority, tenure, and bumping, all of which will be discussed in the section on teachers. In some districts, including New York City, practices like "bumping" have been eliminated, and seniority and tenure are under assault in many states. But many contracts retain seniority provisions, allowing senior teachers to keep jobs during cutbacks even if they are less effective than more junior faculty members. Most districts have yet to eliminate traditional tenure in contract negotiations, although many states are doing so legislatively.

Even teachers seem to favor the idea of school-based hiring, in spite of its implications for such labor protections as bumping. At least one survey found that teachers hired by the principal tended to give much more favorable evaluations to that principal.[9] That makes sense if the idea is that a school's faculty and administration should be a self-selected team, but it is an idea that challenges old-style labor relations.

Additional Staff: Adequate support is far from a minor issue. In a recent survey, principals in high-needs districts reported that *support*, not higher salary, was the most important element needed to attract and keep top-notch administrators.[10]

According to a National Center for Education Statistics (NCES) survey in 2007–2008, public school principals are working approximately fifty-eight hours per week.[11] Loading additional duties, like instructing teachers, makes no sense, unless other duties are removed.[12] Most of the successful districts relieved the overload by adding mentors and subject matter specialists to school staffs. They have either particular expertise in a content area (like reading or math) or broad knowledge of professional development or team building. Rather than looking to the principal, teachers turned for help to these people, who often organized and ran meetings of grade-level or subject matter groups. Long Beach is a model, but a rarity: It staffs its senior high schools with two principals, three vice principals, and several counselors.

Some districts also took over various noneducation management functions (cafeteria, custodial, or landscaping supervision). New York City has developed sophisticated support organizations to allow schools to contract out some of these functions. Most districts, however, left these jobs to the principals, sometimes because they saw no value in doing otherwise, but sometimes because of money. As principals' workloads refocus toward academic leadership, the value of having others do non-core functions may be more obvious. We will return to this subject in chapter 26.

The relationship with the central office is also different. As Chris Steinhauser in Long Beach explained: "The central office is to serve the principals, not the other way round." So when principals have a problem, they can call on the central office for help to relieve their burden. But that requires overturning old attitudes among central office bureaucrats, and that does not come easily.[13] Even Steinhauser, the leader of a model district, agrees.

Give Principals as Much Authority as They Can Handle—but No More

The great challenge for any superintendent, especially a transforming one, is to push or prod the team of principals forward. It is an art. Some of the principals take easily to the new world, some struggle with it. There is no cookie-cutter, one-size-fits-all approach.

The successful superintendents keep in close contact with the principals throughout the year. Most schedule regular meetings with them (or, in larger districts, meetings with regional superintendents or directors). Whether it is a small district like Pearl River, or a large one like Fairfax or Montgomery County, the meetings serve as an important show of support for principals and for the collaborative approach. But the meetings also put pressure on principals: Their world is now being *measured*, and people are watching.

In successful districts (of either the high-performing or transforming variety), the administrative dynamic is a mix of both looser and tighter central office control, in comparison with the old industrial model. Administration is *tighter* in the sense that the principal will now be required to fulfill a series of measurable metrics—such as higher test scores, fewer dropouts, higher teacher retention, or greater parent satisfaction. But administration is *looser* in the sense that, as long as the principal has the trust of the central office, he or she will have flexibility in deciding how to meet the goals.

Jack Dale, the Fairfax County superintendent, for example, expects his principals to be "creatively insubordinate." But with a principal who is struggling or whose scores continue to drag, he maintains tight supervision. Chicago and New York follow a similar path. Elsewhere, most superintendents seem to have evolved an informal version of the same strategy.

Why should reformers, especially those who are not school employees, care about "loose-tight"? If Washington or the state legislature is going to try to dictate how this supervision will occur, they are inevitably going to get it wrong. This is not the place for hard and fast rules, even though legislators are constantly tempted to write them. It is why you hire really good superintendents.

Pay and Bonuses

Do salary levels generally affect the ability to recruit or retain principals? And do bonuses based on performance make a difference in the quality of principals' work?

Unlike teachers' pay, principals' pay has not been attacked as woefully inadequate. The NCES reports that average salary for a public elementary school principal in 2007–2008 was $85,200, and for a secondary principal, $90,300.[14] No one expressed concern that money was keeping teachers from moving into administration.[15]

My sample may not give the full picture. New-style, postindustrial principals have to work a lot harder than their mass-production counterparts. Salaries and salary differentials (between principals and master teachers) therefore may become a bigger issue as time goes on.

Bonuses might be one way to deal with such a problem, but according to those I interviewed, their ability to foster better performance is not yet established. Nevertheless, pay for performance was used in a number of districts either to create incentives to take on management roles or to reward principals' achievements: For example, New York City, Washington, DC, Pearl River, Aldine, and Brazosport all used them.

Are the bonuses worth the money? David Weiner, as principal of a large elementary school in Brooklyn, participated in New York's pay for performance plan. (He is now Philadelphia's deputy superintendent for accountability.) Weiner judges that the plan worked well because New York's measures were clear and logically related to student achievement. In his view, a bonus does not get people to work harder; it gets them to "work smarter," by focusing everyone's attention on what is most important to the district.

None of the superintendents or senior administrators could point to any clear connection between school improvement and a principal's bonus. Bonuses were generally just one of many changes instituted at roughly the same time in districts, and it was hard for the superintendents to evaluate how much impact the bonuses had. The superintendents acknowledged they had value as a form of recognition for work well done. However, no one could say whether a gold watch or a certificate might have done just as well, [16] or whether the threat of firing or the potential embarrassment of having lower test results than their peers would have achieved the same effect without other inducements.

GETTING RID OF PRINCIPALS IS NOT AS EASY AS IT MIGHT SEEM

Even with ample help, many principals in turnaround districts chose to leave. [17] Indeed, all of the transformational superintendents I interviewed (except one, Gerald Anderson) had experienced a large turnover in principals. A 2009 report found that 80 percent of New York City's principals had been hired after 2001. [18]

The superintendents identified a number of reasons that principals failed:

- They could not take the pressure of living in a measured environment, where they were required to improve scores and/or meet other goals.
- They had not been trained to be instructional leaders. They did not know curriculum or pedagogy. They were weak on running professional learning communities that foster teachers' professional development. They did not know what to do *and did not want to learn*.

- They were personally uneasy in a collaborative environment.
- They could not handle being the CEOs of their buildings. They did not know how to prioritize projects and get the most out of the resources available.
- They were simply overwhelmed by organizing meetings, budgeting, planning, evaluating, conferring with parents. The burdens were often compounded by an unwillingness to share leadership with mentors, master teachers, or the faculty in general.

But what if a struggling principal simply does not want to go? Wanting to fire someone and actually doing it are two extremely different things in the world of education.

Approximately one-quarter of school principals have tenure provisions in their contracts.[19] If a tenured principal is failing, reform in that school is effectively stymied, unless the central office can pressure him or her to move on or retire. It is a huge stumbling block. The superintendents unanimously agreed that their ability to fire principals was the biggest motivator—and most important tool—they had to get principals to adapt to the twenty-first century.

Principals, however, have more than their contracts to protect them.

They often have their own power bases. As capable political actors, they can—and do—build up support among parents and teachers to fight off a superintendent's desire to see someone else take his or her place.

Nick Fischer related how he faced just such a problem after arriving in Fall River. The principal at the high school had a terrible track record, with a 44 percent dropout rate, severe underachievement in many courses, and AP classes taught by teachers who had not themselves been trained in how to teach the subjects. Fischer wanted to replace him. However, that had not deterred the principal from approaching Fischer about getting a substantial raise.

When Fischer did not show any interest in giving the principal the raise, calls started coming from parents, some of whom were highly influential locally, who said they did not want to lose their beloved school leader. The school committee and faculty weighed in.

Fischer not only resisted the raise, he fired the principal. (He then brought in an outsider, which offended both the community and the mayor, and undoubtedly contributed to his own firing, recounted earlier.)

In a few places, the problem is further compounded because the superintendent does not even hold the principal's contract. The parents and teachers do.

Although only a few districts I visited (Chicago, Long Beach, and San Diego)[20] currently give some formal authority to school councils in the hiring or firing of teachers, the idea always crops up in discussions of school reform. In 2009, activists in New York City were still demanding

the restoration of Community School Districts, with hiring authority entrusted to school leadership teams.[21]

The battles for local control make interesting reading,[22] but I want to
limit the discussion to the impact of local control on the subject at hand—
terminating failing principals.

The problem with local councils is that their existence divides authority and responsibility in a school district. Advocates of school councils
point out private schools have boards that hire and fire headmasters, but
the analogy is poor. There is no superintendent for a private school. The
board is the ultimate authority. In the public schools, it is different.

School councils that hire or fire principals divide authority. They may
have one idea of what works in a school while the superintendent has
another. Or they may just have different values: As in Fall River, they
may like the principal and just want to keep him on even if the school's
student achievement is miserable.

Especially in a transformational district, where values are not necessarily widely shared, or where principals are about to be measured by a
standard they have previously never had to meet, the likelihood of real
conflict seems great—and counterproductive.

Indeed, in Chicago, the various senior district administrators with
whom I spoke all complained about being stymied by local councils,
which have kept on principals the central office saw as nonperformers. It
seems unfair to hold a superintendent responsible for performance in
such a case—just as it seems unfair to hold principals responsible when
they cannot hire their own faculty.

Reservations about school council control are not inconsistent with
encouraging parents and taxpayers to be proactive. They should make
their views known. If their advice is rejected, they can see whether scores
went up or down after the principal was fired. If the superintendent was
wrong, there is always the recourse of the ballot box.

Finally, even if a superintendent does have the ability to replace a
principal, getting the right person in the job may still be a challenge.

Professor Craig Richards of Columbia Teachers College says that loyalty, rather than ability, is often the major criterion for the selection of
administrators. Even in Montgomery County, where Jerry Weast has
transformed almost every aspect of the district over the past decade, high
school principals were selected by "an old-boy network" until recently.
The obvious problem with such cronyism is that the principals you get
are not likely to be capable of doing the job, whether it is maintaining a
high-performing school or creating one.

FINDING THE RIGHT KIND OF PRINCIPAL

The impediments to firing underperforming principals pale in comparison with the real problem: We really do not have much of a pipeline of good people to put in their place. If we want one, we have a lot of work to do.

Districts recruit badly. They train badly. States hand out licenses cavalierly. In most districts, we do not support new principals at all. The indifference is inexcusable.

If we cannot produce effective principals, we will not have quality districts, whether they are already high performing or transforming. *Without effective principals:*

- Teacher evaluation has no legitimacy.
- Professional development of teachers is useless.
- Individualizing instruction for students is likely impossible.
- Parent outreach and involvement are simply not going to happen.

Self-Selection Produces "Old-Style" Administrators

We need to start at the beginning of the pipeline. Historically, administrators have been teachers who decided they had had enough of the classroom and wanted the additional prestige and salary of an administrator's job. The problem is that teachers, in general, are *not* a good group from which to draw your school's leadership.

I asked interviewees whether teachers tend to make good administrators. They all answered that most teachers do *not* have the right skill set. David Helme (the superintendent in Roslyn, New York) was typical: Teachers tend not to be risk takers because they are too concerned with security, and after years of being isolated in classrooms, they do not "interact enough with adults" to know how to do the job.[23]

Arthur Levine and Craig Richards, both of whom have taught at the Teachers College at Columbia, saw this issue from the perspective of graduate school education: There is effectively no screening of people who apply for graduate programs in education administration. An example of how bad it is: Professor Richards and Becca Knight of the Broad Center for the Management of School Systems (which runs the Broad Superintendents' Academy, a large program to train administrators), both talked about the logic of graduate education administration programs joining with business schools on some type of combined degree. However, neither thought it would work in many places because the entry requirements are so different. The teacher types just could not get into the business schools.

A couple of decades ago, the quality issue was less of a problem: We were not asking much of our principals back then in the mass-production era. That is simply not the case anymore.

Districts Need to Identify Good Candidates and Actively Recruit Them

The overall remedy is obvious: Do *not* rely on self-selection. Many of the high-performing districts have a program to identify and recruit teachers who might make good administrators.[24] So do high-performing systems in other countries.[25]

Almost all the successful superintendents take a personal interest in recruitment, scanning the teaching ranks for people who seem to have the right skill set. For example, Wilfredo Laboy found potential administrators by personally screening those who have taken on some additional responsibilities, such as serving as teacher mentors or department chairs.

Some jurisdictions have designed programs to interest these candidates in applying for the principal's job. Fairfax County runs a seminar to explain the principalship to teachers who might be interested. In Watauga County, the district invites candidates to shadow current principals, to see if they like the job.

Sophisticated districts may employ assessment tools such as multiple interviews, structured management exercises, or simulations to see how well someone interacts with a group.[26] Some districts go further. Recognizing that they are looking for distinct personality types, several districts and charters I visited (including Green Dot, New York City, Fairfax County, and Blue Valley) have used psychologists' personality tests to help identify potentially successful administrators.[27]

Districts Should Reach Out to Noneducators — at Least for Now

Should districts reach out to noneducators as potential administrators? Certainly noneducators can make good superintendents. But do they make good principals?

Unlike superintendents, principals are working *in schools*. They supervise their teachers and the education strategy. Several interviewees expressed great hesitancy about opening the door to noneducators. Tom Payzant put it simply: "Educational leaders should be educators."[28] Indeed, I found no support for using outsiders *as principals* among the superintendents.

Yet, states like Florida and New Jersey now allow outsiders to be hired as principals. The question is whether the model of the principal these states have in mind is the same as what Payzant wants. In mass-production days, where there was no emphasis on principals as education leaders, it would have been easier to make the case. The best argument for what these states have done may simply be that there is no reason to exclude one arbitrarily — provided that those making the selection understand clearly the skill set they are looking for.[29]

The more critical noneducator-administrator issue deals with noninstructional central office jobs, such as the people who head up human resources, information technology, contracting, or construction. Many districts have traditionally awarded such jobs to former teachers.

Los Angeles had several former teachers in such roles before Romer's arrival. They left a legacy of destruction in their wake, from poorly managed construction projects to overpriced computers, to totally one-sided contracts that guaranteed we paid more or got poorer service than we should have. Romer replaced as many of them as he could with outsiders who had the right background. (Our construction chief was a former Navy Seabee.) Until he did, my initial instruction to my new lawyers before they went off to counsel their clients: "Don't let 'em run out of bounds." Enough said, I hope.

TRAINING PRINCIPALS FOR THE TWENTY-FIRST CENTURY

I asked every administrator this simple question: Was your graduate study in education administration useful? The consistent answer was that one or two of the courses were helpful, but the programs were mostly a waste of time.[30]

The comments are consistent with study after study decrying administrators' training. In 2005, Columbia Teachers College's former president, Arthur Levine, who had by then moved to the Woodrow Wilson Foundation, did a major survey. He found some extraordinarily high-quality programs, but his overall conclusion was strongly downbeat:

> This study found the overall quality of education administration programs in the United States to be poor. The majority of programs range from inadequate to appalling, even at some of the country's leading universities.[31]

Working administrators often share these views. In 2007, Public Agenda surveyed principals from high-needs schools, reporting that "Very few had much positive to say about traditional training in its prevailing forms."[32]

And remember, this sad state of affairs is the handiwork of people who, supposedly, train others on how to run high-performing schools.

School districts thus face a major problem. The pipeline is not producing enough quality administrators (and, as we shall see later, teachers) to run twenty-first-century schools. The solution: *Do it yourself.*

Approximately one-quarter of America's school districts have already instituted their own programs to train aspiring administrators.[33] These programs follow one of three tracks: district-run, university-district collaboration, or independent programs that have struck agreements with individual districts.

District-Run Principals' Academies

Many of the most successful districts run their own programs to train principals. Plano, a high-performing suburb of Dallas, has its I LEAD Academy. New York also has a large internal principals' academy, as does Boston. The Knowledge Is Power Program (KIPP), a charter school organization with over eighty affiliates nationwide, has created a program called Pathways, which focuses on internships for principal candidates at high-performing schools. Statistics show that about two-thirds of medium-to-large districts (those with over 10,000 students) have some form of training program, either to train new administrators or to provide professional development for current administrators.[34]

The downside of these programs is that they are costly, both to the school district and to the aspiring administrator. Terry Holliday, in Iredell County, lamented that his budding administrators still had to get a graduate degree, even though the district was going to be teaching them what they needed to know. The graduate degree was, as he rightly growled, a waste of time and money, and he hoped North Carolina would soon change its rules on licensure. Sixteen states, including Louisiana, Maryland, Tennessee, and Wisconsin, have already done just that.[35]

For smaller districts, running such programs is an especially costly burden that would be better spread over multiple districts. Moreover, there is the question of who is going to teach these programs. Districts that use outside programs (such as University of California Santa Cruz's New Administrator Program) still need to provide their own mentors. In New Britain, as I have noted, the main teacher is the superintendent, Doris Kurtz. On top of an already busy schedule, she took on building a corps of competent middle managers, simply because there was no one else to do it in-house and no money to pay for a consultant to do it for her.

District-University Collaborations (Directed by the District)

Another alternative is a partnership with a graduate school, where the district defines the program. Perhaps the closest collaboration in the country is in Long Beach: The school district has co-developed the program with the local branch of the California State University, and it supplies many of its better administrators as professors. In Portsmouth, David Stuckwisch arranged with Regent University to teach his new administrators, according to curriculum he selected. Even some big districts (like Fairfax County) use this approach as part of their principals' academy.[36]

A different way to create collaboration is for districts to offer real, extensive internships for a university's students. Although none of the districts I visited had gone this route, some universities have restructured their traditional programs to incorporate year-long experiences with collaborating school districts.[37] If districts closely scrutinize the quality of the university's part of the program, and if they commit themselves to really educating the interns, these programs might work as an alternative to formal partnerships. (And it would be even better if, as a condition of participation, districts insisted that the programs address their particular concerns.)

Independent Training Programs: Nonprofits Collaborate with Districts

The growth of specialized independent programs, operating in conjunction with school districts, represents a promising variation on the "do it yourself" theme. The most prominent independent programs are the Broad Foundation and New Leaders for New Schools (NLNS), which is funded in part by Broad, and two Broad foundation programs, the Superintendents' Academy and the Broad Residency Program, which places private, public, and civic sector executives into public and charter schools. Both NLNS and Broad focus on producing reform-minded administrators. They carefully screen applicants, reaching out to potential administrators and superintendents to ensure that the training goes to people who will be change agents.[38]

Even after the formal training, all of the programs continue to provide coaching and mentoring for new principals and administrators. NLNS, for example, provides extensive coaching and mentoring in the first year following graduation, and beyond. On top of that, it has begun to use its network of graduates as an ongoing mutual support group, along with online programs, and it tries to place its residents and new graduates in schools where earlier NLNS graduates are senior principals or superintendents.

In some states, these programs can now provide certifications—answering Terry Holliday's criticism about imposing two sets of coursework on candidates. In Maryland, Louisiana, and Wisconsin, NLNS can award administrator certification for principals. In other states, including New York, NLNS is authorized to provide certification, as long as an accredited university has approved the training.[39]

Are These Alternative Programs Adequate?

One important reservation about all these alternative programs is that the amount of coursework is limited—often to no more than several weeks of intense summer sessions plus some weekend coursework during the year. That is brief, not only in comparison with traditional education programs, but also in comparison with traditional business school programs (although Carl Cohn, who sits on Broad's Review Board for the Prize, insists the program's out-of-the-classroom demands makes it more extensive than its few weeks of formal training suggests). An MBA program takes at least one year to prepare students to be hired by a company that will then teach them its business. Schools and school districts are as complex as most businesses. Can one really be prepared with only about one-quarter as much coursework—no matter how intense?

The answer to this question may be that these programs are good enough, especially if that is all the district can afford. Most of the superintendents thought their programs, as short as they are, were meeting their needs. However, I would also note that some programs, like New York's, have come under criticism for producing a significant number of failures.[40]

The better answer may be that administrators' training *never really stops*. For example, Superintendent Ron Friedman (Great Neck) not only supplies his new administrators with mentors and other support,[41] but also regularly meets with even his most experienced principals and administrators to review their performance against their goals. The district policy is to provide them whatever training they need to enhance their effectiveness—whenever they need it.[42] Their early training then morphs into midcareer training that can lead to some form of enhanced credential[43] or organized support systems for continuing personal development.

The process is not limited to single districts. There are regional superintendent roundtables in various places like Massachusetts, Connecticut, and Ohio, where superintendents share ideas and approaches.[44] The key is that people value what they learn because it is relevant to their immediate concerns, and because it really does improve their game.

Improving Graduate Schools—Make Them Accountable and Change Them If They Won't Do It Themselves

The problem with all of the alternative training strategies is that they do not produce anywhere near the number of leaders required. There were approximately 226,000 elementary and secondary school administrators in 2006 (and a projection of roughly 12 percent growth, to 2016).[45] Assuming the historic 5 percent to 10 percent annual turnover rate continues, that suggests a total need for about 12,500 to 25,000 new administrators every year.[46] The alternative training programs cannot meet that number, certainly not in the near future. In 2008, for example, NLNS trained only about 140 principal recruits.

If the alternative programs can't meet the need, we have no choice but to rely on the graduate schools to step up to their mission. What can parents, taxpayers, school board members, and politicians do to make this happen? Here are three strategies to drive improvement:

Track Which Programs Work—and Complain about Those That Don't

We want administrators who can succeed. If some schools do better than others preparing administrators, that is where we want to look for new hires. Sounds sensible, but few districts have done that. With the development of big data systems, districts can now keep track of which university's graduates have been successful as principals (and other administrators). And when they have collected a reasonable amount of data on their own hires, the districts should announce, publicly, that they will now be recruiting candidates *only* from those schools.

At the state level, there should be a similar tracking system for the state's universities: Which ones produce graduates who are successful once they become administrators? Did they raise student test scores? Did they earn good school or district scorecards? The data should also be made public—just like the results for No Child Left Behind. (Louisiana, for example, has such a policy for teacher training programs.[47])

State legislatures should then make their decisions about funding based on *which programs are working and which ones are not*. They should also take the more drastic step of opening up the funding to allow school districts to compete directly for the money. In fact, they should consider a further step: Provide *all* the money to school districts, since they are the institutions really on the line to produce capable administrators. Then let the districts use some of the funds to buy services from graduate schools that they believe give them what they need. Having such discerning buyers choosing among competing programs should improve the quality of graduate school education more rapidly than any strategy employed up to now. I am going to return to this subject when talking about teacher training.

Change the Licensing Requirements for Principals

State licensing requirements can drive positive changes. Based on the results I saw, districts' training programs are fully capable of producing quality administrators. There is no reason for license procedures to require a master's or a doctorate in education administration. Quality district-based programs should be placed on equal footing, as Terry Holliday urged. If nothing else, that dose of competition should get schools of education to start thinking about what they have to do to satisfy their customers.

Also, after you put down this book, take a look at the practice version of the multistate administrator exam, which can be found at www.ets.org, and see how many of the subjects discussed here are thoroughly assessed there. If the adage "what gets measured gets done" is right, the refocusing of what is important to the licensure board should refocus what is important to a university's course offerings.[48]

There is already a move in several states, and in the Obama administration, to revise license qualifications to take into account principals'
effectiveness on the job as well as their formal training. There is even
some survey evidence that superintendents and principals would support such changes.[49] That kind of shift should push the universities to
incorporate fieldwork—that is, placements in school districts—into the
graduate curriculum, driving the kinds of collaboration that good districts are already seeking.

Push State Legislatures to Require a Total Overhaul of Graduate School
Education for Administrators

If that kind of pressure fails to get schools of education to make the
right changes, state legislatures can simply push through the needed
reform. They have the purse strings (at least for public institutions), and
they should not be shy about pulling them if the universities cannot
reform themselves.

Entrance requirements need to be tightened. Several education experts, including Arthur Levine, Craig Richards, and Margaret Terry
Orr,[50] argue that entrance requirements should be tightened. At a minimum, admission standards should include some requirement that applicants demonstrate leadership and management skills, or at least provide
a recommendation from their district attesting to those skills.

Courses need new content. "Old-style" graduate school education
did not produce educational leaders, real managers, or capable political
actors. Indeed, the utter inability of many of the senior administrators at
Los Angeles Unified School District to behave like competent managers
was one of the most disturbing failures of the many I witnessed while
general counsel. The ongoing drumbeat of badly negotiated contracts
and poorly administered operations left me constantly muttering, "they
could not have learned anything about management in graduate school."

The Harvard Graduate School of Education has run the Public Education Leadership Program, an eight-week executive seminar, for many
years in collaboration with the Harvard Business School. In 2009 it expanded to include the Kennedy School of Government.[51] Other institutions should adopt a similar "three-legged" strategy, and use it for more
than just eight-week seminars.

Training needs to happen in the field. As states revise their standards for administrator education, they should specifically require more
time in the field. The change has implications for funding as well: Universities will have to share the program money with their partner school
districts, which will now bear a significant share of the training workload. (Or, if it turns out districts are now the ones given the money for
training, the sharing will happen the other way around, but more of that
later.)

Who Should Pay for Training?

Who should pay for training school administrators? Traditionally, the self-selected future administrator enrolls in a graduate program and pays tuition out of his or her own pocket. That is not true for a district-run internal program, or for independent operations like NLNS. There, teachers do not pay for the training, although they may be obligated to work as an administrator for some number of years.

This alternative approach makes a great deal of sense. After all, the U.S. military sends hundreds of its officers to graduate school every year, picking up both their salaries and tuition as part of its budget. The program works: The Department of Defense has built a sophisticated senior leadership that understands not only military operations, but also politics and management.

Some districts and states are moving in that direction. Mississippi, for example, has adopted a School Administrator Sabbatical Program, which offers full salary and benefits for one year to teachers who enroll in education leadership programs. North Carolina does something similar. Montgomery County covers 50 percent of tuition. A district can identify good administrator candidates, train them to be effective, and guarantee their service for some number of years; paying their tuition (and, if necessary, their salary) is a small price for a potentially huge positive result.

WHAT WE NEED TO DO

Every district must really believe that how it recruits, trains, and motivates its principals is important—*really* important. If not, money set aside one year will disappear the next, and tough issues, like identifying and recruiting quality candidates, will just get put off from now until doomsday. There should be a budget for recruiting and training; probably no more than 0.3 percent to 0.4 percent of the total district operating expense is required (excluding trainees' salaries), and it should be protected through good and bad years.

Now the details: District leadership needs to go out and identify good administrator prospects. Everyone needs to insist that a serious vetting process takes place.

Reformers should insist districts identify quality programs that produce superior candidates and that it recruit—exclusively, if possible—from those sources. Or the district should set up an alternative program, either on its own (if state law allows) or with the cooperation of a quality university or nonprofit. When the new recruits arrive, the district must provide them trained, capable mentors and other support.

Moreover, parents and taxpayers need to let superintendents manage their principals. If everyone has agreed that student achievement is the goal for the district and the means by which the superintendent's performance will be measured, then she has to have the right to terminate ineffective principals. Parents can voice an opinion, but dividing authority between school councils and the superintendent is unfair to the superintendent and counterproductive as well.

At the state level, there are still more important improvements to push for:

- States should allow districts to compete for all funds previously directed toward graduate education administration programs run by state universities.
- State funding should be targeted toward productive universities rather than those that are not graduating good administrators.
- State law should allow districts to create their own alternative programs, or should at least authorize independent programs (like the Broad Superintendents' Academy or NLNS).
- If the colleges of education can't manage to reform their programs, the state should write laws that do it for them.
- Any alternative program that is educating quality principals and superintendents should be allowed to certify new administrators without a requirement they obtain a separate degree from a university.

NOTES

1. Steve Farkas, Jean Johnson, Ann Duffett, and Tony Foleno, *Trying to Stay Ahead of the Game* (New York: Public Agenda, 2001), 7.

2. Louis Kennedy, "Collaborative Teacher Evaluation," in *Recruiting, Retaining, and Supporting Highly Qualified Teachers*, ed. Caroline Chauncey (Cambridge, MA: Harvard Education Press, 2005), 122–23.

3. Sharon D. Kruse and Karen Seashore Louis, *Building Strong School Cultures* (Thousand Oaks, CA: AASA/Corwin Press, 2009), 13.

4. Linda Lambert, *Leadership Capacity for Lasting School Improvement* (Alexandria, VA: Ass'n. for Supervision and Curriculum Development [ASCD], 2003), 5.

5. Ed Fuller and Michelle D. Young, *Tenure and Retention of Newly Hired Principals in Texas* (Austin: University Council for Education Administration, University of Texas at Austin, 2009), 2 (and citations therein).

6. The National Association of Elementary School Principals has a Principals Advisory Leadership Corps to train master principals, as do several state and regional groups (Pete Hall, "Building Bridges: Strengthening the Principal Induction Process through Intentional Mentoring," *Phi Delta Kappan* 89, no. 6 [February 2008]: 449). Other groups, such as the National Institute for School Leadership, provide in-service training directly.

7. William G. Ouchi, *Making Schools Work* (New York: Simon & Schuster, 2003).

8. Many experts and panels have advocated giving schools control over faculty selection for years. See, for example, The Teaching Commission, *Teaching at Risk: Progress & Potholes* (New York: The Teaching Commission, 2006), 19; CPRE (Strategic Management in Human Capital), *Taking Human Capital Seriously: Talented Teachers in Every Classroom, Talented Principals in Every School* (Madison, WI: CPRA, 2009), 12.

9. Dale Ballou and Michael Podgursky, "What Makes a Good Principal? How Teachers Assess the Performance of Principals," *Economics of Education Review* 14, no. 3 (1995): 249.

10. Public Agenda, *A Mission of the Heart: What Does It Take to Transform a School* (New York: Public Agenda, 2008), 8.

11. NCES, *Characteristics of Public, Private, and Bureau of Indian Education Elementary and Secondary Schools in the United States: Results from the 2007–2008 Schools and Staffing Survey, Principals, First Look* (Doct. 2008-323) (Washington, DC: GPO, 2009), table 7.

12. Suzette Lovely, *Staffing the Principalship: Finding, Coaching, and Mentoring School Leaders* (Alexandria, VA: ASCD, 1998), 11.

13. Clayton M. Christensen, *The Innovator's Dilemma* (New York: Collins Business Essentials, 2005), 187–88.

14. NCES, *Characteristics of Public, Private, and Bureau of Indian Education Elementary and Secondary Schools in the United States*, table 5.

15. But in other districts, there may be pernicious problems with salary that are harder to identify. One study found that principals in minority schools were paid $7,000 less on average, even though there were few differences in administrative experience. Leaders for California Schools, *Policy Brief, No. 09-04* (Berkeley: Policy Analysis for California Schools, University of California, 2009), 8.

16. Deming was a strong believer in the power of intrinsic motivation, like a desire to be the best, and doubted that extrinsic motivators—like bonuses—could work as well. W. Edwards Deming, *The New Economics* (Cambridge, MA: MIT Press, 1994), 122.

17. Statistics available from a handful of states, for example, suggest that only about half of beginning principals remain in the same job five years later, and that many leave the principalship altogether when they go. *Education Week*, "Turnover in Principalship Focus of Research," Oct. 26, 2009 (retrieved from www.edweek.org/ew/articles/2009/10/28/09principal_ep.h29.html on Oct. 28, 2009).

18. *New York Times*, "Principals Younger and Freer, but Raise Doubts in the Schools," May 26, 2009 (retrieved from www.nytimes.com/2009/05/26/nyregion/26principas.html on May 27, 2009).

19. NCES, *Characteristics of Public, Private, and Bureau of Indian Education Elementary and Secondary Schools in the United States*, table 12 (SASS).

20. Of the districts I visited, only Chicago and Long Beach give a formal role to members of the community in selecting principals, and in those two districts, the local school councils select from a list of candidates prepared by the district. In San Diego, a school council narrows the list to three candidates, and the superintendent makes the final decision. In all the other districts, the superintendent simply appoints the principals; and even in Long Beach and San Diego, the superintendent still has general authority to remove a principal.

21. Parent Commission on School Governance and Mayoral Control, *Recommendations on School Governance* (New York: Parent Commission on School Governance and Mayoral Control, 2009), 2.

22. See, for example, Jeffrey R. Henig and Wilbur C. Rich, eds., *Mayors in the Middle* (Princeton, NJ: Princeton University Press, 2004).

23. Others agree. See, for example, Vivian Troen and Katherine C. Boles, *Who's Teaching Your Children?* (New Haven, CT: Yale University Press, 2003), 86.

24. Alexander Russo, "Preparing the 'Highly Qualified Principal,'" in *Recruiting, Retaining, and Supporting Highly Qualified Teachers*, ed. Caroline Chauncey (Cambridge, MA: Harvard Education Press, 2005), 129–30.

25. Organization for Economic Cooperation and Development, *Strong Performers and Successful Reformers in Education: Lessons from PISA for the United States* (Paris: OECD, 2010), 241.

26. Linda Lambert, *Building Leadership Capacity in Schools* (Alexandria, VA: ASCD, 1998), 77; Lovely, *Staffing the Principalship*, 41.

27. Lovely, *Staffing the Principalship*, 125–29. Off-the-shelf personality tests, used for hiring teachers and administrators, are available from the Gallup Organization, Ha-

berman Foundation, and Ventures for Excellence some districts, like Durham, NC, have created their own. Charlotte, NC, Dallas, and Denver have used Haberman. New York City, Fairfax County, VA, and Blue Valley, KS, have used Gallup.

28. Surveys of educators agree. See, for example, Public Agenda, *A Mission of the Heart*, 8.

29. *Dallas News*, "DISD Welcomes Bush Institute's Plan to Widen Field of Recruitment of School Leaders," Sept. 30, 2010 (retrieved from www.dallasnews.com/sharedcontent/dws/news/localnews/stories/DN-edannounce_30met.ART.Central.Edition1.333874d.html on Oct. 4, 2010).

30. Broader surveys of superintendents reach the same results. A 2001 Public Agenda survey found 85 percent of superintendents believe overhauling leadership training and education in graduate school programs would improve leadership in the nation's schools. Eighty percent of superintendents in the survey characterized the programs as "out of touch with the realities of what it takes to run today's school district." Farkas et al., *Trying to Stay Ahead of the Game*, 28, 32, 34.

31. Arthur Levine, *Educating School Leaders* (Princeton, NJ: The Education Schools Project, 2005), 21–22.

32. Public Agenda, *A Mission of the Heart*, 10.

33. NCES, *Characterstics of Public, Private, and the Bureau of Indian Education Elementary and Secondary Schools in the United States*, table 12 (SASS)—among districts with more than one school, percentage of principals who were newly hired, average number of days in the normal contract year for principals, percentage of districts that had a tenure system for principals, and percentage of districts that had a training program for aspiring school administrators, by state: 2007–2008, (retrieved from http://nces.ed.gov/surveys/sass/tables/sass0708_2009320_d1s_12.asp on Oct. 2, 2009).

34. NCES, *Characteristics of Public School Districts in the United States: Results from the 2007–2008 Schools and Staffing Survey*, NCES Publication 2009-320 (Washington, DC: U.S. Department of Education, 2009), table 12.

35. Consortium for Policy Research in Education, *Strategic Management of Human Capital: New Leaders for New Schools* (Madison, WI: University of Wisconsin Press, 2008), 12.

36. *Education Week*, "Districts Take Bigger Role in Preparing New School Leaders," Oct. 27, 2010 (retrieved from http://blogs.edweek.org/edweek/inside-schol-research-2010/10/d9stricts-take-bigger-role-in.html on Oct. 28, 2010).

37. Lovely, *Staffing the Principalship*, 45.

38. As of 2008, five states allow national programs like Broad to certify nontraditional administrators. United States Chamber of Commerce, *Leaders and Laggards* (Washington, DC: U.S. Chamber of Commerce, 2009), 29.

39. *Education Week*, "New Leaders Group to Train Charlotte, NC Principals," Jan. 7, 2009, 5; Joseph Murphy, Hunter Moorman, and Martha McCarthy, "A Framework for Rebuilding Initial Certification and Preparation Programs in Educational Leadership: Lessons from Whole State Reform Initiatives," *The Teachers College Record* 110, no. 10 (Oct. 2008): 2176. Council of Chief State School Officers (CCSSO), *State Policy Framework to Develop Highly Qualified Administrators* (Washington, DC: CCSSO, 2005), 6.

40. *New York Times*, "Principals Younger and Freer, but Raise Doubts in the Schools," May 26, 2009 (retrieved from www.nytimes.com/2009/05/26/nyregion/26principals.html on May 27, 2009); *New York Times*, "City Officials Put Academy for Principals under Review," Dec. 20, 2005 (retrieved from www.nytimes.com/2005/12/20/education/20academy.html on December 21, 2005).

41. See Michael Fullan, *Leading in a Culture of Change* (San Francisco: Jossey-Bass, 2001), 127–28; Sharon D. Kruse and Karen Seashore Louis, *Building Strong School Cultures* (Thousand Oaks, CA: Corwin Press, 2009), 127; Public Agenda, *A Mission of the Heart*, 11–12.

42. One cannot overemphasize the importance of continuous professional development for administrators, teachers, and staff. In the worlds of both business and the military, ongoing training is an important ingredient for success. Bernard Rostker, the

former Department of Defense undersecretary for manpower and readiness, explained to me during an interview that the military trains an officer for each job he or she has and is committed to doing it over and over again, all the way up the career ladder. The military assumes that every year a certain percentage of its middle-level office corps will be away full-time earning some form of advanced degree or at least going through some further training for a new duty assignment. General Electric, which is widely admired for its management style, has a commitment to training its managers that is even more extensive. The corporate policy is to train managers either at its own in-house facilities or by paying for them to attend outside graduate schools. A GE manager does not go just once; he or she prepares for each step up the corporate ladder with a new round of training. GE operates a major training center at Croton-ville, NY, where 10,628 of its employees attended 465 classes during 2004. In addition, it has three other facilities in the United States and four overseas. According to GE's website, "through both internal and external training initiatives, GE invests over $1 billion annually in training and development. In addition to internal training and development, GE invests over $38 million annually in tuition reimbursement for employee undergraduate and graduate degree programs."

43. Patricia Reeves, "Superintendents on a Courageous Journey," *Phi Delta Kappan* 90, no. 9 (May 2009): 30–35.

44. Lee Teitel, "Changing Peer Support for Superintendents," *Phi Delta Kappan* 90, no. 9 (May 2009): 24–29.

45. U.S. Department of Labor, Bureau of Labor Statistics, *Occupational Outlook Handbook 2008–09, Education Administrators* (retrieved from http://stats.bls.gov/OCO/OCOS007.htm on August 12, 2009).

46. According to NCES, 9.3 percent of principals are newly hired every year, but many were previously principals elsewhere or were assistant principals who already had their graduate training. NCES, *Characteristics of Public, Private, and Bureau of Indian Education Elementary and Secondary Schools in the United States* , table 12. A RAND Education study prepared for the Wallace Readers' Digest Funds found that between 1983 and 1999 15 percent to 33 percent of administrators left the field every year. Susan M. Gates, Jeanne S. Ringel, Lucrecia Santibanez, Karen E. Ross, and Catherine H. Chung, *Who Is Leading Our Schools?* (Santa Monica, CA: RAND Education, 2003), xv.

47. *New York Times*, "What Louisiana Can Teach," Dec. 12, 2008 (retrieved from www.nytimes.com/2008/12/12/opinion.12fri2.html on December 12, 2008). For a concise summary of Louisiana's program, see The Teaching Commission, *Teaching at Risk: Progress & Potholes* (New York: The Teaching Commission, 2006), 41.

48. Also, compare the standards used by the Interstate School Leaders Licensure Consortium (ISLLC), which effectively drive the licensure exam, with those suggested by the Southern Region Education Board (www.e-lead.org/principles/standards1.asp). The SREB standards, which *unfortunately* are not used for the license exam, are much closer to the type of principal high-performing schools have.

49. Public Agenda, *Rolling Up Their Sleeves: Superintendents and Principals Talk about What's Needed to Fix Public Schools* (New York: Public Agenda, 2003), 40 (74 percent of superintendents and 78 percent of principals think "certification requirements should be changed to include a lot more focus on practical, hands-on experience.")

50. Margaret Terry Orr, "Mapping Innovation in Leadership Preparation in Our Nation's Schools of Education," *Phi Delta Kappan* 87, no. 7 (March 2006): 493.

51. Richard F. Elmore, "Building a Knowledge Base for Educational Leadership," *Education Week*, Jan. 30, 2008 (retrieved from www.edweek.org/ew/articles/2008/01/30/21elmore.h27.html on Feb. 10, 2009); *Lexington Herald-Leader*, "Harvard Ed School Offers 1st New Degree Since 1935," Sept. 15, 2009 (retrieved from www.kentucky.com/513/story/935905.html on Sept. 16, 2009).

Part III

Teachers

In the winter of 2010–2011 the political narrative about school reform focused on teachers. It started with the seemingly universally accepted premise that we want more good teachers. That, in turn, morphed into the "good teacher, bad teacher" narrative. And that, in turn, led to calls to adopt pay for performance (based mostly on how well a teacher's students perform on tests) in order to attract and keep good teachers, and to eliminate tenure to get rid of the worst ones.

We like narratives about people, so we think we "get" this argument. *We would be wrong. Neither pay for performance nor the elimination of tenure is central to reform of our nation's schools. If we think we will have achieved success by legislating them, we are about to be sorely disappointed. They may be useful improvements (although I have some reservations, especially about pay), but they are sideshows to the big idea on which we need to focus.*

In a system of education where we want every child to learn, we need to do what any twenty-first-century business would do to keep in focus each of its customers. We need to empower the workers (teachers) closest to the customers (students) to make decisions that fit each of their needs. That strategy requires more highly trained teachers and relies on them to collaborate in previously unheard-of ways with each other and with their principals, all of which calls for treating them with more respect while demanding they take more responsibility for what they do.

To do that, we need to change the working conditions that have long characterized many of our nation's schools in the mass-production era. In making these changes, we achieve something else: We reduce the turnover that drives out good teachers and leads us to tolerate low performers because we cannot find enough valued ones to fill the ranks. We improve teaching quality and increase quality teachers at the same time. We cannot ask for more.

SIX

A Brave New World

A great school is not about the 10 percent of the teachers who are the best any more than it is about the 10 percent who are the worst. It is about making the most of the 80 percent in the middle—who can deliver quality education if the system will just give them the chance.

Understanding something about the categories—I call them "tiers"—of teacher quality is an essential part of our thinking about how to run a first-rate school.

TIER ONE

These are, naturally, the really good teachers. They know the content. They know how to get a wide variety of students to learn. They get good marks on various standards of accountability. And they can usually do well for their kids despite an unsupportive or depressing school environment.

TIER TWO

The second group can make a solid contribution, but their schools are not organized so that they can be fully effective. For example, a fourth grade teacher may be terrific teaching reading, but awful at math. A school could try to make the teacher a better math instructor. That may work, but there may be a limit to how much improvement that teacher is going to achieve. Instead, if several teachers have a mix of strengths and weaknesses, the school might reorganize all the fourth grade instruction so that the one teacher who is great at teaching math specializes, allowing the other teachers to cover reading, science, and social studies.

TIER THREE

Teachers in Tier Three have potential, but it is not being used. They think they know how to teach and that they have nothing to learn; or they are burned out and just going through the motions.[1]

Either way, they're not getting the job done.[2] Their students may well get by during standardized testing, but these teachers are short-changing their kids with a mediocre effort. They need to commit to continuous improvement and work hard on their practice.[3]

TIER FOUR

These teachers have no place in the profession. The colleges of education they attended were "cash cows," where almost everyone was admitted and almost no one flunked. They got tenure because there was no firm requirement that they demonstrate competence. Or, perhaps, it was one of those hard-to-staff schools where the principal preferred to take her chances with a bad teacher rather than recruit a new one and start all over again.

THE BIG-PICTURE STRATEGY

So here is the strategy: Recruit and keep as many Tier Ones as we can, although there will never be enough. Give Tier Twos better training, and be flexible about the organization so that we get the best out of what we have. Motivate Tier Threes to work hard and improve. Get rid of Tier Fours.

In other words, the key to a realistic strategy for reform today is to incorporate teachers in Tiers Two and Three into a *high-performing system*. Good districts know that. Nick Fischer put the problem this way: "What has to be done is find a middle ground between firing them all and believing they are all wonderful. That middle ground is being willing to learn what you need to [learn]." That means, figure out how to work with and improve what you have.

Throughout the discussion of teachers, three themes—continuous improvement, collaboration, and continuous training—will constantly reappear. In the old days, none of them counted for much. The fact that they do now is as profound a change to a teacher's world as "every child can learn."

Continuous improvement is the subtlest change, and the one most subversive of the old order. To improve means we have to know where we stand. So we need a decision on a vision, benchmarks to see if we are achieving it, means of measuring them, and a will to act in response to what we find. All of that turns the old order on its head, some of which is obvious and some of which is so subtle it is overlooked by all but the most astute observers.

Collaboration is the antithesis of teachers doing "their own thing," which is what old-style teacher autonomy is all about. In the world of every child can learn, we need to start thinking of schools as collaborative organizations, teams of teachers figuring out how best to use their collective talents to improve their skills and the overall function of the school. It's the sculling analogy: For the boat to move forward everyone has to be rowing in the same direction; the more synchronized the strokes, the faster you go.

The other key ingredient in the transition from "old schools" is continuous training. Teachers—and others—often think that their training happens in college. Erase that idea. As we learned about leadership training in chapter 5, professional development does not end with a bachelor's or master's degree. Learning how to teach is—or should be—a demanding and tough-minded process that goes on as long as that teacher continues to teach. And since schools and school districts are the institutions being held accountable for student learning, they cannot simply stand by and allow teachers to do their own thing.

Committing to continuous improvement and changing just these old-style assumptions about teaching—that teacher training happens in college and that teachers are masters of their classrooms—will produce remarkable results. They do not provide all the answers, but you will be surprised by how many successful school goals depend at least in part on schools being committed to training, collaboration, continuous improvement, and joint teacher–administrator responsibility for student achievement.

NOTES

1. Burnout is not simply an American problem triggered by poor schools. Other countries see burnout, even though their national education systems are held in high regard. The point is that it is a universal problem for long-serving workforces that should not be dismissed as a trivial issue. Michael Huberman, "The Professional Life Cycle of Teachers," *The Teachers College Record* 91, no. 1 (1989): 31–57.

2. One national study of teacher attitudes done by the National Center for Education Statistics found that 34 percent of teachers would not choose teaching as a career again, and a majority of those felt it "was a waste of their time to try to do their best as a teacher." See National Center for Education Statistics, *Job Satisfaction among America's Teachers: Effects of Workplace Conditions, Background Characteristics, and Teacher Compensation* (Washington, DC: U.S. Department of Education, 1997), 11.

3. Barbara Benham Tye and Lisa O'Brien, "Why Are Experienced Teachers Leaving the Profession?" *Phi Delta Kappan* 84, no. 1 (Sept. 2002): 24–32. ("Whatever their age, discouraged and unhappy teachers do not always leave the profession, and herein lies one of the potential dangers for the nation. Some will simply stay on, doing a poor job and feeling helpless, negative, and overwhelmed. [footnote omitted] They're not bad teachers; most do what they can under the circumstances. But they are not doing the *best* they can. And in the gap between what they *are* doing and what they are *capable* of doing—if the working conditions were less onerous and if they felt valued and respected—lie a huge waste of talent and an even greater loss of possibility for our children. If one were to attach a dollar value to these losses, the total would be staggering. Isn't it possible that improving working conditions would be less expensive to school districts than the costs of losing—and replacing—unhappy teachers? [footnote omitted] Why can't we see this?" [Italics in the original.])

SEVEN

Keeping — and Working with — Those You Have

In any "good teacher, bad teacher" narrative, the discussion inevitably leads to the conclusion that we have a shortage of good teachers, and that, in turn, leads to the seemingly logical economic proposition that the way to fix the shortage is to pay teachers more across-the-board. It is a misguided strategy.

It is not that pay is irrelevant, but trying to fix the problem with pay will cost more than we can afford — and would not work anyway.

Until the 1960s, women and minorities had few job options, so they often wound up teaching. Not surprisingly, in 1964, 21 percent of new women teachers scored in the top 10 percent of SAT or ACT college entrance tests. However, one of the great victories of the civil rights movement was to open up opportunities, so that by 2000, the number of new women teachers with top scores had fallen to 11 percent. Conversely, the number of new women teachers coming from bottom-tier colleges increased from 16 percent in 1963 to 36 percent in 2000.[1]

Unfortunately, we don't have the money to pay enough to reverse those numbers. One recent study by McKinsey & Company calculated what it would take to increase just the percentage of "top third" college graduates teaching in low-income schools. It estimated that to raise the percentage from today's 14 percent to 68 percent would require increasing overall salaries and expenses $100 to $250 million for the average, large urban school district.[2] Not likely. That translates to billions of dollars nationwide.[3]

And then there is the "status" question. Experts who have investigated why foreign education systems do so much better recruiting high-quality teachers have concluded that in those countries, teaching has a much higher social status than it does in the United States.[4] Like pay, we are not going to solve the status issue any time soon.

There are also specific shortages. We are significantly short of teachers in science, technology, engineering, and math (a set of disciplines referred to by their acronym, STEM). The shortfall, roughly 200,000 over the next decade,[5] is generally attributed to the ability of people with those skills to make far more money in the private sector than in teaching.[6]

Some think that the perennial shortage of special education teachers might also be solved by money. It is not clear how much pay would have to be put on the table to remedy that deficit, but given that we are talking about teaching almost 10 percent of our school population, it is going to be substantial.

However, even if we paid STEM and special education teachers more, we likely would not solve the problem, because we would not be able to keep them in the system. Money is not our only problem.

We know that, historically, public schools need to hire some 240,000 new teachers annually just to stay even.[7] But because of the growth of the student population and the retirements of the last of the baby boomer teachers, the size of the annual number of teacher replacements needed will rise to perhaps as high as 275,000 to 300,000 per year for at least the next several years.[8]

We also know that somewhere between 33 percent and 50 percent of new teachers leave the profession within the first five years of teaching (depending on the school or the district), with the problem concentrated, not surprisingly, in low-income, urban schools.[9] An extraordinarily small percentage of these teachers leave because they are not given tenure (although that is changing slightly);[10] most depart for a host of other reasons.[11]

Those "other reasons" are the frustrating, unreasonable, and eventually intolerable working conditions that pervade too much of the education system.

We have inadequate numbers of quality special education teachers not only because of their salaries but also because special education is a bureaucratic nightmare that pushes even the best intentioned from the classroom. The same problem faces STEM teachers. Even if we get more of them into the system by paying higher salaries, we may lose them back to other professions after these new recruits have suffered through the lack of training, mismanagement, and bureaucracy they would never face in their old workplaces. And we have bottom-of-the-barrel faculty in hard-to-staff schools because of the toxic combination of destructive labor rules and a deplorable lack of money, support, or decent leadership. Together, they guarantee that any competent teacher will flee at the first opportunity.

This high turnover inflicts two pernicious effects on our struggling schools. We need so many teachers that we cannot be selective in whom we hire, and many of those who leave are precisely the people we want to stay. Their above-average capability makes them good teachers, but it also gives them the freedom to find a more congenial place to work.

It is like trench warfare in World War I. You can recruit more and better, but it does not matter. You still send them into the same trenches. Still get them chewed up. And still carry them out not long after. The right answer is not improving the quality of people being chewed up. It is finding an effective alternative to trench warfare.

We should not, therefore, frame the issue generally as a shortage of teachers. We should think of it as a supply-and-demand problem, where, if we cut the demand by reducing the number of good teachers who leave, we could be more selective in hiring. And we would be under less pressure to keep underperformers because of a fear we might not be able to replace them.

And there are two further benefits from focusing on bad working conditions. By making specific changes in working conditions, which will likely involve continuous improvement, collaboration, and continuous training, we wind up providing a better environment to deliver on the promise that every child can learn. And there is an even bigger and better benefit — it costs far less.

IT'S THE SYSTEM, STUPID: WORKING CONDITIONS TRUMP SALARY ISSUES

As you might expect, the connection between pay and teacher quality has been studied to death. Low salaries, though a regularly cited problem, [12] are rarely the most important culprits. [13] Several prominent experts [14] and the National Center for Education Statistics [15] have analyzed the volumes of data and reached the same conclusion as the districts I visited: Fixing working conditions will have greater impact on teacher retention and quality than broad salary increases.

The best way to make sense of what is going on may well be the analysis in a recent study of California teachers. It found seemingly inconsistent survey results: Those who left teaching complained that salaries were too low, while those who stayed were much more likely to be satisfied with what they were paid. The investigator, Professor Ken Futernick, reconciled the findings in a commonsense way that underscores the relationship between working conditions and salary. When a teacher thinks working conditions are so bad that he or she wants to leave, the conclusion is that "they are not paying me enough to endure what I am going through." Among those who stay, the reaction is the reverse, that "the work is so satisfying that I am happy with my job, including my pay."[16]

Casting further doubt on the value of focusing on salaries is that there is little correlation between them and high student performance. An example is the District of Columbia. Prior to Michelle Rhee's arrival, the District had among the highest salaries in the nation and some of the country's worst test scores (and, as of this moment, still does, although it is starting to improve[17]).

The converse is also true. Lots of districts with high performance do not pay teachers high salaries:

- In Pearl River, the starting salary (in 2009) was around $43,000, while some districts in neighboring Westchester start at around $51,000. Nonetheless, according to Sandy Cokeley, the district's director of quality and community relations, Pearl River attracts high-quality talent because of the favorable work environment and collegial support.
- In New Britain, Doris Kurtz reported that the salary structure was good, but not great. Nonetheless, she has a large number of high-quality recruits because of the district's reputation for progressiveness.
- Brett Springston, the superintendent in Brownsville, had the same view: Even though it is at the southern tip of Texas and in one of the poorest counties in the country, the district draws a large number of quality teacher prospects because teachers can make a meaningful contribution.

The most powerful point about pay is that teachers in private schools are often the most satisfied and yet earn less than their public school counterparts.[18] It is all about workplace conditions.

EARLY EXITS: "YOU CAN'T PAY ME ENOUGH TO WORK HERE" AND OTHER TALES

What drives out teachers—and keeps them out[19]—includes:

- Insufficient mentoring or other training at a teacher's new school, leaving them lost about how to teach.
- Feeling isolated in their classrooms without the professional or emotional support of a collaborative environment of their peers.
- Principals who do not support them either emotionally or professionally, or who are unethical or make decisions based on cronyism.
- Being shut out of decision making, and otherwise not feeling as if they have any control over their working environment.

- Burdensome accountability (testing) and bureaucratic requirements; among the most troublesome are the paperwork and hearing requirements for special education under the Individuals with
  Disabilities Education Act.
- Curriculum not aligned to state standards, or no curriculum at all.
- Excessively difficult assignments: in the most troubled schools;
  with the most difficult kids, especially an unfair share of special
  education students; heavy teaching loads; or teaching subjects or
  grades they are not prepared to teach.
- Violence or a generally disorderly environment that is not focused
  on learning.
- Not feeling supported by parents or respected by students.[20]

Except for issues surrounding parents and students, all of the working
conditions listed above are subject to a principal's control. In fact, the best
principals understand that and don't wait to hear complaints or suggestions from teachers before acting.[21] But the problem persists.[22]

FIXING THE TURNOVER PROBLEM: WHAT ARE WE WAITING FOR?

It makes sense for every district to reduce the loss of teachers, especially
new ones. If we cut the loss of those who leave before retirement, especially those who leave within the first five years, by just 25 percent annually, we would reduce hiring needs by 60,000 to 70,000 teachers per year.
Even assuming *no* increase in the number of top-third students going into
teaching, that would mean that the share of top-third teachers in the
annual class of new recruits would rise from our current figure of roughly one-quarter of the total to approximately one-third.

The fact that districts devote so little attention to the turnover problem
suggests that they just don't appreciate how much it costs them . In 2005,
Boston estimated the cost of replacing a third-year teacher to be $25,000.[23]
Nationally, the Alliance for Excellent Education reported in 2004 that the
cost was $12,546 per teacher,[24] and a 2008 *Time* special report placed the
total yearly price tag at $7 billion.[25]

These numbers don't begin to count what it costs in the loss of conti-
nuity in the academic lives of students. Michael Lach, who is in charge of
Chicago's Office for High School Teaching and Learning, bemoaned the
fact that the high turnover there caused the district to be constantly training new people. The eventual effect of the turnover wave is to worsen the
achievement gap. The poor, urban districts with high teacher turnover
wind up spending more money on "induction"—the training of new
first- or second-year teachers—(see chapter 8) than their suburban neigh-
bors (and therefore less on instruction or salaries). Even then, these districts have a harder time providing new teachers with the same level of

support. One study found 65 percent of new teachers in low-income schools had mentors, compared to 91 percent in high-income schools.[26]

There is one more cost from the failure to fix the underlying working-condition problems that lead to high turnover: It gives teachers who stay an excuse for poor performance, whether it is their students' or their own. Why didn't the students do well? "There was too much paperwork," or "I am an English teacher but was forced to teach math." A high-performing district gives its teachers and students as few reasons to excuse poor performance as possible. "Headspace"—a teacher's perceptions, values, and the related conversation constantly going on in his or her head—is as important, if not more important, as any other working condition in education.

If the damage from turnover is so serious, then why have so many districts not fixed the problem? Most of the causes can find their way back to the industrial view of teaching:

- Older teachers prize their autonomy.[27]
- Teachers see themselves as equals, resisting the notion that they can learn from their peers.[28]
- Mentors and master teachers, who are essential to training, are seen as breaking "solidarity," making them "pawns of the administration" and not true colleagues.[29]

Autonomy, pride, and habituation to the old system simply thwart efforts to make working conditions more professional.[30] Tom Payzant, who spent eleven years building up teacher collaboration as part of reforming Boston, thinks teachers still work far too much on their own. Even Blue Valley, the most innovative district I visited, faced a huge problem when it sought to develop a learning community. According to Elizabeth Parks, the district's director of assessment and research, there was serious resistance from scores of teachers who just wanted to be left alone.

Districts are not without sin either. They want to believe (or at least rationalize) that they do not have to do more. Even if a state requires a new teacher support program, they see no need for quality mentors and extensive mentoring, or any other training new teachers need. Their principals are not, in any event, capable of providing guidance since they were never trained to do so and never saw it as part of their job description. Their rationalization has one further advantage: It saves districts money.

WHAT WE NEED TO DO

The first thing is about what *not* to do. Do not think that across-the-board salary increases can solve the issue of teacher shortages. It may well be that higher salaries will eventually help, especially for STEM and special education teachers. But they are not a short-term panacea. The focus has to be on continuous improvement and working conditions and all that flows from them, like teacher collaboration and professional learning communities.

That is the argument that sets the table for the rest of the chapters in this section. Fixing working conditions, creating learning communities, and revising outworn labor rules are the most important changes that have to be made. Money, specifically salaries, plays a subsidiary role, and only in support of these more important steps.

NOTES

1. Caroline M. Hoxby, "Wage Distortion: Why America's Top Female College Graduates Aren't Teaching," *Education Next* 5, no. 2 (March 22, 2005): 50.

2. McKinsey & Co., *Closing the Talent Gap: Attracting and Retaining the Top Third Graduates to Careers in Teaching* (Washington, DC: McKinsey & Co., 2010).

3. The biggest problem with increasing salaries across the board is that it is not possible politically, largely because it is not rational fiscally. Giving every teacher a 20 percent raise, roughly $10,000 plus related benefits, would require school budgets to increase by about 12 percent, or $70 billion. Taxpayers are not about to swallow that increase. More importantly, it is not clear whether average wages of $60,000 attract an entirely new class of teacher. And, if $70 billion were available, we are going to see that there are much more effective ways of spending that money.

4. OECD, *Strong Performers and Successful Reformers in Education: Lessons from PISA for the United States* (Paris: OECD, 2010), 238.

5. *Christian Science Monitor*, "Wanted: More Science and Math Teachers in the US," Dec. 29, 2008 (retrieved from www.csmonitor.com/USA/2008/1229/p02s01-usgn.html on Jan. 19, 2010).

6. These numbers leave out the issue of quality, which is unfortunate. One recent study concluded that America's future math teachers earned on average a C on a new test comparing their skills with their counterparts in fifteen countries. *New York Times*, "U.S. Falls Short in Measure of Future Math Teachers," April 14, 2010 (retrieved from www.nytimes.com/2010/04/15/education/15math.html on April 15, 2010).

7. The total number of teachers hired is more than double that number, but that includes approximately 300,000 teachers who move from one school to another. Richard M. Ingersoll, *Is There Really a Teacher Shortage* (Seattle: Center for the Study of Teaching Policy, University of Washington, 2003), 10; Linda Darling-Hammond and Gary Sykes, "Wanted: A National Teacher Supply Policy for Education: The Right Way to Meet the 'Highly Qualified Teacher' Challenge," *Education Policy Analysis Archives* 11, no. 33 (Sept. 2003): 14.

8. Press Release, United States Department of Education, "U.S. Secretary of Education Arne Duncan Says Colleges of Education Must Improve for Reforms to Succeed" (Washington, DC: U.S. Department of Education, October 22, 2009) (retrieved from www.ed.gov/news/pressreleases/2009/10/10222009a.html on Nov. 13, 2009) (200,000 required annually); *Time*, "How to Make Great Teachers," Feb. 25, 2008, 28 (2.8 million between 2008–2016).

9. Gene Budig, "A Perfect Storm," *Phi Delta Kappan* 88, no. 2 (Oct. 2006): 114; *Washington Post*, "Half of Teachers Quit in 5 Years," May 9, 2006 (retrieved from www. washingtonpost.com/wp-dyn/content/article/2006/05/08/AR200605801344_pf.html on June 3, 2006); Elaine Allensworth, Stephen Ponisciak, and Christopher Mazzeo, *The Schools Teachers Leave, Teacher Mobility in Chicago Public Schools* (Chicago: Consortium on Chicago School Research, 2009), 30.

10. According to the NCES, in 2007–2008, the average American school district had 211.4 teachers. Each district dismissed 1.4 untenured teachers per year. NCES (IES), table 8 of Student and Staffing Survey (SASS) (*Average number of public school teachers and average number of public school teachers who were dismissed in the previous year or did not have their contracts renewed based on poor performance, by tenure status and state: 2007–08*) (retrieved from www.nces.ed.gov.surveys/sass.tables.sass0708_2009320_d1s.08.asp on Dec. 4. 2009).

11. See, for example, McKinsey & Co., *How the World's Most Improved School Systems Keep Getting Better* (New York: McKinsey & Co., 2010).

12. See, for example, Liza Gonzalez, Michelle Brown, and John Slate, "Factors Involved in Teachers Leaving the Teaching Profession," presentation at the Hilton New Orleans Riverside, New Orleans, LA, Feb. 7, 2008 (retrieved from www.allacademic.com/meta/p207189_index.html); Allensworth, Ponisciak, and Mazzeo, *The Schools Teachers Leave*, 7; NCES, *Job Satisfaction among America's Teachers: Effects of Workplace Conditions, Background Characteristics, and Teacher Compensation* (Washington, DC: U.S. Department of Education, 1997), 23.

13. One survey found that salary was the most important reason current teachers were thinking of leaving, but for those teachers who had already left, the prime issue was the pressure from accountability testing. Barbara B. Tye and Lisa O'Brien, "Why Are Experienced Teachers Leaving the Profession?" *Phi Delta Kappan* 84, no. 1 (Sept. 2002): 24–32.

14. Richard M. Ingersoll and Thomas M. Smith, "The Wrong Solution to the Teacher Shortage," *Educational Leadership*, May 2003, 34. See also Richard M. Ingersoll, *Who Controls Teachers' Work? Power and Accountability in America's Schools* (Cambridge, MA: Harvard University Press, 2003); Richard M. Ingersoll, "The Teacher Shortage: A Case of Wrong Diagnosis and Wrong Prescription," *NASSP Bulletin* 86, no. 631:16–30.

15. NCES, *Job Satisfaction among America's Teachers*, ix.

16. Ken Futernick, *A Possible Dream: Retaining California Teachers So All Students Learn* (Sacramento: The Center for Teacher Quality, California State University Sacramento, 2007), 47–48. Another analysis of teachers who were ambivalent about the role of pay in their decision to leave teaching suggested that although the low pay was a problem, the larger issue was that it represented a lack of respect for teachers and their effort. Karianne Sparks and Leslie Keiler, "Why Teachers Leave," in *Keeping Good Teachers*, ed. Marge Scherer (Alexandria, VA: ASCD, 2003), 213, 216.

17. *Washington Post*, "D.C.'s Progress Report," editorial, Oct. 15, 2009 (retrieved from www.washingtonpost.com/wp-dyn/content/article/2009/10/14/AR2009101403265_pf.html on Dec. 15, 2009); *Washington Post*, "District Leaps Forward in Math," Dec. 9, 2009 (retrieved from www.washingtonpost.com/wp-dyn/content/article/2009/12/08/AR200912081570.html on Dec. 9, 2009); NCES (IES), *The Nation's Report Card* (Washington, DC: U.S. Department of Education, 2009) (retrieved from http://nces.ed.gov/nationsreportcard/states/profile.asp on Dec. 15, 2009).

18. NCES, *Job Satisfaction among America's Teachers*, 32; Public Agenda, *Our Money, Our Schools: Ten Top Findings from Our Research Team* (Washington, DC: U.S. Department of Education, 2009), 35.

19. One survey asked those who had left the profession what it would take to get them to come back. Seventeen percent said they would come back for a sufficiently high salary, without any change of working conditions, but 28 percent said they would come back if working conditions were corrected, even if no higher salary was offered, and 29 percent said they would only come back if there were both sufficiently high salaries and better working conditions. Futernick, *A Possible Dream*, 26.

20. For example, in a 2009 report, Public Agenda surveyed teachers, asking them to choose between two schools in otherwise identical districts. One school had better student behavior and parental support. The other had a significantly higher salary. The school with better student behavior and parental support won: 83–16 percent among elementary teachers and 83–15 percent among secondary teachers. When asked the same question where the variable was "administrators who are strongly

supportive" versus higher salary, the school with the better administrators was favored: 82–17 percent. Public Agenda, *Our Money, Our Schools*, 19. Susan Moore Johnson, *Finders and Keepers: Helping New Teachers Survive and Thrive in Our Schools* (San Francisco: Jossey-Bass, 2009), passim; Carol P. Choy, "Creating a 'Finders and Keepers' Relationship," *HGSE News*, 2009 (retrieved from www.gse.harvard.edu/news/features/johnson09012004.html on June 9, 2009); NCES, *Job Satisfaction among America's Teachers*, 25; National Commission on Teaching and America's Future, *What Matters Most: Teaching for America's Future* (Washington, DC: NCTAF, 1996), 39–40; Public Agenda, *Our Money, Our Schools*, 5–6 (64 percent of new teachers entering through alternative certification and 41 percent of traditionally trained teachers in high-needs schools believe they have been given the hardest-to-teach students); Eric Hirsch and Ken Church, *North Carolina Teacher Working Conditions Survey Brief: Teacher Working Conditions Are Student Learning Conditions* (Santa Cruz, CA: UC Santa Cruz New Teacher Center, 2009) (retrieved from www.newteachercenter.org on Dec. 21, 2009); Susan L. Swars, Barbara Meyers, Lydia C. Mays, and Brian Lack, "A Two-Dimensional Model of Teacher Retention and Mobility: Classroom Teachers and Their University Partners Take a Closer Look at a Vexing Problem," *Journal of Teacher Education* 60, no. 2 (March/April 2009): 168–83, 172–77; Futernick, *A Possible Dream*, passim; Tye and O'Brien, "Why Are Experienced Teachers Leaving the Profession?," 24–32; Jack Buckley, Mark Schneider, and Yi Shang, *The Effects of School Facility Quality on Teacher Retention in Urban School Districts* (Washington, DC: National Clearinghouse for Educational Facilities, 2004) (retrieved from www.edfacilities.org).

21. A great website for a list of articles and books on how to retain teachers is http://retainingteachers.com.

22. Donald Boyd, Pamela Grossman, Marsha Ing, Hamilton Lankford, Susanna Loeb, and James Wyckoff, *The Influence of School Administrators on Teacher Retention Decisions* (retrieved from www.teacherpolicyresearch.org/ResearchPapers/tabid103 on Dec. 21, 2009); Helen Ladd, *Teacher Perceptions of Their Working Conditions: How Predictive of Policy-Relevant Outcomes?*" (Santa Cruz, CA: UC Santa Cruz New Teacher Center, 2009), 27 (retrieved from www.newteachercenter.org on Dec. 21, 2009; Michael Fullan, *Turnaround Leadership* (San Francisco: Jossey-Bass, 2004), 28.

23. *Boston Globe*, "School Is Out," Aug. 27, 2006 (retrieved from www.boston.com/news/globe/magazine/articles/2006/08/27/school_is_out/ on May 11, 2009).

24. Alliance for Excellent Education, *Tapping the Potential: Retaining and Developing High-Quality New Teachers* (Washington, DC: Alliance for Excellent Education, 2004).

25. *Time*, "How to Make Great Teachers," Feb. 25, 2008, 31.

26. Susan Moore Johnson, Susan M. Kardos, David Kauffman, Edward Liu, and Morgaen L. Donaldsen, "The Support Gap: New Teachers' Early Experiences in High-Income and Low-Income Schools," *Education Policy Analysis Archives* 12, no. 61 (Oct. 29, 2004): 10–11.

27. NCES, *Job Satisfaction among America's Teachers*, 18; Susan Moore Johnson, *Teachers at Work: Achieving Success in Our Schools* (New York: Basic Books, 1990), passim.

28. Dan C. Lortie, *Schoolteacher* (Chicago: University of Chicago Press, 1975), 192–96; Susan Moore Johnson, *Second-Stage Teachers and Coaching: Building School Capacity and a Teaching Career* (paper presented for the 2009 Annual Meeting of the American Educational Research Association, San Diego, CA, April 13–17, 2009), 5; Susan M. Kardos and Susan Moore Johnson, "On Their Own and Presumed Expert: New Teachers' Experience with Their Colleagues," *The Teachers College Record* 109, no. 9 (2007): 2083–2106; Elizabeth Campbell, "Challenges in Fostering Ethical Knowledge as Professionalism within Schools as Teaching Communities," *Journal of Educational Change* 6, no. 3 (2005): 209; Katherine C. Boles and Vivian Troen, "Mamas Don't Let Your Babies Grow Up to Be Teachers," in *Recruiting, Retaining, and Supporting Highly Qualified Teachers*, ed. Caroline Chauncey (Cambridge, MA: Harvard Education Press, 2005), 20 (asking for help is seen as "patently ridiculous"); Lambert, *Leadership Capacity for Lasting School Improvement*, 39.

EIGHT

Training New (and More) Teachers Inside the System

Deborah Meier, famous for propelling her poor and minority students' achievement upward at her New York Central Park East public school in the 1980s, once said, "Show me a school where teachers are learning, and I'll show you a school where kids are learning."[1]

The most significant strategy in the short term for improving school quality in many districts may be elevating the performance of Tier Two and Tier Three teachers (and thereby making more of the good ones want to stay). That is not going to happen in schools of education. It is going to happen, if it happens at all, school by school and district by district, where they are already working.

TRAINING AND THE ROAD TO HIGH PERFORMANCE—STEP ONE: INDUCTION

In the world of education, induction refers to the period from when a teacher first shows up at a school district to the end of that teacher's first or second year, or to the time when he or she is granted tenure.

Amazingly, until relatively recently, this induction period had been largely overlooked. In the "old days," teachers fresh out of college were brought in, given a couple of days of orientation about how things were done in a district, then sent out to their classrooms. New teachers have simply been woefully unprepared on their first day of school. Inexcusable, but true.

"WHO ARE YOU?" WHAT WE DON'T KNOW ABOUT
THE TEACHERS WE PUT IN THE CLASSROOM

By the time a teacher sets foot in a classroom, both the district and the teacher should have satisfied themselves that they are meant for each other. Most often, it does not work that way.

There are exceptions. According to John Rogers, the dean of studies at the legendary Phillips Andover Academy in Massachusetts, one of the most highly respected boarding schools in the nation, the school puts new hires through eight to ten rigorous interviews. Some districts I visited do as well. Long Beach, for example, draws many of its new teachers from California State University–Long Beach. Those students do most of their student teaching in the Long Beach schools, giving the district the opportunity to have an extensive look at potential recruits. Unfortunately, that kind of extensive screening is often confined to high-income districts, like Great Neck, where there is a detailed interview process with principals and occasionally teachers and parents.[2]

However, in other cases, even among some of the high-performing districts I visited, on the first day of school, the school principal does not know much about the teacher, and the teacher does not have a clue about the school. Some districts were not even able to manage having the central office—and perhaps a principal—watch a recruit give a demonstration lesson or review a portfolio of lesson plans. On a national level, in fact, only a small percentage do that much.[3]

This utter lack of knowledge is not remedied by the introductory programs that districts hold for new teachers in the summer prior to the start of school. No district I visited provided more than twelve days of preschool instruction, and some were as short as three or four days.[4] There is not much information about curriculum or pedagogy and no way to instill any sense of excellence. Nor do the schools get a sense of whether the new teachers fit with the needs of their new school,[5] and teachers have no idea what a new school is like or what is expected of them.[6]

Here is one important difference with some of the larger and more successful charters. Both the Knowledge Is Power Program and Green Dot place more emphasis on the summer period. Even though most of their teachers have experience, they bring them in for three weeks or more to learn the charter's method and to bond with their colleagues. What the charters understand, and what most districts seem to have forgotten, is that good teaching comes from identifying with a good organization and absorbing its values. New teachers cannot be productive if they are simply slotted into positions and told to do their thing.

USEFUL IDEAS FROM THE MARINES: BOOT CAMP

Before joining the Los Angeles Unified School District, I served as deputy general counsel/legal counsel of the U.S. Department of Defense. As I interviewed superintendents about induction, I contrasted what they were saying with the "boot camp" that the military, particularly the Marine Corps, has used over many decades to transform civilians into committed soldiers.

I asked the superintendents what they thought of the following idea: New teachers would begin in early June. They would teach (or even better, coteach with an experienced teacher) summer school during part of the day, during which they would be observed and mentored, and receive training on district curriculum and learning strategies during the rest. Over the course of several weeks, principals and teachers might view these new teachers directly in order to assess if they were a good fit—and vice versa.

The idea had a second element as well. Based on how well the new teachers performed, they would be placed either in a "tenure-track" position (assuming tenure exists) or not. The rest would be treated as "non-tenure-track" or permanent substitutes who would have to earn a tenure-track position during the coming year. (If nothing else, giving substitutes some real training would be a helpful departure from the shameful way they are currently thrust into classrooms without a clue about the school, the curriculum, or even the class.[7])

The point about making a "cut" at the end of the summer session is similar to boot camp. The Marines feel free to dismiss people who do not measure up. The culling process instills a sense of excellence in those who remain and creates a bond with the Corps and fellow Marines. Making a similar "cut" in a school's pre-service program can have the same impact: a sense of bonding and excellence that can motivate teachers once in a school setting.

Nearly everyone interviewed liked the idea (albeit with varying degrees of enthusiasm). There was unanimous agreement on the value of giving new teachers more training in the summer. There were two problems. The first was obvious: money—although a district that is already conducting alternative certification training (see chapter 11) during the summer would have few additional costs.

The second problem was that no district could afford to use boot camp to differentiate among recruits unless all districts did. Otherwise, new teachers would gravitate to those districts where hiring assured them a full-time position that was not further contingent upon doing well at "summer school."

I agree with both reservations, particularly with the second. I offer the boot camp idea here to stimulate the discussion about early training,

which is a worthwhile goal for most districts, regardless of the final result.

LEARNING WHILE TEACHING: THE FIRST YEAR

Some people, unfortunately, are still not convinced about the need for an
induction program.[8] Amanda Rivera, who is responsible for Chicago's
professional development, told me in 2009 that there were still principals
who refused to get on board with the one the district had rolled out in
2002–2003.

But in most cases, superintendents and school boards will piously nod
their heads in support of the accepted wisdom. However, a head nod is
different from really digging in and doing it right. That is what this
discussion is all about.

Various states, like Connecticut, have specific mandates for what the
programs should include.[9] For-profit companies and universities like the
University of California–Santa Cruz's New Teacher Center[10] offer numerous induction programs that a district can buy off-the-shelf,[11] and
there are multidistrict, multiuniversity collaborations with well-defined
programs that other districts may join.[12] The differences that exist among
them are far less significant than the fundamental strategies common to
most of them. Every superintendent I interviewed acknowledged the importance of such strategies but worried about finding the money, and,
more importantly, qualified and dedicated trainers.[13]

The most important of the trainers are most often teachers who have
been designated "mentors." The mentor advises a new teacher on how to
deal with practical problems in the classroom and gives emotional support. The mentors generally observe teaching and sometimes "model"
instruction by having a new teacher watch them, but the number of observations and other help varies widely.

For example, one recent survey from North Carolina, which has a
strong, state-supported induction program, reported that only 51 percent
of new teachers said they had any contact with their mentors at least once
a week.[14] That is not enough; some mentoring models suggest first-year
teachers should talk to mentors at least once or twice a week throughout
the year.[15] The data supports that frequency.[16] According to a National
Center for Education Statistics survey, 66 percent of new-teacher mentees
who met with their mentors at least once a week said they were helped "a
lot." However, for those who met their mentors only two or three times a
month, the share that said they were helped "a lot" fell to 38 percent; if it
was only once a month, the share was 31 percent.[17]

Time is not the only issue. What the mentors do, and how they interact with their new teachers, is just as important. Harvard's Susan Johnson
notes that some mentors do not provide much teaching help, limiting

their assistance to emotional support.[18] Kaya Henderson, Michelle Rhee's successor in Washington, added another caveat: If there is not good personal chemistry between mentor and mentee, the process is not going to work; yet it is difficult at times because of labor rules or a shortage of good mentors to change pairs even when it is clear that the two people are a bad match.

Henderson told me she prefers to rely on a new teacher's colleagues to provide guidance and help. Studies from the National Bureau of Economic Research and the Harvard Graduate School of Education Project on the Next Generation of Teachers support her. They found that teachers who are surrounded by more capable peers raise the test scores of their students more than those whose colleagues are not as skilled.[19] And there is a similar positive effect when principals mentor.[20]

So is it mentoring or collaboration? The right answer is neither one nor the other. It is most often both.

SHOULD NEW TEACHERS USE A SCRIPT?

The term "curriculum" can refer to both the content taught (the "what") and the method of instruction (the "how"), which is formally referred to as pedagogy. There is generally a consensus that in a standards-based era, a central office (and the state) will have control over much of what is taught (although teachers like to be asked for their views), but there is considerable disagreement about the degree to which a district should try to dictate the "how."[21]

Paul Vallas, the superintendent in New Orleans's Recovery School District (and formerly of Chicago and Philadelphia), strongly believes in having teachers use a curriculum that provides detailed guidance over not only the content of the curriculum, but also the pedagogy. So did Alan Bersin and his deputy for instruction, Anthony Alvarado, when they first arrived in San Diego, although they eventually restored more flexibility after meeting stout teacher resistance.

The heavy scripting of classroom pedagogy is what raises most teachers' hackles.[22] Carl Cohn, who followed Bersin as San Diego's superintendent, told me:

> San Diego [when I got there] was doing managed pedagogy. Pedagogy is the third rail of education. If you want trouble go into a good teacher's classroom and say I am going to deconstruct your teaching and require *b* after *a*. That will get you war.

Detailed scripting can make sense for new teachers, who often desire the guidance,[23] but it may not make sense for more accomplished educators who have developed their own effective styles.[24] Harvard's Next Generation of Teachers Project found that significant numbers of new teachers in

both low-income and high-income schools want more curricular guidance, but they also found that in low-income schools, the guidance is too
prescriptive, which reduces satisfaction and makes these teachers want to
leave.[25] Dictating the selection of instructional approaches contradicts the
core of teachers' sense of professionalism.[26] It undermines teacher self-
respect.[27] It is inconsistent with the transition from mass production to
artisanal education.

A more insidious, adverse impact is that an administration that is
overly prescriptive about pedagogy may undercut any attempt to build a
collegial, collaborative culture where teachers assume a greater role in
school leadership. Charlotte Danielson, a consultant and academic who
has written extensively about "teacher professionalism," notes that dictating how things should be taught ignores that expertise and destroys
any hope of mutual respect and collaboration.[28]

All of which means that if you are a reformer, the subject has to be
approached with nuance. Give enough guidance to help those who need
it, but not so much that you undercut the professionalism you are trying
to foster.

THE NEED FOR CONTINUED SUPPORT

Many of those I interviewed, including Jack Dale in Fairfax County and
Montgomery County's associate superintendent, Jody Leleck, agree with
Harvard's Johnson on the absolute necessity of principals providing a
supportive atmosphere for new teachers.[29] Unlike older teachers, new
ones want guidance. They want to be observed. They want the principal
and master teachers to take an interest in how well they are doing. However, in too many districts they still feel isolated and alone.[30]

And they should not be placed in untenable classroom situations, but
often are. Stephanie King, a Miami-Dade teacher and the Florida Teacher
of the Year in 2000, told me that she was the mentor for a new teacher
who was given a class of fifty-five, half of whom were special education
students. There was supposed to be a coteacher who was a special education specialist, but he only came by occasionally to ask the new teacher
how she was doing. And the new teacher was afraid of complaining for
fear of getting fired. King went over the head of everyone at the school to
Miami's central office. The problem was fixed—in January. It confirmed
her experience with new teachers: Unless something really awful happens, or someone with more clout than a new teacher complains, new
teachers can be abused.

Finally, new teachers need continuing coursework. Most high-performing districts provide additional classes for them directly or at local
universities during their first year or two of teaching. Sometimes the
courses are in response to state requirements, but often they reflect the

district's thinking about what its new teachers need. For example, Sandy Cokeley in Pearl River reported that her district's new teachers attend training sessions one afternoon a month during their first year. Most of the courses deal with practical issues like classroom management or understanding assessments and standardized test scores. Amanda Rivera said that Chicago provides new teachers with instruction on ten high-need topics—again focused on the classroom.

If you look back about why new teachers leave, the lack of these three supports—collaborative mentors and fellow teachers, better guidance, and continuing assistance—figure prominently on the list. They may look like "nice to haves," but they are really serious necessities—and better at boosting retention than salary increases.[31]

WHAT WE NEED TO DO

We need to ensure that new teacher support programs include:

- A coherent and focused description of what it takes to be a good teacher rather than a haphazard set of directions about how to fill in grade books or take attendance.
- Serious interviewing of potential new teachers, including observing their teaching.
- A meaningful amount of training, before the start of a teacher's first year (i.e., boot camp).
- A program to support and advise the new teacher. What a program is *not* is just the mentor or specialist, with everyone else ignoring the new teacher.[32]
- A collegial support structure that involves both teachers and the administration, including grade or subject matter meetings where time is allocated to discuss new-teacher issues.
- Real clinical support, which means: (1) at least one meeting with a mentor or coach every week, preferably more; (2) a regular series of classroom observations of the new teacher, weekly or biweekly at first and at some greater interval as time goes on; and (3) opportunities for a new teacher to work with a master teacher, either co-teaching or at least observing.
- Mentors who are trained to provide guidance and have time to give it.
- Classroom assignments appropriate for a *new* teacher, including a reasonable class size and mix of students that a new teacher can handle. More generally, new teachers should not be given the meanest and most difficult jobs merely because they are lowest in the pecking order.

- Coursework focused on problems new teachers encounter in the classroom. The good news is that these courses are useful for more than just new, traditionally trained teachers. They will be relevant for anyone being alternatively trained, and, as discussed in chapter 9, they may help struggling, veteran teachers who need to relearn the basics.[33]

Merely acknowledging the value of induction does not get a district far along in meeting all these requirements. What it will take is a fundamental belief in the importance of districts as the place where teachers are trained. It is the theme that animates the next three chapters.

NOTES

1. Quoted in Katherine K. Merseth, "Arming New Teachers with Survival Skills," in *Recruiting, Retaining, and Supporting Highly Qualified Teachers*, ed. Caroline Chauncey (Cambridge, MA: Harvard Education Press, 2005), 29.

2. Susan Moore Johnson, Susan M. Kardos, David Kauffman, Edward Liu, and Morgaen L. Donaldsen, "The Support Gap: New Teachers' Early Experiences in High-Income and Low-Income Schools," *Education Policy Analysis Archives* 12, no. 61 (Oct. 29, 2004): 7–8.

3. Merseth, "Arming New Teachers with Survival Skills," 29 (citing a study that reported 7.5 percent of the teachers in the four states surveyed teach a sample lesson as part of the hiring process); Kenneth D. Peterson, *Effective Teacher Hiring: A Guide to Getting the Best* (Alexandria, VA: ASCD, 2002), 43.

4. Pittsburgh has just begun a three-week summer session for new teachers. *Pittsburgh Post-Gazette*, "Pittsburgh Schools Outline Plans for Teacher Training," July 20, 2010 (retrieved from www.post-gazette.com/pg/10201/1073901-298.stm on July 22, 2010).

5. In this kind of truncated hiring process, there is likely no time for the administration of personality tests to identify if the new teacher has the traits necessary to be a good teacher. Advocates of personality tests believe they can identify which traits are relevant to teaching, Peter B. Swanson, "Ready, Set, Recruit for Teaching," *Phi Delta Kappan* 91, no. 2 (Oct. 2009): 28–32, although, as noted in the section on administrators, the idea has many detractors.

6. Deborah Meier created the highly respected Central Park East High School in New York in the 1980s. She has described five qualities she would look for in prospective teachers. Here they are: "(1) a self-conscious reflectiveness about how they themselves learn and (maybe even more) about how and when they *don't* learn; (2) a sympathy toward others, an appreciation of differences, an ability to imagine one's own "otherness"; (3) a willingness, better yet a taste, for working collaboratively; (4) a passion for having others share some of one's own interests; and then (5) a lot of perseverance, energy, and devotion to getting things right!" Deborah Meier, *The Power of Their Ideas: Lessons for America from a Small School in Harlem* (Boston, MA: Beacon Press, 1995), 142.

7. See, for example, Carolyn Bucior, "The Replacements," *New York Times*, Jan. 3, 2010 (retrieved from www.nytimes.com/2010/01/03/opinion/03bucior.html on Jan. 4, 2010).

8. The overall number of districts providing some form of mentoring has increased significantly in the last decade. As of 2008, twenty-two states funded induction programs for new teachers, and twenty-five specifically funded mentoring programs. *Education Week*, "State Highlight Reports 2009" (Bethesda, MD: Editorial Projects in

Education, 2009), 9; NCES (IES), table 3.7 (SER)—Requirements for participation in state-funded induction programs and mentoring programs for beginning teachers, whether standards exist for mentors, and reduced-workload policies for first-year teachers, by state: 2007–08 (retrieved from http://nces.ed.gov/programs/statereform/tab3_7.asp on Oct. 2, 2009).

9. Susan M. Kardos, "New Teacher Induction," in *Recruiting, Retaining, and Supporting Highly Qualified Teachers*, ed. Caroline Chauncey (Cambridge, MA: Harvard Education Press, 2005), 72–73. As of 2009, twenty-two states required participation in an induction program. But even where they do exist, the quality of these programs is painfully uneven. Only 56 percent of new teachers receive basic mentoring and supportive communications from the school or the department, and only 26 percent enjoy basic support plus the collaboration of colleagues, common planning time, and seminars for new teachers. Michael Strong, *Effective Teacher Induction and Mentoring: Assessing the Evidence* (New York: Teachers College Press, 2009), 3; Kardos, "New Teacher Induction," 65–66.

10. *Mentoring New Teachers: The Santa Cruz New Teacher Project* (Washington, DC: U.S. Department of Education National Conference on Teacher Quality, 2010) (retrieved from www2.ed.gov/inits/exemplary practices/d-1.html on Dec. 14, 2010).

11. Learning Point Associates, *Quality Teaching in At-Risk Schools* (Naperville, IL: Learning Point Associates, 2008) (retrieved from www2.tqsource.org/strategies/atrisk/Induction.pdf); see also www.thefreelibrary.com/ETS's+PATHWIDE+New+Teacher+Induction+Program+Selected+for+DOE.

12. Carol Giles, Barbara Davis, and Sheryl McGlamery, "Induction Programs That Work," *Phi Delta Kappan* 91, no. 2 (Oct. 2009): 42–47 (describes the Comprehensive Teacher Induction Consortium, which involves the University of Missouri, the University of Nebraska at Omaha, and Texas State University at San Marcos).

13. One study has concluded that a district can see a return of $1.66 after five years for every dollar invested in quality induction. Strong, *Effective Teacher Induction and Mentoring*, 99.

14. Eric Hirsch, *North Carolina Teacher Working Conditions Research Brief: Supporting New Teachers* (Santa Cruz, CA: UC Santa Cruz New Teacher Center, 2009), 2 (retrieved from www.neteachercenter.org on Dec. 21, 2009). The NCES data from the year 2000 showed that only 11 percent of teachers who were mentoring met with their mentees at least once a week, and only 8 percent of those mentees said they met with their mentors that frequently. Table 33-2 (percentage of public school teachers who participated in various collaborative activities during the past 12 months, by focus of activity and frequency of participation: 2000), in NCES, *The Condition of Education 2002* (Washington, DC: U.S. Department of Education, 2002), 188. Another, older study of California's Beginning Educator Support and Training (BEST) program reported over half the new teachers reported they did not have contact with their mentor even once a month. Linda Darling-Hammond and Gary Sykes, "Wanted: A National Teacher Supply Policy for Education: The Right Way to Meet the 'Highly Qualified Teacher' Challenge," *Education Policy Analysis Archives* 11, no. 33 (Sept. 2003): 26.

15. See, for example, Barry Sweeney, *The New Teacher Mentoring Process: A Working Model* (retrieved from www.teachermentors.com/Mprocess.php on Dec. 4, 2009); John Myers, *A Model Teacher Mentoring Program for Districts* (retrieved from www.associatedcontent.com/article.1741386/a_model_teacher_mentoring_program_for.html on Sept. 4, 2009); *Chicago Tribune*, "Schools Focus on Training New Teachers," Dec. 6, 2010 ("[M]entors must spend at least 60 hours of 'face-to-face contact' with the new teacher every year, whether observing in class, planning lessons or prepping for parent conferences.") (retrieved from www.chicagotribune.com/news/education.ct-met-teacher-coaching-hechinger-201012106,0,1188861.story on Dec. 8, 2010).

16. Stephen Fletcher, Michael Strong, and Anthony Villar, "An Investigation of the Effects of Variations in Mentor-Based Induction on the Performance of Students in California," *Teachers College Record* 110, no. 10 (Aug. 2008): 2271–89.

17. Table 33-4 (Percentage of public school teachers indicating the extent to which participation in various collaborative activities during the past 12 months improved their teaching, by focus of activity and frequency of participation: 2000) in NCES, *The Condition of Education 2002* (Washington, DC: U.S. Department of Education, 2002), 188.

18. Johnson, *Finders and Keepers, supra, passim.*

19. C. Kirabo Jackson, Elias Bruegmann, *Teaching Students and Teaching Each Other: The Importance of Peer Learning for Teachers* (Cambridge, MA: National Bureau of Economic Research, 2009).

20. Anita M. Varrati, Mary E. Lavine, Steven L. Turner, "A New Conceptual Model for Principal Involvement and Professional Collaboration in Teacher Education," *The Teachers College Record* 111, no. 2 (Feb. 2009): 480–510.

21. Dan C. Lortie, *Schoolteacher* (Chicago: University of Chicago Press, 1975), 240–42; David Kauffman, *Curriculum Prescription and Curriculum Constraint: Second-Year Teachers' Perceptions* (Cambridge, MA: Next Generation of Teachers Working Paper, 2005), 19.

22. Susan Moore Johnson, *Second-Stage Teachers and Coaching: Building School Capacity and a Teaching Career,* (paper prepared for the 2009 Annual Meeting of the American Educational Research Association, San Diego, CA, April 13–17, 2009), 27; Susan Moore Johnson, Susan M. Kardos, David Kauffman, Edward Liu, Morgaen L. Donaldsen, "The Support Gap: New Teachers' Early Experiences in High-Income and Low-Income Schools," *Education Policy Analysis Archives* 12, no. 61 (Oct. 29, 2004): 12; *Quality Counts 2008,* "Working Conditions Trump Pay" (Bethesda, MD: Education Week, 2008), 32–35; Arthur T. Costigan, Karen K. Zumwalt, Margaret S. Crocco, *Learning to Teach in an Age of Accountability* (Mahwah, NJ: Lawrence Erlbaum Assocs., 2004).

23. David Kauffman, Susan Moore Johnson, Susan M. Kardos, Edward Liu, Heather G. Peske, "'Lost at Sea': New Teachers' Experiences with Curriculum and Assessment," *Teachers College Record* 104, no. 2 (March 2002): 278; Johnson et al., "The Support Gap," 13; David Kaufman, *Curriculum Support and Curriculum Neglect: Second-Year Teachers' Experiences,* (Cambridge, MA: Harvard Graduate School of Education Project of Next Generation Teachers, 2005); Peter Rennert-Ariev, "The Hidden Curriculum of Performance-Based Teacher Education," *Teachers College Record* 110, no. 1 (2008): 105–38.

24. Pam Grossman, "Teaching: From *A Nation at Risk* to a Profession at Risk," in *Recruiting, Retaining, and Supporting Highly Qualified Teachers,* ed. Caroline Chauncey (Cambridge, MA: Harvard Education Press, 2005), 13; Karen Chenoweth, *How It's Being Done, Urgent Lessons from Unexpected Schools,* (Cambridge, MA: Harvard Education Press, 2009), 191.

25. IGrossman, "Teaching," 15; Ken Futernick, *A Possible Dream: Retaining California Teachers So All Students Learn* (Sacramento, CA: The Center for Teacher Quality, California State University Sacramento, 2007), 19, 57 (One in four teachers leaving the profession cited "over-scripting and a narrow curriculum" contributed to their decision.); Barbara Benham Tye, Lisa O'Brien, "Why Are Experienced Teachers Leaving the Profession?" *Phi Delta Kappan* 84, no. 1 (Sept. 2002): 24–32.

26. Charlotte Danielson, *Enhancing Professional Practice: A Framework for Teaching* (Alexandria, VA: ASCD, 1996), 24.

27. Linda Darling-Hammond, *The Right to Learn* (San Francisco: Jossey-Bass, 1997), 93.

28. Charlotte Danielson, *Teacher Leadership That Strengthens Professional Practice* (Alexandria, VA: ASCD, 2007), 22–23.

29. Johnson, *Finders, Keepers, passim.*

30. Susan M. Kardos and Susan Moore Johnson, "On Their Own and Presumed Expert: New Teachers' Experience with Their Colleagues," *The Teachers College Record* 109, no. 9 (2007): 2083–2106.

31. Deborah Reed, Kim S. Rueben, and Elisa Barbour, *Retention of New Teachers in California* (San Francisco: Public Policy Institute of California, 2006), vi; Harry K.

Wong, "Induction Programs That Keep Working," in *Keeping Good Teachers*, ed. Marge Scherer (Alexandria, VA: ASCD, 2003), 42.

32. Kardos, "New Teacher Induction," 73.

33. California's Beginning Teacher Support and Assessment (BTSA) program, which is a relatively robust induction effort, cost the state $3,675 for a first year teacher and $3,357 for a second year teacher in 2005–2006. Districts added an additional $2,000 in-kind. Reed, Rueben, and Barbour, *Retention of New Teachers in California*, 14.

NINE

The Rest of Your Life—Good Teachers Can Always Get Better: The Professional Learning Community

Historically, professional development has been an underfunded, often ineffective sideshow.[1] District central offices provided courses on what they thought teachers should know. They were most likely "one-shot" affairs, with no follow-up. Teachers attended these sessions, sat passively in their seats, looked at the clock, and then went back to school doing the same things they had done before the course.[2]

The information was often somebody else's idea of what was important. It bore little relationship to teachers' needs as they saw them,[3] because it was "too isolated from classroom realities to have an impact."[4] Its inadequacies justified, in teachers' minds, their determination to accept or ignore instructional directives as they saw fit, and nothing was in place that would make them do otherwise. It was loose coupling epitomized.

With the arrival of accountability and the ability to track student achievement data, all that changed. Ignoring advice and hiding out are no longer possible.[5] Good teaching now counts. But that leaves the tough questions: What training will really improve teaching? How is it demonstrated? How to get it accepted? And, just to complicate things, how to do it in a way that fosters artisanal and professional instruction rather than mindless mass production?

THE "NEW WORLD"

Just as isolation thwarts excellence in the modern education system, there is substantial evidence that collaboration and sharing can improve teacher performance and, equally importantly, retention.[6] Paul Vallas went so far as to say that he thinks year-round, data-driven professional development, coupled with better recruitment and promotion on merit, is a "silver bullet" for education reform. ("Silver bullet" is his characterization, not mine.)[7]

THE PROFESSIONAL LEARNING COMMUNITY EXPLAINED

Although often identified with one team of proponents, Richard and Rebecca DuFour and Robert Eaker,[8] the concept of the professional learning community has evolved around the nation over the last twenty years and taken many forms.[9]

The key concept is that teachers work proactively and collaboratively on much of their own training in order to improve their practice and enhance student learning.[10] Gerald Anderson, who won national acclaim for closing the achievement gap in the Brazosport district during the 1990s, explained why that is so valuable:

> Teachers are working as hard as they can work within the system . . . .
> But a teacher is only as good as she is—given time and money available. Say six or seven algebra teachers are shutting their doors, doing their thing, all independent of one another, not collaborating. Those kids are going to come out of that as well as that teacher's ability allows. A poor teacher does not know what a better teacher knows. There is tremendous potential when you harness the skills of seven versus one.[11]

A superintendent, like Anderson, still makes clear what he believes quality teaching looks like, but he works on creating a joint vision rather than imposing a top-down directive. When that is done well, teachers are more willing to accept what they are taught because it focuses on what they see as their own needs and circumstances.[12]

Learning communities depart from the "old world" in other ways as well. It is all about continuous improvement. That means the focus is on a vision of good teaching and timely student data, first to identify where teachers need to improve and later to test what works effectively. And it is not just about the short-term problems of students or teachers. There is a long-term focus on extended training, which works, rather than the old "one-shot" programs, which do not.[13]

For some principals, running a learning community means a painful break with how they have always approached their job. They have to win over teachers to the whole idea of meaningful collaboration, which means they have to believe in it themselves. And they have to accept one other profound change: They have to learn to live with data. If the numbers convey bad news, the response has to be "how do we fix this?" rather than "heads are going to roll." "Spinning" bad news, a long-time forte of many adept bureaucrats, is definitely out. Principals have to know how to guide the work, support it, and give teacher organization and leadership time to develop.[14]

Any district with a group of principals willing to do all those things is not your "old time" district any more.[15] It has abandoned mass production in favor of a twenty-first-century vision.

THE CHALLENGES IN CREATING A LEARNING COMMUNITY

Although there is widespread praise for professional learning communities,[16] a 2009 study from the National Staff Development Council led by Stanford's highly respected Linda Darling-Hammond concluded, "Most teachers in the United States do not have access to [quality] professional development...."[17] Here is why:

Labor Contracts

Although unions have long acknowledged the importance of key features of the learning community, union policies often inhibit the learning communities that would otherwise deliver what they say they want. Seniority clauses disrupt collegial groups, a subject we are about to discuss in the chapter on hard-to-staff schools (see chapter 16). The commitment to a single salary schedule makes it impossible to pay mentors and master teachers more. Union work rules are often too inflexible to allow collaboration time. Union commitments to "worker solidarity" make them refuse to allow teachers to help evaluate other teachers.[18] Like many other problems caused by union straddling between mass production and professionalization, what unions say they want and how they act are often at odds.

Getting the Data Accepted

Teachers' acceptance of the legitimacy of student achievement data is a linchpin for making this professional development work.[19] Without that acceptance, there is no basis for any data-driven decision making, including identifying how a teacher's instruction might be improved. Right now, teachers are distrustful.[20]

For example, "Ed Man" blogged in response to an article in the online *Houston Chronicle* about creating a statewide system for standardizing education data: "Anyone who agrees with these guys that in education 'the truth is in the numbers' needs to go back to school—this particular bit of 'hey, aren't we cute' is 110% pure pig poop—the buzzwords sound good, but it's ALL ka ka—in Beaumont, the instrument of choice is a series of fatally flawed 6 week tests—teachers waste weeks each year teaching and then administering The Test—then we waste even more time in meetings disaggregating the data which is then ignored—and yes, it is all about the money."[21]

Whatever the truth in the posting, Ed Man's diatribe is useful: It is a reminder that convincing people that data is legitimate and useful is not a slam-dunk. It takes careful work and planning—and credible data. As we shall discuss shortly, that last point—credibility—is not a small issue.

Convincing Teachers to Accept Observation and Advice

Teachers have to accept that others, primarily the principal, but also their colleagues, have a right, and indeed an obligation, as part of a commitment to the students to ensure that the good practices demonstrated are in fact incorporated into real teaching.[22] It means the end of old-style autonomy and loose coupling.[23]

The problem is not theoretical. Paul Hegre is the Minneapolis coordinator of Q Comp, Minnesota's ambitious salary overhaul program. When I talked to him, he told me Q Comp districts rely heavily on the Milken Family Foundation's System for Teacher and Student Advancement Project (TAP), which connects professional development and pay benefits. Even though TAP is showing good results in the district, there are still teachers who feel they do not need help—even when it is in their financial interest to do so. They do not want to collaborate; they just want to remain as isolated and autonomous as ever.

If teachers can be won over, there are real benefits. They may agree to form Peer Assistance and Review committees, which were first created by districts working with local unions affiliated with the Teachers Union Reform Network, the reform-oriented organization of teacher union locals. These groups of teachers and administrators assist both new teachers and old ones to become better educators, but, if they are unsuccessful, the committees can recommend terminating those who are not working out.

More importantly, if teachers will listen to one another, they really can improve their practice. Probably the best single case of such teacher-to-teacher improvement occurred in Long Beach. According to Carl Cohn, the former Long Beach superintendent, one classroom teacher developed the district's prized math curriculum (called MAP2D). That teacher showed the curriculum first to the rest of the school and then to other schools in the district. Cohn is convinced that its success is the reason Long Beach has been a repeated finalist for, and winner of, the Broad Prize.

The Greatest Challenge Is Time

John Simmons, the president of Strategic Learning Initiatives, which has taken over several Chicago schools and turned them into successful charters, told me that time for collaboration is key. Although the amount of time available has increased over the last twenty years,[24] it is not yet enough.

Stanford's Linda Darling-Hammond, among others, has suggested ten hours a week would be a reasonable amount of time for planning and collaboration time,[25] and she has written approvingly about Singapore's commitment to giving teachers twenty hours per week to collaborate and one hundred hours a year for professional development.[26] Sadly, no district I visited (or have read about) has been able to build in that kind of program. Doug Otto in Plano gives his elementary school teachers one period weekly for collaboration, and he has been able to carve out that much time for secondary teachers. And that is from someone who is a firm believer in collegial professional development.[27]

Caveat: Can You Trust the Teachers?

When I spoke with her in the spring of 2009, Kaya Henderson resisted much of this idea of teacher-directed self-improvement. She pointed out that it is premised on having teachers with enough skill and understanding of the learning process to be able to identify problems and work on them.

Stephanie King agreed. She has spent many years coaching others and has much the same concern as Henderson. "Teachers cannot identify the right professional development," she said, "unless they are adequately skilled and not demoralized by a process that demands change without explaining why."

Luckily, those were exceptions—at least among those I interviewed. Nonetheless, Henderson's point is noted: If there is not a broad-based level of basic competence, this strategy is not likely to succeed.

One More Caveat: Money!

The final challenge to the professional learning community is cost. While expenses ranged widely from district to district among those that I visited, several districts, such as Aldine, Brownsville, and Long Beach, provided collaborative time, mentors, and coursework within the limited budgets of districts dependent on state aid, sometimes supplemented with grants from special state funds or foundations. Blue Valley and Plano, both of which are richer districts, clearly had the capacity for extensive professional development without significant budget increases, although they, too, found outside grant support.

Those who have advocated professional learning communities have estimated the direct cost to the district (excluding salary enhancements) at roughly $6,000 to $8,000 per teacher per year.[28] The National Commission on Teaching and America's Future estimates alternatively that the figure is about 3 percent of a typical district's budget,[29] although that figure may be low if one includes things like arranging for adequate planning time.

Several sources of support exist, including the Milken Foundation's TAP program, Title II of the No Child Left Behind Act, and the new dollars released by the Obama administration's Race to the Top incentives. In addition, some of the current money for training can be used more productively. But these sources pale in comparison with two other pots of money.

One is the billions of dollars state legislatures appropriate every year to operate state-supported colleges' and universities' teacher training programs. Although I cannot find an estimate of how large that pot is for all fifty states and the District of Columbia, it is significant.[30] Total spending by states and localities for higher education in 2007–2008 was over $70 billion.[31] The share of those funds that are directed to schools of education should now be opened up to school districts that provide new teacher training, either on their own or in collaboration with universities or nonprofit organizations. They should be allocated a fair share of that money if they can demonstrate that their professional development programs are more cost-effective than traditional ones.[32]

However, even that pot may not be the biggest source of money associated with professional development that could be used to sustain learning communities. As we will discuss in chapter 14, it is now estimated that teachers currently receive approximately $30 billion built into their salaries in compensation for additional postcollege coursework or advanced degrees. But there is little evidence that the degrees bought with those funds actually improve student learning. It can be put to better use—paying either for salary supplements tied to mentoring or master teaching or for the professional development programs themselves.

WHAT WE NEED TO DO

We need to demand that districts become professional learning communities. But that is only the beginning. It is almost inevitable that if a superintendent does not initiate the program, he or she will respond to a demand by parents or taxpayers by saying that the district is *already* a professional learning community. Do not accept that statement at face value.

Make the superintendent prove the claim. And here is what the proof should include:

- A continuous improvement plan that includes professional development
- A commitment to teacher-teacher and teacher-administrator collaboration
- Adequate training for mentors, master teachers, and principals
- A Peer Assistance and Review committee
- Principal and teacher evaluation standards that take into account how well they participate in, or manage, professional learning communities
- Enough mentors, master teachers, facilitators, and consultants to provide the training
- Revisions to union contracts if their provisions inhibit the development of professional learning communities
- Enough money in the budget to fund all of these steps—somewhere between 3 percent and 5 percent of district operating expenses—and a commitment that the community will not be dismantled at the first sign of a budget shortfall

Finally, be part of the continuous improvement process by looking at the numbers. If the data says that something is not right, participate in the conversation about how to fix it.

NOTES

1. Katherine S. Neville, Rachel H. Sherman, and Carol E. Cohen, *Preparing and Training Professionals: Comparing Education to Six Other Fields* (Washington, DC: The Finance Project, 2005); Hayes Mizell, "The Misuse of Professional Development," *Education Week*, Sept. 20, 2010 ("[T]he change required is to make professional development responsive to the objective learning needs of teachers and their students, needs supported by student- or teacher-performance data.") (retrieved from www.edweek.org/ew/articles/2010/09/22/04mizell_ep.h30.html on Nov. 23, 2010).

2. Milbrey W. McLaughlin and Joan E. Talbert, *Building School-Based Teacher Learning Communities* (New York: Teachers College Press, 2006), 68.

3. National Commission on Teaching and America's Future, *What Matters Most: Teaching for America's Future* (Washington, DC: NCTAF, 1996), 40–41.

4. Vivian Troen and Katherine C. Boles, *Who's Teaching Your Children?* (New Haven, CT: Yale University Press, 2003), 54.

5. There is no better proof of this change than the *Los Angeles Times'* posting Los Angeles Unified School District student test score data *sorted by teacher* in the summer of 2010. Jason Felch, Jason Song, and Doug Smith, "Who's Teaching LA's Kids?," *Los Angeles Times*, Aug. 14, 2010, and "Meet L.A.'s Most Effective Teachers—and Find Out How Your Child's Teacher Performs," *Los Angeles Times*, Aug. 29, 2010. The latter story included data on six thousand teachers and the "Top 100 'Value-Added' Teachers."

6. A recent survey of Chicago teachers found that teacher retention at the city's high schools is strongly related to "collective responsibility and perceptions of innovation among colleagues," and retention at all city schools was 4 percent to 5 percent higher "where there is a shared commitment among the faculty to improve the school so all students can learn. . . ." Elaine Allensworth, Stephen Ponisciak, and Christopher

Mazzeo, *The Schools Teachers Leave: Teacher Mobility in Chicago Public Schools* (Chicago: Consortium on Chicago School Research, 2009), 25.

7. National Commission for Teaching and America's Future, *No Dream Denied: A Pledge to America's Children* (Washington, DC: NCTAF, 2003), 7.

8. See, for example, Richard DuFour, Rebecca DuFour, and Robert Eaker, *Revisiting Professional Learning Communities at Work* (Bloomington, IN: Solution Tree Publishing, 2008); Richard DuFour, Rebecca DuFour, Robert Eaker, and Gayle Karhanek, *Whatever It Takes: How Professional Learning Communities Respond When Kids Don't Learn* (Bloomington, IN: Solution Tree Publishing, 2004).

9. The National Staff Development Council has standards for professional development that are similar (www.nsdc.org/standards/index.cfm).

10. Karen Seashore Louis, "Creating and Sustaining Professional Communities," in *Sustaining Professional Learning Communities*, ed. Alan M. Blankstein, Robert W. Cole, and Paul D. Houston (Thousand Oaks, CA: Corwin Press, 2008), 42.

11. See also Karen Seashore Louis, Kenneth Leithwood, Kyla L. Wahlstrom, and Stephen E. Anderson, *Investigating the Links to Improved Student Learning* (Minneapolis: University of Minnesota Press/University of Toronto Press, 2010), 19–36; Tom Carroll, "The Next Generation of Learning Teams," *Phi Delta Kappan* 91, no. 2 (Oct. 2009): 10 ("The idea that a single teacher, working on her own, should be expected to know and do everything to meet the diverse learning needs of 30 students for a year is an idea whose time has passed.").

12. Steve Farkas, Jean Johnson, and Ann Duffett, *Stand By Me: What Teachers Really Think about Unions, Merit Pay and Other Professional Matters* (New York: Public Agenda, 2003), 30; Council of Chief State School Officers, *Current Models for Evaluating Effectiveness of Teacher Professional Development* (Washington, DC: CCSSO, 2008), 2.

13. *Education Week*, "Staff Development for Teachers Fragmented," Feb. 11, 2009, 7.

14. McLaughlin and Talbert, *Building School-Based Teacher Learning Communities*, 39, 58.

15. Christopher Steel and Elizabeth Craig, "Reworking Industrial Models, Exploring Contemporary Ideas, and Fostering Teacher Leadership," *Phi Delta Kappan* 87, no. 9 (May 2006): 676–80.

16. *MetLife Survey of the American Teacher* (New York: Metropolitan Life Ins. Co., 2008), 30.

17. Linda Darling-Hammond, Ruth Chung Wei, Alethea Andree, Nikole Richardson, and Stelios Orphanos, *Professional Learning in the Learning Profession: A Status Report on Teacher Development in the United States and Abroad* (Washington, DC: National Staff Development Council, 2009), "Key Findings."

18. McLaughlin and Talbert, *Building School-Based Teacher Learning Communities*, 114–15.

19. McLaughlin and Talbert, *Building School-Based Teacher Learning Communities*, 57; Sharon D. Kruse and Karen Seashore Louis, *Building Strong School Cultures* (Thousand Oaks, CA: Corwin Press, 2009), 55.

20. Jean Johnson, Andrew Yarrow, Jonathan Rochkind, and Amber Ott, *Teaching for a Living: How Teachers See the Profession Today* (New York: Public Agenda, 2009), Question 6e Results.

21. Chron.com, "Data System Would Help Schools Focus on Success," Sept. 22, 2009 (retrieved from www.chron.com/disp/story.mpl.editorial.outlook.6632044.html on Sept. 22, 2009).

22. *Usable Knowledge*, "Rounds for Teachers" (Harvard Graduate School of Education) (retrieved from www.uknow.gse.harvard.edu/teaching/TC103-607.html on Feb. 16, 2009); Megan Charner-Laird, *Ready and Willing: Second-Stage Teachers and Professional Collaboration* (paper presented at the Annual Meeting of the American Education Research Association, Chicago, IL, 2007), 10; Council of Chief State School Officers, *Current Models for Evaluating Effectiveness of Teacher Professional Development* (Washington, DC: CCSSO, 2008), 8; Michael Fullan, *Turnaround Leadership* (San Francisco: Jossey-Bass, 2004), 51–52.

23. Richard Elmore, *School Reform from Inside Out* (Cambridge, MA: Harvard Education Press, 2004), 82.

24. Council of Chief State School Officers, *Does Teacher Professional Development Have Effects on Teaching and Learning?* (Washington, DC: CCSSO, 2008), 5.

25. *eSchool News*, "Congress Schooled on STEM Teaching Crisis," Aug. 1, 2007 (retrieved from www.eschoolnews.com/news/tpl-news/index.cfm on Nov. 25, 2009).

26. *Time*, "How They Do It Abroad," Feb. 25, 2008, 34.

27. One way to push the creation of more time is to follow North Carolina's example. In 2001 it established thirty working condition standards for public schools. Among them were standards providing teachers adequate time for the development of curriculum, collaboration, and professional development. Ken Futernick, *A Possible Dream: Retaining California Teachers So All Students Learn* (Sacramento: The Center for Teacher Quality, California State University Sacramento, 2007), 66–67.

28. *Education Week*, "Full Cost of Professional Development Hidden," Nov. 10, 2010 (retrieved from www.edweek.org/ew/articles/2010/11/1-/11pd_costs.h30.html on Nov. 29, 2010).

29. See, for example, National Commission on Teaching and America's Future, *What Matters Most: Teaching for America's Future* (Washington, DC: NCTAF, 1996), 84.

30. Part of the problem in coming up with a number is that education programs are often "cash cows" whose tuition money is siphoned away to support other university activities. It makes coming up with a definitive figure particularly difficult.

31. NCES (IES) — table 281 — State and Local Financial Support for Higher Education by State: 2005 to 2008.

32. Strategic Management of Human Capital/Consortium for Public Research in Education, *Taking Human Capital Seriously: Talented Teachers in Every Classroom, Talented Principals in Every School* (Philadelphia: CPRE, 2009), 7.

TEN

Training New (and More) Teachers: Working the Pipeline into the Classroom

While writing the book, I had lunch with a friend who is a health care expert. He observed that one of the challenges for any health care reform in America is getting doctors to think about the world differently from the way they were taught to see it in medical school. I said, "That's the same problem we have in education. Unlearning or relearning things is a lot tougher than learning them right in the first place." Reform, no matter how successful it may seem at any one moment, will be under constant threat if teachers first learn the mass-production model and adopt its attitudes. Districts cannot be forever burdened with getting teachers to unlearn things and then relearn them the right way. We have to do it right from the start.

New teachers are trained in one of two ways. In this chapter, we focus on colleges of education, where students earn a degree with a major or minor in education. (In the next chapter, we talk about alternative certification programs,[1] which train those who have already graduated from college in another discipline.)

INADEQUATE UNDERGRADUATE TEACHER TRAINING

The principal critiques of teacher education have not changed much over the past two decades. The coursework is fragmented, too theoretical, and too narrowly focused.[2] It is not tied to specific teaching settings, even though there is agreement that that is how teachers learn best.[3] Students dismiss this coursework as bureaucratic mumbo-jumbo, favoring the

practical instead; they parrot educational theory without believing it just
to graduate, initiating them into loose coupling even before they get
hired at their first school.[4] Student teaching placements are haphazard,
the amount of time spent student teaching is too short,[5] and the quality of
the student teaching experience is poor.[6]

More generally, traditional training programs are accused of lacking
any commitment to excellence. They take in poor-quality students, whose
abilities, as we discussed earlier, have been declining for much of the past
fifty years. Not only have they failed to step up their game to compensate
for these undergraduates' lower skills, they have failed to weed them out.
Even great schools like Harvard inflate grades and pass their students
along in order to sustain these "cash cows" that feed the rest of their
school's programs.[7] (The graduation rates average 96 percent.[8])

In 2006, former Columbia Teachers College president Professor Arthur Levine, the author of the scathing critique of administrator education referred to in the chapter on principals, wrote a major report on
teacher education, which included the following assessment:

> Today, the teacher education curriculum is a confusing patchwork. Ac-
> ademic instruction and clinical instruction are disconnected. Graduates
> are insufficiently prepared for the classroom. And research on teacher
> education is criticized by the academic community for its low quality
> and is ignored by policy makers and practitioners.[9]

I called Professor Levine while writing this book to see if anything had
yet changed. His answer was simple: "No change."[10]

Secretary of Education Arne Duncan was even blunter. In October
2009, he told an audience at Teachers College, Columbia University,
"Many, if not most of the nation's . . . schools, colleges, and departments
of education are doing a mediocre job of preparing teachers for the realities of the 21st-century classroom."[11] A few weeks earlier, his comments
were even saltier. He called education schools "the Bermuda Triangle of
higher education."[12]

DISTRICTS AS AGGRESSIVE AND VOCAL CONSUMERS

What do districts do? The first option: They should identify which
schools are doing the job and target recruitment there.

David Stuckwisch in Portsmouth does not like the quality of many of
the graduates of universities in his state. So he has reached out to the
Midwest and brought those teachers to his district. According to Priscilla
Ridgeway, Aldine's deputy superintendent, they also look to the Midwest for teachers. In both cases, the districts recognize that it costs them
money to recruit outside their home states, but they value the quality
they get in return for their effort. New York City has now followed suit,

teaming with the State University of New York at Albany and Stanford to track thirty-one teacher preparation programs sending elementary teachers to the district. If enough districts adopt the idea, maybe colleges of education will finally get the message.

If so, they can follow Doane College in Crete, Nebraska. The college offers a guarantee to the employing school system. If the district finds the new teacher deficient, the college will allow the person to take additional courses to improve skills without charge.[13] Some states, like Georgia, are following the same path.[14] Now there is a real customer satisfaction commitment!

Beyond that, districts should push states to follow Louisiana's lead in gathering and publishing information about the quality of university teacher education. Secretary of Education Arne Duncan has pushed states to do exactly that.[15] Ohio has followed suit.[16] Others, like Texas, are considering similar proposals as of the time of this writing.[17]

The other place where districts should make known their views is the National Council for Accreditation of Teacher Education (NCATE), which accredits colleges of education.[18] Districts do not relate to NCATE often, let alone complain en masse. That is a mistake. They need to make their views known.[19] In fact, they should do more than just explain what they want colleges of education to do. As Rick Hess, a well-known education scholar, has suggested, it is time for districts to tell NCATE that it should recognize them as a primary, if not *the* primary, focus of teacher preparation in America.[20]

DISTRICT-UNIVERSITY COLLABORATION

A second option for improving teacher education outside district premises is to follow the lead of districts like Long Beach, which has worked with California State UniversityM Long Beach to design an undergraduate curriculum that is specifically tailored to the district's needs. Almost 75 percent of its teachers come from the program. The advantage is obvious: The district gets exactly what it wants—and it has an inside track on recruitment.

There are real possibilities to expand these collaborations. Because of the long-standing criticism about a lack of practical training for new teachers, these university-school arrangements appeal to reformers and philanthropists. For example, the Carnegie Foundation's Teachers for a New Era grants require close cooperation between a university and participating schools, characterizing the training as "academically taught clinical practice."[21]

The Clinton and Bush administrations used money from Title II of the Higher Education Act to fund such projects until 2005, and the Obama administration has used money from Title II of No Child Left Behind, which is to improve teacher quality, to fund the development of new university-district training partnerships.[22] Various states, including Alabama, Arkansas, and Louisiana, are using state funds for the same purpose. At this point, however, state and federal agencies see such collaborations as experimentation.

Their thinking is behind the times. Long Beach and others have had these arrangements for many years. Governments need to think less about such partnerships as innovations needing testing and more as good ideas worthy of implementation. The concept is proven; funding should follow.

For "What We Need to Do," see the end of the next chapter. The one set of recommendations on training new teachers really covers the discussion in both this chapter and the next one.

NOTES

1. In this context, "alternative certification" means providing whatever training is required to obtain a basic teacher's license and, in many cases, credentials or certificates demonstrating the ability to teach specific subjects or grades.

2. Joseph Murphy, "Questioning the Core of University-Based Programs or Preparing School Leaders," *Phi Delta Kappan* 88, no. 8 (2007): 582–84.

3. Milbrey W. McLaughlin and Joan E. Talbert, *Building School-Based Teacher Learning Communities* (New York: Teachers College Press, 2006), 9.

4. Peter Rennert-Ariev, "The Hidden Curriculum of Performance-Based Teacher Education," *Teachers College Record* 110, no. 1 (2008): 105–38.

5. As of 2007–2008, thirty-nine states have some minimum requirement for student teaching, but some like New York require only eight weeks. Maryland requires the most, twenty weeks, and Wisconsin eighteen weeks, but no other state requires more than fifteen. NCES (IES), table 3.2 (SER)—State initial licensure requirements for teacher education in subject area taught written teacher assessments, and clinical training experiences, by state: 2007–2008 (retrieved from http://nces.ed.gov/programs/statereform/tab3_2.asp on Sept. 25, 2009).

6. National Commission on Teaching and America's Future, *What Matters Most: Teaching for America's Future* (Washington, DC: NCTAF, 1996), 31–33; Linda Darling-Hammond, "Reforming Teaching: Are We Missing the Boat?" *Education Week*, March 30, 2009 (retrieved from http://nces.ed.gov/programs/statereform/tab3_2.asp on Oct. 5, 2009); Linda Darling-Hammond, "Constructing 21st Century Teacher Education, *Journal of Teacher Education* 57, no. 3 (2006): 300–314.

7. Vivian Troen and Katherine C. Boles, *Who's Teaching Your Children?* (New Haven, CT: Yale University Press, 2003), 41–43.

8. David Leal, "Assessing Traditional Teacher Preparation: Evidence from a Survey of Graduate and Undergraduate Programs," in *A Qualified Teacher in Every Classroom? Appraising Old Answers and New Ideas*, ed. Frederick Hess, Andrew Rotherham, Kate Walsh (Cambridge, MA: Harvard Education Press, 2004), 25.

9. Leal, "Assessing Traditional Teacher Preparation," 26.

10. He is not alone. In March 2009, Katherine Merseth, director of teacher education at the Harvard Graduate School of Education, told a conference that "of the nation's 1,300 graduate teacher training programs, only about 100 were doing a competent job and 'the others could be shut down tomorrow.'" *New York Times*, "Do Teachers Need Education Degrees?," Aug. 16, 2009 (retrieved from http://roomfordebate.blogs.

nytimes.com/2009/08/16/education-degrees-and-teachers-pay found on August 17, 2009).

11. U.S. Department of Education, "U.S. Secretary of Education Arne Duncan Says Colleges of Education Must Improve for Reforms to Succeed" (Press Release, Oct. 22, 2009) (retrieved from www.ed.gov/news/pressreleases/2009.10/10222009a.html on Nov. 13, 2009).

12. *Education Week*, "Duncan Cites Shortcomings of Teacher Preparation," Oct. 23, 2009 (retrieved from www.edweek.org/ew/articles/2009/10/23/09teachered.h29.html on Oct. 23, 2009).

13. See www.doane.edu/academics/education; Troen and Boles, *Who's Teaching Your Children?*, 52.

14. *Atlanta Journal Constitution*, "Georgia Teachers Now Guaranteed," Dec. 4, 2002; see http://education.gsu.edu/main/2820/htm.

15. U.S. Department of Education, "Teacher Preparation: Reforming the Uncertain Profession—Remarks of Secretary Arne Duncan at Teachers College, Columbia University" (Press Release, Oct. 22, 2009). Kate Walsh, *Steps That Congress Can Take to Improve Teacher Quality—without Overstepping Its Bounds* (Washington, DC: National Council on Teacher Quality, 2007) (a proposal to impose the requirement nationally as part of the Higher Education Act).

16. The Teaching Commission, *Teaching at Risk: Progress & Potholes* (New York: The Teaching Commission, 2006), 42.

17. *Education Week*, "Two on Teacher Preparation," Nov. 3, 2009 (retrieved from http://blogs.edweek.org/edweek/teaacherbeat/2009/11/two_on_teacher_preparation. html on Nov. 4, 2009).

18. The much smaller Teacher Education Accreditation Council is merging with NCATE at the time of this writing. *Education Week*, "Teacher-Prep Accrediting Groups to Merge," Nov. 1, 2010 (retrieved from www.edweek.org/ew/articles/2010//10/25/ 10merge.h30.html on Nov. 3, 2010).

19. Harold Levy, the former chancellor in New York, has suggested taking the idea one step further: making a school's often candid and rigorous accreditation reports available to potential students so that they could see for themselves which schools of education were highly ranked by professional evaluators. Harold O. Levy, "Five Ways to Fix America's Schools," *New York Times*, June 8, 2009 (retrieved from www.nytimes. com/2009/06/08/opinion/08levy.html on June 8, 2009).

20. Frederick Hess, "Not Yet Sold on NCATE's 'Transformative' Clinical Vision," *Teachers College Record*, Dec. 6, 2010 (retrieved from www.tcrecord.org/Content.asp? ContentID=36253 on Jan. 22, 2011).

21. Carnegie Corporation of New York, "After 20 Years of Reform, Progress, but Plenty of Unfinished Business," *Carnegie Results* 1, no. 3 (Fall 2003).

22. *Education Week*, "Teacher 'Residencies' Get Federal Boost," Oct. 5, 2009 (retrieved from http://blogs.edweek.org//edweek/teacherbeat/w009/10/teacher_residencies_get_a_boos.html on Oct. 6, 2009).

ELEVEN

Creating More Alternative Training and Certification Programs

If colleges of education are not providing well-trained teachers, there is a second path: alternative certification programs.

When I spoke to then education secretary designate Arne Duncan back in 2008, he told me that, based on his seven years as superintendent in Chicago, he considered these alternative programs key to future school improvement.

There are now approximately six hundred of them in all fifty states and the District of Columbia.[1] They do not all follow the same design, but here are their most common characteristics:

- Approximately two-thirds of the alternative certification programs require an interview or basic skills test for entry, and a majority of them test for proficiency in a subject matter.[2]
- Most begin with a five- to seven-week summer session that introduces the new teachers to pedagogy, classroom management, and content.[3] The session may take place in a district, at a university, or at an organization that has been structured to do such training.
- Approximately 90 percent of the programs place the recruits into schools as teachers of record immediately following the short training period.[4] During that first year (or two years, in some cases), the teachers take academic courses either at a university, on site, or online to fulfill the academic requirements associated with state licensure.[5]
- The key feature of these alternative programs is the support provided by a mentor, who is (or at least should be) a master teacher on whom the new recruit can rely for guidance and advice.

- Some programs pay a stipend for the summer work, and some require a commitment of a certain number of years of teaching in return.

Among major cities, New York, Chicago, and Boston all have teaching fellows or residency programs. In 2005–2006, alternative teacher training programs graduated 59,000 new teachers, which is approximately 20 percent of the total.[6] Over three-quarters of these recruits are trained in just five states: California, Georgia, New Jersey, New York, and Texas.[7]

Various types of institutions operate alternative programs. Universities run approximately half. Another fifth are operated by school districts. The rest are the responsibility of states, community colleges, regional organizations, or nonprofit groups.[8]

WHY WE NEED ALTERNATE PROGRAMS: THEY WORK!

Because of the diversity of alternate certification programs, broad conclusions about their impact and effectiveness are probably suspect. Nonetheless, certain results are not in dispute. The programs, on the whole, do well turning out science and math teachers and teachers of color.

In a 2005 study, 20 percent of alternatively certified teachers taught math and 28 percent some branch of science,[9] although another survey found that only 5 percent of the recruits switched from careers in math or science and 6 percent from finance or accounting.[10] In 2009, with the downturn in the economy, several states used alternative certification to expand math and science training programs in response to an unexpected influx of high-quality talent.[11]

The programs also helped with minority recruitment; one report estimates that 32 percent of alternative certification candidates in 2005 were nonwhite, in comparison with 16 percent of the teaching force.[12] Finally, almost all alternate route teachers wind up teaching after certification, while only 40 percent of the 200,000-plus graduates of conventional programs do in their first year following graduation.[13]

IS ALTERNATIVE CERTIFICATION READY FOR PRIME TIME?

The five- to seven-week introductory training period given new teachers in 90 percent of alternative certification programs is regularly—and loudly—criticized as the academic version of throwing the Christians to the lions. The detractors, many of whom are closely associated with traditional colleges of education, argue that these teachers are simply woefully unprepared.

Aldine's Priscilla Ridgeway told me her schools will not use Teach for America or other alternative certification program teachers because their student teaching experience is not enough. Studies come down on both sides of the question, but there is clearly concern that the lack of pre-service training may do a disservice to students.[14]

Approximately 10 percent of the current alternative programs follow an approach that might be a compromise between the warring sides. The new teachers spend either a semester or a full year working with a master teacher while continuing a significant level of coursework.[15] That may be more coursework than some would like,[16] but even ardent traditional training advocates like Linda Darling-Hammond acknowledge that such a model, emphasizing coursework surrounding a strong clinical experience, might provide a satisfactory amount of traditional training to new teachers before they assume responsibility for a full class of students.[17]

THE ARGUMENT FOR EVERY DISTRICT TO PARTICIPATE IN ALTERNATIVE CERTIFICATION

So, if a compromise is accepted, should we encourage more alternative certification? Absolutely. Susan Johnson, the Harvard education professor, told me the focus of teacher training now has moved from traditional university programs to alternative certification. They are simply faster and capable—at least—of offering cheaper and better training.

You may stop short at that last sentence and say: How can training that is so much shorter than traditional coursework be "better"? Here is how:

Learning by Doing

With their focus on training while teaching, alternative programs are all about "learning by doing." Katherine Merseth of the Harvard Graduate School of Education explains why learning by doing works: "I am a huge proponent of practice-based learning from the first day. To stand in front of a classroom of kids has a way of focusing your thinking and grounding your experience. Then everything you try to do is in the service of the question of how this plays in the real world, rather than what contribution this makes to the literature."[18]

Accepting Feedback and Making It Meaningful Enough to Be Accepted

Another benefit of hands-on learning is the feedback that teachers receive as a result of classroom observations.[19] Just as important, someone has to observe. Historically, principals rarely observed teachers, and other teachers did so even less frequently. If alternative certification is going to work, it means that teacher evaluation will have to be more thorough and more accurate than ever. That, in turn, requires that principals and perhaps teachers are going to have to be trained on what good teaching looks like and how to observe and evaluate it. Collectively, that is another great improvement from the unproductive past that has ramifications for all sorts of important reforms, as we shall see when we discuss teacher evaluation in the next chapter.

Smart Placement

As I noted during the discussion of why teachers leave prematurely, one problem is the placement of new teachers in tough schools or difficult classes. If the desire for a successful alternate training program promotes recognition that new teachers need to be placed somewhere consistent with their skill level,[20] it will be an acknowledgment that might lead to other, far more important changes at hard-to-staff schools.[21] (See chapter 16.)

All of those advantages of alternative certification training should intrigue even the most traditional superintendents. However, if advocates of alternative certification have not yet convinced the doubters, there are other advantages worth noting:

- A district gets a chance to create a new teacher in the image of the district rather than have to make over someone who has learned all sorts of practices the district wants to avoid.[22]
- And then there is the one thing that should absolutely seal the deal for any district that has had trouble recruiting. If you operate a quality alternative certification program, you won't be last in the pool. Many districts, especially poorer ones, suffer because they are often late recruiting new teachers, leaving no choice but to draw from the bottom of the barrel. Also, because they are late, they hire without knowing much about the candidate, so it is difficult to anticipate what skills she has, and whether she will fit in with a particular group of teachers.[23] Good alternative certification fixes all that.

RELYING ON OTHER ALTERNATIVE CERTIFICATION PROGRAMS: TEACH FOR AMERICA

Many districts seek out other alternative certification programs as sources of new teachers.

That brings me to one final loose end regarding recruitment: the well-known Teach for America (TFA) program. It began in 1990 by recruiting five hundred recent graduates of highly competitive universities to teach in difficult urban schools for two years. Currently, it has 7,300 corps members in the field, training about 3,600 per year. As with many other alternative programs, TFA trains its teachers during a five-week summer session, which is followed up with additional training during the two-year commitment period, with the courses often focused on meeting a state's requirement to obtain a master's degree.[24]

There are studies about the effectiveness of TFA teachers that come down on both sides.[25] Regardless, the larger point is how much districts want smart, high-quality TFA members even though their commitment is to stay only two years (although approximately one-third now stay for longer periods).

Teachers in those first two years are still learning their craft. If a district permanently holds open slots for TFA, it means that some percentage of its faculty never reaches full potential. That is acceptable now only because the alternatives are worse. The long-run goal of American public education has to be to put TFA out of business. Not because we dislike TFA, but because we have found a way to recruit, train, and retain equally high-caliber teachers who are intending to stay far longer than TFA requires.

WHAT WE NEED TO DO

Districts, not colleges of education, need to rethink their attitude toward training. They have to seize control of the process from colleges of education, either by being more aggressive consumers or by doing it themselves (or in collaboration with others) through alternative certification programs. That will not happen until they control much of the state and federal money that supports teacher training. There are two key requirements to make all this happen: School districts have to accept the idea they are the center of all teacher training, and federal and state legislation has to be revised to encourage them to bid for training money that now goes elsewhere.

As I said early in the book, the best structure is where money, authority, and responsibility are all in one place. When it comes to training, that is the school district.

NOTES

1. *New York Times*, "When Career Switching . . . ," July 26, 2009 (retrieved from www.nytimes.com.2009/07/26/education/edlife/26contedBOX-t.ht on July 26, 2009).

2. C. Emily Feitstritzer, *Profile of Alternate Route Teachers* (Washington, DC: National Center for Education Information, 2005), 66.

3. One recent study reported that alternative certification teachers in "low coursework programs" took 115 hours of coursework before starting their teaching, while "high coursework" programs required 150 hours. Mathematica Policy Research, Inc.,

An Evaluation of Teachers Trained through Different Routes to Certification (Washington, DC: U.S. Department of Education, 2009), xviii.

4. Feitstritzer, *Profile of Alternate Route Teachers*, 39.

5. Mathematica Policy Research, *An Evaluation of Teachers Trained through Different Routes to Certification* ("The total hours required by [alternative certification] programs ranged from 75 to 795, and by [traditional certification] from 240 to 1380.") However, according to one survey, only 61 percent of alternative certification teachers actually took college education courses, and at least 50 percent of those people took fewer than twenty-four semester hours. Feitstritzer, *Profile of Alternate Route Teachers*, 40. We will return to this point in a moment. Urban Teacher Residency United (URTU), an organization that promotes teacher residency programs that provide alternative certification, has developed a set of standards for such programs. See www.urtu.org. However, there is no current obligation that they be followed.

6. National Center for Alternative Certification, *Alternative Teacher Certification: A State by State Analysis* (Washington, DC: National Center for Alternative Certification, 2007) found at www.teach-now.org/intro.cfm on September 8, 2009.

7. C. Emily Feistritzer and Charlene K. Haar, *Research on Alternate Routes Education Research* (Washington, DC: National Center for Alternative Certification, 2006), 16.

8. Feitstritzer, *Profile of Alternate Route Teachers*, 64.

9. Feitstritzer, *Profile of Alternate Route Teachers*, 12; Feistritzer and Haar, *Research on Alternate Routes Education Research*, 12.

10. Daniel C. Humphrey, Marjorie E. Wechsler, and Health J. Hough, "Characteristics of Effective Alternative Teacher Certification Programs," *The Teachers College Record* 110, no. 1 (2008): 1–63.

11. *Education Week*, "STEM Talent Increases, Jobs Decrease," Aug. 26, 2009, 1.

12. Feitstritzer, *Profile of Alternate Route Teachers*, vi.

13. Steve Farkas, Jean Johnson, Ann Duffett, Tony Foleno, *Trying to Stay Ahead of the Game* (New York: Public Agenda, 2001), 4.

14. Chifeng Dai, Paul T. Sindelar, David Denslow, James Dewey, and Michael S. Rosenberg, "Economic Analysis and the Design of Alternative-Route Teacher Education Programs," *Journal of Teacher Education* 58, no. 5 (2007): 422; Think Tank Review Project, "Mathematica Study of Alternative Teacher Certification Does Not Apply to Vast Majority of American Classrooms, Experts Say" (press release, Education and the Public Interest Center, Boulder, CO, and Tempe, AZ, March 10, 2009, retrieved from http://epicpolicy.org/newsletter/2009/03/mathematica-study-alternative-teacher-certification-does-not-apply-vast-majority on Oct. 5, 2009); Susan Moore Johnson and Susan M. Kardos, "Keeping New Teachers in Mind," in *Keeping Good Teachers*, ed. Marge Scherer (Alexandria, VA: ASCD, 2003), 25, 28.

15. Milwaukee has such a program. Felicia Saffold, "Renewing Urban Teachers Through Mentoring," in *Keeping Good Teachers*, ed. Marge Scherer (Alexandria, VA: ASCD, 2003), 81. Vivian Troen and Katherine C. Boles, *Who's Teaching Your Children?* (New Haven, CT: Yale University Press, 2003), 146–47 (similar proposal).

16. Kate Walsh, *Steps That Congress Can Take to Improve Teacher Quality—without Overstepping Its Bounds* (Washington, DC: National Council on Teacher Quality, 2007), 2.

17. Professor Darling-Hammond was executive director of the National Commission on Teaching for America's Future and produced *What Matters Most: Teaching for America's Future* in 1996. The report cites several alternative certification programs with approval (p. 93).

18. Katherine K. Merseth, "Arming New Teachers with Survival Skills," in *Recruiting, Retaining, and Supporting Highly Qualified Teachers*, ed. Caroline Chauncey (Cambridge, MA: Harvard Education Press, 2005), 28. Another expert, David C. Berliner, has said virtually the same thing: "Only through experiencing the complexity of the classroom does a teacher learn." Marge Scherer, "Improving the Quality of the Teaching Force: A Conversation with David C. Berliner," in *Keeping Good Teachers*, ed. Marge Scherer (Alexandria, VA: ASCD, 2003), 14.

19. Scherer, "Improving the Quality of the Teaching Force," 14.

20. NCES (IES), table 3.7 (Requirements for participation in state-funded induction programs and mentoring programs for beginning teachers, whether standards exist for mentors, and reduced-workload policies for first year teachers, by state: 2007–08) (retrieved from www.nces.ed.gov/programs/statereform/tab3_7.asp on May 8, 2009).

21. There are many articles and books summarizing the key elements of a successful alternative certification program. See, for example, North Central Regional Education Laboratory, *Alternative Certification: A Review of Theory and Research, Characteristics of Effective Programs* (Naperville, IL: North Central Regional Education Laboratory, 2002) and citations therein.

22. Debra Viadero, "Nontraditional Paths to Teaching," in *Recruiting, Retaining, and Supporting Highly Qualified Teachers*, ed. Caroline Chauncey (Cambridge, MA: Harvard Education Press, 2005), 51.

23. These alternative programs can even benefit new teachers coming out of colleges of education. As we discussed earlier, too many districts, even high-performing ones, give new, traditionally trained teachers only a short introduction before sending them off to their new schools. If some or all of the alternative certification's summer training is extended to the traditional teachers, the administrators and principals can do a better job conveying what they think teaching is all about, and, more importantly, the new teachers can teach summer school or otherwise demonstrate and improve their skills. And, since the program is already running, they can do it for little additional cost.

24. See www.tfa.org.

25. Zeyu Xu, Jane Hannaway, and Colin Taylor, *Making a Difference? The Effects of Teach for America in High School* (Washington, DC: National Center for Analysis of Longitudinal Data in Education Research and the Urban Institute, 2009), 2 ("The findings show that TFA teachers are more effective, as measured by student exam performance, than traditional teachers."); Thomas J. Kane, Jonah E. Rokoff, and Douglas O. Staiger, *What Does Certification Tell Us about Teacher Effectiveness? Evidence from New York City*, Working Paper No. 12155 (Cambridge, MA: National Bureau of Economic Research, 2006), 4 ("[C]lassrooms of students assigned to Teach for America corps members scored .02 standard deviations higher relative to certified teachers."); but see Linda Darling-Hammond, Debora J. Holtzman, Su Join Gatlin, and Julian Vasquez Heilig, "Does Teacher Preparation Matter? Evidence about Teacher Certification, Teach for America, and Teacher Effectiveness," *Education Policy Analysis Archives* 13, no. 42 (Oct. 12, 2005): 20 ("Although some have suggested that perhaps bright college graduates like those who join TFA may not require professional preparation for teaching, we found no instance where uncertified Teach for America teachers performed as well as standard certified teachers of comparable experience levels teaching in similar settings.")

TWELVE

What Is a Good Teacher?: Evaluation in a Professional World

As I previously said, the current "hot" policy topics, pay for performance and tenure, have little to do with how good school districts have improved education. However, there is one thing that both the political solutions and the ongoing work in the field have in common: They both need to be able to evaluate teacher effectiveness.

THE OLD DAYS OF MASS-PRODUCTION EVALUATION

By now, it should be apparent that in the old days of mass-production education, evaluation of individual teacher effectiveness was not as central to the enterprise as it is today. After all, the entire system was constructed on the premise that teachers had limited ability. They were given a script and told to follow it. No great skill or knowledge required.

Teachers were evaluated essentially at two points in their careers. First, they had to obtain a license to teach upon graduation from college and a couple of years later, they might obtain a permanent one. None of that acted as much of a filter.[1]

Licensing schemes varied from state to state, and collectively they offer a confusing set of requirements on which we don't need to dwell. The details won't add much to our understanding of the one universal truth common to virtually every scheme: None set a high bar.

Even when Congress dipped its toe into this swamp, it did not help things much. No Child Left Behind required schools to employ teachers certified to teach their grades or subjects, whom the act designated as "highly qualified." However, since the states still set the standards, the actual quality of the teachers did not change. The one value of the designation was that it highlighted when the gym teacher wound up teaching physics.

Over time, the authorities did become troubled because these evaluations could not accurately predict whether a teacher actually was good at what she did. Some states began to put more stress on evaluating an undergraduate's student teaching. But, since most districts did not put much effort into those evaluations, that did not add much knowledge either.

In the 1980s, Albert Shanker and others created the National Board for Professional Teaching Standards (NBPTS). The NBPTS set standards for what it thought good teaching should look like and invited veteran teachers to send in videos and portfolios of their work to be evaluated according to those standards. As an incentive, teachers who received NBPTS certification were often given a salary increase, which was mandated in some states and authorized by local collective bargaining agreements in others.[2]

The NBPTS concept then led various states to include the evaluation of portfolios and other evidence of in-classroom performance as part of the licensing process. They required that, as a condition for initial or final, permanent licensure, teachers had to submit to observation and/or provide portfolios and videos, like NBPTS candidates.[3]

The problem with these assessments is that they did not correlate well with student test scores. According to several studies, even NBPTS teachers' students do not do appreciably better on exams,[4] although many of the superintendents firmly believe in the value of NBPTS. It is the one credential they are willing to pay for because they think the process by which a teacher acquires NBPTS certification is worthwhile professional development.

The tenure process added little value (or, more to the point, subtracted few unqualified teachers).[5] How could it? Principals, who were the most likely evaluators of new teachers, were not trained in instruction or evaluation. In any event, they observed teachers only a few times a year. In most districts, schools granted tenure to over 90 percent of teachers, year after year.[6]

Because of that lack of knowledge of instruction among midlevel management, districts have historically done a miserable job at earlier attempts at today's two hot policy options. Firing people because they were incompetent rarely worked because there was no agreement on what good teaching looked like, and, in any event, few principals could explain what it was or document its absence. Cases involving the revocation of tenure rarely turned on whether a teacher was merely incompetent; short of criminal or bizarre behavior, everyone kept their job.

The same was true for earlier pay-for-performance schemes. Prior to the development of standardized testing, performance bonuses were often based heavily on principals' observations of teachers. After all, not only were there no test scores available, there was not even much peer interaction, where a quality teacher could demonstrate skills to the benefit of the rest of the group. So these bonus schemes tended to fall apart because no one was confident they were awarded on merit rather than on favoritism or intraschool politics.[7]

EVALUATING TEACHER EFFECTIVENESS IN THE TWENTY-FIRST CENTURY: STARTING WITH A CLEAN SLATE

Let's just assume that, instead of all the confusing rules and regulations now in force, we have a clean slate with which to work.

First, what is it that we are trying to do? We are in the business of creating good teachers. That means we need to identify quality candidates. Then, we have to know what good teaching looks like, so we can provide the right instruction.

That leads to the second step. We need to be able to evaluate how well new faculty are absorbing what they are supposed to be learning. That requires assessments that can measure accurately teacher effectiveness. It may be student test scores, principal observations, or something else. The fundamental goal, whatever the means, is that it be accurate.

However, that word, "accurate," flags the final issue. To the extent the measures are not fully "accurate," we need to understand their limitations and use them cautiously in order to get the benefit of what they can reasonably tell us without burdening them with the assumption of more accuracy than they can fairly bear. Otherwise, they lose legitimacy. Then we need to work over time to make them better tools for their intended purpose.

A TEACHER EVALUATION STRATEGY FOR THE TWENTY-FIRST CENTURY

Let's approach this subject from the perspective of a school superintendent. She wants to recruit first-rate people, and consistent with those earlier chapters on professional development, wants to build a first-rate faculty. She wants a teacher evaluation strategy that helps her.

Conservative, free-market advocates often oppose increasing basic licensure or certification requirements for fear that by constricting the market, it will drive up the price of teachers without necessarily increasing the quality of teacher candidates—or improving student test scores. They argue that superintendents should have a free hand to hire whom they want, which is a freedom accorded to private schools in many states. After all, the superintendents can be trusted to choose wisely because, if test scores go down as a result of bad teaching, they are the ones who will be held accountable.

However, the superintendent is still going to want information about the candidates before she hires them. Basic state licensure and subject matter certification might provide that information (although they are still low bars in most places). Without them, a diligent superintendent might simply create her own version of the same.

In the districts I visited, the details of licensure and certification drew little interest. Tellingly, *no one* talked about either eliminating or tightening licensure or certification. It was not integral to their strategies for high performance.

What was far more important was whether the new teacher was likely to be effective. To assess that, they wanted a recruit to demonstrate teaching a lesson and perhaps present a portfolio of earlier work. That was the critical part of the selection process.[8]

Test Scores and Observations

After hiring, we have options. We can continue to observe teachers to see if they are instructing according to our notions of what good teaching looks like. Or we can see how their students perform on standardized tests.

Some educators in the real world, like Jody Leleck in Montgomery County, say things like "A good principal knows what good teaching looks like,"[9] or "I can tell pretty quickly in an interview or observation who is going to make a good teacher."[10]

On the other hand, Secretary of Education Arne Duncan has said that it is difficult to predict who would become a good teacher because it is hard to capture what knowledge and skills are essential.[11] He clearly takes that position seriously. It was the rationale offered as the reason that the Department of Education demanded in 2009 that states remove any barriers to the use of student achievement or growth data in teacher evaluations as a condition to receipt of some of the $4 billion in Race to the Top grants.[12]

The Traditional Evaluation

The most fundamental element in managing any business's talent is to define, and agree upon, what type of performance is needed.[13] One of the amazing facts (at least to an outsider) about many districts is that they have never actually spelled out what they expect good teaching to look like. It may have been the consequence of the "mass production" vision of teaching, or the despair administrators felt in the face of loose coupling. As a result, Chicago's Amanda Rivera told me that the district had not had any agreed-upon vision for its teachers in its 150-year history until it adopted a matrix developed by a well-known education academic, Charlotte Danielson, which maps one view of the fully rounded teacher.[14]

New York has adopted Danielson as well. Now, and only now, both districts finally have a basis for evaluating whether their teachers actually demonstrate quality.[15]

However, the failure to have a standard is not the only problem. Someone has to do the observations. Mostly, that is going to be principals, and, as noted in chapter 5, no one has pushed them to be education leaders until recently. So if the evaluations are to be effective, we need to educate those who are going to do them to ensure they know what constitutes good teaching. Of equal importance, we have to teach the evaluators how to rate people consistently, so that two different people give two teachers of equal quality the same score (something called "inter-rater reliability").

Such training has started, but it is not even close to complete. We are simply not in a position to subject all 3,200,000 active teachers to evaluations because we do not have enough skilled evaluators or a consistent system of evaluation. We may be able to do it for small groups, like NBPTS teachers or the districts I visited. However, that is a small slice of the total pie. Merely decreeing that there shall be evaluations is a lot different from actually being able to do them successfully.

If there is any good news, it is that there are interesting developments in the wings that may take the pressure off principals—at least to some extent. The Bill and Melinda Gates Foundation, for example, has funded a program that videotapes teachers in classrooms and then has the tape reviewed by specially trained evaluators, which answers both the skill and "inter-rater reliability" questions.[16] But, like principal training, it is an idea in its infancy. Even if it works, it is not likely to be widely available for several years.

The Use of Student Achievement Data in Evaluating Teachers

The hottest education topic since No Child Left Behind, the use of student achievement data in teacher evaluations, threatened to swamp Race to the Top discussions in 2009–2010. The grant competition gave extra points to states like Ohio, which was one of eighteen states that passed legislation requiring the consideration of student achievement teacher evaluations.[17]

In terms of the amount of ink used to report the debate, it is a *huge* question. Should it be?

The idea has the aura of precision and reliability that traditional evaluations lack. It is also something that is already widely available—at least for reading and math and for the years where such testing is required by NCLB.[18] Although proponents always say they want test scores used in combination with evaluations, the data's simplicity and ubiquity threaten to overwhelm the process. Unfortunately, neither ubiquity nor simplicity guarantees accuracy. Using data makes sense because it works—as I saw in the districts I visited. But using the data *with sense* is the key—which is what every superintendent will tell you.

Using Data Is Not as Simple as It Sounds

As we have seen, it is easy to be seduced by the idea of using data in teacher evaluations. It suggests looking at some straightforward result, like "90 percent of your students made a full year of progress or better this year, but 10 percent did not," and then deciding whether that result supports licensure, promotion, tenure, or a pay bonus.

It is not that simple.

At the outset, we have to understand that we cannot simply adopt the accountability measures created by NCLB. The act has all sorts of limitations and problems with what it is measuring. It will not fairly evaluate teachers.

NCLB mandates that all students be proficient in reading and mathematics by 2014 and that each school make "adequate yearly progress" (AYP) toward the goal. That progress had to be measured every year in grades 3 through 8 and once in high school, and not just for a school as a whole, but also for disaggregated groups of students according to income, race, gender, English language ability, and special education status. If any of the subgroups failed, the school failed for that year. (Starting in 2007–2008 there was a separate science assessment requirement, but it does not trigger the same consequences as failure to make AYP in math or reading.)

Some of the problems are obvious. Some are not.

First, the obvious issues: NCLB testing does not cover all subjects or all grades. It can only provide data on the teachers whose students are tested. Also, when it was set up, there was no way to track individual students, so it was impossible to track individual teachers. AYP was about how the various subgroups in each grade in a school had done collectively.

The less obvious problems make reliance on the test even less appropriate. Because the standards were to be set by the states, those standards could—and did—vary wildly. Moreover, some states "dumbed down" the standards to avoid the embarrassment of large-scale failures.[19] Then slight changes in Department of Education rules turned previously satisfactory schools into failing ones, creating more doubt about the rules than the schools.[20]

Some states became embarrassed by how far the standards had deteriorated and recalibrated them upward.[21] That produced a new set of problems. For example, in 2010, New York State issued new and more stringent standards, resulting in much worse test results for students.

New York chancellor Joel Klein and New York mayor Michael Bloomberg were left scrambling to explain how, notwithstanding the numbers, they had done well. And that left New Yorkers wondering what, if anything, to make of the test results, or the school and teacher evaluations that Klein had insisted be based on the data.

The way the tests are constructed raises a further set of issues. The big payoff on these tests is to get students just below proficiency to score slightly better, which means that teachers ignore those students who are clearly doing well or badly, contrary to the goal that every child can learn. Moreover, it does not track a student's progress. AYP is based on what this year's fifth-graders have done in comparison with last year's. The scoring makes no accommodation if the kids come from wildly different backgrounds, leaving the feeling that the comparison may be "apples" to "oranges," as often as not.

The test is also just a snapshot. It fails to take into account results over time, accommodating for one-time aberrations. It does not address the possibility of significant differences in test-taking skills or the possibility that students might better demonstrate achievement through portfolios or other work. It makes no allowance for the impact of poverty and other socioeconomic factors, which may well be the right answer, but, as we shall discuss shortly, that judgment has pros and cons.

The full list of deficiencies is far more extensive. The obvious question: What is the alternative?

The testing design most often associated with current evaluation protocols is called "value-added" testing, pioneered by William Sanders, a former professor at the University of Tennessee and now a researcher at the SAS Institute in Cary, North Carolina. His work has progressed to the point where several states, such as Tennessee, North Carolina, Ohio, and Pennsylvania, and individual districts in fifteen other states had adopted his methods as of 2008,[22] and many more have done so in the wake of 2010–2011's spate of reform legislation. The measure used by "value-added" analysis is how much learning a student has achieved in a given subject during the school year, that is, how much "value" the teacher has added to the child's store of learning.

Sanders's current measurement ideas have attracted a host of critics, including (as of the fall of 2010) the chair of the National Academies Board of Testing and Assessment, Edward Haertel, who worries about things like mismeasuring the outputs and inputs and the untrustworthiness of the data themselves.[23] Similarly, Paul Hegre, the Q Comp pay plan coordinator, says Minneapolis started with Sanders's work but has now moved on to an internal growth model that it judges fairer.

The objective in all this, lest we forget, is to assess how much students have learned in the September to June (or thereabouts) school year and determine if it is the result of a teacher's effort.

Most teaching situations are not that straightforward. There is almost universal agreement on something called "summer learning loss," which means that kids lose some of what they have learned in July and August, when they are not in school. Middle-class kids, however, with their activity opportunities over the summer, do not lose as much as poor kids. No test given in one May can fairly tell how much a child has learned by the next May unless it can take into account summer learning loss. [24]

And that is not the only problem. What happens when various teachers are involved? Suppose the elementary school has "departmentalized," so one teacher teaches the fourth grade math, while another teaches reading. Do we assume that there are no cross-discipline effects that impact both teachers' results? Or what happens when the school employs a reading specialist who assists teachers with reading instruction. Whose work is being assessed at the end of the year?

These tests have to come to grips with all sorts of other kinks as well. For example, poor kids move a lot. Does one include in a test a child who has been with the teacher half a year? Is someone going to take into account that student placement in classes is often not random, so even between two new teachers teaching the same grade at the same school, meeting the student achievement standard may not be the same? [25]

Or what do you do with the teacher who has more than a fair share of special education kids who are simply more challenging to teach? And how much stress should be placed on a single test? Does that result overrule all other facts?

Another complication is the demographic one. What constitutes a fair standard when measuring both majority, middle-class, and minority, low-income schools? Is a new teacher in a majority, middle-class school in the suburbs going to be held to the same level of student achievement as a teacher working in the inner city where too many students do not have supportive parents, a place to study, or enough to eat? Vincent Gray, who defeated Adrian Fenty in 2010 to become Washington's mayor, has questioned Michelle Rhee's evaluation system, called IMPACT, for precisely this reason. [26]

Even if the teachers are only measured against teachers in similar schools, are the two sets of standards truly comparable? Is a new teacher in a school with extremely capable colleagues who create a wonderful synergy that stimulates student learning across-the-board going to get the same credit for boosting achievement as someone who works in a school with a dismal faculty whose net effect on kids is to depress them?

Finally, the use of data may have nasty, unintended consequences. If, as a new teacher, I am going to be evaluated based on student test scores, why would I want to teach at a school where it is far more challenging to get good test results? That new teacher will want to play it safe and go to a nice, majority, middle-class school where the kids are likely to perform well even if the teacher does not. The net effect is to make staffing hard-to-staff schools even more difficult (see chapter 16). However, if one somehow tries to adjust for the differences, does that stigmatize lower-socioeconomic-status schools, suggesting to teachers that they should not have high expectations about the kids in the first place?

The other unintended consequence is that value-added may lock in a vision of teaching that is disappearing. As I said before, it likely works best with elementary school teachers, who, at least for the moment, are generally the people largely responsible for all of a child's education for a given year. But what if elementary schools departmentalize? Or what if they team teach? If we become heavily dependent on a value-added model that cannot accommodate these variations, do we wind up with an evaluation, or pay, or tenure system that prevents us from making changes that we really want to make to improve schools?

Even Secretary Duncan concedes that such data should not be an exclusive determinant,[27] but part of a broader evaluation based on the more traditional observations of teachers—and other factors, not all of which are, as of this writing, agreed to.[28] The best one can say, at the moment, is that there are multiple efforts to create better data-driven assessments.[29]

A Caution about Using What We Have Now

Opposition to the tests might be lessened if they were recognized as imperfect and used with some caution.[30] Making fine distinctions using data that is imprecise is bound to cause dissatisfaction. (That is, it might be reasonable—and acceptable—to use the data to separate teachers into three groups, but not six.) Or the caution might take the form of recognizing that the more serious the decision, the greater the number of factors in addition to value-added data should be taken into account. Instead of one year's data for evaluations, two or three might be used. Or different sorts of data might be included.

The danger of simply spreading around numbers is well illustrated by the series of stories the *Los Angeles Times* ran in the summer of 2010 in which it analyzed student testing data over several years using Sanders's value-added method to determine the effectiveness of over six thousand Los Angeles Unified School District teachers. There was no other form of evaluation, like scores of principal observations. The stories drew national attention and created a furor that highlighted the debate about the value of such calculations[31] and set off demands for the release of similar data elsewhere.[32]

In early 2011, the National Education Policy Center, which reviews research studies in various public policy areas like education, evaluated the *LA Times*'s methodology using a model that included additional variables. It concluded that "[o]nly 46.4% of teachers would retain the same effectiveness rating under both models." If nothing else, that raises questions about how strongly anyone should rely on the findings.[33]

Why Do We Use Student Data?

Virtually every district I visited used some aspect of student achieve-ment data to drive professional development. The lesson learned, howev-er, is that data is important, but not king. In these districts, there are not only frequent student assessments, but also frequent teacher collabora-tions and teacher-administrator contact. Unlike the *LA Times* series, the numbers do not exist in a vacuum. The people interpreting them can take all sorts of factors into account.[34] They do not make serious judgments about effectiveness based on a one-time snapshot.

* * *

The section on "What We Need to Do" regarding evaluations is incorpo-rated at the end of the next chapter, which deals with tenure. Many of the points overlap, so there is no need to repeat them twice. However, there is one point that is fundamental to evaluation that should be underscored here: *In the high-performing districts I visited, evaluation was all about improv-ing performance. It was not a punitive exercise designed, first and foremost, to get rid of Tier Four teachers.*[35] If that is the goal, it undercuts the collabora-tion, mutual respect, and continuing professional development necessary to building a quality school.

NOTES

1. Brandeis's Vivian Troen and Harvard's Katherine Boles, among others, bluntly dismiss licensure as a major failure in the larger, dysfunctional process of teacher preparation: "It is our contention that the overall quality of teacher preparation is at a historic low and shows no prospects for improvement any time soon. The general quality of teachers entering the classroom is kept low by the complicity of the two major agencies in the supply chain—those programs and institutions charged with the training of teachers, and those at the state and local levels charged with creating and upholding the standards for admittance into the classroom. Both are derelict in their responsibilities to the public." Vivian Troen and Katherine C. Boles, *Who's Teaching Your Children?* (New Haven, CT: Yale University Press, 2003), 39.
2. Since 1987, NBPTS has granted 74,000 certificates in twenty-five areas, such as "adolescence and young adulthood mathematics."
3. National Commission on Teaching and America's Future, *What Matters Most: Teaching for America's Future* (Washington, DC: NCTAF, 1996), 68.
4. Studies of NBPTS, for example, have reached mixed conclusions about whether those who are certified have a more positive impact on student achievement than other teachers. Douglas N. Harris and Tim R. Sass, *The Effects of NBPTS-Certified Teach-ers on Student Achievement*, Working Paper No. 4 (Washington, DC: National Center for Analysis of Longitudinal Data in Education Research, 2007) ("[W]e find evidence that NBPTS certification provides a positive signal of a teacher's contribution to student achievement only in a few isolated cases."); George K. Cunningham and J. E. Stone, "Value Added Assessment of Teacher Quality as an Alternative to the National Board for Professional Teaching Standards: What Recent Studies Say," in *Value Added Models in Education: Theory and Applications*, ed. Robert Lissitz (Maple Grove, MN: JAM Press,

2005) ("Four recent studies have examined the annual increases in student achievement produced by NBPTS teachers and found them to be slightly larger than the average of their non-certified peers. However, relative to the achievement gaps identified by the No Child Left Behind Act, the advantage associated with NBPTS certification is trivial."); Steven Cantrell, Jon Fullerton, Thomas J. Kane, and Douglas O. Staiger, *National Board Certification and Teacher Effectiveness: Evidence from a Random Assignment Experiment* (Cambridge, MA: National Bureau of Economic Research, 2008) ("There was no statistically significant difference in scores in math and language arts between students assigned to NBPTS certified teachers and teachers who did not apply for certification, but students of teachers who applied for certification and failed did worse than those who did."); Dan Goldhaber and Emily Anthony, *Can Teacher Quality Be Effectively Assessed?* (Washington, DC: Urban Institute, 2004), 27 ("Many of our findings appear to confirm that the NBPTS assessment process is successful in identifying the more effective teachers among applicants to the program. . . . While we consistently find that teachers who will eventually be NBPTS certified are more effective, there are mixed findings about their effectiveness after being identified as [a National Board Certified Teacher]."); Linda C. Cavaluzzo, *Is National Board Certification an Effective Signal of Teacher Quality?* (Alexandria, VA: CNA Corporation, 2004) (found positive effect).

5. For example, in 2009, Ramon Cortines, LAUSD's superintendent, admitted what has long been true in Los Angeles and in many other districts as well: There had been a total failure in adequately evaluating new teachers' performance. *Los Angeles Times,* "L.A. Schools Chief Orders Weak New Teachers Ousted," Dec. 18, 2009 (retrieved from www.latimes.com/news/local/la-me-laused-teachers18-2009dec18,0,0945 293,print.story on Dec. 21, 2009).

6. See, for example, *New York Times*, "Fewer Public School Teachers Receive Tenure," July 29, 2010 (retrieved from www.nytimes.com/2010/07/30/nyregion/30tenure.html on July 30, 2010).

7. Richard J. Murnane and David K. Cohen, "Merit Pay and the Evaluation Problem: Why Most Merit Pay Plans Fail and a Few Survive," *Harvard Education Review* 17, no. 1 (Feb. 1986): 1–17.

8. Civil rights groups regularly litigate the lack of "highly qualified" teachers in low-income schools. If certification continues to exist, it should stress evaluating what a teacher knows, rather than what courses he or she has taken. That is the approach taken by alternative certification programs, and it has generally worked to ensure a minimal level of competence.

9. Eric A. Hanushek and Steven G. Rivkin, "How to Improve the Supply of High-Quality Teachers," in *Education Policy 2004*, ed. Diane Ravitch (Washington, DC: Brookings Institution, 2004), 24. (Ms. Leleck has lots of company: There are several surveys that have reflected the same view.)

10. The process is not as much guesswork as the quote might suggest. For example, Martin Haberman, a professor of education at the University of Wisconsin–Milwaukee, has developed a set of questions that can help principals predict success among urban teachers. The questions have been widely used. www.altcert.org.

11. See also Frederick M. Hess, *Tear Down This Wall: The Case for a Radical Overhaul of Teacher Certification* (Washington, DC: Progressive Policy Institute, 2001).

12. 74 Fed. Reg. 37806 (July 29, 2009).

13. Edward E. Lawler III, *Strategic Talent Management: Lessons from the Corporate World* (Madison, WI: Strategic Management of Human Capital/Consortium for Policy Research in Education, 2008), 26.

14. Charlotte Danielson, *Enhancing Professional Practice: A Framework for Teaching* (Alexandria, VA: Association for Supervision and Curriculum Development, 1996), 3–4. (There are twenty-two components clustered into four domains: planning and preparation, classroom environment, instruction, and professional responsibilities.) Each of those domains is in turn broken down into components. For example, one component of "the classroom environment," is "managing classroom procedures."

And one element of that component is "management of instruction groups." Teachers are evaluated on that element as "unsatisfactory," "basic," "proficient," or distinguished," using guidelines. For example, to be distinguished in the management of instructional groups, an evaluator has to find that "small group work is well organized, and students are productively engaged at all times, with students assuming responsibility for productivity." Charlotte Danielson, *Enhancing Professional Practice*, 2nd ed. (Alexandria, VA: ASCD, 2007), 72.

15. In addition to matrices like Danielson's, there are all sorts of instructional manuals that describe strategies for various aspects of instruction. See, for example, *New York Times Sunday Magazine*, "Building a Better Teacher," March 7, 2010 (retrieved from www.nytimes.com/2010/03/07/07teacher-t.html on March 7, 2010) (describing Doug Lemov's suggestions for good teaching included in his book, *Teach Like a Champion*).

16. *New York Times*, "Teacher Ratings Get New Look, Pushed by a Rich Watcher," Dec. 3, 2010 (retrieved from www.nytimes.com/2010/12/04/education/04teacher.html on Dec. 4, 2010).

17. *Washington Post*, "States That Lost School Money Face Reform Dilemmas," Dec. 5, 2010 (retrieved from www.washingtonpost.com/wp-dyn/contentarticle/2010/12/05/AR2010120502384_pf.html on Dec. 8, 2010).

18. Some states require considerably more testing, covering other subjects and other grades, but the scope of such other testing varies widely from state to state.

19. *New York Times*, "Federal Researchers Find Lower Standards in Schools," Oct. 30, 2009, A18.

20. *Los Angeles Times*, "New State Rules Raise the Bar on School Scores," March 27, 2007, A1.

21. The most important evidence of the problem was the wide disparity in how well states did on a nationwide test, the National Assessment of Education Preparedness, and two international tests, the Trends in International Mathematics and Science Study (TIMSS) and the Progress in International Reading Literacy Study (PIRLS). The comparisons showed that while many states claimed high "proficiency" for their students on their own tests, many of them did poorly on the national and international tests. Gary W. Phillips, *International Benchmarking: State Education Performance Standards* (Washington, DC: American Institutes for Research, 2010).

22. *Time*, "How to Make Great Teachers," Feb. 25, 2008, 31.

23. See, for example, Eva L. Baker et al. *Problems with the Use of Student Test Scores to Evaluate Teachers* (Washington, DC: Economic Policy Institute, 2010); *Education Week*, "Testing Experts Cautious on 'Race to Top' Rules," Oct. 8, 2009 (retrieved from www.edweek.org/ew/articles/2009/10/08/07academies.h29.html on Oct. 20, 2009). For a direct attack on Dr. Sanders's work and his rebuttal: Charles Barone, *Are We There Yet? What Policymakers Can Learn from Tennessee's Growth Model* (Washington, DC: Education Sector, 2009), and William L. Sanders, *Tennessee Growth Models: A Response from Dr. William Sanders* (retrieved from www.quickanded.com/2009/03/tennessee-growth-models-response-from.html on Dec. 31, 2009). See also Richard Rothstein, "The Influence of Scholarship and Experience in Other Fields on Teacher Compensation Reform"; Daniel F. McCaffrey, Bing Han, and J. R. Lockwood, "Turning Student Test Scores into Teacher Compensation Systems"; and Derek Neal, "Designing Incentive Systems for Schools," in *Performance Incentives, Their Growing Impact on American K–12 Education*, ed. Matthew Springer (Washington, DC: Brookings Institution, 2009), 87–110.

24. The problem is not solved by a test in September. Various academics doubt that kids will take the test seriously, and a teacher could easily depress the results by telling them that it merely sets a "baseline" for the test at the end of the year.

25. Stephanie King, the former Florida Teacher of the Year, e-mailed me a list of situations she had experienced as a teacher that would undercut the idea that there was a level field for assessing teachers' abilities. For example, what if a well-off teacher solves a problem with a lack of textbooks by using her own money to buy enough for

the class? Or a teacher might be friendly with the person running the copy room, so that she could reprint copies of books or articles, avoiding copyright rules. Or the teacher sleeps with the assistant principal and has an easier time getting large classes leveled. King, however, does not oppose using data. Rather she argues for using data principally for the purpose of continuous improvement in teaching skills, as we will discuss later.

26. *Washington Post*, "Gray: IMPACT Teacher Evaluation System Has 'a Long Way to Go' for Fairness," Jan. 17, 2011 (retrieved from http://voices.washingtonpost.com. dcschools/2011/01/gray_teacher_evaluation_system.html on Jan. 18, 2011).

27. *Education Week*, "Duncan Calls for Multiple Measures in Evaluation," Oct. 30, 2009 (retrieved from http://blogs.edweek.org/edweek/teachersbeat/2009/10/duncan_calls_for_multiple_meas.html on Nov. 4, 2009).

28. Even strong advocates of using student achievement data acknowledge that the use of more holistic metrics, such as principal or peer evaluations, alone or in combination with data would be a distinct improvement over the status quo. Hess, *Tear Down This Wall*.

29. Stanley N. Rabinowitz, "Next-Generation Assessments Systems," *Education Week*, Feb. 22, 2010 (retrieved from www.edweek.org/ew/articles/2010/02/24/22rabinowitz_ep.h29.html on Feb. 22, 2010); Stephen Sawchuk, "Experts Hope Federal Funds Lead to Better Tests," *Education Week*, Aug. 5, 2009 (retrieved from www.edweek.org/ew/articles/2009/08/05/37measure.h28.html on Aug. 13, 2009).

30. Raegen Miller, *Adding Value to Discussions about Value-Added* (Washington, DC: Center for American Progress, 2009); Steven Glazerman, Susanna Loeb, Dan Goldhaber, Douglas Staiger, Stephen Raudenbush, and Grover Whitehurst, *Evaluating Teachers: The Important Role of Value-Added* (Washington, DC: Brown Center on Education Policy at the Brookings Institute, 2010).

31. David Leonhardt, "Stand and Deliver: When Does Holding Teachers Accountable Go Too Far?," *New York Times Magazine*, Sept. 5, 2010, 13–14.

32. *New York Times*, "Union Loses Suit over Teacher-Ranking Data," Jan. 10, 2011 (retrieved from http://cityroom.nytimes.com/2011/01/10/union-loses-suit-over-teacher-ranking--data/?ref=nyregion on Jan. 10, 2011).

33. National Education Policy Center, *Due Diligence and the Evaluation of Teachers: A Review of the Value-Added Analysis Underlying the Effectiveness Rankings of Los Angeles Unified School Teachers by the* Los Angeles Times (Boulder, CO: School of Education, University of Colorado at Boulder, 2011), 3.

34. For example, the Gates Foundation now is promoting using students' assessments of teacher effectiveness as part of the overall evaluation process. Bill and Melinda Gates Foundation, *Working with Teachers to Develop Fair and Reliable Measures of Effective Teaching* (Seattle: Bill and Melinda Gates Foundation, 2010).

35. Larry Ferlazzo, a teacher in Sacramento and a member of the reform-minded Teacher Leaders Network, wrote an opinion piece in the *Washington Post* in November 2010, which summarized what he believed to be the right way to do assessment. His list included observations by instructionally savvy supervisors; using data to inform decisions rather than letting the data drive decisions; multiple types of data; regular feedback from students, colleagues, and parents; and a hefty dose of self-reflection. *Washington Post*, "The Best Kind of Teacher Evaluation," Nov. 23, 2010 (retrieved from http://voices.washingtonpost.com/answer-sheet/guest-bloggers/the-best-kind-of-teacher-evalu.html on Nov. 23, 2010).

THIRTEEN

Tenure

In the winter of 2010–2011, the elimination of tenure was at the top of some politicians' list of school reforms. The sometimes stated—and sometimes unstated—message is that there are thousands of no-good teachers out there who are shirking their duties, stealing our money, and ruining the lives of our children. Just fire them and all will be well.

Not so. None of the superintendents I talked to like current tenure rules. As a former general counsel of a school district who had to try to work within its arcane and unfair procedures, nor do I. But its elimination is not a panacea. We are not about to fire our way into nirvana.

WHAT IS TENURE?

The grant of tenure gives teachers significant procedural protections against dismissal for cause. Those protections are in most cases so convoluted and the standards so difficult to meet that it effectively gives lifetime employment to individual teachers—absent completely bizarre or criminal conduct. Virtually no teacher gets fired for merely being lousy at his job.[1]

However, tenure is not about group terminations. When districts have to fire dozens or hundreds of teachers because of budget shortfalls, as they have had to do in 2010–2011, tenure is irrelevant. Seniority, which is an entirely different contractual right, is key. In most districts around the country, seniority provisions have guaranteed that teachers with fewer years on the job will be fired before those who have served longer, regardless of who is more effective.

It is this last problem that has driven people into a frenzy. Parents and politicians object as younger, highly qualified teachers are laid off and

133

successful faculties broken up to accommodate seniority systems. And, as usual, the burden falls on low-income, hard-to-staff schools, which have larger numbers of newer teachers. Parents have fought back. In early 2011, the Los Angeles Unified School District (LAUSD) settled a suit brought by the American Civil Liberties Union to stop seniority-based layoffs because they were having a disproportionate effect on poor kids, who attended schools with above-average numbers of young teachers.[2]

Even if tenure were eliminated, it would not affect this order of firings. And if seniority were eliminated, it would not make dismissing a single incompetent or criminal teacher any easier.

TENURE'S IMPORTANCE TO SCHOOL IMPROVEMENT—OVERSTATED?

In my discussions with superintendents, everyone dutifully announced he or she did not like tenure, but had moved forward nonetheless. In essence, the repeated story line was that the superintendents refocused professional development and school procedures so that he or she got the most out of Tier Two or Three teachers. That solved most problems. The Tier Four teachers, or those who just did not want to work in the new, collaborative, and data-driven environment, found themselves facing a great deal of pressure, not just from principals but from their peers as well. The superintendent or one of the principals could likely "counsel" that teacher out of the district rather than institute a formal proceeding. It may not have been perfect, but it was good enough.

Where this story line breaks down is in districts without the peer pressure of learning communities and in big cities. Whether it is the number of poor teachers, the strength of the unions, the lack of data, or the lack of enough well-trained principals to get the job done, urban superintendents like Michelle Rhee and Joel Klein considered tenure not merely an irritant, but a real problem. They were two of seventeen superintendents who wrote a "manifesto" in 2010 that called for its elimination.[3]

There is one other fact to keep in mind. Remember the number of teachers we already need every year: 275,000 to 300,000. We are struggling to find that many, and it requires us to dig far deeper in the barrel than we want. If we think we are going to eliminate tenure so we can fire thousands of additional teachers and replace them with something better, the new-teacher pipeline is going to disappoint us.

WHY TENURE BUGS US

The first thing about tenure that should bug us: There have been no serious quality standards used in most districts to decide who should receive it. Even many teachers acknowledge that the grant of tenure has little to do with a teacher's basic skills.[4] Granting what is in essence permanent job protection without even getting the assurance of competent teaching is, simply put, nuts.

What makes people even angrier is a process that is so time consuming and creates so much hostility between teachers and administrators that the administrators simply take a pass on invoking disciplinary proceedings against all but the worst of the worst teachers.[5] In the summer of 2009, there was a series of articles in the *Los Angeles Times* about LA teachers who had been removed from the classroom for misconduct. They were in "the rubber room," literally a room where they sat all day doing nothing but drawing salary because they could not be placed back in teaching until their cases were decided.[6] Some of those teachers were people who were initially removed from teaching when I was still the general counsel, six years earlier. The same thing happens in many other districts, with the same theme repeated by all the observers: the delay and difficulty of resolving contested firings is inexcusable.[7]

Other than university professors, no one has this kind of protection. There is a good reason. Given employment law in the twenty-first century, tenure is unnecessary to ensure due process for teachers in the event the district wants to fire them. While I was general counsel, LAUSD terminated a probationary teacher. She resisted and sued, claiming that she was terminated to punish her for exercising her free speech rights. She lost on the facts, but what was absolutely clear was that under California law she had plenty of protections of the sort that the unions like to argue come only with tenure.

I expect that many other states would have afforded this teacher similar rights that allowed her a day in court. Labor protections have come a long way since tenure rights were first granted. There are a host of laws against discrimination based on age, gender, race, religious affiliation, and sexual orientation. There is considerable First Amendment jurisprudence that did not exist in 1950, including protections against retaliation because of political activity. Teachers no longer need the special rules, and they certainly do not need them at such a high cost to taxpayers.

PROCEDURAL REFORM

In January of 2010 Randi Weingarten of the American Federation of Teachers offered to begin discussions about how to make student data part of the teacher evaluation process. She also offered to work to make the due process provisions of tenure "fair and efficient,"[8] proposing a streamlined process several months later. And in April of that year her successor in New York, Michael Mulgrew, made a deal with Chancellor Klein to close the city's rubber rooms.[9]

The redesign of the New York tenure evaluation process—as well as termination procedures—is not, as of this writing, fully resolved.[10] The National Education Association is nowhere near as forthcoming, but they may have no choice because of the tide of legislation in many state capitols.

CURRENT LEGISLATIVE EFFORTS

Tenure has become a flash point for education reform. Eliminating it was at the heart of SB 6, for example, a Florida reform measure in 2010 that would have also barred payments to teachers for years of service or advanced degrees. Governor Crist vetoed it in the spring of 2010, after a noisy campaign by the Florida teachers' union.[11]

But the issue did not go away. Several states followed those that had changed their rules on the use of student achievement data as part of a teacher's evaluation during 2009–2010. On top of that, legislators responded to superintendents' and mayors' complaints that they were forced to fire highly effective younger teachers in favor of longer-serving ones simply because of union seniority rules.[12] Colorado, Oklahoma, and Arizona passed legislation in 2010 requiring that layoffs be based primarily on performance instead of seniority,[13] and others had it on their agenda in 2011.

TAKING ADVANTAGE OF AN OPPORTUNITY

The prime benefit of this focus on tenure may be pushing districts to get serious about the issue of evaluation. Traditionally, state rules about the standards for granting tenure have been useless. For example, until recently, more states focused on whether teachers attended meetings than on whether their students demonstrated learning.[14] In essence, the decision was left to districts, and districts rarely had clear ideas about what they wanted to do. They now need to follow places like Chicago and New York and adopt Danielson or some other set of teaching standards.

And while legislatures are focused on the grant of tenure, they should rethink the currently common legislative provision that tenure is granted in two or three years. That makes little sense; it is far too arbitrary. Rather, the laws should be rewritten to authorize the grant of tenure based on the demonstration of competence at any point up to some number of years, say five, after a teacher is hired by a district.

This concentration on demonstrating quality teaching should also energize Peer Assistance and Review (PAR). As discussed previously, PAR teachers work with struggling peers to improve performance to an acceptable level.[15] If not, the panel may counsel a teacher to leave, or it can recommend to a joint teacher-administrator panel that a teacher be removed. Montgomery County's Jody Leleck told me that the district's PAR teams have done well at convincing failing teachers that they would be better off doing something else. While the success rate may not be 100 percent, she was satisfied they could live with the results.

Finally, we need to reflect on the fact that this discussion of tenure and seniority is really a discussion about providing some employment benefit in exchange for a demonstration of teaching competence. The spring of 2010 saw legislatures across the country propose various forms of such a bargain. Here are several ideas, some of which were among those the lawmakers considered:

1. Guarantee teachers a full year of pay in the event their position is eliminated or they are asked to leave their current position, and they cannot find a new one in the short term. If they cannot secure a position over the year, they must leave. This idea is essentially what is now in place in Washington and Chicago.[16]
2. Guarantee that teachers who have a consistent track record of a certain level of student achievement every year for a set period of years are protected against layoff for the following two to four years. So long as the teacher's student achievement data remains above level, they will remain employed (or at least at the bottom of any list of people being fired). It is the premise of the Colorado, Arizona, and Oklahoma legislation noted earlier.
3. Guarantee a teacher will not be laid off for a period of years in exchange for volunteering for some extraordinary service. For example, offering a teacher who has taught for at least three or four years the following deal: Teach at a hard-to-staff school for the next four years, and the district will guarantee employment for the five years or ten years after that.

Whatever is selected represents a "win-win." Teachers have an incentive to teach better or take on tougher assignments in exchange for a benefit that costs a district no money out of pocket. Certainly it is cheaper than pay for performance, which we will discuss in the next chapter.

WHAT WE NEED TO DO

Because tenure is merely part of the larger issue of teacher evaluation, this "to do" list incorporates ideas from the prior chapter as well:

- Insist that the district have a clear idea of what good teaching looks like. Point to Charlotte Danielson's matrix or other similar attempts at cataloguing the traits necessary for good teaching.
- Make sure that the principals and others who evaluate understand the standards. And the observers have to be able to rate consistently so any two principals are likely to rate the same teacher at least approximately the same.
- Insist on having the process focus on continuous improvement. No one should be evaluating teachers in order to fire them.
- Push for a system that uses multiple sources for evaluation. Data should be only one of them.
- Recognize the need to keep working on the testing underlying the data. It is currently useful, but not perfect.
- Support the elimination of tenure. However, it is not as critical as adopting the other systemic reforms necessary to evaluate teachers properly. You can probably get most Tier Four teachers to leave even with tenure in place.
- Keep professional learning communities robust. They make all of this discussion sensible.

NOTES

1. According to the National Center for Education Statistics, in 2007–2008 the average American school district, which has 211.4 teachers, dismissed three tenured teachers a year. NCES (IES), Table 8 of Student and Staffing Survey (SASS)—Average number of public school teachers and average number of public school teachers who were dismissed in the previous year or did not have their contracts renewed based on poor performance, by tenure status and state: 2007–2008 (retrieved from www.nces.ed.gov. surveys/sass.tables.sass0708_2009320_d1s.08.asp on Dec. 4, 2009). New York had a similar percentage as recently as 2005. *Wall Street Journal,* "City Gets Tough on Tenure," Sept. 28, 2010 (retrieved from http://online.wsj.com/article/58100014240527 4804654004575518390126045142.html on Sept. 29, 2010).

2. *Los Angeles Times,* "Judge OKs Settlement That Limits Use of Seniority in L.A. Teacher Layoffs," Jan. 21, 2011 (retrieved from www.latimes.com/news/local/la-me-lausd-aclu-20110122,0,7405675,print.story on Jan. 22, 2011); Rob Manwaring and Tim Sullivan, "When School Improvement and Teacher Seniority Collide," *Education Week,* Oct. 8, 2010 (retrieved from www.edweek.org/ew/articles/2010/10/13/07manwaring. h30.html on Nov. 23, 2010).

3. Partnership for Learning, *Rhee, Klein Release Education Manifesto* (Washington, DC: Parternship for Learning, 2010) (retrieved from www.partnership4learning.org/node/2850 on Oct. 14, 2010).

4. Scholastic, Inc., Bill and Melinda Gates Foundation, *Primary Sources: America's Teachers on America's Schools* (Seattle: Gates Foundation, 2010), 41.

5. Public Agenda, *Rolling Up Their Sleeves: Superintendents and Principals Talk about What's Needed to Fix Public Schools* (New York: Public Agenda, 2003), 32 (80 percent of superintendents and 67 percent of principals thought removing a terrible, tenured teacher was "difficult but doable," while 16 percent of superintendents and 30 percent of principals thought it was virtually impossible").

6. The *Los Angeles Times* series included the following stories: "Failure Gets a Pass: A *Times* Investigation," April 22, 2009; "Firing Tenured Teachers Can Be a Costly and Tortuous Task," May 3, 2009; "L.A. Unified Pays Teachers Not to Teach, May 6, 2009; "Teacher Loses Fight to Keep Job," May 7, 2009; "Accused of Sexual Abuse, but Back in the Classroom," May 10, 2009; "Teacher Loses Fight to Keep Job," July 14, 2009. Jason Song wrote all articles. They can all be found at www.latimes.com/news/local.

7. Steven Brill, "The Rubber Room," *New Yorker*, Aug. 31, 2009 (retrieved from www.newyorker.com/reporting/2009/08/31/090831fa_fact__brill?on Dec. 29, 2009); David Brooks, "The Sidney Awards II," *New York Times*, Dec. 29, 2009, A31; Nicholas D. Kristof, "Democrats and Schools," *New York Times*, Oct. 15, 2009 (retrieved from www. nytimes.com/2009/10/15/opinion/15kristof.html on Oct. 15, 2009); *New York Times*, "A New Effort to Remove Bad Teachers," Nov. 15, 2007 (retrieved from www.nytimes. com/2007/11/15/education/15teacher.html on Nov. 24, 2009); *St. Petersburg Times*, "It Takes a Lot to Dismiss a Teacher," March 28, 2009 (retrieved from www.tampabay. com/news/education.k12/its-hard-to-fire-teachers-even-if-they-bad/987898 on Nov. 30, 2009).

8. *Washington Post*, "Union Head to Propose Tying Test Scores, Teacher Evaluations," Jan. 12, 2010 (retrieved from www.washingtonpost.com/wp-dyn/content/article/2010/01/11/AR2010011103691_pf.html on Jan. 12, 2010); *Education Week*, "AFT Chief Vows to Revise Teacher-Dismissal Process," Jan. 12, 2010 (retrieved from www. edweek.org/ew/articles/2010/01/12/18aft_ep.h29.html on Jan. 12, 2010).

9. *New York Times*, "Teachers Set Deal with City on Discipline Process," April 15, 2010 (retrieved from www.nytimes.com/2010/04/16/nyregioin/16rubber.html on April 16, 2010); Steven Brill, "The Teachers' Unions' Last Stand," *New York Times*, May 17, 2010 (retrieved from www.nytimes.com/2010/05/23/magazine/23Race-t.html on May 19, 2010).

10. New York's United Federation of Teachers and the New York State United Teachers have agreed to a proposed law that would eventually evaluate teachers on a 100-point scale, with 25 points based on how much students improve on standardized state exams and 15 percent to locally selected measures, with the rest locally determined. The deal also provides for a sixty-day hearing process. That leaves significant issues open, but it is a strong start for the AFT. *New York Times*, "A Better Deal for Schools," May 11, 2010 (retrieved from www.nytimes.com/2010/05/12/opinion/12wed3.html on May 12, 2010); *New York Times*, "Agreement Will Alter Teacher Evaluations," May 10, 2010 (retrieved from www.nytimes.com.201005/11/nyregion/11teacher/html on May 11, 2010).

11. *New York Times*, "Florida Governor Splits with G.O.P. on Teacher Pay," April 15, 2010 (retrieved from www.nytimes.come/2010/04/16/us/16teachers.html on April 16, 2010).

12. See, for example, National Public Radio, "In Teacher Layoffs, Seniority Rules. Should It?," June 2, 2010 (transcript retrieved from www.npr.org/templates.story. story.php?storyId=127373157&ps=rs on Oct. 18, 2010); *New York Times*, "Last Teacher In, First Out? City Has Another Idea," April 24, 2010 (retrieved from www.nytimes. com/2010/04/25/education/25seniority/html on Jan. 21, 2011).

13. *New York Times*, "Governor Thrusts New Jersey to Fore on Education," Jan. 12, 2011 (retrieved from www.nytimes.com/2011/01/13/education.13jersey.html on Jan. 13, 2011).

14. For example, as of 2007, only four states required that classroom effectiveness be the preponderant criterion for evaluating teacher performance in anticipation of tenure; other states give weight to things like attending faculty meetings. National Council on Teacher Quality, *State Teacher Policy Yearbook, 2007* (Washington, DC: NCTQ, 2007), 10.

15. Michael Strong, *Effective Teacher Induction and Mentoring: Assessing the Evidence* (New York: Teachers College Press, 2009), 13–16.

FOURTEEN

Motivating Teachers: Is Pay the Be-All and End-All?

A recent McKinsey & Co. study on employee motivation and change issued a simple warning worth keeping in mind throughout this discussion: "Money is the most expensive way to motivate people."[1]

Remember in chapter 1, there was a long discussion of "headspace," where the message was that teachers' attitudes and perceptions influence their performance as much as their skills of instruction. In chapter 7 we already discussed that a school's working conditions and attitudes will often trump money as an incentive to keep teachers from leaving. The question now is whether pay for performance based on student achievement data can be a dominant motivator to improve classroom performance, or will those same working conditions and attitudes again turn out to be the real drivers that cause a teacher to do well?

ARE TEACHERS UNDERPAID? A QUESTION WITH NO CLEAR RIGHT ANSWER

The average salary of a teacher in 2006–2007 was $50,816. According to a 2008 *Education Week* study[2] that used similar numbers, teachers nationwide earned about 88 percent of those in comparable occupations (i.e., nurses, computer programmers, psychologists, counselors, editors, architects, accountants).[3] In ten states, salaries met or exceeded comparable careers, and even in the state with the worst comparison, North Carolina, the figure stood at 83 percent.

Those salaries do not include the generous health, dental, life, and disability benefits most teachers receive; nor does it take into account widespread pension plans, most of which still guarantee fixed payments at the time of retirement.[4] In 2007, those represented about 24 percent of total compensation, while private sector workers' benefits averaged only 17 percent.[5] (The seeming 7 percent difference may understate the real value of schools' benefits packages in light of districts' habitual under-funding of their pension accounts.[6]) Finally, none of this compensation package takes into account that most teachers have essentially two months of summer vacation. Nor does it consider the extraordinary bene-fit that tenured public school teachers are far less likely to be fired than those in comparable occupations, especially in years like the 2009–2010 recession.[7]

When all of that is taken into account, it may not be surprising that the 2008 *MetLife Survey* reported 66 percent of teachers now think that they already have the opportunity to make a decent salary. Similarly, a 2009 Public Agenda/Learning Point Associates survey found that 62 percent of teachers saw low salaries as either "no drawback" or only a "minor drawback" in teaching.[8]

Here, then, is the situation we face. We do not have to pay more simply because teachers are so unhappy with their salaries that, regard-less of what else we might do, they will not be motivated to perform. More money might help, but are there better and cheaper alternatives? And if we use money, how do we do that most effectively? What works?

MOTIVATORS IN TEACHERS' HEADS — NOT THEIR WALLETS

This chapter poses two distinct questions. The first: how to get teachers to do the best they can in what we have already asked them to do. That is the principal question for "pay for performance." The second: how best to get them to do something new or in addition to what they already do. That is the discussion of "merit pay." The distinction is significant. The facts suggest that a well-functioning district has plenty of incentives *al-ready in place* for teachers to work as hard and as smart as they can at what they do. Enticing them to do something else is another thing entire-ly.

The Love of Teaching

Every teacher will tell you that she teaches because she loves to help children learn. In any survey of teacher attitudes, the same message al-ways surfaces as the prime motivation for why educators are in the busi-ness of teaching. Teaching is a calling.[9] However, that does not answer the widely acknowledged problem of teacher demoralization and burn-out.[10] And it overlooks that teachers are not independent actors. They are part of organizations. Their attitude toward their work is not simply shaped by their conception of themselves; it is hugely influenced by their perception of the school where they teach and the district that employs them.

The Power of the Right Vision

A school's vision, which can drive its culture, can also foster effectiveness, productivity, community, and improvement.[11]

The first part of "vision" is the story that explains a school's purpose and drives its mission. Everyone wants to be part of something bigger than himself or herself. But the vision has to mean something.

A visit to a Catholic school like St. Ignatius Loyola in Baltimore gives a visitor a sense of what can motivate teachers. Loyola's faculty is mostly white, while its students are African American. They live in different neighborhoods, indeed in different worlds. The faculty, not all of whom are Catholic, is motivated by the Jesuit vision of the development of the "whole child" into a caring, active participant in society. The school has found a way to carry out that mission by taking young boys who are struggling in Baltimore City elementary schools, turning around both their attitudes and academic skills in middle school, and sending them off to quality parochial and private high schools that can give them first-rate educations.

Blue Valley may do even better. In talking with teachers, they repeated what is clearly a "secret sauce" that makes their district special. Blue Valley is the "biggest, baddest, most innovative," cutting-edge district they can find, said one teacher, and he and his colleagues want to be part of creating such an extraordinary learning space for kids. Superintendents elsewhere would kill for this kind of enthusiasm.[12]

What the visions have in common is that they are grounded in something teachers can see and feel.[13] Blue Valley teachers love information technology. They find new things, are encouraged to try them out, and constantly tinker to get better results. They *know* they are the biggest, baddest guys in the neighborhood because they act that way every day. A good vision is a virtuous circle.

There is a second part to vision. It is the part about being part of an organization. Think of the Marines. An individual Marine believes in the mission. But even more importantly, he believes in his buddies, his platoon, and his company. And he believes in the Corps.[14]

In a world where teacher isolation is passé and collaboration is the order of the day, part of the vision has to be that the group of teachers assembled in that school is a great team. Teachers have to want to wake up each day and go to school to see their fellows. They have to believe there is something special about their team.

One example from my travels: Sam Williams in Brazosport walked into a dysfunctional elementary school. Among other bad habits, teachers fiercely defended their autonomy, which was going to be a problem for his vision of a high-performing school where everyone collaborated. Sam got them to agree that some teachers seemed better at teaching some subjects, especially math, than others. Then he got everyone to agree to let those teachers teach all of the kids' math. It worked; scores rose. And Sam went on from there.

But what if a failing school has no vision—or a toxic one, and the principal cannot find a way to turn it around?

The Obama administration has been clear in its preference to fix failing schools by closing them, firing the principal and much of the faculty, and starting over. They call it "reconstitution."

It is not popular. Parents often object to firing the principal and getting rid of beloved teachers. Yet it may be necessary. David Weiner summed up the problem as succinctly as anyone I talked to. He does not believe that closures are necessary simply because there is a large group of incompetent teachers. Rather, he believes districts often have to close low-performing schools because "the school culture is both so negative and so strong" that it can frustrate all other efforts to reform what happens in the building. The prime evil is not incompetence, but obstinacy.

Vision, in other words, cuts both ways.

Three Organizational Motivators

There are a host of other traditional motivators that can occupy a teacher's headspace.[15] For example, parents and students can love teachers, and teachers can respond by wanting to please them.[16] I intend to spend some time on these kinds of traditional motivators later in the book; for now, I want to focus on how the current organizational efforts at restructuring schools profoundly affect teacher motivation.

The Positive Effects of Team Building

No one is better at building staff loyalty than Southwest Airlines, which has become the only consistently profitable airline in the United States—in large part because of its conscious and extensive effort to empower and celebrate workers and make them a family.[17]

In the old top-down industrial version of schools, thanking teachers and celebrating their success was not unknown; it was just not a principal's priority. However, where teachers are appreciated, their satisfaction increases.[18]

Blue Valley, which may have the most enthusiastic workforce and the one most receptive to change among all those that I visited, has nurtured teacher motivation by respecting and appreciating them. Bob Moore, the district's executive director of IT services, said: "My people bust their butts because . . . they want to be part of something good. . . . Everything is not top down, we listen to teachers."

The change may have something to do with the finding in the 2008 *MetLife Survey* that 48 percent of teachers believe they are recognized for good performance, up from just 33 percent in 1984.[19] In comparison with the "old days," the change is a genuine motivator.

Accountability

In the "old days," teachers were rarely held accountable.[20] That has changed radically over the past twenty years, and with it, teacher motivation. The presence of great volumes of student data is a powerful incentive for improvement.[21]

That pressure is simply going to increase over time as more and more data systems become sophisticated enough to track every child—which also means to track every teacher.[22] The Obama administration set aside $250 million in 2009 to support states developing data systems that include unique student identifiers, and the Race to the Top, the administration's $4 billion competitive grant program begun in 2009–2010, has included progress on data systems as one of the selection criteria.[23]

Brad Jupp, who negotiated the innovative Pro Comp pay incentive agreement for the union in Denver, told me, "The union wants to save its teachers, even those who are in the lowest quartile of performance, but that may not be possible. Once people have individual data they start seeing things differently. Giving this data to parents is devastating [to underperforming teachers]." Witness the *Los Angeles Times* series on teacher effectiveness in 2010.

The same dynamic works inside schools. In Blue Valley, for example, the fifth grade teachers will gather every week to review data on recent quiz-like mini-assessments. The purpose is to see how each child is doing and to figure out how to provide assistance to those who are struggling before they get too far behind. No one is focusing on the data as a measure of a teacher's performance, but if the data shows that three of the four classes are doing well in, say, long division, but the fourth class is collectively in trouble, it does not take much for anyone to conclude that it is likely a problem with the teacher and not the students. That is motivation, both positive and negative.[24]

The Professional Learning Community

The idea of the collegial learning community requires teachers to share ideas with each other every week. It exposes their skills and abilities (or lack of them), and, in so doing, creates a previously nonexistent peer pressure.[25] Those who know what they are doing are asked to help others, or they simply offer ideas they have found useful in their classrooms. Conversely, those who do not know what they are doing are found out. They cannot avoid exposure by hiding out in their classrooms anymore. That simply creates more peer pressure to do well.

If there is a limitation on the effects of accountability or the professional learning community, it is likely the result of a district's not yet having fully introduced either into their schools. That arguably makes the case for pay for performance as a motivator, but the more logical argument is to take that dollar and put it into better data and more collaboration. Both likely have a more direct impact on learning.

PAY DEPENDENT ON STUDENT PERFORMANCE

Currently the Federal Teacher Incentive Fund and the Milken Family Foundation's System for Teacher and Student Advancement Project (TAP), as well as several smaller projects, are funding dozens of experiments with compensation that include some form of teacher pay that is dependent on student performance.[26] As of this writing, there is no consensus about the programs' impact.[27] However, in the last half of 2010, three studies raised doubts about the effectiveness of such incentive pay,[28] and those districts I visited with such a plan were similarly uncertain about its effects. When the final results are in, there may be some agreement about their value, but in the absence of those conclusions, I believe that the following observations make sense:

In the districts I visited, few tied merit pay to student performance. Most districts, including places like Brownsville and Aldine, recent Broad winners, had done well without it. Brownsville's Brett Springston told me that everyone in the district looks at how schools are rated every year, and that those rankings drive a great deal of effort even without dollars attached.[29]

Other superintendents, like New Orleans Recovery District's Paul Vallas, heartily dislike this kind of pay for performance. Vallas views it as building in "pay for mediocrity" because it essentially telegraphs to teachers who do not earn a bonus that they are still getting paid for doing a poor job. David Stuckwisch, who has done so much in Portsmouth without pay for performance, worries that it will just cause cheating and dissension, a problem confirmed by investigations in several cities in 2010 and 2011.

The fact that dollars are tied to standardized test scores also tends to highlight the problems with the tests themselves. There is no question that there are various flaws in the tests prescribed by No Child Left Behind, many of which were enumerated in chapter 12. When the flaws influence how much people get paid, there is going to be more resistance to them than otherwise.[30]

One final problem is the same one that dogs every attempt to use student performance data, whether for licensing, tenure, or pay. If it is

not adjusted to take into account the different levels of expected performance in low- and high-poverty schools, its use may drive teachers away
from hard-to-staff schools rather than toward them. A study of North
Carolina's experimental pay program concluded, "If teachers perceive
bonus programs as yet another factor making jobs in advantaged schools
more attractive, increased turnover rates in low-performing schools are a
predictable consequence."[31]

Should Performance Pay Be Awarded Individually or Collectively?

Whether or not to award merit pay individually or collectively is a
good question.[32] Although it may seem a minuscule issue in the larger
scheme of things, it is not. If a pay scheme is done badly, it threatens the
push for increased teacher collaboration that is fundamental to virtually
every other aspect of a twenty-first-century school.

Brad Jupp told me that he was surprised that Denver teachers wanted
the pay awarded individually, rather than collectively. His conclusion
was that teachers still saw themselves as working in isolation; they
wanted to control their own fate since they had little influence on others.

William Hite, the superintendent in suburban Washington's Prince
George's County, found the same thing. In 2008–2009, the first year of
this district's voluntary trial of a bonus plan, which is in part based on
individual awards tied to student achievement, teachers told him they
had decided to participate because they felt the district was finally giving
them a way to be acknowledged for performances superior to those of
their peers.

Kaya Henderson in Washington also argued for individual awards.
Her concern focused on low-performing schools. In trying to entice outside teachers to transfer, it might diminish the appeal if any bonus were
tied not only to their performance but also to that of their low-performing
colleagues.[33]

Still, are individual awards a good idea? Here is the trade-off: We
want individual teachers motivated. We also want collaboration and collegial effort. Will individual awards promote individual effort, and even
if they do, will it be to the detriment of the collegiality and collaboration
that are at the heart of high-performing schools?

The three structural motivators (praise, accountability, and learning
communities), plus the teacher's own sense of wanting to see kids do
well, will likely provide plenty of incentive for individual teachers with
regard to the quality of their own teaching. However, *collegial pay* for
performance may be an effective incentive to get them to spend additional time or effort on helping others.[34]

Nick Fischer of New London put the problem this way: "People need
to see the difference between what they do now, and what we want them
to do in the future. And then we have to pay them that way. If you want

collaboration, for example, then the financial model has to take that into account."

If teachers' income is in part based on how well their colleagues perform, they have a greater interest in reaching out to them than they would have otherwise. For example, if all four fifth-grade teachers in a school can earn some additional money if the entire fifth grade does well, the three teachers in the group who are capable will have an incentive to work with the struggling fourth teacher to pick up performance.[35]

Individual bonuses, on the other hand, may stifle the impulse. One survey found that, by a 63 percent to 22 percent margin, teachers thought individually awarded merit pay would foster "unhealthy competition and jealousy" among colleagues. One teacher is reported as having said, "I think you might have less sharing. In my building, the fourth grade team that I work with, we lesson plan together. You might be a little more competitive. Then you're, like, 'I'm not giving her this idea because I want this to make me look better.'"[36]

Collegial bonuses also finesse the problem of student assignments. They are rarely random. There are still some places that track children by ability, and even if the practice is formally abandoned, assignments are still often a function of parental pressure or principals just playing favorites. Indirectly tying some part of pay to a principal's decision where to assign a child seems far more counterproductive than helpful.

TAP schools and some cities, like Houston,[37] have tried a combination of individual and collegial awards tied to evaluation and/or performance, but there has been little assessment of what, if any impact, the individual awards have on collaboration (in part, no doubt, because other parts of their system are pushing in exactly the opposite direction—toward working together). Still, any individual award that cuts down sharing of information, or makes teachers think only about their kids and not everyone's kids, simply undermines the collegial atmosphere at the heart of the learning community.

There are pay experiments that try to straddle to avoid the worst of individual awards.

Some plans, like New York City's, have a bonus awarded to the school as a whole, and teachers and/or the principal, or both, decide how the money should be divided.[38] They avoid some of the worst problems of individual awards by still requiring a group effort to get the money in the first place. Alternatively, individual awards not based on student performance but on something else, such as the Long Beach teacher's development of a terrific math program, are great incentives. While they recognize individual achievement, they do not compromise collegiality.

THREE MORE WORDS ABOUT PAY: SINGLE SALARY SCHEDULE

Notwithstanding our interest in promoting collaboration, we do want teachers to step up, take on new roles, and excel at them. That means we have to create a system for *merit pay* that focuses on rewarding individual teachers for their unique contributions as master teachers, mentors, and leaders. The entire twenty-first-century school structure is dependent on it, and, if there is any hope of enticing better-qualified people into the schools with the prospect of more money, these changes are how we are going to have to do it.

This kind of merit pay system cannot easily coexist with one of the most sacred and long-standing artifacts of mass-production education: The single salary schedule should be consigned to the trash bin—now.

The single salary pay structure for teachers has been in use since the 1920s and now covers 96 percent of public school districts.[39] The logic was that it prevented discrimination, curbed favoritism, and gave everyone a fair way to earn more money.[40]

It is the ultimate in "collegiality." Everyone earns the same amount of money, with the only variations based on years of service and additional coursework or advanced degrees.

The problem is that none of those pay increments are tied to student achievement or school improvement. In discussing with superintendents what were the ingredients of their district's improved performance, I was struck by the fact that, while they wanted strong professional learning communities, no one mentioned having more teachers with advanced degrees.

Similarly, there is agreement that a teacher's skills are likely to improve through the first three, and maybe four to five, years,[41] but districts continue to incur pay increases thereafter without concurrent increases in teacher effectiveness. In Boston, an exception to the rule, the pay package roughly reflects teachers' learning curve; it flattens out after eight years.[42]

The evil of the single salary schedule is not simply that it is wasteful. It actually is a barrier to everything a good district wants to do.

The single salary schedule makes the collegial learning environment more difficult. At first blush, that may seem counterintuitive, but it is not. A learning environment relies on mentors, master teachers, team leaders, facilitators, and deans. The single salary schedule interferes with paying these people for their effort. On top of that, it prevents paying more for science, technology, engineering, and math (STEM) teachers or special education teachers, any pay for performance scheme, or those willing to teach in hard-to-staff schools (see chapter 16).[43]

Having ruled out large, across-the-board pay increases as a way to lure better-qualified candidates into the profession, these new payments become the only monetary incentive available. Rather than being locked into the single salary schedule, potential teachers can foresee becoming mentors or leaders in a few years and being compensated for their willingness to assume the additional work.[44] And after becoming teachers, the new salary structure is more likely to keep them in teaching. One of the great concerns about the single salary schedule was that the only way a teacher could earn significantly more was to leave teaching for administration—which was exactly what experts want to avoid.[45]

HOW TO PAY FOR A NEW COMPENSATION SYSTEM

During 2009–2010, various cities, including New Haven, Baltimore, and Pittsburgh, signed new labor contracts that ended the single salary structure.[46] They paid for the new deal by abandoning much of the old structure's reliance on step increases for years of service and advanced degrees.

If districts did not pay for experience or advanced education, as they do now, collectively they would have approximately $50 billion to put into a revamped salary structure.[47] That money could then reward mentors, STEM and special education teachers, hard-to-staff school faculties, and those whose students excel.[48]

Here is how I calculated that $50 billion figure. First, let's start by considering the money paid to teachers for advanced coursework or degrees, which I briefly mentioned back in chapter 9.

As of 2008, approximately 49 percent of all American teachers earned enhanced pay based on having completed advanced degrees or additional coursework.[49] In Los Angeles alone, in the mid-1990s, 22 percent of teachers' salaries, then $253 million, could be attributed to salary point credits earned by taking courses, and, at the time, the total nationwide was approximately $19 billion.[50] Today those salary point and degree credits are probably worth roughly $30 billion a year.[51]

There is little evidence justifying the current system of paying teachers for earning an advanced degree of their choosing, without regard either to the district's needs or their own skill deficiencies. Confirming my discussions with the superintendents, independent studies have been unable to find that people with such degrees improve student achievement.[52] Patricia Wasley, dean at the University of Washington's College of Education, and Marguerite Roza, a professor at the college, who have studied the effects of the master's "pay bump," explain why most advanced degrees seem to have no effect:

> Current pay-bump policies invite a cynical, wasteful, and expensive logic: Since the compensation incentive is automatic, why not simply obtain the cheapest, most expedient degree? After all, if there is no link between the subject matter of the degree and what the teacher does,

nor an imperative to improve teacher performance in return for higher pay, the current compensation system rewards the path of least resistance.[53]

Since this sum of money is spent in pursuit of professional development, it is fair to rethink how to use it most effectively. Some of it will have to go to expenses that will not affect the salary structure, like providing for collaboration time, mentor training, and additional professional development assistance. Assume, therefore, that half the total, approximately $15 billion, is available for overhaul of the salary structure.

Second, if a district takes some of that experience-based pay back, it can be an extremely large sum.[54] A 2007 study estimated the experienced-based pay supplements accounted for 10 percent of all K–12 expenditures,[55] and Stanford economist Eric Hanushek recently put the number at 27 percent of total salaries, which are currently about $295 billion.[56] Based on current spending,[57] that means somewhere between $60 and $80 billion annually is paid to teachers based on their years of service.[58]

A fair alternative to the current salary system would still recognize that teachers should be paid more as their quality improves. However, those payments stop when improvements stop. As a result, a new system might be like Boston's, paying an experience supplement for the first five, or maybe eight, years. Even after subtracting the amount left to fund this new shorter, experience-based learning package, there should be about $35 billion of experience-based spending that could be put to other uses. That amount, plus the $15 billion of reallocated payments for advanced degrees, gets us to $50 billion.

The proposed pot represents approximately 15 percent to 18 percent of total teacher pay. It may not be enough to meet all the objectives behind this proposed pay structure, but it is a good start.

WHAT WE NEED TO DO

The conclusions a parent or taxpayer (or even better, a superintendent or state school official) should draw from the foregoing discussion should be these:

- Reforming the single salary schedule is vital. Professional learning communities and high-performing schools need money for mentors, master teachers, and STEM and special education teachers.
- Ending pay supplements for advanced degrees or coursework and longevity are the best source for the additional amounts to be paid mentors and others.
- Pay for performance is not vital. It may be helpful, but the right working conditions are likely to do more. And any pay for perfor-

mance scheme needs to be carefully constructed to make sure that it does not undermine collaboration and collegiality.

- Negotiations over such pay packages are going to be difficult. Teachers will fight to hold on to their education and longevity payments. To get around the problem in Denver and Minnesota, new pay plans came from a fund based on a surtax (in Denver) and a state-funded program (in Minnesota). That should not be the favored solution. Realignment of current pay structures makes far more sense. If the 15 percent to 18 percent generated does not do the job, then taxpayers can decide if they want to tax themselves more.

NOTES

1. Carolyn Aiken and Scott Keller, "The Irrational Side of Change Management," *The McKinsey Quarterly* 2 (2009): 106.

2. *Quality Counts 2008*, "Teacher Salaries, Looking at Comparable Jobs," *Education Week*, 2008, 16–17.

3. But see Sylvia A. Allegeto, Sean P. Corcoran, and Lawrence Mishel, *The Teaching Penalty* (Washington, DC: Economic Policy Institute, 2008) (finding teacher wage erosion in the period 1996–2006); same authors, *How Does Teacher Pay Compare* (Washington, DC: Economic Policy Institute, 2004) (finding a relative erosion of teacher salaries in comparison with what the authors deem comparable jobs in the period 1983–2003).

4. As of 2007–2008, 98 percent of districts provided general medical insurance; 85.2 percent, dental insurance; 80 percent, group life insurance; and 83 percent a defined-benefit retirement plan. In twenty-nine states, 100 percent of the districts provided general medical insurance, and in thirteen states, 100 percent of the districts provided dental insurance. NCES (IES), table 4 (SASS)—Percentage of public school districts that offered various benefits to teachers, by state: 2007–08 (retrieved from http://nces.ed.gov/surveys/sass/tables/sass0708_2009320_d2s_04.asp on Oct. 2, 2009).

5. NCES (IES)—table 7 (Revenues and Expenditures for Public Elementary and Secondary Education) Current instruction and instruction-related expenditures for public elementary and secondary education, by object and state or jurisdiction: Fiscal year 2007) (retrieved from http://nces.ed.gov/pubs 2009/expenditures/tables/table_07.asp); Frederick R. Hess, "Teacher Quality, Teacher Pay," *Policy Review* 124 (April/May 2004) (retrieved from www.hoover.org/ppublications/policyreview/3438676.hrml on Oct. 2, 2009). An older study by the Bureau of Labor Statistics found that in the late 1990s, businesses spent $.92 per hour worked on retirement and savings benefits for white-collar workers, but districts spent $2.40 an hour for teachers. The ratios of benefits to salaries, which were based on the average salaries at the time, were equally tilted toward teachers: a ratio of .054 for white-collar workers and a ratio of .09 for teachers. Douglas N. Harris and Scott J. Adams, "Understanding the Level and Causes of Teacher Turnover: A Comparison with Other Professions," *Economics of Education Review*, 2005, 16.

6. *Education Week*, "Personnel Costs Prove Tough to Contain," Jan. 5, 2011 (retrieved from www.edweek.org/ew/articles/2011/01/12/16personnel.h30.html on Jan. 12, 2011).

7. When all of that is taken into account, it may not be surprising that the 2008 *MetLife Survey* reported 66 percent of teachers now think that they already have the opportunity to make a decent salary. Similarly, a 2009 Public Agenda/Learning Point Associates survey found that 62 percent of teachers saw low salaries as either "no

drawback" or only a "minor drawback" in teaching. Jean Johnson, Andrew Yarrow, Jonathan Rochkind, and Amber Ott, *Teaching for a Living: How Teachers See the Profession Today* (New York: Public Agenda, 2009), question 6 results. However, the NCES found only 45.9 percent of public school teachers were "satisfied" with their salaries in 2003–2004. NCES (IES), table 72 (2008 Tables and Figures)—Teachers' perceptions about teaching and school conditions by control and level of school: 1993–94, 1999–2000, and 2003–04.

8. Johnson, Yarrow, Rochkind, and Ott, *Teaching for a Living*, question 6 results.

9. Public Agenda, *A Sense of Calling: Who Teaches and Why* (New York: Public Agenda, 2000), 10.

10. A fall 2009 Public Agenda/Learning Point Associates survey of America's teachers found that 40 percent of them were "disheartened." *Education Week*, "State of Mind: America's Teaching Corps Is Made Up of Three Groups with Distinct Attitudes about Their Profession, Which Has Implications for Policymakers," Oct. 21, 2009, 21; Johnson, Yarrow, Rochkind, and Ott, *Teaching for a Living*.

11. Terence E. Deal and Kent D. Peterson, *Shaping School Culture* (San Francisco: Jossey-Bass, 1999), 7.

12. Charlotte has taken significant steps to reduce its hard-to-staff school problem by turning staffing such schools into a "mission," which gives principals more authority and the schools greater access to technology, staff, and new programs. *New York Times*, "When the System Works," April 26, 2010 (retrieved from www.nytimes.com/2010/04/26.opinion.26mon2.html on April 26, 2010).

13. Michael Fullan, *Leading in a Culture of Change* (San Francisco: Jossey-Bass, 2001), 19.

14. A Marine who was blinded by a roadside bomb in Iraq wrote in a blog in the *New York Times* about his attitude to the Corps and to his platoon: "I have a tattoo over my left breast (where my heart is) that says 'Semper Fidelis' the Marine Corps motto. It is Latin for 'Always Faithful' and refers to always accomplishing the mission. Around the 'Semper Fidelis' are four names, 'Thompson,' 'Belchik,' 'Cockerham,' and 'Hodshire.' All great guys that I would let date my sister." *New York Times*, March 2, 2010 (retrieved from http://opinionator.blogs.nytimes.com2010/030/02/home-fires-the-war-movie=you-don't-want-to-see/on March 2, 2010). Without taking a position on tattoos, schools should—and would—die for that kind of commitment and motivation among teachers toward their mission, their fellow faculty, and their school.

15. The great educational change guru Michael Fullan has written that one of the elements of successful change is "establish conditions for the evolution of positive pressure." Michael Fullan, *Transformational Leadership* (San Francisco: Jossey-Bass, 2006), 45.

16. Elaine Allensworth, Stephen Ponisciak, and Christopher Mazzeo, *The Schools Teachers Leave: Teacher Mobility in Chicago Public Schools* (Chicago: Consortium on Chicago School Research, June 2009), 32; NCES, *Job Satisfaction among America's Teachers: Effects of Workplace Conditions, Background Characteristics, and Teacher Compensation* (Washington, DC: U.S. Department of Education, 1997), 34.

17. Kevin Freiberg and Jackie Freiberg, *Nuts* (New York: Broadway Books, 1996); Jody Hoffer Gittell, *The Southwest Airlines Way* (New York: McGraw Hill, 2003).

18. NCES, *Job Satisfaction among America's Teachers: Effects of Workplace Conditions, Background Characteristics, and Teacher Compensation* (Washington, DC: U.S. Department of Education, 1997), 28; Susan L. Swars, Barbara Meyers, Lydia C. Mays, and Brian Lack, "A Two-Dimensional Model of Teacher Retention and Mobility: Classroom Teachers and Their University Partners Take a Closer Look at a Vexing Problem," *Journal of Teacher Education* 60, no. 2 (March/April 2009): 178.

19. *MetLife Survey of the American Teacher* (New York: Metropolitan Life Ins. Co., 2008), 25.

20. Vivian Troen and Katherine C. Boles, *Who's Teaching Your Children* (New Haven, CT: Yale University Press, 2003), 75–76.

21. Michael Fullan, *Six Secrets of Change* (San Francisco: Jossey-Bass, 2004), 95; Brett D. Jones and Robert J. Egley, "Looking through Different Lenses: Teachers' and Administrators' Views of Accountability," *Phi Delta Kappan* 87, no. 10 (2006): 770.

22. *Quality Counts*, "Data Yield Clues to Effectiveness," *Editorial Projects in Education* 27, no. 18 (Jan. 10, 2008): 20.

23. *Education Week*, "States Said to Be Progressing on Data Systems," Nov. 23, 2009 (retrieved from www.edweek.org/ew/articles/2009/11/23/13data.h29.html on Nov. 23, 2009).

24. I am comfortable with this assertion, even though there are researchers who claim that there is no "credible evidence" based on scientific research to support the claim. *Education Week*, "'Race to Top' Said to Lack Key Science," Oct. 2, 2009 (retrieved from www.edweek.org/ew/articles/2009/10/07/06research_ep.h28.html on Oct. 7, 2009).

25. Michael Fullan, *Six Secrets of Change* (San Francisco: Jossey-Bass, 2008), 63–64; Kent Peterson, *Building Collaborative Cultures* (Naperville, IL: North Central Regional Educational Laboratory Monograph, 1994), 3–4 (retrieved from www.ncrel.org/sdrs/areas/issues/educatrs/leadershp/le)pet.htm on Oct. 5, 2009), 6–7; Michael Fullan, *Leading in a Culture of Change* (San Francisco: Jossey-Bass, 2001), 118.

26. As of 2008, ten states provided for some type of pay for performance. United States Chamber of Commerce, *Leaders and Laggards* (Washington, DC: U.S. Chamber of Commerce, 2009), 24. *See also* NCES (IES), table 5 (SASS)—Percentage of public school district that used pay incentives for various reasons, by state: 2007–08 (retrieved from http://nces.ed.gov/surveys/sass/tables.Sass0708_2009320_d1s_05.asp on Oct. 2, 2009); *Quality Counts 2008*, "States Experiment with Pay for Performance," *Education Week*, 2008, 31 (A useful summary of the seven state pay-for-performance programs in existence in 2008).

27. "Performance Pay Studies Show Few Achievement Gains," in *Education Week's Spotlight on Pay for Performance*, May 2009.

28. Mathematica Policy Research, Inc., *An Evaluation of the Teacher Advancement Program (TAP) in Chicago: Year Two Impact Report* (Washington, DC: Mathematica Policy Research, Inc., 2010); National Center on Performance Incentives, *Teacher Pay for Performance* (Nashville: Vanderbilt University, 2010) (Nashville, TN, schools); Sarena F. Goodman and Lesley J. Turner, *Teacher Incentive Pay and Educational Outcomes: Evidence from the New York City Bonus Program* (New York: Columbia University, 2010) (New York City).

29. One survey of superintendents and principals asked: "Which of these would be a better way to improve the quality of teaching?" Forty-nine percent of superintendents and forty-four percent of principals said "expand professional development." Only 10 percent of superintendents and 9 percent of principals said "implement merit pay for teachers." Public Agenda, *Rolling Up Their Sleeves: Superintendents and Principals Talk about What's Needed to Fix Public Schools* (New York: Public Agenda, 2003), 30.

30. Some critics of tying pay to student performance suggest an alternative: pay increases that use performance assessments based on classroom observations or portfolios, like those associated with licensure or NBPTS certification. Nation Commission on Teaching and America's Future, *What Matters Most: Teaching for America's Future* (Washington, DC: NCTAF, 1996), 100.

31. Jacob L. Vigdor, "Teacher Salary Bonuses in North Carolina," in *Performance Incentives: Their Growing Impact on American K–12 Education*, ed. Matthew Springer (Washington, DC: Brookings Institution, 2009), 246.

32. *Quality Counts 2008*, "States Experiment with Pay for Performance," *Education Week*, 2008, 31 (Of the seven states with pay-for-performance programs as of 2008, two were based exclusively on whole school performance, and the rest were a mixture of individual and group awards).

33. The contract Washington finally negotiated with its union after two years of contentious bargaining reflects that view: The parties have agreed to a two-track system, where teachers can elect to join a pay for performance track that will make bonus

payments to individual teachers, with student test scores one of multiple evaluation measures. *Education Week*, "Foundations to Subsidize Merit Pay in D.C. Teachers' Pact," April 21, 2010, 11.

34. United States Chamber of Commerce, *Leaders and Laggards* (Washington, DC: U.S. Chamber of Commerce, 2009), 30–31 ("Ron Wilke, the principal of a Q Comp [Minnesota's pay for performance plan] school in La Crescent-Hokah School District, explains that the program has changed how the school operates. Teachers are collaborating more and keeping their eye on the school's central goal. 'We rely heavily on student achievement data and focusing on student need,' Wilke says. 'That's what really drives things.'").

35. These examples do point out one concern that Professor Johnson had with group bonuses. If the group upon whose performance the award is based is too large—an entire high school, for example—it may seem to any individual teacher that her effort is not likely to influence the final results. However, if the award is made to a group that is small enough, like those fifth grade teachers, an individual teacher may think her effort will significantly increase the possibility of qualifying and will be more likely to stimulate the desired behavior.

36. Public Agenda, *Stand By Me: What Teachers Really Think about Unions, Merit Pay and Other Professional Matters* (New York: Public Agenda, 2003), 26. A more recent survey of teachers confirms the same perception. Scholastic, Inc., Bill and Melinda Gates Foundation, *Primary Sources: America's Teachers on America's Schools* (Seattle, WA: Gates Foundation, 2010), 42.

37. See, for example, The Teaching Commission, *Teaching at Risk: Progress & Potholes* (New York: The Teaching Commission, 2006), 30.

38. *New York Times*, "Teachers Agree to Bonus Tied to Scores," Oct. 18, 2007 (retrieved from www.nytimes.com/2007/10/18/education/18schools.html on Oct. 18, 2007).

39. The Teaching Commission, *Teaching at Risk*, 26.

40. Susan Moore Johnson, *Second-Stage Teachers and Coaching: Building School Capacity and a Teaching Career* (paper presented for the 2009 Annual Meeting of the American Educational Research Association, San Diego, CA, April 13–17, 2009), 5.

41. Jonah E. Rockoff, "The Impact of Individual Teachers on Student Achievement: Evidence from Panel Data," *American Economic Review* 94, no. 2 (May 2004): 247–52; Eric A. Hanushek and Steven G. Rivkin, "How to Improve the Supply of High-Quality Teachers," in *Education Policy 2004*, ed. Diane Ravitch (Washington, DC: Brookings Institution, 2004), 16.

42. Most places are not as reasonably structured. For example, Broward County, Florida, gives teachers a $320 bonus for their first ten years on the job, but "backloads" $20,000 of experience-based pay increases between years eighteen and twenty-one. That certainly boosts teacher pensions, but it is equally certain not to have any effect on student performance. Chad Alderman, *Ladders of Success: Keeping Teacher Pay on Schedule* (Washington, DC: Education Sector, 2009) (retrieved from www.educationsector.org/analysis/analysis_show.htm on Dec. 29, 2009).

43. National Commission on Teaching for America's Future, *What Matters Most: Teaching for America's Future* (Washington, DC: NCTAF, 1996), 97.

44. In the chapter on ethics, we are going to return to this subject in the context of identifying those who move up the career ladder based on merit, rather than cronyism. Prior career ladders have failed when they have not been fairly administered. Morgaen L. Donaldson, "Building a Better Career Ladder," in *Recruiting, Retaining, and Supporting Highly Qualified Teachers*, ed. Caroline Chauncey (Cambridge, MA: Harvard Education Press, 2005), 80.

45. Adam Urbanski and Carl O'Connell, *Transforming the Profession of Teaching: It Starts at the Beginning* (Washington, DC: NCTAF, 2006) (retrieved from www.nctaf.org/article/?g=0&tsc=3&tsc-13&tssc=0&ta=39 on Dec. 21, 2009).

46. *New Haven Register*, "City Teachers Contract Hailed as Model," Oct. 27, 2009 (retrieved from www.nhregister.com/articles/2009/10/27/news/new_haven/a1_--re-

formforum_1027.txt on Dec. 9, 2009); *Education Week*, "Three New Pay Elements in Pittsburgh Teacher Pact," June 15, 2010 (retrieved from www.edweek.org/edweek. teacherbeat/2010/06/philly_contract_contains_new_p.html on Dec. 3, 2010); *Education Week*, "Baltimore Teacher Union Signs Performance-Pay Pact," Dec. 13, 2010 (retrieved from www.edweek.org/ew/articles/2010/12/11/392500mdbaltimoretap.html on Dec. 13, 2010).

47. Bill Gates, along with many education reformers, has argued the approach has extraordinary implications for reform across the country. *New York Times*, "Gates Urges School Budget Overhaul," Nov. 19, 2010 (retrieved from www.nytimes.com/2010/11/19/us/19gates.html on Nov. 19, 2010).

48. See, for example, Bryan C. Hassel and Dan Katzir, "Teacher Incentive Fund: Trivial or Transformative?" *Education Week*, April 20, 2010 (retrieved from www.edweek.org/ew/articles/2010/04/21/29hassel_ep.h29.html on April 23, 2010).

49. NCES (IES), table 67 (Digest of Education Statistics)—Highest degree earned, years of full-time teaching experience, and average class size for teachers in public elementary and secondary schools by state: 2003–04 (retrieved from www.nces.ed. gov/programs/digest/d08/tables.dto8_067.asp on Dec. 7, 2009).

50. Randy Ross, *Effective Teacher Development through Salary Incentives* (Santa Monica, CA: RAND Corp., 1994), cited in National Commission on Teaching and America's Future, *What Matters Most: Teaching for America's Future* (Washington, DC: NCTAF, 1996), 84, 120.

51. *Education Week*, "Districts Try Out Revamped Teacher-Pay Systems," Nov. 9, 2010 (retrieved from www.edweek.org/ew/articles/2010/11/10/11degress_ep.h30.html on Nov. 9, 2010).

52. Eric A. Hanushek and Steven G. Rivkin, "How to Improve the Supply of High Quality Teachers," in *Education Policy 2004*, ed. Diane Ravitch (Washington, DC: Brookings Institution, 2004), 14.

53. Patricia Wasley and Marguerite Roza, "The 'Master's Pay Bump': Why Ending It Shouldn't Frighten Ed. Schools," *Education Week*, Dec. 1, 2009 (retrieved from www.edweek.org/ew/articles/2009-12-02/13roza.h29.html on Dec. 2, 2009).

54. Recent NCES data showed that the average teacher starting salary increased only $3,100 for a master's, but $9,400 for ten years teaching experience, and the highest possible step increase on the typical salary schedule, which would be a combination of years and degrees, was worth $28,600. NCES (IES)—table 2 (SASS)—Percentage of public school districts that had salary schedules for teachers and among those that had salary schedules, the average yearly teacher base salary, by various levels of degrees and experience and selected public school district characteristics: 2007–08.

55. Marguerite Roza, *Frozen Assets: Rethinking Teacher Contracts Could Free Billions for School Reform* (Washington, DC: Education Sector Reports, 2007), 3. That is roughly the same conclusion reached by a different 2002 study that estimated that 17 percent of public K–12 *expenditures on instruction* are spent on teacher seniority, Dale Ballou and Michael Podgursky, "Returns to Seniority among Public School Teachers," *Journal of Human Resources* 37, no. 4 (2002): 893. The study also suggests looking at other parts of teachers' contracts, such as paid professional development days, paid sick leave, class-size limitations, required use of teachers' aides, and benefits as sources of additional funds. However, collectively, all these expenditures do not come close to experience and education salary supplements in size, and the merits of reducing or eliminating these sources requires a discussion beyond the scope of this book. At least one, paid professional development days, which the report estimates at just over 1 percent of all K–12 school spending, or $5.5 billion, probably stays dedicated to professional development, although the way it is used may be new. In any event, the study's suggestion that there are other sources of possible funds in teacher's contracts is worth keeping in mind if the proposed pot is not large enough to do everything one wants.

56. *Education Week*, "Personnel Costs Prove Tough to Contain," Jan. 5, 2011 (retrieved from www.edweek.org.ew.articles.2011/01.13/16personnel.h30.html on Jan. 12, 2011); *Education Week*, "Districts Try Out Revamped Teacher-Pay Systems," Nov. 9,

2010 (retrieved from www.edweek.org/ew/articles/2010/11/10/11degrees_ep.h30.html on Nov. 9, 2010).

57. NCES (IES), Fast Facts, http://nces.ed.gov/fastfacts/display.asp.

58. A review of salary schedules should convince even skeptics that experience pay is costly. For example, under the current North Carolina salary schedule, a teacher at the first step of the M schedule will make $33,700, while someone on step 30 will make $56,680, a difference of $23,020, or 41 percent (www.ncpublicschools.org/fbs/finance/salary).

FIFTEEN

The Coleman Report Effect on Motivation: Do Teachers Have Low Expectations of Poor Kids?

We cannot leave the subject of teacher motivation without touching on one more troublesome issue.

Section 402 of the Civil Rights Act of 1964 required the writing of a report concerning "the lack of availability of equal education opportunities . . . in the United States. . . ." The report, entitled *Equality of Education Opportunity*, has subsequently become known as the "Coleman Report," after its principal author, Professor James S. Coleman.[1]

Coleman found that minority students who believed they would be able to control their environments through reasonable effort did better on achievement tests than those who did not.[2] Perhaps even more importantly, Coleman concluded that schools have less influence over students' achievement than do their backgrounds and homes:

> Taking all these results together, one implication stands out above all: That schools bring little influence to bear on a child's achievement that is independent of his background and general social context; and that this very lack of an independent effect means that the inequalities imposed on children by their home, neighborhood, and peer environment are carried along to become the inequalities with which they confront adult life at the end of school.[3]

That conclusion reverberates in school hallways all over the country—as it has for most of the last forty-five years. It has a fundamental, negative effect on teachers' expectations for their students. That attitude undercuts everything else, like pay for performance, that a school might do to motivate teachers to give it their best shot.

For example, a review of five studies of successful turnaround schools found that when, during meetings, teachers discussed things going on at a child's home or other problems over which they exercised little control, they were discouraged.[4] The 2008 *MetLife Survey* confirms the extent of the problem: 83 percent of urban principals and 65 percent of urban teachers (and 49 percent of teachers overall) say that poverty hinders learning for at least a quarter of their students.[5]

It may also be why pay tied to student performance elicits a strong, negative response among some teachers. One 2009 Public Agenda survey found that 54 percent of teachers do not think teacher pay should be tied to student performance because they believe so much of that achievement is dependent on parents and home life.[6]

The difficulty of coming to grips with the problem has shot through hearings on the reauthorization of No Child Left Behind.[7] For example, the National Council on State Legislatures has issued a position paper blaming the federal government for failing to take all consequences of poverty into account in its design of No Child Left Behind testing and accountability.[8] The problem with that position and many put forward by other critics: They offered no clear, alternative version of accountability where all those issues were taken into account.

SO WHAT? LIVING IN A "NO EXCUSES" WORLD

What most distinguishes the districts I visited that had succeeded in becoming good or great districts without more money, without pay for performance, and without doing away with tenure was that they had succeeded in instilling the belief that every child can learn. They truly were "no excuses" districts. They did not just say "we're a no excuses district." They meant it.

Gerald Anderson in Brazosport may have taken the most hard-line approach, but in some ways it makes sense. I asked him to describe his program to reach out to uninvolved parents. He told me he did not have one. I was shocked. Here was a successful superintendent. How could he not have had a parent outreach program? His reason: Outreach programs rarely succeeded in bringing in large numbers of parents from low socioeconomic groups. He was not going to try such a program and fail, because if he did, it would give his teachers an excuse to rationalize failure with their kids. He had a no-excuses district; his kids were going to succeed. Period.

Jean-Claude Brizard, the superintendent in snowy Rochester (and, as of 2011, the superintendent in Chicago), did something similar in 2008, when he arrived in the district. To emphasize there were "no excuses," he kept schools open even when temperatures fell to subzero in the middle of the winter. According to him, the kids did not have a day to lose.[9]

Even if no one else demonstrated the point in such dramatic fashion, all the highly successful districts are, in their own ways, "no excuses" districts.[10] Districts like Long Beach, Brownsville, and Aldine have simply made it their mission that every child *will* learn. It is now an accepted part of the belief system.

Many teachers actually agree that it is possible to overcome the barriers facing low-income kids. There is considerable evidence they believe that good teachers can overcome poverty's obstacles.[11] Those reports are no secret. The same 2009 Public Agenda survey cited above found that 54 percent of new teachers believe teacher quality is just as important for student achievement as parents and socioeconomic factors.[12] Another 2009 Public Agenda survey found that 75 percent of teachers agreed with the statement that "good teachers can lead all students to learn, even those from poor families or who have uninvolved parents."[13]

There is one thing "no excuses" is not. It is not an excuse to be used in the larger political education wars. Liberals are not excused from having high expectations for student achievement despite all of the country's social problems. And conservatives are not excused from an obligation to address those problems, even if the schools do well in the face of the daunting challenges they create.

The bottom line is probably a message like this one, to be given new teachers during their summer induction:

> Look, teaching poor kids is a challenge. No doubt. It is hard, but if you teach at a school filled with poor kids, you are not going to be cut any slack. Whatever the problems these kids face, we know good teaching and good schools can make a difference in their lives. We are not going to lower the bar for how we measure success. The best you are going to get is the knowledge that when you celebrate your victories, they are going to be sweeter than if you had worked elsewhere because you will know that the success is because you and your students walked through the fire and came out the other side.

NOTES

1. James S. Coleman et al., *Equality of Education Opportunity* (Washington, DC: U.S. Department of Health, Education, and Welfare, 1966).
2. Coleman, *Equality of Education Opportunity*, 320–21.
3. Coleman, *Equality of Education Opportunity*, 325.
4. Daniel L. Duke, "What We Know and Don't Know about Improving Low-Performing Schools," *Phi Delta Kappan* 87, no. 10 (June 2006): 732.
5. *MetLife Survey of the American Teacher* (New York: Metropolitan Life Ins. Co., 2008), 28, 29.
6. Public Agenda, *Our Money, Our Schools: Ten Top Findings from Our Research Team* (Washington, DC: Public Agenda, 2009), 23. See also Public Agenda, *Stand by Me: What Teachers Really Think about Unions, Merit Pay and Other Professional Matters* (New York: Public Agenda, 2003), 15 (Fifty-nine percent of teachers said it was not fair to hold teachers accountable for things that affect student learning but are beyond their con-

trol. However, the same survey found that 48 percent of teachers believe that classroom effort is mainly determined by what teachers do to motivate them, versus 42 percent who believe it is determined by the motivation that students bring with them from other sources.)

7. *Education Week*, "Needs of 'Whole Child' May Factor in ESEA Renewal," April 27, 2010 (retrieved from www.edweek.org/ew/articles/201/04/28/30esea_ep.h29.html on April 27, 2010).

8. National Conference of State Legislatures, *Education at a Crossroads: A New Path for Federal and State Education Policy* (Denver, CO: National Conference of State Legislatures, 2010), 7.

9. *Rochester Democrat Chronicle*, "Jean-Claude Brizard Driven to Improve Schools," Oct. 25, 2010 (retrieved from www.democratandchronicle.com/article/20101025/NEWS01/10250305/Brizard-driven-to-improve-schools&referrer=-NEWSFRONT CAROUSEL on Oct. 28, 2010).

10. Others have made the same observation about other highly successful districts. Karen Chenoweth, *How It's Being Done: Urgent Lessons from Unexpected Schools* (Cambridge, MA: Harvard Education Press, 2009), 186.

11. William L. Sanders and June C. Rivers, *Cumulative and Residual Effects of Teachers on Future Student Academic Achievement* (Knoxville, TN: University of Tennessee Value-Added Research Center, 1996) ("Differences in student achievement of 50 percentile points were observed as a result of teacher sequence after only three years"); Steven G. Rivkin, Eric A. Hanushek, and John F. Kain, *Teachers, Schools, and Academic Achievement*, Working Paper No. 6691 (Washington, DC: National Bureau of Economic Research, 2001), 449 ("The issue of whether or not there is significant variation in school quality has lingered, quite inappropriately, since the original Coleman Report. This analysis identifies large differences in the quality of instruction in a way that rules out the possibility that the observed differences are driven by family factors."); Byron Auguste, Bryan Hancock, and Matt Miller, "America's Permanent Education Recession," *Teachers College Record*, Nov. 3, 2009 ("So while the price of the systems gap is remarkably high, the dramatic differences in student achievement between schools and school systems serving similar students are reason for hope. . . . California and Texas for example are two large states with similar demographics. Yet Texas students perform one to two years ahead of California students at the same age, even while having less income per capita and spending less money per pupil."); Linda Darling-Hammond, "How Teacher Education Matters," *Journal of Teacher Education* 51, no. 3 (2000): 51, 166; Linda Darling-Hammond and Gary Sykes, "Wanted: A National Teacher Supply Policy for Education: The Right Way to Meet the 'Highly Qualified Teacher' Challenge," *Education Policy Analysis Archives* 11, no. 33 (Sept. 2003): 10 (various studies cited).

12. Darling-Hammond and Sykes, "Wanted: A National Teacher Supply Policy for Education,", 33.

13. Jean Johnson, Andrew Yarrow, Jonathan Rochkind, and Amber Ott, *Teaching for a Living: How Teachers See the Profession Today* (New York: Public Agenda, 2009), question 21 results.

SIXTEEN

The Special Challenge of Hard-to-Staff Schools

All the issues about recruiting, training, and motivating teachers come together when we talk about how to fix hard-to-staff schools—a shorthand euphemism for those schools with high levels of poverty, parental disengagement, and fiscal and leadership deficits. In these schools, we absolutely have to get teacher recruiting, training, and motivating right.

THE BIGGEST PROBLEM: RECRUITMENT

All districts recruit teachers; but there all similarities end. Twenty-eight percent of new teachers in low-income schools are hired after the school year has already started while only 8 percent of new teachers in high-income schools are.[1] A teacher is not going to go somewhere unless asked, and low-income schools just do not ask before many of the good teachers are long gone.

Effective recruitment turns on three factors. First, the human resources department must be up to the task of advertising openings, collecting and sorting résumés, vetting candidates, and possibly participating in selection. Second, the district's (or state's) labor policies must help, rather than hinder, the job of filling the vacancies with competent teachers.[2] Third, as we discussed in chapter 3, *when* districts find out how much money they have to spend is as critical as *how much* it turns out to be. If some districts know earlier than others how much money they have, they are going to have an unfair advantage in making offers first.

One thing that recruitment and placement does not turn on is the definition of a "highly qualified" teacher, which we discussed in chapter 13. Those who have promoted a stringent test for "highly qualified" teachers somehow see the enforcement of a strict application of the standard as a way to fix the problem of hard-to-staff schools.[3] It is not. Even if a state raises the overall quality of teachers by enforcing the rules or making the definition more stringent, the hard-to-staff schools are still going to have the worst teachers. There will be no change in equities. The kids who need the best teachers still will not get them.

The Human Resources Department as a Pothole

During the 1990s and the early years of the twenty-first century, some reform superintendents focused on the woeful performance of their district's human resources departments, which were a major problem on the road to reform. They failed to advertise, lost résumés, delayed sending out offers. The list of sins is long.[4]

On top of the best recruits going elsewhere, those who did sign up were more likely to be surprised by workplace conditions or not have their expectations met. And they were more likely to leave.[5]

Districts' business processes (see chapter 26) have often been a weak link in school reform, although they rarely receive the attention they deserve. These business departments are starved for funds that are always prioritized for instruction and are often led by former teachers who have no business being on the business side of the district. In many other departments that play a supporting role, their weak performance principally translates into districts wasting money. Here it is worse: Districts with poor human resources departments waste opportunity.[6]

Tom Payzant faced an acute human resources problem in Boston.[7] A significant part of his reform effort there focused on getting that department to function better. He installed professional management, a much-enhanced computer system, and pushed to get vacancies established, and recruiting started, earlier than had been done before.

The key way to test an HR department's efficiency: Just ask by what dates were half, three-quarters, and finally all tenure-track teachers hired in the prior year. If the dates are March, April and June, HR is doing fine. If the dates are June, August, and October, HR is not.

The Havoc of Outdated Labor Policies

Although the precise terms may vary, teachers have three contract rights that bedevil hiring, especially in urban districts, and most particularly in schools that are hard to staff.[8]

First, in many states, law guarantees teachers the right to resign at any time on some relatively short notice, like sixty or ninety days. And if the law does not provide the right, a contract may. In schools with low turnover, it is not a problem. But hard-to-staff schools have, by definition, high turnover. There are just more people leaving, and the law allows them to do so in unpredictable fashion.

Second, current teachers often have the right to bid on vacancies before the positions can be opened to outsiders. So even if a teacher gives notice in January that he or she is not intending to be back the next September, by the time the job is posted and the time required for other teachers to bid for it has passed, it may be late spring before outside candidates are aware of its existence. And if a current district teacher gets the job, the process repeats. . . .

Finally, many districts have historically given tenured teachers various rights to jobs even where there are no vacancies. It is the practice of "bumping," which has been discussed before. If a school closed, a displaced senior teacher might be able to "bump" a more junior teacher out of a position at another school. That in turn, of course, would lead to a cascading effect, depending on how the contract was written. Many districts, including New York, have now won union agreement to do away with some or all bumping, but it is not completely eliminated.[9]

Where it has not been eliminated, it has disastrous consequences. Eric Gordon, the chief academic officer in Cleveland (and now the CEO), where the district has faced declining enrollment, told me that these contract obligations have made an already troubling situation even worse. As enrollment declined, teachers had to be laid off. That meant forcing young teachers to leave, no matter how good they were, and it broke up teams of teachers who were used to working together. It forced schools to accept teachers who, although certified to teach the subjects they were assigned, often did not have the additional training and professional development of those who were displaced, such as Montessori training or training in a new school model. That left everyone demoralized.

In Los Angeles in 2010 the same issue led to legal action. A combination of seniority and bumping meant that up to half the teachers in at least three low-income, hard-to-staff schools were replaced as a consequence of the district's decision to cut staff in response to its budget distress.[10] The lawsuit's settlement stopped the practice in those schools, but the union has vowed to oppose any further erosion of seniority rights.[11]

These rules foster "the dance of the lemons." Teacher A is not doing well in School Z. The principal does not want to go through the problematic exercise of writing up a poor evaluation or trying to get the teacher fired. The teacher does not want the bad evaluation. They agree that it is best for all concerned for the teacher to find a position at some other school. Teacher A now gets to inflict some more bad teaching on School Y. School Y's principal may harbor doubts about A's competence but has no record on which to object and a contract provision with which to comply.[12] So the bad teaching just gets imposed on a new set of kids.

The late funding of poor districts that are heavily dependent on state aid compounds all of these contract issues. States' tax bases have historically been far less stable than those of local jurisdictions that rely on property taxes. As a consequence, school districts relying on state aid often will not act on hiring until late spring or summer, when their actual appropriation is established. Richer districts with stable funding sources do not suffer the same fate; they will have been out recruiting the best and brightest of the current crop since early in the year.

THE REST OF A STRATEGY TO STAFF HARD-TO-STAFF SCHOOLS

Recruiting early and effectively is good. It is not enough. According to one recent California survey, 20 percent of teachers who were staying in the profession expressed interest in transferring to a high-poverty school if teaching and learning conditions were improved and if additional compensation were offered.[13]

The most important way of keeping teachers in any school is to do the things we discussed at the beginning of the section on training (see chapter 8). All of these things are true for any school.[14] For hard-to-staff schools, however, there are some additional needs.[15]

School Safety

Thankfully, school violence has declined as an issue for teachers over the past decade. However, retention studies still often note that teachers leave schools where they are concerned for their physical safety, either in school or in the neighborhood in which the school is located.[16]

The more important point is that schools can employ strategies starting in elementary school that do remarkably well at steering kids away from violence. "Not losing sight of a student," which we discuss next, can make a big difference. Sometimes, it is as simple as making the effort to have an adult focus on every child, treat that child with respect, and offer advice and support when needed. The Green Dot charter organization took over Locke High School in Los Angeles in 2008. Locke is infamous for its gang violence, which had often been out of control when the school was part of Los Angeles Unified School District. Green Dot's different and respectful approach to kids has thus far calmed the waters and refocused kids on learning.

An Attractive Place to Teach

Kaya Henderson pointed out that Washington schools have tried to recruit accomplished teachers to join troubled schools' faculties. They do not want to go, she says, not just because it may be a more challenging group of kids than the ones they currently have, but also because they are not looking forward to working with the principal and faculty. The district can unilaterally deal with the principal, but teachers are different.

Henderson suggested that it might be easier in some cases to offer to let teachers organize a group that would collectively take over an entire fourth grade or high school English department.[17] Arlene Ackerman has done much the same thing in Philadelphia.[18]

Charlotte, North Carolina, has been one of the most successful districts dealing with school turnarounds. Superintendent Peter Gorman ran a contest to identify the best principals in the district, and then made them an offer "they could not refuse." He proposed they take over the worst schools in the district, and he allowed them to pick an eight-person transformation team. And they could transfer up to five teachers out of the school in order to build a collaborative team. Scores in the first seven schools transformed rose significantly in just the first year of the program.[19] Other cities, including Boston, have followed the same route, if not in such a sweeping way.[20]

No Child Left Behind's reconstitution remedy, where a school is closed and faculty fired, highlights another problem for hard-to-staff schools.[21] Teachers already at the school have an incentive to leave before the place is closed down, and outsiders question why they should go.[22] Individual teachers, or even small groups, may not want to transfer to a place where their presence is not sufficient to turn things around because the school may be closed, leaving them to find another position somewhere else. The law and local labor contracts need to be able to afford good teachers adequate security that assures them they will not be caught up in a sanctions process.

No More Budget Tricks: When Treating All Schools Equally Is Not Equal

Then there is the issue of "combat pay." Should districts try to attract and hold teachers to hard-to-staff schools by paying them more?

Before getting to that issue, however, there is a preliminary financial issue that should first be resolved: Many districts employ something called "salary cost averaging," which treats every faculty member as if he or she costs the district the same amount of money. It is a fraud that hurts the schools that need the money most.

Here is how "averaging" works: One school may have an *actual* average salary of $50,000 and another may have an *actual* average salary of $70,000, but the district's books *record* that the faculties at both schools average $60,000. What looks like equal support to both schools really is not. As a result, schools with younger faculty (that is, the hard-to-staff ones) do not even get an equal amount of financial support for teachers. They actually receive *less* money than schools with older faculty (to which senior teachers have fled). By the trick of "averaging," those discrepancies are not publicly reported, hiding how much less is actually devoted to educating kids in hard-to-staff schools.[23]

Districts argue that they do not want principals to have to take into account the cost of particular teachers when choosing staff, but the concern is misplaced. What the policy really does is allow attractive schools to accumulate older, more experienced—and higher-paid—teachers because it does not cap the total amount of money available to that school for faculty pay and benefits. Averaging simply makes the central office's budgeting operation complicit in denying hard-to-staff schools a lever to get more experienced faculty.

That leaves the larger question: What to do with the schools in the district that have more needs?

The first point is that there has to be recognition that lock-step equity among schools is not real equity. Otherwise, there is no philosophical or moral basis for additional financial support. Both Jerry Weast in Montgomery County and Gerald Anderson in Brazosport initially faced budgeting systems that treated all schools equally. Both knew they had to change the system, and they were lucky. They had school boards that understood the need for providing more resources for high-poverty schools and had the courage to vote for budgets that recognized the difference.

It is more likely to happen if superintendents can recast the policy in a way that continues to acknowledge the importance of "equity," while still reaching the conclusion that every child is properly served. Both Weast and Anderson found a similar rationale: In essence, their districts' commitment is that every student receives the same education: If someone needs help, they get it; if someone should be pushed ahead with enrichment programs, they get that, too. It just happens that low-performing, high-poverty schools need more of the resources so that every one of their children gets the same help offered in more middle-class schools.

Alternatively, Arlene Ackerman in Philadelphia has been an advocate of "weighted student" budgeting, which bases allocations on student characteristics, such as poverty, that track what it actually costs to educate such children. That winds up sending more money to schools with more poor kids and gives principals some greater flexibility.

Long Beach has solved the matter in another way: aggressively pursuing open enrollment. By spreading the problems out, equalizing the demographics, differences in school populations have shrunk and with them the need for differences in budget allocations.

Paying More for Teaching in Hard-to-Staff Schools

Paying more to teachers in hard-to-staff schools, known as "combat pay," has attracted much attention, especially in 2009 when the Obama administration made it part of its Race to the Top discussion. As of 2008, twelve states provided pay incentives to teach in high-poverty schools;

ten others had incentives for teaching in low-performing poor schools (which were also generally high poverty, although they did not have to be).[24] In other states, districts like Memphis are tackling these problems head-on, approaching unions for contract modifications and foundations for additional money.[25] Unfortunately, few of these programs have been in place long enough to determine whether the idea is effective.[26]

In one of the only studies thus far, North Carolina researchers found that an annual $1,800 bonus for teaching in a high-poverty school (or for being certified in math, science, or special education) reduced turnover among targeted teachers by 17 percent.[27] However, that number may be low. An older Texas study estimated that, assuming no improvement in working conditions, it would take a salary differential of 25 percent for new female teachers, and 40 percent for those with three to five years' experience, to prevent them from switching from an urban to a suburban district.[28]

Joel Packer, a lobbyist at the National Education Association when I interviewed him, told me that he thought combat pay was not the right way to solve the problem. The important issues, in Packer's view, are working conditions and the caliber of the principal in the school. If both are good, then there will not be significant turnover of teachers already there.

Some of the districts I visited support his view.[29] David Stuckwisch in Portsmouth, Virginia, for example, won accreditation for eighteen of his twenty-three schools without combat pay by improving working conditions and finding better principals. San Diego proves the same point—in reverse. When Carl Cohn tried to get good teachers to go to San Diego's hard-to-staff schools, the issue was not money. They refused because those schools had the worst principals.

Other districts, like those in Chicago and Philadelphia, have tried to move forward with reform on a broad scale for over a decade, but still have only had mixed results. Until we fix the working conditions at these schools, we may never know whether "combat pay" has an impact. For the moment, continuing to experiment with what might work seems to make a lot of sense.

CELEBRATE WALKING THROUGH THE FIRE

One final point about hard-to-staff schools. We need to think hard about what really is a good school.

In Los Angeles, administrators and teachers would call Warner Avenue Elementary, located in the heart of tony Westwood, a good school. It had to be; its students, the kids of the wealthy lawyers and doctors and UCLA academics who lived in the neighborhood, got great scores on their standardized tests and eventually went to college. People rarely spoke in the same way about 52nd St. or 95th St. Elementary Schools, both of which are located in the heart of South-Central Los Angeles, although their Latino and African American kids scored far better than anyone might expect.

At a poor school it is a success of immense proportions to get 80 percent of ninth graders to graduate in four years and to have even 70 percent of the class go on to college—any college. Is this a "good school"? And then there are—there really are—the "90-90-90" schools, where 90 percent of the students are minority, 90 percent are free and reduced lunch, and 90 percent are performing at or above proficient on standardized tests.[30] These are not just good schools. These are great schools. But they are rarely celebrated beyond the few people who work in them or send their kids to them.

If our goal is for teachers to *want* to go to hard-to-staff schools, we have to rethink what a great school is. We need to start focusing on those where success comes after a walk through that fire, not a ride in an air-conditioned limousine.

WHAT WE NEED TO DO

In order to solve the problems of hard-to-staff schools, we have a great deal of work to do:

- A "no excuses" policy is essential in a hard-to-staff school.
- The human resources operation has to be efficient. Figure out when teachers are hired and make a ruckus if more than a few are hired after June.
- Go to the state legislatures and lobby to make state labor policies consistent with putting student achievement first. Enshrine principals' and incumbent teachers' rights to pick the teachers with whom they want to work.
- Commit to a policy that every child is afforded the same opportunities. If it happens that more money needs to be spent at some schools in order to fulfill the promise, support that commitment.
- Focus on school working conditions and school safety. Remember, it is not just about money. It is about how the money is used.
- Experiment with "combat pay," and, if it seems to work, make it a permanent part of a compensation overhaul.
- Remember to celebrate the low-income schools that really do a good job. They are what education should be all about.

NOTES

1. Susan Moore Johnson, Susan M. Kardos, David Kauffman, Edward Liu, and Morgaen L. Donaldsen, "The Support Gap: New Teachers' Early Experiences in High-Income and Low-Income Schools," *Education Policy Analysis Archives* 12, no. 61 (Oct. 29, 2004): 8.

2. National Commission on Teaching and America's Future, NCTAF State Partners, *Unraveling the 'Teacher Shortage' Problem: Teacher Retention Is the Key* (Washington, DC: NCTAF, 2002), 6.

3. See, for example, *New York Times*, "The 'Highly Qualified Teacher' Dodge," Nov. 13, 2009 (retrieved from www.nytimes.com/2009/11/13/opinion/13fri2.html on Nov. 13, 2009).

4. National Commission on Teaching and America's Future, *What Matters Most: Teaching for America's Future* (Washington, DC: NCTAF, 1996), 36; Strategic Management of Human Capital/Consortium for Public Research in Education, *Cross-Case Analysis* (Madison, WI: CPRE, 2008).

5. Johnson et al., "The Support Gap," 4.

6. Strategic Management of Human Capital/Consortium for Public Research in Education, *Taking Human Capital Seriously: Talented Teachers in Every Classroom, Talented Principals in Every School* (Philadelphia: CPRE, 2009), 14.

7. Strategic Management of Human Capital, *Boston* (Madison, WI: CPRE, 2008) (retrieved from www.smhc-cpre.org).

8. Jessica Levin, Jennifer Mulhern, and Joan Schnuck, *Unintended Consequences: The Case for Reforming Staffing Rules in Urban Teachers Union Contracts* (New York: The New Teacher Project, 2005); Jessica Levin and Meredith Quinn, *Missed Opportunities: How We Keep High-Quality Teachers Out of Urban Classrooms* (New York: The New Teacher Project, 2003).

9. Payzant's principals in Boston tried to get around the problem by hiding the existence of the vacancy until the bidding period had passed, when they would be free to hire an outsider. Payzant was able to make some changes in the union contract to speed the process, but even his efforts did not eliminate it entirely. A study by The New Teacher Project found that Boston was not alone in being hamstrung by labor rules. In a survey it conducted to assess the effect of such provisions, it discovered that in one of the five districts it investigated, 47 percent of surveyed principals did the same thing. Levin, Mulhern, and Schnuck, *Unintended Consequences*, 5. In Philadelphia Arlene Ackerman made doing away with seniority in hiring a major goal of her 2009 bargaining with the teachers union, but the union resisted. *Education Week*, "Leader in Phila. Seeks Changes in Teacher Rules," Sept. 2, 2009 (retrieved from www.edweek. org/ew/articles/2009/09/02.philadelphia.h29.html on Sept. 10, 2009). In the winter of 2010, the two sides reached agreement, with Ackerman winning the right to have school sites control 90 percent of their hiring. In troubled locations, designated as "Renaissance Schools," according to the new agreement, all faculty would have to reapply for positions and no more than 50 percent could be rehired. *Philadelphia Inquirer*, "Philadelphia Teachers Approve Contract," Jan. 21, 2010 (retrieved from www. philly.com/phully/education/20100121Philadelphia_teachers_approve_contract.html on April 14, 2010).

10. *Los Angeles Daily News*, "LAUSD Teacher Seniority Settlement Paves the Way for Real Reform," October 8, 2010 (retrieved from www.dailynews.com/opinions.ci_16284442 on Oct. 18, 2010). (LAUSD settled an American Civil Liberties Union suit challenging the practice by agreeing to renegotiate layoff rules.)

11. The combination of seniority and bumping can also be particularly toxic in urban districts, which are good places for a robust alternative certification program. In one of the districts studied by The New Teacher Project, any position filled after June had to be posted for voluntary transfer the next year. In another, it was any position after September 1. In another district, any position held by an alternatively certified teacher had to be posted when the alternatively certified teacher's program was com-

pleted, even if that new teacher had done well. In all three districts, these teachers could be "bumped." Levin, Mulhern, and Schnuck, *Unintended Consequences*, 24.

12. Levin, Mulhern, and Schnuck, *Unintended Consequences*, 16–17. (In two of the districts surveyed, NTP found 26 percent and 37 percent of principals had encouraged a poorly performing teacher to transfer.)

13. Ken Futernick, *A Possible Dream: Retaining California Teachers So All Students Learn* (Sacramento: The Center for Teacher Quality, California State University Sacramento, 2007), 30 (8 percent said they would transfer without increased salary if the conditions were right).

14. Facilities, supplies, and administrative support are frequently cited by teachers as being far more significant problems in low-income schools. Louis Harris, *New Survey of California Teaches Reveals Serious Problems in Classrooms: Starkly Unequal Conditions for African American, Latino Students, and Broad Teacher Support for Transferring More Control, Accountability from Districts to Schools* (San Francisco: Peter Harris Research Group, 2004).

15. One good summary of all the required changes is the Learning First Alliance's *A Shared Responsibility: Staffing All High-Poverty, Low-Performing Schools with Effective Teachers and Administrators* (Washington, DC: Learning First Alliance, 2005).

16. Elaine Allensworth, Stephen Ponisciak, and Christopher Mazzeo, *The Schools Teachers Leave, Teacher Mobility in Chicago Public Schools* (Chicago: Consortium on Chicago School Research, June 2009), 20, 23; Public Agenda, *Stand by Me: What Teachers Really Think about Unions, Merit Pay and other Professional Matters* (New York: Public Agenda, 2003), 11 (35 percent of teachers in mostly minority schools believe their schools are safe, orderly, and respectful, while 68 percent of teachers in schools with few minority students believe that.).

17. One survey suggests that teachers may doubt whether this strategy can work. A 2003 Public Agenda survey found that 65 percent of teachers believe that truly good teachers can overcome barriers such as poverty or uninvolved parents to get their students to learn, but only 26 percent of teachers in an earlier, 2000 Public Agenda survey said a group of exceptionally talented teachers on their own could turn things around in a school with low achievement. Public Agenda, *Stand by Me*, 16.

18. *Education Week*, "Leader in Phila. Seeks Changes in Teacher Rules," Sept. 2, 2009 (retrieved from www.edweek.org/ew/articles/2009/09/02.philadelphia.h29.html on Sept. 10, 2009).

19. *Charlotte Observer*, "Struggling Students + Best Teachers = Success," Sept. 16, 2010 (retrieved from www.charlotte observer.com/2010/09/16/1695566/struggling-students-best-teachers.html on Nov. 23, 2010); *Newsweek*, "An Offer They Wouldn't Refuse," Oct. 12, 2010 (retrieved from www.newsweek.com/2010/10/12/how-one-district-fixed-its-failing-schools.html on Jan. 21, 2011).

20. *New York Times*, "Lesson Plan in Boston Schools: Don't Go It Alone," Aug. 8, 2010 (retrieved from www.nytimes.com/2010/08/09/education/09winerip.html on Aug. 9, 2010).

21. Allensworth, Ponisciak, and Mazzeo, *The Schools Teachers Leave*, 20.

22. Linda Darling-Hammond and Gary Sykes, "Wanted: A National Teacher Supply Policy for Education: The Right Way to Meet the 'Highly Qualified Teacher' Challenge," *Education Policy Analysis Archives* 11, no. 33 (Sept. 2003): 24; Futernick, *A Possible Dream*, 60.

23. Marguerite Roza and Paul T. Hill, "How Within-District Spending Inequities Help Some Schools to Fail," in *Education Policy 2004*, ed. Diane Ravitch (Washington, DC: Brookings Institution, 2004), 201–23; Education Trust—West, "Study of the State's 112 Largest School Districts Shines Spotlights on Hidden Teacher Spending Gap at Individual Schools" (News Release, Sept. 14, 2005); Kelly Warner-King, "Salary Averaging Unfair to Teachers," *Seattle Post-Intelligencer*, May 29, 2003 (retrieved from www.seattlepi.com/opinion/124013_seattleschools29.html on Dec. 8, 2009).

24. *Quality Counts 2008*, "Human Resources a Weak Spot," *Education Week*, 2008, 17.

25. *Memphis Commercial-Appeal*, "Memphis City Schools Plan to Hire Teachers Early," Oct. 5, 2009 (retrieved from www.commercialappeal.com/news/2009/oct/05/mcs-pans-to-hire-teachers-early on Oct. 5, 2009).

26. In 2007–2008, 5.7 percent of districts had some pay incentive to get teachers to teach in a less desirable location. NCES (IES), table 5 (SASS)—Percentage of public school district that used pay incentives for various reasons, by state: 2007–08 (retrieved from http://nces.ed.gov/surveys/sass/tables.Sass0708_2009320_d1s_05.asp on Oct. 2, 2009).

27. Charles Clotfelter, Elizabeth Glennie, Helen Ladd, and Jacob Vigdor, "Would Higher Salaries Keep Teachers in High-Poverty Schools? Evidence from a Policy Intervention in North Carolina," *Journal of Public Economics* 92 (2008): 1352–70.

28. Eric A. Hanushek, John F. Kain, and Steven G. Rivkin, "The Revolving Door: A Path-Breaking Study of Teachers in Texas Reveals That Working Conditions Matter More Than Salary—Research," *Education Next*, Winter 2004 (retrieved from http://findarticles,com.p/articles/mi_m0MJG/is_1_4/ai_111734755/?tag=content;col1 on Dec. 29, 2009).

29. One recent study in Alabama reported the same result. Supportive school leadership, engaged community and parents, high-quality professional development, and an atmosphere of trust and respect, among other things, were more important than high salaries in influencing decisions to teach at low-performing schools. Michelle Exstrom, *What Teachers Need* (Santa Cruz, CA: UC Santa Cruz New Teacher Center Issue Brief, 2009) (retrieved from www.newteachercenter.org on Dec. 21, 2009).

30. Douglas B. Reeves, *Accountability in Action* (Englewood, CO: Advanced Learning Press, 2000), 185–208.

Part IV

Customers

No business will ever last if it loses sight of its customers. But schools regularly do. Students and their parents are systematically ignored.

The failures are simply stated. Students have different skill levels, different interests, different learning styles, and different temperaments and attitudes. Teachers have traditionally ignored the differences, using one curriculum (theirs or the district's), taught one way. But if we believe every child can learn, then we need more differentiated instruction. And we need a better way to follow each student's progress that will allow us to respond flexibly when individual students fall behind or run ahead, or just lose faith in their own abilities, or in the opportunities of a great education.

The other part of the customer base for schools is, not surprisingly, parents, who are also the schools' partners and owners. Unfortunately, schools really want just one kind of parent, who will be "just right." That is, educators do not want parents to be highly involved in school life, which would peel back their insulation from accountability. But they also do not want parents underinvolved, which would leave them with the job of mentoring students and ensuring kids embrace positive attitudes about themselves and their education.

All those failings, piled one on top of the other, leave schools with a lot of work to do.

SEVENTEEN

Do Not Lose Sight of the Student

Doris Kurtz says bluntly, "The old way is 'the way I do it.' The new way is 'satisfy the customer.' We need to change a self-serving culture that is employee based. We cannot put ourselves first; we do what is best for them."

THE "OLD DAYS" IN EDUCATION

Unfortunately, we have a system built on an industrial model. It virtually guarantees we lose sight of students.

One can trace the origins of the system to 1891, when the National Education Association, which was then dominated by university leaders, decided it needed a report on secondary school curriculum and the requirements for college admission.[1] The response was the 1893 report of the powerful Committee of Ten on Secondary School Studies, chaired by Harvard's president, Charles W. Eliot. One key conclusion:

> Every subject which is taught at all in a secondary school should be taught in the same way and to the same extent to every pupil so long as he pursues it, no matter what the probable destination of the pupil may be, or at what point his education is to cease.

The report was perhaps the most prominent single push—among many—for standardizing elementary and secondary education, which was rapidly expanding to serve large masses of students. The committee saw the virtue in applying the concepts of the country's industrial revolution to education. So did many others.

There were dissenters. John Dewey, who was the most prominent critic, attacked the growing industrialized style of mass education. He deplored rote learning and the dividing up of curriculum into six or twelve years of school life. To him, that meant that the focus of education was wrongly placed "outside the child." He argued that all children are different and had to be treated differently. Learning was to be "child centered."[2]

His valiant effort to change the tide of education has always had its adherents. But the Committee of Ten prevailed.

One Size Fits All

In the "old days," a subject or a class generally focused on a given textbook (or perhaps a tightly scripted "program") and maybe a related workbook. The book was built around a set of facts and skills that "experts" believed appropriate for a student of a given age. That often made the books bland, superficial, and quickly outdated.[3] Moreover, their product was printed on paper and bound, effectively the equivalent of being written in stone.

The books were also based on key assumptions the authors had made. When it came to a ten-year-old in fifth-grade math, for example, the textbook publishers assumed that the student could read at the fifth-grade level, and that was how the book was written. (See chapter 18, about curriculum issues.) They assumed that the students had absorbed successfully all the math skills they were presumably taught in grades 1 through 4. The accompanying teachers guide generally assumed all students learned the same way. If the student had a different learning style, different interests, or inadequate knowledge to deal with the level of the book, nothing could, or would, be done.

The attitude fit a world in which teachers were deemed something akin to Henry Ford's autoworkers toiling on a production line producing one Model T after another. They were not expected to tailor instruction. No variation in content. No variation in pedagogy.

Students who did not fit all the assumptions were left adrift. Teachers might have sensed that a child was struggling, or, for that matter, that a child was well beyond the material and totally bored. Even if the teachers wanted to help, they were likely not equipped to do much about personalization, and they rarely have had any organizational support even if they wanted to. They might think about keeping a child after school to give him help or time to work on a special project, but it was not likely when there was only one bus home and it left right after the last regular class.[4]

The Rationalization for Ignoring the Obvious

Teachers and many administrators understood the problem. But they did little. Instead, they rationalized.

Ted Sizer, who was a Harvard education professor and the headmaster at Phillips Andover Academy, became famous in the 1980s and 1990s for a series of books about "Horace," a teacher at mythical "Franklin High." Sizer told Horace's story as a way to describe the failings of American secondary education and to propose the way to fix it. In *Horace's Compromise*, Sizer took direct aim at high schools' claim that they individualized education:

> Franklin High School uses plenty of public relations talk about "taking each child individually," but the school's practices belie the boast. . . . May as well treat 'em all the same. Or accept someone else's judgment about how swift a kid is, and go with it. Expect more, expect less. Compromise with your common sense: the kids are different, but we can't admit it, even to ourselves.[5]

Others saw students' failure as a sign they were "uneducable." Whatever that meant. The bottom line was that rather than working to adapt education to children's needs, educators justified inaction on the ground that it was the children's fault,[6] not the school's quality of service.

Most troublingly, there was race, and, to a lesser degree, class bias. People said such kids could not, or did not want to, learn. Several education researchers have in the last two decades directly accused districts of racism in overidentifying minority students as having learning disabilities. Rather than seeing themselves as failing to understand how these children learn, or what motivates them, educators simply categorize them as "special needs."[7]

Finally, there was an incentive to keep rationalizing. Mass-production teaching was—and is—simply easier.[8] One curriculum, one style of instruction, no effort at customization. It is also safer.[9] Just make sure kids know specific answers to tests, and no one will be criticized. And it is probably cheaper.

THE END OF THE OLD DAYS

Two things ended the old days. One was the change in the American economy. As low-skilled jobs dried up and high-skilled jobs became the order of the day, it became clear that mass-production education was not going to work. People needed real academic skills to get a job.

The other was more profound because it was not just about economic necessity. It was all about civil rights. In 1954, the Supreme Court decided *Brown v. Board of Education*[10] and its companion cases. Legal segregation of the races in education was in theory over.

Once African Americans demonstrated the power of civil rights to remake schools, other groups took up their own causes. First were those who spoke little or no English. Then came parents with children with physical or learning disabilities—the deaf, the blind, the autistic, the dyslexic—who decided to fight for better treatment. Until then, such children were excluded from the public schools, sent to specialized schools where the education was, at best, poor, or just dismissed as "slow" and consigned to classes guaranteed to produce not much learning at all. The movement ultimately resulted in the Education for All Handicapped Children Act of 1975 (renamed the Individuals with Disabilities Education Act [IDEA] upon a reauthorization in 1990).[11]

As it turned out, IDEA was a much more powerful leveler than *Brown v. Board of Education* was.

Schools were required to identify special needs children and design individual education plans for them. To the greatest extent possible, those plans were to be delivered in regular classrooms. If parents did not like the plans, they could seek legal redress. If their objections were upheld, schools had to change plans or pay for students to attend private schools that could provide a more appropriate education.

Suddenly, there was a group of students the law required schools not to lose sight of. Although the law only affected about 10 percent of all children (6.6 million, to be exact, in 2008), indifferent, mass-production education was out.

IDEA's impact has been profound. First, it forced schools and teachers to acknowledge that some students learn differently and that new and different ways had to be found to teach them. They could not be relegated to special schools, and after the passage of NCLB, their test score results had to show the same improvement as those of other students.

However, IDEA had far broader effects. Teachers were required to identify struggling students and have them tested to see if they qualified as "special needs." The process drove home the idea that children might need different instruction in order to succeed even if they did not qualify for an individual education plan.

Then Came Multiple Intelligences and the Push for Personalized Education

At almost the same time as the passage of IDEA, psychologists focused on the differences in how students learn and express themselves. The discussion began in earnest in the 1980s, when Harvard professor Howard Gardner published his theory of "multiple intelligences."[12] He eventually identified eight of them: linguistic, logical-mathematical, bodily kinesthetic, interpersonal, intrapersonal, musical, naturalist, and spatial. He argued that these "intelligences," which we might consider talents or skills, should be nurtured in schools in order to bring out the fullest development of each child.[13]

Some have taken his reasoning further, arguing that such intelligences should be taught in schools or used as different ways of presenting material. That extension of Gardner's reasoning[14] has been disputed,[15] and I am not going to attempt to argue one side or the other here. However, the lasting impact has been to make accepted the idea that children are different and should be treated that way.[16] Moreover, a child's emotional profile, sociological needs (like working alone or with peers), physical capabilities, and cultural background are no longer dismissed as irrelevant differences, but rather are influences that teachers have to address.[17]

Various school reform advocates picked up the idea. Among them were Ted Sizer, who began the Coalition for Essential Schools,[18] and Deborah Meier, who created Central Park East School in New York City.[19] Both emphasized personalized education. Taking on Dewey's mantra, schools were to be "learner centered." Teaching and learning were "personalized." Students were "active workers" and teachers "facilitators and performance coaches." Personalized assessments, which were diagnoses of an individual student's knowledge and skills, were the foundation of instruction. Academic progress was measured in a variety of ways to capture the full picture of student skills, not merely what they might do on standardized tests.[20] Sizer and Meier focused on students teaching themselves by doing projects, and they favored evaluating student progress based on portfolios of their work, including those projects.

Gardner, Sizer, Meier, and other advocates of personalized instruction[21] have had an enormous influence on education thought and practice in the last twenty-five years. In 1996, for example, the National Association of Secondary School Principals proposed that high schools focus on six themes, the first of which is personalization.[22] In 2010, the Institute for the Study of Knowledge Management in Education held a "Big Ideas Fest," which brought together 175 teachers, educational innovators, and leaders from schools, colleges, research labs, government, science, and philanthropy. Their consensus, too, focused on individualized instruction and projects that would better harness students' self-motivation.[23]

However, like so many ideas in education, implementing ideas comes far more slowly than their intellectual acceptance. There are places like Pueblo, Colorado, that have individualized education plans for *every* student, not just those with special needs, and that use computers aggressively to differentiate instruction.[24] But such districts are still the ones subject to "special reports." The vast majority of districts are not yet there.

The other important and highly practical result of IDEA was the development of computer databases for education. Schools needed information technology (IT) capable of accommodating the vast amounts of data essential to make the implementation of thousands of those individual education plans actually happen. Although computer databases were proliferating across American business, the revolution in IT came slowly to schools. One of its principal drivers was getting the administration of IDEA under control. And once one built a system that could keep complicated records for 10 percent of the student population, one could build a system for the other 90 percent as well.

TWO CAUTIONS WORTH KEEPING IN MIND

So now you know the history. But before we embark on a discussion of how "not to lose sight" of anyone, two cautions are worth keeping in mind:

Teachers and Students Have Personality Issues, Too

One impediment is simply the vagaries of human relationships. Some teachers make up their minds about students' potential before they actually get to know them.[25] They do not lose sight of students; they never have them in focus in the first place.

Two examples come to mind from current popular literature.

Frank McCourt, the gifted Irish-American storyteller best known for his Pulitzer Prize–winning book, *Angela's Ashes*, was for most of his life an English teacher in the New York City public schools. He wrote a book about his experiences, *Teacher Man*,[26] which candidly paints a picture in lyrical prose of the day-to-day life of a journeyman teacher. Early in his career, McCourt taught at a vocational high school in Staten Island. As he described it, he pretended to teach, and his students pretended to learn. The kids had low expectations for themselves, and he, in time, had low expectations of them. Later, he moved to the city's renowned Stuyvesant High School, which was filled with overachievers who had tested in to what is one of the best public high schools in America. Neither they nor their teacher had to pretend about anything. They wanted to learn, and McCourt was excited to teach them. As drab as existence had been on Staten Island, it was glorious just a few, short blocks from the other end of the ferry in Manhattan.

The other example is the comparison Malcolm Gladwell draws between the unknown Christopher Langan and celebrated Robert Oppenheimer in his best seller, *Outliers*.[27] Gladwell describes Langan as brilliant, but never able to get anyone to give him a hand that would propel him to a success that eluded him throughout his life. In contrast stands Oppenheimer, the great scientist who led America's work on the Manhattan Project, which developed the atom bomb. He found his way to an illustrious career even though he had a dark streak that included attempting to kill one of his tutors at Cambridge. Somehow Oppenheimer was able to win over his teachers to support and defend him despite his repeated bad behavior. Langan could not even get help trying to arrange a change to his schedule in college.

When you say, "do not lose sight of any child," you are asking McCourt on Staten Island to charge into that crowd of blue-collar kids and make them excited about Shakespeare. And you are wagging a finger at the teachers who failed to give the talented Langan even half the breaks they gave the troubled Oppenheimer.

Advocates of individualizing instruction stress that the classroom has to be "safe and affirming for each learner."[28] What McCourt and Gladwell remind us is that it is easier to say those words than to make them happen.

The Mobile Poor Are Always with Us

The second problem with not losing sight of the kids is that they move. A seemingly inexorable fact of life in America is that the poor constantly change where they live. In some low-income schools, one-third of the children present on opening day are not there in June.[29] Losing sight of these kids is not figurative; it is literal. Kids who move frequently do not perform as well as their peers.[30]

What Does "Not Losing Sight of Any Child" Really Mean?

Okay, you say, I agree we are not going to lose sight of any child. But what exactly does that mean?

First

The system has to accept every child as he or she is, not as how the system thinks they should be.

From curriculum to grade configuration to course design, school districts have to be willing to look at every child as an individual and work with what they find. It is in part the one-textbook, one-pedagogy problem, but it is far more complicated than that. We need to recognize that many other practices, such as having grades (i.e., fourth grade), or de-tracked classrooms, can be as much of a problem as a class taught only from a single textbook. What we need to create is a learning environment that can respect children for who they are, not ignoring them by caricaturing them as who we would like them to be.

Second

Each child's progress is closely assessed.

No one is allowed to fall far behind or to get bored because he or she is ready to move on with nowhere to go. Teachers closely follow students' progress. They then immediately act on what they find with some kind of tailored help.

Third

Every child has a supporter and mentor.

Whether it is a parent or a teacher or community volunteer, every child has someone to bolster their confidence, foster their self-respect, encourage them to aim high, and give them a helping hand.[31] At a minimum, they need a teacher who knows them, how they think, and what interests they have.[32] That "personalization" of education may, in fact, be the aspect of private schools, with their significantly lower student-teacher ratios, most appealing to parents.[33] However, let us leave this last part until the chapter on parents, since so much of kids' headspace revolves around their mothers, fathers, and grandparents, as well as their school.

NOTES

1. For the complete text of the full report see http://tmh.floonet.net/books/commoften/mainrpt.html.

2. John Dewey, *The School and the Society & The Child and the Curriculum*, 1915 ed. (New York: BN Publishing, 1915), 22–25.

3. Allan C. Ornstein and Francis P. Hunkins, *Curriculum: Foundations, Principles, and Issues*, 3rd ed. (Boston, MA: Allyn and Bacon, 1998), 358.

4. Linda Darling-Hammond, *The Right to Learn* (San Francisco: Jossey-Bass, 1997), 79.

5. Theodore R. Sizer, *Horace's Compromise* (Boston, MA: Houghton Mifflin, 1992), 6.

6. Deborah Meier, *The Power of Their Ideas: Lessons for America from a Small School in Harlem* (Boston, MA: Beacon, 1995), 72.

7. See, for example, Suzanne M. Donovan and Christopher T. Cross, eds., *Minority Students in Special and Gifted Education* (Washington, DC: Committee on Minority Representation in Special Education, National Academy Press, 2002).

8. Allen C. Ornstein, "Critical Issues in Teaching," in *Contemporary Issues in Curriculum*, 4th ed., ed. Allen C. Ornstein, Edward F. Pajak, and Stacey B. Ornstein (Boston, MA: Pearson, 2007), 88.

9. Howard Gardner, *The Unschooled Mind* (New York: Basic Books, 1991), 140, 150.

10. 347 U.S. 483 (1954).

11. 20 USC § 1400.

12. Gardner, *The Unschooled Mind*; Howard Gardner, *Multiple Intelligences* (New York: Basic Books, 1993).

13. Gardner's and Daniel Goleman's works are part of the larger study of "cognitive neuroscience," which has resulted in significant insights into the differences in how children learn. *New York Times*, "Studying Young Minds and How to Teach Them," Dec. 21, 2009 (retrieved from www.nytimes.com/2009/12/21/heath/research/21brain.html on Dec. 21, 2009).

14. In *The Unschooled Mind*, Gardner wrote: "I argue that a contrasting set of assumptions is more likely to be educationally effective. Students learn in ways that are identifiably distinctive. The broad spectrum of students—and perhaps the society as a whole—would be better served if disciplines could be presented in a number of ways and learning could be assessed through a variety of means" (p. 12).

15. Compare Daniel T. Willingham, *Why Don't Students Like School?* (San Francisco: Jossey-Bass, 2009), 122–25; Harold Pashler, Mark McDaniel, Doug Rohrer, and Robert Bjork, "Learning Styles," *Psychological Science in the Public Interest* 9, no. 3 (Dec. 2008): 106–17; Mike Schmoker, "When Pedagogic Fads Trump Priorities," *Education Week*, Sept. 29, 2010, 22–23, with Carol Tomlinson, "When Pedagogical Misinformation Trumps Reason," *Education Week*, Nov. 17, 2010, 28; *Wall Street Journal*, "Beyond the Test-Prep Bounds," July 12, 2010 (retrieved from http://online.wsj.com/article/SB10001424052748704799604575357332322937668.html on July 12, 2010).

16. See, for example, Marie Carbo, "Match the Style of Instruction to the Style of Reading," *Phi Delta Kappan* 28, no. 18 (Jan. 2009): 373, 375.

17. Robert W. Cole, "Educating Everybody's Children: We Know What Works—and What Doesn't," in *Educating Everybody's Children*, 2nd ed., ed. Robert W. Cole (Alexandria, VA: ASCD, 2008), 15, 21.

18. Theodore Sizer, *Horace's Compromise* (Boston, MA: Houghton Mifflin, 1984); Arthur G. Powell, Eleanor Farrar, and David K. Cohen, *The Shopping Mall High School* (Boston, MA: Houghton Mifflin, 1985); Robert L. Hampel, *The Last Little Citadel: American High Schools since 1940* (Boston, MA: Houghton Mifflin, 1986).

19. Deborah Meier, *The Power of Their Ideas: Lessons for America from a Small School in Harlem* (Boston, MA: Beacon, 1995).

20. James Keefe, "What Is Personalization?," *Phi Delta Kappan* 89, no. 3 (Nov. 2007): 217.

21. There are more education reformers who also focused on personalization. For example, Ron Edmonds and Lawrence Lezotte's Effective Schools Movement, which started in 1982, also focuses on regular formative assessments and constant adjustment of instruction depending on individual progress.

22. Edmonds and Lezotte, Effective Schools Movement.

23. Lisa Petrides, "Big Ideas and Reform Fatigue," *Education Week*, March 23, 2010 (retrieved from www.edweek.org/ew/articles/2010/03/23/27petrides.ht9.html on March 25, 2010).

24. Panasonic Foundation, American Association of School Administrators, "Strategies," *AASA Journal* 14, no. 1 (May 2009): 1–15.

25. John M. Bridgeland, Robert Balfanz, Laura A. Moore, and Rebecca S. Friant, *Raising Their Voices* (Washington, DC: Civic Enterprises, 2010), 17.

26. Frank McCourt, *Teacher Man* (New York: Scribner, 2005), 66–110, 183–231.

27. Malcolm Gladwell, *Outliers* (New York: Little, Brown, 2008), 69–115.

28. Carol Ann Tomlinson, *The Differentiated School* (Alexandria, VA: ASCD, 2008), 47.

29. See, for example, Kai A. Schafft, *Low Income Student Transiency and Its Effects on Schools and School Districts in Upstate New York: The Perspective of School District Administrators* (Ithaca, NY: Cornell University, 2002); David Kerbow, *Patterns of Urban Student Mobility and Local School Reform* (Chicago: University of Chicago Press, 1996).

30. Government Accountability Office, *K–12 Education: Many Challenges Arise in Education Students Who Change Schools Frequently* (Washington, DC: GPO, 2010).

31. Tracy Kidder, *Among Schoolchildren* (Boston, MA: Houghton Mifflin, 1989), 312–13.

32. Allan C. Ornstein, Edward F. Pajar, and Stacey B. Ornstein, *Contemporary Issues in Curriculum* (Boston, MA: Pearson, 2007), 84.

33. Theodore R. Sizer, *The Red Pencil* (New Haven, CT: Yale University Press, 2004), 42. The current ratio at Sizer's old school, Phillips Andover, is 5:1. In comparison, the ratio at 2009 Broad winner Aldine is 29:1.

EIGHTEEN

Seeing Every Child for Who They Are, Not Who We Assume Them to Be— Replacing One Curriculum Taught One Way

After eight years in office, Joel Klein resigned as New York's chancellor in the fall of 2010. He then wrote an op-ed titled "What I Learned at the Education Barricades."[1] One of those pieces of knowledge: "The classroom model we have used since the 19th century, in which one teacher stands in front of a room of 20 to 30 kids, is obsolete." Agreed. So where do we go from here?

Let's start with curriculum, always the most visible issue, reserving the rest of the challenges for the next chapter.

Before beginning this discussion of curriculum, I need to make a disclaimer. There is no inconsistency in believing children need instruction tailored to their interests or needs and favoring a core curriculum of knowledge and skills that every child must learn. I do not want to take sides, however, on what that core knowledge and skill set might be. The point of this book is that whatever the content might be, it is more effectively taught in a system that has both high expectations for every child and an appreciation that every student has different interests, different ways of learning, and different emotional attitudes.

BUILDING A CURRICULUM CAREFULLY

Every curriculum should be coherent, demanding, and content rich. The goal for math and reading is real mastery of the content, not just getting by NCLB testing, and other subjects should receive equally significant attention and thoughtful treatment. That commitment is critical to the successful districts I visited, and it is what all successful foreign systems do.[2]

A curriculum designed to meet that goal has to manage three problems inherent in instruction. It has to be logical, teaching the basic elements first and then gradually growing more complex and demanding (which educators call "scaffolding"). It has to be organized well so that the overall progress of instruction gives most kids enough, but not too much, time to master the material (called "pacing"). On top of that, the disciplines like reading, math, and science recognize their interdependence on each other and are coordinated both across subjects and between grades (called "mapping"). You cannot ask sixth graders to solve a math problem if they cannot read or understand what is presented to them.

Because of the complexity in constructing a curriculum that meets all these objectives, it is obvious why schools make assumptions about kids. But because of the complexity of the students, it is apparent why curricula constructed with lots of those assumptions will not work.

As Ted Sizer said, "to run a school on the basis of One Best Curriculum and One Best Pedagogy and One Best Pace of Learning . . . is . . . profoundly discriminatory."[3]

TEXTBOOKS

Since so much of our current curriculum is still textbook driven, the discussion should begin with them.

Textbooks or some electronic equivalent are still with us, and they are likely to have a role for many years. If nothing else, it makes economic sense. Many educators, and, more importantly, most of those creating standards, agree there is core content that is fundamental for every student to know and understand.[4] If that content can be conveyed in a way that is both interesting and substantive for large numbers of students, it is reasonable to use a textbook or electronic equivalent as a starting point, or base, for classroom instruction.

Similarly, textbooks can make sense if they reflect a manner of instruction that works for most students. In fact, Long Beach, which is a consistently highly rated district with a majority of minority and low-income students, nonetheless uses Open Court, a highly structured reading program. Chris Steinhauser, the superintendent, told me that its use does not conflict with the district's stress on differentiated instruction. He does not see Open Court as a straitjacket, but as "great strategies and great assessments," which his teachers adapt to individual needs.[5]

Can Steinhauser and Sizer be reconciled? Probably not entirely. The middle view may be using textbooks or programs where they are helpful, while being savvy enough to appreciate their limits. That, in turn, requires knowing when and how to supplement them or use different teaching methods when they are insufficient. In terms of the great debate between the "industrial" and "professional" views of teaching, it requires a far more "professional" vision of what it takes to be a good educator than many districts, or teachers, have historically embraced.[6]

THE INTERNET HAS CHANGED EVERYTHING: CONTENT AND CONNECTION IN THE DIGITAL AGE

In any event, textbooks are never going to play the role they have historically played because of the IT revolution. Textbook publishers can, themselves, reduce some of the rigidity by offering electronic variations.[7] That is just the start, though.

The deficit that commercial software firms have most aggressively tried to fill is the market for remedial materials. Dozens of commercial developers have programs designed to help "recover" students who had been struggling or just dropped out. The diverse approaches arguably can reach a variety of learning styles.[8] Students can work on them alone, at home, or with the remote assistance of a teacher or mentor—as well as with a teacher in the same room. A student can also spend as much time on them as he or she needs to master material.

However, "recovery" has not been the only use. In districts like Plano, Pearl River, and Broward County, computerization had enabled them to teach more courses, expose students to more of the real world, and facilitate more individual and group projects. In Florida, the state has gone so far as to approve a "Virtual Academy," which is a K–8 education delivered entirely over the Internet.[9] In New York City, the "School of One" program is an experimental instruction strategy where every student has a unique daily schedule that is a mix of teacher-led instruction, one-on-one tutoring, independent learning, and work with virtual tutors.[10]

Computer-based learning is clearly attractive. One forecast is that by 2015, schools will be spending $4.9 billion on all sorts of "self-paced" programs.[11]

As good as some of this software is, many superintendents still favor at least some traditional classroom time. The key to their success was the smooth integration of computer material with classroom lecture or discussion. It was not a disconnected "add-on."

Achieving that integration is not easy. Blue Valley has worked hard on training teachers how to do it, and even in that innovative district, the process was costly and time consuming. But it has been, in their view, worth it. They have now developed a series of courses that they think are more effective than just a teacher lecturing or a student sitting at a computer.

There is one other flexibility that arises from the Web. Schools are not limited to commercial developers for material. Teachers, principals, and students themselves can use the Internet to substitute for, or supplement, a textbook that does not fit a need.[12] It might be a lesson plan one teacher buys from another over the Internet. Or it might be material students independently find to support a project or homework assignment.

The increasing sophistication of IT makes the strategy easier every day. Pre-Internet, for example, a student project required the time and effort needed to go to the library, take notes, photocopy pages, and then write or type up something. Now, a project means Google, Yahoo, and Bing. It also means the ability to compile all that material while sitting in a classroom or the comfort of a kid's room at home.

The new opportunities are not only about content, but also about how that content can be transmitted and used. Some districts are now streaming video on demand to their students,[13] who can receive it on their Kindle, iPad, or advanced PDA. They are also creating collaborative environments, like Facebook or Edmodo, where students can work together over the Internet; these are already available, and single-player, game-based learning is going to be a reality by 2012.[14]

The Obama administration has grasped the significance of all of these developments, both those increasing access to information and those that change the way students learn, and incorporated all of them in an ambitious proposal, its 2010 National Education Technology Plan[15] to expand IT use in schools. If the plan is implemented, individualized instruction should be easier than ever.[16]

A recent survey of teachers by Scholastic and the Gates Foundation underscores the importance of using differentiated assignments to engage students in learning. Sixty-four percent of elementary teachers, 52 percent of middle school teachers, and 40 percent of high school teachers "strongly agree on their importance."[17]

And it is all due to the Internet. Fifty-seven percent of those same teachers strongly agree that digital resources engage students, while only 6 percent strongly agree that traditional textbooks are as effective.[18] One key reason: Digital resources can be tailored to be relevant to a student's world. Kids then become more engaged because they understand that there is a practical payoff if they master the content or skill on offer.[19] That in turn attacks the two predominant reasons kids cite for leaving high school early: boredom and a perception that what they were being taught lacked relevance in their lives.[20]

Computer-based materials have one other powerful feature: They are also more interactive. Some of us can absorb material easily enough from the printed page, but learning with something—anything—with which you *interact individually* is so much more engaging. Recent news reports fret about the amount of time kids spend Twittering, blogging, and "Googling," but the interaction engages each student on a personal level.[21]

There are still a host of reasons to rely on teachers, classrooms, and whole class instruction, but this connection to a machine that responds to a child immediately adds greatly to what that child wants to do.

All of which leads us to Gary Gordon. He is an educator who worked at Blue Valley and who has written a book, *Building Engaged Schools*.[22] Blue Valley administrators love to cite him, as do other people with whom I spoke, like Marsha Leyles, New York's deputy chancellor for instruction.

Gordon starts with the reasonable premise that we like doing those things we do well. Echoing Gardner's "multiple intelligences," Gordon argues that each of us (or at least most of us) has some skill we do well and which, as a consequence, we like to do. Yet schools often focus on what we do badly and, in the era of NCLB, relentlessly concentrate on potential failure rather than success. So rather than lure kids into learning because it is associated with things they like, we berate them about where they fail, making schoolwork painful drudgery.

Gordon is not suggesting we ignore things with which kids struggle. Nor is he suggesting we abandon the challenging parts of a curriculum in favor of dumbed-down pabulum. He is merely doing what a good salesperson would do: Think about how to wrap the good parts around the more difficult ones so that the child eagerly embraces mastering the package.[23] The connection to the ability to tailor elements of the curriculum to capture children's individual interests is obvious.

COLLABORATION COUNTS

There is a caveat about access to all this Internet material. Allowing teachers individually to create content raises the dual concerns of quality control and consistency in the teaching throughout the school, let alone the district. Textbooks, at least, guaranteed a certain level of quality—at the price of flexibility.

If one is going to try to achieve similar quality *and* flexibility, teachers and administrators have to work together. That collaboration broadens the knowledge base about what is available, which in turn should create a higher-quality and more consistent product. Without that joint effort, turning isolated teachers loose to create flexible content is a virtual guarantee some kids will unnecessarily receive an even worse experience than they would with that inflexible textbook. In other words, teachers' "doing their own thing" does not go with flexible curriculum.[24]

THE END OF THE TEXTBOOK WARS

The power of the Internet in altering the role of textbooks has one other implication worth noting, even if its impact seems far removed from the classroom.

In Texas, California, and Florida, state school boards decide on textbooks for all their districts. They have great influence on textbooks sold throughout the United States because of the buying power of their decisions, and that has caused considerable controversy every few years. For example, Texas conservatives have fought their way on to the elected state school board to try to force textbooks to include creationism, or at least the slightly watered-down "intelligent design" theory. More recently, they have resolved that the books emphasize the role and importance of Christianity in the founding of the United States.[25]

Liberals fret. Science and history teachers object. Even if their own state's standards are different, they worry they are going to be saddled with textbook materials that they do not want to teach because of Texas's inordinate power over the nation's textbook content decisions. Multiplying the sources of content and manner of instruction may just make much of the passion on both sides go away.

ONE OTHER OUTCOME WORTH A MOMENT'S REFLECTION

There is one other likely outcome of the ability to access vast amounts of material through the Internet that may have an even more profound, although perhaps not as obvious, an effect. Starting in the 1970s, there has been almost a fixation on finding the one right curriculum (including both content and pedagogy) for reading, or math, or history. It was, in its own way, a new manifestation of mass production.

The fixation distracted from the really fundamental, and far more difficult, challenges of training, collaboration, assessment, and mentoring that have produced real results. Because we did not fix any of these things in the hope the new curriculum would solve everything, we just wound up changing curriculum again a couple of years down the line.

Now, rather than looking for the one best way, the new Internet world allows people to look for a variety of materials and ways to teach. We can concentrate on assessing if the content and methods of teaching proposed by various curricula meet the interests and needs of our kids. If they do, that is fine. If not, we move on or add something else.

* * *

Because the recommendations for "What We Need to Do" are closely connected to the discussions in the next two chapters, the entire agenda for students is at the end of chapter 20.

NOTES

1. Joel Klein, "What I Learned at the Education Barricades," *Wall Street Journal,* Dec. 4, 2010 (retrieved from www.wsj.com/article/SB100014205274870410 4575622800493796156.html on Dec. 6, 2010).

2. See, for example, Common Core, *Why We're Behind: What Top Nations Teach Their Students But We Don't* (Washington, DC: Common Core, 2009).

3. Theodore R. Sizer, *Horace's Compromise* (Boston, MA: Houghton Mifflin, 1992), 32.

4. During the "curriculum wars" of the 1970s and 1980s, there was great dispute about whether there was a core curriculum. Critics of people like Sizer and Meier contended that "child-centered" education meant that instruction would not include the conveying of fundamental content that every child should know. Disputes about core curricula continue at some level today, although now the disagreements are more about the content of the core rather than whether schools should strive to convey a common body of knowledge for all students. E. D. Hirsch Jr., *The Making of Americans* (New Haven, CT: Yale University Press, 2009).

5. Other scholars, like Linda Darling-Hammond and Jonathan Kozol, would disagree. They have argued heavily scripted teaching leads to "skill and drill" instruction in low-income schools. Children in middle-income schools, on the other hand, are less likely to face scripting and more likely to receive engaging, meaningful, and individually tailored instruction that helps them develop the thinking, reading, and writing capacities they need in the current world. Seth Parsons, Ann Harrington, "Following the Script," *Phi Delta Kappan* 89, no. 10 (June 2009): 748, 749–50.

6. Carol Ann Tomlinson, *The Differentiated School* (Alexandria, VA: ASCD, 2008), 25.

7. As I write this book, some Ohio legislators have introduced a bill requiring college textbook publishers to offer electronic versions of textbooks. *Columbus Dispatch,* "Bill Calls for e-Book Versions of Textbooks," March 23, 2010 (retrieved from www.dispatchpolitics.com/live/content/local_news/stories/2010/03/23/bill-calls-=for-e-versions-of textbooks.html on March 25, 2010), and in 2009 Indiana's School Board was so displeased with available social studies textbooks that it sent districts a letter advising them to seek material online. *Education Week,* "Texas' Clout over Textbooks Could Shift with Market," April 22, 2010 (retrieved from www.edweek.org/ew/articles/2010/04/22/30textsep.ht9.html on April 22, 2010).

8. In 2009, San Diego adopted its i21 computer learning initiative, which follows the principals of Universal Design for Learning (UDL). UDL's computer based strategy focuses on multiple means of presenting material, multiple ways for students to demonstrate mastery, and multiple ways to tap into learners' interests. *eSchoolNews,* "Reinventing Education," Sept. 9, 2009 (retrieved from www.eschoolnews.com/news/special-reports/special-reports-articles/indec.cfm?on Nov. 30, 2009). For a more extensive explanation of UDL, see www.cast.org/research/udl.

9. See www.flva.org; *New York Times,* "In Florida, Virtual Classrooms with No Teachers," Jan. 17, 2011 (retrieved from www.nytimes.com/2011/01/18/education/18classrooms.html on Jan. 18, 2011).

10. See http://schools.nyc.gov/community/innovation/SchoolsofOne/default.html; *eschoolNews,* "School of One Boosts Individual Learning," Oct. 13, 2010 (retrieved from www.eschoolnewls.com/2010/10/13/school-of-one-boosts-individual-learning on Nov. 29, 2010).

11. *T-H-E Journal*, "PreK–12 Dominates Growth in e-Learning," Jan. 20, 2011 (retrieved from http://thejournal.com.Articles/2011/01/20/PreK12-Dominates-Growth-in-E-Learning.aspx on Jan. 20, 2011).

12. *Education Week Digital Directions*, "The Personal Approach," Winter 2010, 16–20; *Education Week*, "E-Curriculum Builders Seek a Personalized Approach," April 23, 2010 (retrieved from www.edweek.org/ew/articles/2010/04/28/30edtech_21century.h29.html on April 27, 2010).

13. *eSchoolNews*, "Texas District Streams Video Wirelessly on Demand," March 31, 2010 (retrieved from www.eschoolnews.com/2010/03/31/texas-district-streams-video-wirelessly-on-demand on April 2, 2010).

14. L. Johnson, R. Smith, A. Levine, and K. Haywood, *The 2010 Horizon Report: K–12 Edition* (Austin, TX: The New Media Consortium, 2010).

15. *Transforming American Education: Learning Powered by Technology* (Washington, DC: Office of Educational Technology, U.S. Department of Education, 2010).

16. Chris Dede, "Transforming Schooling via the 2010 National Educational Technology Plan," *Teachers College Record*, June 2, 2010 (ID Number 15998, retrieved from www.tcrecord.org/Content.asp?/Content=15998 on July 18, 2010).

17. Scholastic, Inc., and Bill and Melinda Gates Foundation, *Primary Sources: America's Teachers on America's Schools* (Seattle: Gates Foundation, 2010), 34.

18. Scholastic, Inc., and Bill and Melinda Gates Foundation, *Primary Sources: America's Teachers on America's Schools*, 35.

19. Linda Darling-Hammond, *The Right to Learn* (San Francisco: Jossey-Bass, 1997), 81.

20. John M. Bridgeland, Robert Balfanz, Laura A. Moore, and Rebecca S. Friant, *Raising Their Voices: Engaging Students, Teachers, and Parents to Help End the High School Dropout Epidemic* (Washington, DC: Civic Enterprises, 2010), 6.

21. *Fast Company* magazine ran a story shortly after I wrote these words that brought my observation up to date. In an article titled "'A' Is for App," the magazine describes how the use of the Internet through mobile phones and handheld computers may be creating a revolution in childhood creativity. It started the story with a short vignette: "When the Singer sisters were just 6 months old, they already preferred cell phones to almost any other toy, recalls their mom, Fiona Aboud Singer: 'They loved to push the buttons and see it light up.' The girls knew most of the alphabet by 18 months. . . ." *Fast Company*, "'A' Is for App," April 2010, 68.

22. Gary Gordon with Steve Crabtree, *Building Engaged Schools* (New York: Gallup Press, 2006).

23. Gordon and Crabtree, *Building Engaged Schools*, 47.

24. The National Commission on Teaching and America's Future, *Unraveling the "Teacher Shortage" Problem: Teacher Retention Is the Key* (Washington, DC: NCTAF, 2002), 13.

25. *New York Times Sunday Magazine*, "How Christian Were the Founders?," Feb. 14, 2010, 36; *New York Times*, "Texas Conservatives Win Curriculum Change," March 12, 2010 (retrieved from www.nytimes.com/2010/03/13/education.13texas.html on March 16, 2010).

NINETEEN

Ending a System Designed to Lose Track of Kids—Paying Attention to Real Students, Not to the Assumptions We Make about Them

Even with adapted, tailored content and pedagogy, schools are not out of the woods. Not only is their curriculum "industrialized," so is the way they do business. Grading by age, classroom assignment, and class size have all been influenced by mass-production models. Left untouched, they will undercut whatever progress schools make in tailoring content and pedagogy.

THE EVILS OF BUILDING A SCHOOL STRUCTURE THAT ASSUMES KIDS ARE ALL LEARNING AT THE SAME PACE

We assume that kids in a certain grade are at a certain level of achievement. That is, we assume that learning takes place at a certain speed so that, for example, all nine-year-olds should be at a particular point in mastering math or English language arts. We provide materials and instruction accordingly. The problem is that the assumption ignores reality at times. Even for children who are not where we *want* them to be, we still hand them the materials appropriate for where we *assume* they are. At its extreme, we call the problem "social promotion" and tie ourselves in knots because we cannot figure whether it is best to leave a child back or promote him even though he is not ready for the work.

Ted Sizer characterized grades "as an administratively useful concept," but one that may be more harmful to students than it is helpful to teachers: "Age grading hurts some kids, swelling the heads of those who appear, for whatever obvious or mysterious reasons, to be 'swift' and humiliating the 'slow.' Pigeonholing honors, regular, and special needs students sets up self-fulfilling prophecies."[1]

"Ungraded" schools are one possible answer. They do exist.[2] (Kansas City schools adopted ungraded schools for 17,000 students in 2010.[3]) At least five superintendents with whom I spoke about how "not to lose sight of your customer" eventually observed that doing away with graded education would have some real benefits. But none of them were ever going to propose that because it was a political third rail no one wanted to grasp. Too radical for most parents. In deference, these five shall go nameless here.

One reason grades exist is that they do make some sense. Kids' mental and emotional maturities progress along relatively common paths. Looking for a structure different from "grades" is difficult because those eternal truths draw one back to something like a graded system.

So, if grades continue to exist, what do we do? The most useful innovation I saw to deal with the problems of graded education was Jerry Weast's approach to structuring curriculum in Montgomery County. He calls grade levels "an artifact of the past" and constructed a curriculum with an approach that largely ignored them.

He started by setting a goal that the Montgomery County Public Schools should try to get as many students as possible to score "3" or better on one or more college-level advanced placement (AP) tests. The curriculum for K–12 was built backward from that goal, identifying what had to be taught and learned to get to that end point.

Instead of thinking about learning in twelve (or thirteen or fourteen) discrete segments, learning is a smooth curve, beginning in first grade or kindergarten (or pre-kindergarten) and building toward those AP exams. Weast believes this shift in conceptualizing learning made it much easier to deal collectively with each student's unique issues.[4]

Passing that child along to the next grade does not mean that the district suddenly acts as if he or she has actually mastered writing appropriate for the higher grade level. Regardless of the class in which that child sits, he or she is going to get instruction or remediation that focuses on where that child actually stands along the curve.[5] Of course, that requires good data on every child, which Montgomery County has.

There are real advantages to Weast's approach. No child is made to repeat content and skills that he or she has mastered. Where that child had made adequate progress, he or she is still challenged by curriculum that is appropriate for his or her skill level. The student's opportunity for new learning is not sacrificed in order to fix problem areas.

Most importantly, the damage to a student's "headspace" is limited. He or she remains with his or her peers. There is no humiliation from being "left back." Equally significant, if the child can find areas in which he or she can do well or excel, it sustains a level of confidence and hope that is almost inevitably crushed by being forced to redo an entire grade.[6]

COPING WITH THE "DE-TRACKED" CLASSROOM

Schools have historically tried to ease the burden of teaching by "tracking" students. For most of the twentieth century, schools maintained different tracks into which they sent children depending on their perceived ability. There was the college-bound track and one or more tracks for kids whom teachers and administrators thought had only the capacity to work in factories or the trades (which we used to call "vocational education," but which now is often referred to as "career technical education").

In its day, this tracking was schools' attempt at not losing sight of the child. The problem was that kids were often wrongly sorted based on race or class or current level of mastery, not true capability.[7] And everyone's expectations were adjusted accordingly.[8] Frank McCourt on Staten Island is an obvious example.

In the era of No Child Left Behind, it has meant that those kids perceived to be bright have gotten courses focused on higher-order thinking, while those considered more at-risk were fed "skill and drill" exercises, where the primary goal was just getting them through their standardized test.[9] At the end of the day, then, tracking not only allowed schools to lose sight of children, it caused children to lose sight of themselves.

Over time, civil rights groups successfully brought pressure to end tracking.[10] So schools started to "de-track." Rather than make judgments about innate ability that would stigmatize students and undermine their self-confidence, they were thrown together. As a result, it expanded the range of interests, learning styles, attitudes, and levels of mastery a teacher faces.

Juggling the Competing Problems of De-tracking

De-tracking classes requires navigating between two competing problems. De-tracking eliminates the stigma associated with classes organized around the principle that students are (or are not) smart or are not going to college. On the other hand, de-tracking confronts teachers with students of such varied abilities and goals that it may be difficult, if not impossible, to teach them all at once.[11] In the pursuit of "every child can learn," the system built itself an obstacle to not losing sight of every customer.

In the high-performing districts I visited, they have largely de-tracked in the traditional sense of the term. In trying to draw together their diverse experiences and strategies for coping with a more diverse classroom, one way to characterize the new strategy is to focus on the following question: When and why do we want to use whole class instruction? That is, when is it worthwhile to bring together this group of much more diverse, de-tracked kids, notwithstanding the increase in the range of skills and achievement?

Improving Whole Class Instruction

The simplest answer is that teachers are still going to stand at the front of the class at times and lecture or lead discussions. It can be efficient, and, in the hands of a good teacher, effective.[12] It facilitates common learning and promotes social interaction. None of the districts I visited has abandoned it.

It can work, notwithstanding the increased student diversity.[13] According to one survey, 73 percent of teachers said they were able to differentiate instruction for diverse learners; only 26 percent said their class's sizes were too large to do that.[14] For example, Atlanta's University Community Academy, which is 88 percent low income, achieved a 100 percent pass rate on Georgia's standardized tests in 2009. The principal attributed the success at least in part to classroom teaching adapted to students' various methods of learning.[15]

So it is possible. But it is not the only answer. There are lots of other options, all of which focus on something other than whole class instruction.

More Resources, More Time

The first option for solving the de-tracked classroom is that students at either extreme are identified and provided additional help or opportunity before or after school, on Saturday, or during the summer. In other words, rather than rely on the classroom teacher to solve the problem, other teachers or tutors help out at other times. More about this aspect of dealing with the diverse classroom in the next chapter on assessment.

Better Matching of Teachers and Students

The second option deals with carefully staffing classes and student assignments to them.[16] Several districts have adopted a strategy in elementary school of identifying "block time" for a subject, that is, setting aside a specific hour or two during the school day where students who are struggling in reading or math are regrouped. A particularly good teacher can then concentrate on helping those who are most in need of assistance. The regrouping is not permanent; it lasts only as long as the child has not mastered the material. Or, if teachers have different styles, a student might be reassigned to a class with a teacher whose method better suits the student's learning style. Or two teachers might jointly teach a class where their combined approach is better than the one either pursued individually.[17]

Savvy Use of Information Technology

Differentiated computer-based learning is also relevant to coping with the diverse classroom. Those who are advanced can work on materials or projects that are at their level. The same kind of differentiation is an option for struggling students as well. And everyone can work in small groups. They might be in the same room, but the groups can be connected by social networking technology as well. Virtually every good district I saw regularly broke down large classes at times so that individuals or groups could learn new material or practice a skill on a computer.

One Idea Not Used: Sacrificing Advanced Classes

One great fear of those who mourn the loss of old-style tracking is that these diverse classrooms will undercut high school AP and International Baccalaureate (IB) classes or otherwise undermine the education of the most gifted students.[18] No district I visited has been so cavalier to open these sorts of courses up to everyone without regard to their actual level of skill. What they have done at times is to test their assumptions about what is in fact necessary to function well in AP or IB settings and revise their thinking.

Under Jerry Weast's system, Montgomery County has made a serious attempt at figuring out what skills are necessary and pushed kids who meet the mark to enter such classes. Of course, it works better in Montgomery than in most places because they have the kind of database system and education strategy that can closely monitor how well each student is doing mastering the prerequisites. It has, according to Weast, worked out well in the sense that more minority students are taking and passing advanced courses in Montgomery County than anywhere else in the country. However, there is still a substantial gap between white and Asian students and African Americans and Hispanics. Whether his system will completely eliminate any bias in the system probably needs several more years of experience before we all know the answer.

Don't Just Change Teaching Strategies, Change Schools

There is a larger, more systemic approach to the de-tracked classroom: Not all schools have to look the same. Open up the range of schools to which kids can apply.

The idea is not new. It already happens in districts with magnet schools, or high schools built around particular themes, like a health-sciences academy. Doris Kurtz in New Britain, a relatively small district, prides herself on how she has created a range of schools that satisfy a wide variety of needs, including those of her dwindling number of white middle-class children, while still keeping many schools integrated. Other districts have taken a somewhat similar tack: Long Beach has adopted districtwide "open enrollment." While originally done for integration, the existence of open enrollment gives kids the opportunity to look for school communities that are closest to meeting their needs.

In a few districts, there are schools for exceptionally gifted kids, like New York's Stuyvesant or Fairfax's Thomas Jefferson Science High. Where they exist, they offer one way to deal with the highest-performing students.[19] Alternatively, many districts have dealt with high performers by building partnerships with universities or community colleges, where students can take courses even though they are still officially in high school. Or the district allows them to graduate early if they are academically ready for a full college workload.[20]

Another variation focuses students on the world outside of schools, where they can identify interesting projects or work and build their knowledge and skills around them. The "multiple pathways" career-technical education strategy promoted by ConnectEd, a California education think tank, and UCLA, to which we will return in a moment, relies heavily on working with adults and organizations outside school.[21] Paul Vallas at New Orleans's Recovery School District believes in the approach; the district has a comprehensive work-study program to expose kids "to working and to people who are working."

One variation of the approach incorporates service to the community. Catholic schools traditionally have a volunteer service program.[22] So do many public schools. Miami's Janis Klein-Young, who was the 2003 Miami-Dade County Teacher of the Year, runs the Young Men's Academy for Academic and Civic Development at MacArthur South High. The 180 to 300 at-risk young men live in single-parent households or foster care. They are overwhelmingly minority and poor and have a history of problems. Each Thursday, the classes work at a homeless assistance center, a school for handicapped children, Head Start, or other civic projects. On the average, each participant shows, on a year-to-year basis, a 10 percent increase in school attendance, a 10 percent decline in behavioral referral rates, a 5 percent increase in grade point average, and an 80 percent decrease in suspensions.

Now, that range of choice has been further expanded by the advent of charter schools. They are offering another range of options. For example, Knowledge Is Power Program (KIPP) schools are distinguished by their highly structured learning environment, which is filled with chants of the multiplication tables and much longer school days, weeks, and years. KIPP's doubters question whether middle-class kids need that kind of structure and seat time, but many experts, like Howard Gardner, see the value in such settings for those particularly impoverished kids who need more support and discipline.[23] The schools may not be for everyone, but they are a useful option for at least some students.

In chapter 1, I noted that school districts are not like typical businesses because they cannot limit their services to those whom they think they can serve well. However, districts are different from schools. No one school must deal with every interest, learning style, or skill level. Instead, the district has to be a system where there is reasonable choice to all students that will allow them to find a classroom that fits what they need.

CAREER TECHNICAL EDUCATION: A VERSION THAT IS NOT AN EDUCATIONAL BOOBY PRIZE

De-tracking created more obstacles to not losing sight of the customer, the most prominent of which was vocational education. In many places, it virtually disappeared.

A case in point: my own Los Angeles Unified School District. At LAUSD, in reaction to perceived racial bias, vocational education (as it was then known) "went missing" in the 1980s and 1990s in the words of Santiago Jackson, who later became head of the district's "career technical education" programs.[24]

Giving Kids a Way to Find Their True Calling without Sacrificing Education

In one scene in the 1991 movie *City Slickers* the old cowboy Curly, played by Jack Palance, sits on his horse, holding one finger in the air. "Think about the one thing," he says to Billy Crystal, the city slicker who has come out West for a two-week adventure on a cattle drive, "that will be the secret to your life." If budding carpenters and electricians think those careers are the secret to their lives, we need to honor that with an education that prepares them just as well as it prepares a doctor or a lawyer.

So here is the conundrum. How do we respect kids' desires to go into the trades or other careers without winding up with the same kind of invidious tracking that now causes us to wince? The best answer probably has two parts.

First, we quit thinking about career technical education as if it were the consolation prize for the academically weak. Rather, let's start from the assumption that even really bright students might want to be mechanics or carpenters.

Second, we implement step one by eliminating distinct types of coursework. One recent study found that a majority of the dropouts surveyed "said they were not motivated or inspired to work hard, and many said they would have worked harder if more had been demanded of them."[25]

That means that in many districts I visited, there is no more "university prep" algebra for one group and "algebra for dummies" for the other.

Various reformers have, for years, advocated a challenging curriculum for all students.[26] For example, ConnectEd and UCLA's Institute for Democracy, Education, and Access have proposed a strategy called "multiple pathways." Even those who are focused on technical education take at least a core set of courses that will satisfy university entry requirements rather than the less-difficult "general education" courses to which they are often directed.[27]

Where their education parts company with college-bound students then is not about the academic level of the subject matter they study, but how they round out their coursework and other activities beyond the core. If it turns out that they decide accountancy holds more life promise than engine work, they can shift gears without great effort.[28]

For those who do in fact struggle academically, we do not shield them from demanding coursework. And we do not allow students to indulge themselves in the self-defeating notion that they cannot do better.[29]

We just understand it may take them longer to make it through, or require higher-quality classroom instruction, or additional tutoring.[30] So long as they get the material required to graduate, which in many states is at tenth- or eleventh-grade level, by the end of twelfth grade, there is no problem.

The Obama administration seems to understand. In early 2010, it proposed national standards in math and reading, calling the requirements "College and Career-Ready."[31] It enjoined those working on the standards to acknowledge "all students must have the opportunity to learn and meet the same high standards if they are to access the knowledge and skills necessary in their post-school lives."[32] That is a great start. However, it is not a guarantee of delivery.

HOW SCHOOL SIZE AND CLASS SIZE HELP—SOMETIMES

Size is an obvious problem when thinking about losing sight of students.

One version of the problem is about class size. Even if students were tightly grouped in old-style tracking, there was always the possibility that so many of them were crammed in a room that a teacher lost sight of some of them in the crowd. Then there is the other version: school size. High schools in particular are often accused of being so large that students just get lost in their cavernous halls.

De-tracking arguably made the issue of size worse. One obvious response to de-tracking is to cut down the extent of diversity by making the class size smaller. Dennis Littky and Elliott Washor have explained that there are four reasons their Big Picture Learning Company method of school design works. The first of those is "The Advisor works with the *15-member* class to find what interests and motivates each student."[33] (Emphasis added.) Many states in the last twenty years followed that reasoning, mandating reduced class sizes, especially in grades K–3.[34]

But the issue of size needs to be taken with a grain of salt—actually several.

The entire issue of class size may now be outdated—made an artifact of another age not only by IT and computers, but also by a more flexible, professional approach to teaching, as we have just discussed. Also, super-intendents see value in small classes, especially for early grades (K–3) and for low-income students. But they have concluded that rather than try to replicate small classes in later years, they will get better results putting the money elsewhere—like better assessments, more interventions to help struggling kids, and longer school days. In fact, without doing all those other things even in K–3, there are not likely to be great changes. Those are what turn out to be key.

You might not catch the importance of the "other things" when listening to school reform advocates. But then you just have to listen more closely to what they are in fact saying.

For example, after I spoke to Marco Petruzzi, CEO of Green Dot charter schools, I sent him an e-mail asking if he might summarize the strategy his organization was using to turn around Locke High School, one of the most dysfunctional in Los Angeles. His first point: "break down into small schools so all adults get to know every student on a personal level."

On its face, the way Petruzzi has characterized the strategy suggests that merely by getting to know everyone better, Green Dot has gotten improved results.

That is wrong. While getting to know every student certainly helps the adults, literally, to not lose sight of students, that is only step one. What Petruzzi has done is to shorthand an explanation. So do many other advocates of "small schools."[35]

What is important in not losing sight of the customer is not just "knowing students better." It is what you do once you have that knowledge. It is about tailoring instruction, regular assessment and intervention, and talking to, and mentoring, students.[36] Smaller classes or smaller schools can make those easier to do, but smallness is not a guarantee that they will happen.[37]

The recent experience with the small high school movement suggests the same conclusion.[38] The Bill and Melinda Gates Foundation has been a strong advocate for small high schools over the last decade. They have poured hundreds of millions of dollars into the creation of new small high schools and the conversion of larger ones into several smaller ones. In 2003 the foundation received a report that the success of the small schools varied. Many redesigned high schools, especially those that were

"schools-within-schools," were having particular difficulties, often focused on getting teacher buy-in to new ways of doing things.[39]

Gates's ongoing review of its grantees continued to find similar results. In his 2009 *Annual Letter* on behalf of the foundation, Bill Gates
wrote, "Many of the small schools that we invested in did not improve
students' achievement in any significant way. These tended to be the
schools that did not take radical steps to change the culture, such as
allowing the principal to pick the team of teachers or change the curriculum."[40] Other studies have reached the same conclusion.[41]

The converse is also true: Large schools can work. Brett Springston,
the superintendent in Brownsville, ran a 5,000-student high school before
coming to south Texas. He believes that with the right focus, even a
school of that size can succeed in keeping every child in focus. The size
may make it a challenge, but the key is the commitment. David Weiner,
who is now in Philadelphia, previously ran a 2,200-student elementary
school in New York City. His view is essentially the same as Springston's.
The key is the determination not to lose sight of the child's needs and to
respond accordingly, not the size of the school.

Fairfax County also has big high schools. Its smallest is 1,500 students.
The district splits the students in various ways to build social cohesion,
like grouping core academic classes in the same wing, but these are still
large schools. Even with 40 percent English language learners, the district
has maintained its reputation as a great district with middle- and upper-
middle-class parents moving in just for access to the schools.[42]

Where this history leads me is the following: Quality instruction lies
in getting the mission clear and the instruction, assessment, collaboration,
and mentoring right.[43] When those strategies are in place, it is likely, if
not inevitable, that someone will say that if classes or high schools were
smaller, we could make these changes work even better.[44] About that, I
agree.

NOTES

1. Theodore R. Sizer, *Horace's Compromise* (Boston, MA: Houghton Mifflin, 1992), 5.

2. In 2006, 281,000 out of 64,375,000, or 0.43 percent, of American elementary and
secondary students were in ungraded schools. New York led with 59,822 elementary
and 64,152 high school students. Most of the others were in New Jersey and Michigan.
Thirty-two states had no ungraded elementary schools and thirty-four had no ungraded high schools. NCES (IES), table 34 (Digest of Education Statistics)—Enrollment
in public elementary and secondary schools, by level, grade, and state or jurisdiction:
Fall 2006 (retrieved from http://nces.ed.gov/programs/doigest/d08/tables/dto8_034.asp
on Nov. 8, 2009).

3. Associated Press, "Forget Grade Levels, KC Schools Try Something New," July
3, 2010 (retrieved from www.google.com/hostednews/ap/article/ALeqM5iakmp
80Wihbmx)dpv5ItOD7guYQD9GNNCN00 on July 12, 2010).

4. Deborah Meier's Central Park East and other schools associated with the Coalition of Essential Schools followed a similar pattern. Students understood from seventh grade what they would have to do to graduate, and each had the opportunity to practice the process each semester. Deborah Meier, *The Power of Their Ideas: Lessons for America from a Small School in Harlem* (Boston, MA: Beacon, 1995), 60.

5. Weast is not alone in adopting this strategy, for example, *Kansas City Star*, "A Standards-Based Revolution Arrives in the District," Aug. 26, 2010 (retrieved from http://saving17000kids.kansascity.com/articles/remaking-schools/#ixzz06h1LzV   on Nov. 23, 2010).

6. There are students in Montgomery County who are not in their age-appropriate classes. Most are recent arrivals to the district who are so far behind that they cannot fairly be placed—at least in the first instance—with their peers. And there are a rare few who for whatever reason are failing in so many ways that pushing them ahead is not fair to anyone. However, the existence of the continuum in the curriculum gives the district a way to explain to parents the rationale for the decision and a path that explains, notwithstanding current circumstances, how a child can get back on track.

7. Jeannie S. Oakes, "Limiting Students' School Success and Life Chances: The Impact of Tracking," in *Contemporary Issues in Curriculum*, 4th ed., ed. Allen C. Ornstein, Edward F. Pajak, and Stacey B. Ornstein (Boston, MA: Pearson, 2007), 208–27.

8. For a thoughtful piece on what a teacher feels like when grouped in a computer class based on expected performance, see Cris Tovani, "I Got Grouped," *Education Leadership* 67, no. 6 (March 2010): 26. ("As a result of being grouped, I realized that people I respected didn't have a lot of confidence in my computer abilities. This public declaration almost forced me to give up my goal of becoming proficient with technology. My initial reaction was, why try? Because no one believed in my abilities, there was no pressure to perform. I was off the hook.")

9. Mark W. Ellis, "Leaving No Child Behind Yet Allowing None Too Far Ahead: Ensuring (In)Equity in Mathematics Education through the Science of Measurement and Instruction," *Teachers College Record* 110, no. 6 (2008): 1330–56; Maike Watanabe, "Tracking in the Era of High-Stakes Accountability Reform: Case Studies of Classroom Instruction in North Carolina," *Teachers College Record* 110, no. 3 (2008): 489–534.

10. While writing this book I ran into an African American member of Congress whom I have known for over thirty years. I said I was writing a book on education reform and was much taken with what many districts had done differentiating instruction for students. The congressperson jumped. "That's tracking. We don't want tracking." Now, here was someone who has known me and known that I was committed to equal opportunity. Yet the trigger reaction said, "No, I don't want to hear more. That is a bad idea." The discomfort over prior abuses of data is a problem whose significance is underestimated by many superintendents.

11. Once IDEA forced schools to accept "mainstreaming," classrooms became far more diverse places, even if nothing else happened. While schools with enough money and capable staff can provide special education teachers to help relieve the burden, the presence of special education children complicates teaching strategies.

12. Sean Kelly and Julianne Turner, "Rethinking the Effects of Classroom Activity Structure on the Engagement of Low-Achieving Students," *Teachers College Record* 111, no. 7 (2009): 1665–92.

13. Different learning styles may include a variety of strategies, some of which may relate to how an individual learns on his or her own, while others relate to the best social environment in which to put children. For example, some children may do fine with typical teacher-directed instruction, while others learn best with peers or while reading alone. Robert W. Cole, "Educating Everybody's Children: We Know What Works—and What Doesn't," in *Educating Everybody's Children*, 2nd ed., ed. Robert W. Cole (Alexandria, VA: ASCD, 2008), 9.

14. Public Agenda, *Teaching for a Living: How Teachers See the Profession Today* (New York: Public Agenda, 2009), 5 (retrieved from www.publicagenda.org/pages/teaching-for-a-living on Dec. 21, 2009).

15. *Atlanta Constitution,* "Family Atmosphere Promotes Learning," July 15, 2009. Other districts have claimed to lift results for similar reasons. For example, Clifton, New Jersey, showed significant improvement in scores in 2007; the superintendent attributed the improvements to several factors, one of which was teaching according to each child's learning styles. *Bergen Record,* Aug. 1, 2007, L-5.

16. This paragraph compels a parenthetical note of caution. Every teacher and every principal has at least one story about a parent pushing to have a child transferred to a teacher who is perceived to be "better." The parents who seem to have more influence tend to be the more affluent, and, as race follows wealth, more likely white. Tom Loveless, *Tracking and Detracking: High Achievers in Massachusetts Middle Schools* (Washington, DC: Thomas B. Fordham Institute, 2009), 27. The result may be "re-tracking," where magically some classes are more filled with white, or wealthy, kids than others. Acquiescing in such pressure, however, undercuts the system. On top of the problems giving in to "re-tracking" will cause in terms of student learning, it will undercut the fairness of any pay plan that gives teachers tenure or individual bonuses based on the student achievement data for their own class. As I discussed in the prior chapter, such plans have a difficult time adjusting student achievement data when students are not randomly assigned to classes.

17. Vivian Troen and Katherine C. Boles, *Who's Teaching Your Children?* (New Haven, CT: Yale University Press, 2003), 150. One study has found that within-class ability tracking in kindergarten persists in many schools. In high-minority schools, the practice seems to achieve better results in reading achievement. Anthony Buttaro Jr., Sophia Catsambis, Lunn M. Mulkey, and Lala Carr Steelman, "An Organizational Perspective on the Origins of Instructional Segregation: School Composition and Use of Within-Class Ability Grouping in American Kindergartens," *Teachers College Record* 112, no. 5 (2010): 4–5 (ID Number 15670, retrieved from www.tcrecord.org/PrintContent.asp?ContentID=15670 on Nov. 27, 2009).

18. Loveless, *Tracking and Detracking.*

19. These schools raise interesting questions about how to balance two competing interests. On the one hand, high-performing students are well served by these specialized schools. However, there is evidence that low-performing students, particularly minorities, benefit from having higher-performing peers, in their schools. Douglas N. Harris, "How Do School Peers Influence Student Educational Outcomes? Theory and Evidence from Economics and Other Social Sciences," *Teachers College Record* 112, no. 4 (2010): 8–9. Paul Vallas cited this peer effect as one reason he favored pushing the spread of quality AP and IB classes throughout high schools rather than creating an admission-test-based school for high-performing students.

20. See, for example, *New York Times Sunday Magazine,* "Class Dismissed," Feb. 28, 2010, 11.

21. Jeannie Oakes, Marisa Saunders, "Multiple Pathways: Bringing Schools to Life," *Education Week,* July 20, 2009 (retrieved from www.edweek.org/ew/articles/2009/07/20/37oakes.h28.html on July 24, 2009).

22. Anthony S. Bryk, Valerie E. Lee, and Peter B. Holland, *Catholic Schools and the Common Good* (Cambridge, MA: Harvard University Press, 1993), 139.

23. Howard Gardner, *The Unschooled Mind* (New York: Basic Books, 1991), 197.

24. *Los Angeles Times,* "LAUSD Sees a Future in Career Ed," April 27, 2007, C1; Many districts continue to fail to provide adequate career-technical education according to students and parents surveyed in a study of four school districts: Baltimore, Maryland; Kingsport, Tennessee; Dallas, Texas; and Indianapolis, Indiana. John M. Bridgeland, Robert Balfanz, Laura A. Moore, and Rebecca S. Friant, *Raising Their Voices: Engaging Students, Teachers, and Parents to Help End the High School Dropout Epidemic* (Washington, DC: Civic Enterprises, 2010), 13.

25. John M. Bridgeland, Robert Balfanz, Laura A. Moore, and Rebecca S. Friant, *Raising Their Voices* (Washington, DC: Civic Enterprises, 2010), 6.

26. Carol Corbet Burris, Ed Wiley, Kevin G. Wilner, and John Murphy, "Accountability, Rigor, and Detracking: Achievement Effects of Embracing a Challenging Cur-

riculum as a Universal Good for All Students," *Teachers College Record* 110, no. 3 (2008): 571–607.

27. EdSource, *Levers for Change: Opportunities to Strengthen California's High School Curriculum* (Mountain View, CA: EdSource, 2007), 22; EdSource, *Multiple Pathways in California: An Emerging Option for High School Reform* (Mountain View, CA: EdSource, 2009); Hugh Meghan, *Restructuring and Reculturing Schools to Provide Students with Multiple Pathways to College and Career* (Los Angeles: UCLA Institute for Democracy, Education, and Access, 2007), 11.

28. Such a strategy addresses another survey result reported by *USA Today* in 2010: "A recent national survey of high school teachers by ACT Inc., the educational testing company, found 71% agreed 'completely' or 'a great deal' that high school graduates need the same set of skills and knowledge whether they plan to go to college or enter the workforce, yet 42% said teachers reduce academic expectations for students they perceive as not being college-bound." *USA Today*, "What If a College Education Just Isn't for Everyone?," March 16, 2010 (retrieved from www.usatoday.com/news/education/2010--03-06-1Acollegeforall16_CV_N.htm on March 18, 2010).

29. Theodore R. Sizer, *Horace's Compromise* (Boston, MA: Houghton Mifflin, 1992), 34–35.

30. Christopher Mazzeo, Elaine Allensworth, and Valerie Lee, "College Prep for All? What We've Learned in Chicago," *Education Week*, April 27, 2010 (retrieved from www.edweek.org/ew.articles.2010/04/28/30mazzeo.h29.html on April 28, 2010).

31. See www2.ed.gov/about/overview/budget/budget11/summary/edlite-section3a.html#overview (retrieved on March 2, 2010). As the standards have evolved, they have focused on a single set of standards for all children.

32. Core Standards Initiative, "The Standards—Mathematics" (retrieved from www.corestandards.org/the-standards/mathematics on Dec. 6, 2010).

33. Dennis Littky and Elliott Washor, "Big Picture Learning" (brochure) (Providence, RI: Big Picture Learning), 12.

34. Florida's requirement is now fixed in the state's constitution. Article IX, Section 1(a), Florida Constitution. A modification of the provision, Amendment 8, was rejected by voters in 2010.

35. Petruzzi is not alone. Stanford's Linda Darling-Hammond is an accomplished education academic and skillful writer. In summarizing why the Coalition Campus Schools Project was successful, she lists "small size" as the first factor, followed by "structures that allow for personalization and strong relationships," carefully constructed curriculum," "pedagogical approaches," "school-wide performance assessment," "flexible supports for learning," and "collaboration." Linda Darling-Hammond, "Reinventing High School: Outcomes of the Coalition Campus Schools Project," *American Education Research Journal* 39 (2002): 653. Anthony Bryk does *not* make the same mistake in his discussion of Catholic schools. It may be true that all the schools were small, but without all the other features, they would not have been a success. He calls size a "facilitating factor," for the informal faculty-student interactions that occur because it is the schools' philosophy that there should be the extensive engagement of parents and faculty in extracurricular life of the school. Anthony S. Bryk, Valerie E. Lee, and Peter B. Holland, *Catholic Schools and the Common Good* (Cambridge, MA: Harvard University Press, 1993), 145.

36. Small size is often equated with a lower student-teacher ratio. One does not automatically follow the other, however. In fact, the other way to deal with size is to decrease the student-teacher ratio. Phillips Andover has 1,111 students. It is not a small school. Nonetheless, it has close student-teacher relationships because the student-teacher ratio is 5:1. By way of contrast, Green Dot's Locke ratio is 21:1.

37. Students may feel more comfortable in a smaller atmosphere, even if there are no other improvements in how the school functions.

38. As with so many other education subjects, there is a divide among researchers about whether small class size *alone* has an impact on learning. For example, Eric A. Hanushek, "The Impact of Differential Expenditures on School Performance," *Educa-*

tion Researcher 18 (1989): 45–51 (no effect); S. L. Pong and A. Pallas, "Class Size and Eighth-Grade Achievement in the United States and Abroad," *Educational Evaluation and Policy Analysis* 23 (2001): 251–73; Spyros Konstantopoulos, "What Is the Impact of Class Size on Student Learning?," *Teachers College Record*, Feb. 5, 2009 (electronic article) (positive effect). However, unlike many other subjects where I do not take a position between the differing views, here the most recent analyses make, in my view, a compelling case for a more nuanced view.

39. David Merkowitz, *Ready for College: How Small High Schools Can Provide Under-served Students the Support They Need to Prepare for Higher Education* (Washington, DC: Strategic Communications, 2003). See also Linda Shear et al., "Contrasting Paths to Small-School Reform: Results of a 5-Year Evaluation of the Bill and Melinda Gates Foundation's National High Schools Initiative," *Teachers College Record* 110, no. 9 (2008): 1986–2039; Floyd Hammack, "Off the Record—Something Old, Something New, Something Borrowed, Something Blue: Observations on the Small Schools Movement," *Teachers College Record* 110, no. 9 (2008): 2067–72; Douglas Ready, Valerie Lee, and Kevin G. Weiner, "Educational Equity and School Structure: School Size, Overcrowding, and Schools-Within-Schools," *Teachers College Record* 106, no. 10 (2004): 1989–2014.

40. Bill Gates, *2009 Annual Letter of the Gates Foundation* (Redmond, WA: Gates Foundation, 2009), 11.

41. See, for example, Chrysan Gallucci, Michael S. Knapp, Anneke Markholt, and Suzanne Ort, "Converging Reform 'Theories' in Urban Middle Schools: District-Guided Instructional Improvement in Small Schools of Choice," *Teachers College Record* 109, no. 12 (2007): 2601–41; Thomas Toch, Craig Jerald, and Erin Dillon, "Surprise—High School Reform Is Working," *Phi Delta Kappan* 88, no. 6 (Feb. 2007): 433, 437; Consortium on Chicago School Research, *If Small Is Not Enough: The Characteristics of Successful Small High Schools in Chicago* (Chicago: University of Chicago Press, 2008), 17 ("This work highlights that how adults work together in small schools is a crucial factor in raising student achievement. In particular, it suggests that collective work on improving instruction is a key lever for raising achievement. In addition, it points to the benefits of balancing the direction and initiative provided by principals with teacher voice and leadership. Given that reducing size does not automatically lead to such developments, however, schools will need to intentionally focus on creating these key organizational characteristics.").

42. There are more examples. *New York Times*, "4,100 Students Prove 'Small Is Better' Rule Wrong," Sept. 27, 2010 (Brockton, Massachusetts, high school has 4,100 students and has become an exemplary school in the last ten years.) (retrieved from www.nytimes.com/2010/09/28/education/28school.html on Sept. 27, 2010).

43. Deborah Meier also argues that in order to facilitate the kind of collaborative decision making among teachers and administrators that is essential to succeed, the school *must be* small. Deborah Meier, *The Power of Their Ideas: Lessons for America from a Small School in Harlem* (Boston, MA: Beacon, 1995), 108. My investigations suggest that large schools with committed, understanding principals can create the necessary collaborative environment, although I agree that it would seem logical, on its face, to assume that such collaboration should be easier to achieve in a smaller school environment.

44. Linda Darling-Hammond, *The Right to Learn* (San Francisco: Jossey-Bass, 1997), 335; Vivian Troen and Katherince C. Boles, *Who's Teaching Your Children?* (New Haven, CT: Yale University Press, 2003), 159.

TWENTY

Assessing Students: Never Letting Them Fall Too Far Behind

The most profound change in public education may be the new ability of school districts to keep children and their learning needs in focus. Rather than being limited to private schools or districts with extremely small student/teacher ratios, such personalized service can now be done in every public school. The improvements in our ability to assess student learning may do more to create effective, personalized instruction than any of the other changes discussed in this book.

THE OLD WAY OF KEEPING STUDENTS IN FOCUS

When I spoke with John Rogers, the academic dean at Phillips Andover Academy, I asked him whether he in fact had adopted any of the fancy databases and computerized assessments that characterized some of the high-performing districts I had visited. "No," he said, "but we know how our students are doing all the time."

He went on to describe the close contact that students and teachers have on Andover's residential campus. Every faculty member has eight to ten kids for whom he or she serves as an advisor. There are extensive and regular contacts. The admissions office tracks new students from their first arrival on campus, and for those poor or minority students who may be at risk of isolation, the school goes out of its way to connect each one with a nurturing house counselor or advisor.

No struggling student goes unnoticed. Although there is no formal program for interventions or enrichments, there is an academic support center staffed with two full-time and two part-time people, a lot of peer tutoring, and peer and faculty support groups.

Billie Hicklin, who is an associate superintendent of the Watauga County Schools, said much the same thing. I visited the small, rural district, which is in the mountains in northwest North Carolina, because I had been surprised to find that it had the second-highest test scores in the state. I wanted to know what they were doing right.

I asked Hicklin if the district employed any of the high-tech assessments I had seen at places like Blue Valley. She echoed Rogers almost word for word. "No," she said, "we do not do that, but our schools are pretty close-knit. Teachers know their kids." She went on to describe a system of eight schools, which, because of the rural nature of the district, were largely self-governing and closely tied to their communities. More importantly, the county provided the district with enough money to hire 170 additional staff (at least in 2009) to supplement what the district could have funded with its regular sources of local and state revenue. There were enough teachers in close enough contact with their students that they knew them well, even without regular assessments. All the district had to do was push teachers to help those who were struggling. No one fell behind because they got lost.

KEEPING TRACK OF KIDS IN YOUR HIGH-PERFORMING PUBLIC SCHOOL: ASSESSMENTS

Welcome to the world of the computerized "formative assessment." A formative assessment might look like a quiz or test, but its purpose is different.[1] Instead of being used to determine a grade or evaluate school accountability (in education speak these are "summative assessments"), formative assessments are used for feedback to help "form" teachers' future instructional practices and/or students' future learning strategies.[2]

The whole idea would have floundered without the information revolution, which offered new possibilities for what the assessments might look like, how they could be evaluated, and how the results would be recorded. They are no longer limited to paper and pencil tests. Math quizzes can be taken and scored electronically. So can reading and English language arts assessments, which, as technology has advanced, can evaluate even writing samples.[3] The information is available in "real time." In the distant past of, say, 2009, that meant it was quickly available to the principal, and depending on the school or district, to the teachers.[4] Now there are systems, like clickers handed out to every student in a class, that can give feedback to a teacher in the blink of an eye.[5]

As a result, districts have built in "mini-assessments" as frequently as weekly or biweekly. And that, in turn, means that interventions (to help stragglers) and enrichments (to push those who are already ahead) can be adjusted just as often. Professor Margaret Heritage of UCLA, who has studied assessment for many years, believes the frequency of the formative assessment is key. If they are given only every six to nine weeks (which is the pattern even in some of the districts I visited), their value diminishes. They still can help answer the question, "How are we doing?" but they are much less useful providing guidance for interventions. The information is too stale and the students may have fallen much further behind before the first help arrives.[6]

The impact of timely mini-assessment data is clear. A recent survey of teachers by Scholastic and the Gates Foundation found 75 percent of teachers use student performance data "very often" to identify students who need supplemental services, and 71 percent use it "very often" to differentiate instruction.[7] A second study, of successful California middle schools, identified the extensive use of assessment data to evaluate individual student achievement and to modify instruction as one of the key practices of higher-performing schools.[8] Douglas Reeves, who has studied the "90-90-90" schools where overwhelming majorities of poor and minority kids do well, has written that one of the five keys to their success is "frequent assessment of student progress and multiple opportunities for improvement."[9]

Don't Just Test Students, Ask Them

The assessments, however, are not the only means some districts use to determine how a student learns. Education experts like Carol Ann Tomlinson, who has been a long-time advocate of differentiated instruction, like to talk about "sharing responsibility for teaching and learning" between teachers and students.[10] Some districts have followed her idea; when they want to know how students are doing, they ask them.[11]

One of the most fascinating couple of hours I spent on the road was my visit to Third Creek Elementary School in Statesville, North Carolina. Terry Holliday, who was then Statesville-Iredell County's superintendent,[12] is a great devotee of the Baldrige cycle of "Plan, Do, Study, Act," which translates into: Plan something, do it, study if it worked, and if necessary, revise it and try it again.

The district applies the cycle to student learning in a fascinating way. Starting in *kindergarten*, teachers take time at the end of the week to go over with the class what they are going to learn the following week and how they are going to learn it. When they convene at the end of the next week, they review whether everyone succeeded on the assessments given that week. If anyone did not do well enough, there is a discussion about how they all could learn better.[13]

Remember, this conversation starts with five-year-olds. Yet it seems to work. For example, the principal, Amy Rhyne, reported that one of the kindergarten classes had recently considered the problem that they had not all succeeded in counting from one to twenty. The number thirteen had presented some difficulty. So one girl suggested painting a button on the class door and having every child say "thirteen" when they came or went from class. It worked. One to twenty now included thirteen.

Teachers in Iredell County repeat the same process for individual children. Principal Rhyne and I went over to a corner of a third-grade classroom, and she pulled one of several little loose-leaf books from the shelf. In it, a child had recorded what he was learning, and how he was learning it, in a careful, deliberate hand interspersed with the occasional colorful drawing.

Superintendent Terry Holliday explained that these discussions are a way for children to understand their own learning and take responsibility for it. More importantly, it is a way for teachers to learn about everyone's interests and needs. It is hard to think of a better road map to not losing sight of a child.

Iredell County is not alone. The *New York Times* reported that middle school students in North Brunswick, New Jersey, were doing essentially the same thing as their peers in North Carolina:

> All 428 sixth graders at Linwood Middle School in North Brunswick, NJ, are charting their own academic path with personalized student learning plans—electronic portfolios containing information about their learning styles, skills, career goals and extracurricular activities.
>
> These new learning plans will follow each sixth grader through high school, and are intended to help the students assess their own strengths and weaknesses as well as provide their parents and teachers with a more complete profile beyond grades and test scores. [14]

BUILDING A SYSTEM OF ASSESSMENTS AND INTERVENTIONS

At some point in the future, mini-assessments and intervention strategies are going to be ubiquitous, and teachers' understanding of how to use them commonplace. Not yet, however. Some districts, like Blue Valley and Iredell County, rely heavily on them. Others would like to but have not developed good tests, or properly trained teachers, or just do not have the money for after-school help sessions. And some are simply not yet convinced.

We are still experimenting with what they should look like, [15] and many teachers do not understand how to use them. [16] Is a child's problem merely a need for more seat time while doing the same thing, or is there another learning style that will best help the child master the material? Is the problem with the teaching, or is some emotional issue getting in the way?

The amount of teacher learning required makes the process a challenge. [17] Most districts—and most experts [18] —continue to work out how to interpret mini-assessment results and what to do in response. [19] So do teachers. Their work needs to be encouraged. *Using formative assessment is the heart of the new artisanal form of instruction and an ideal use of the professional learning community.*

Secretary of Education Arne Duncan has recognized the challenges of building a system of mini-assessments that districts can use. As part of the package of Race to the Top funds, Duncan proposed in 2009 that $350 million be set aside to develop common academic [summative] assessments.[20] Both multistate consortia that received grants under the program promise some of that money is supposed to go for "formative" ones as well.[21] Even if that does not happen, then the least one can hope is that the better-constructed summative assessments will eventually help both.[22]

Because mini-assessments are at the heart of the measured environment, they are likely to be the object of attack from those teachers who do not like this new world. Gerald Anderson's Brazosport is a perfect example. After Anderson retired, Texas changed its standards, which led to a change in curriculum. Teachers pressed the new superintendent that there had been altogether too much "testing" and that the district needed to reconsider whether it was worthwhile to commit to the expense of redoing all the mini-assessments. The superintendent agreed.[23] The achievement gap reopened over time in Brazosport, a fact Anderson attributes at least in part to the loss of mini-assessments and the ability to provide kids with the kind of immediate support they had previously received.

INDIVIDUAL INSTRUCTION MEANS MORE TIME AT SCHOOL

That brings us to the larger problem of the length of the school day and the school year. About half of America's parents oppose students putting in extra time after school, on Saturdays, or in the summer.[24] Without a change in those views, there is no reasonable way to create the kind of individualized education that mini-assessments can drive.

Several of the superintendents with whom I spoke believe firmly that there should be a longer school day and more of them, extending school into the summer. The Knowledge Is Power Program has both a longer day, 7:15 a.m. to 5 p.m., and a longer year. So does the Promise Academy run by the Harlem Children's Zone. So does St. Ignatius Loyola in Baltimore, as does the Recovery School District in Louisiana, where every student receives either enrichments or interventions during the last two hours of the day.[25] According to the National Center on Time and Learning, eight hundred charter schools and two hundred traditional public schools have expanded their schedules by more than one to two hours a day, or three hundred hours a year.[26] The Broad Foundation, among others, has given money to push the idea even further.[27] Several prominent education researchers advocate for longer school days and school years.[28] President Obama and Secretary of Education Duncan do as well.[29]

In school, the longer day has real benefits beyond enrichments and interventions: Nick Fischer, the former Fall River superintendent who oversaw adding extra time at one of his failing middle schools, said it gave students a time and place for homework, for playing safely on school grounds, and for joining clubs or other extracurricular activities students could not find elsewhere. The result was increased attendance and fewer students arriving after the start of class.[30]

Finally, the longer year limits "summer learning loss," which we previously discussed in conjunction with value-added testing. For middle-class children who have plenty of stimulation during the summer, the effect is minimal. For poor kids, the loss can be severe, with some estimates as high as 25 percent to 50 percent of a prior year's learning.[31] It may account for as much as 80 percent of the reading achievement gap by ninth grade.[32] They read less, go to fewer museums, and are less likely to go on summer vacations that are learning experiences.

The longer day or year should not be limited to those in academic trouble. Increasing the school day or lengthening the school year for all students removes the peer pressure that is inevitable when some kids have to stay after others go home. In Miami-Dade, one of the problems with the "Zone" experiment that former superintendent Rudy Crew created to test out many ideas, like mini-assessments, was that students in Zone schools had longer days and longer years than other Miami-Dade students. "Why," they complained, "do I have to go to school when no one else does?" It should have been no surprise that students skipped the later classes and ignored summer school days.[33]

WHAT'S ALL THIS INDIVIDUALIZED EDUCATION GOING TO COST?

The good news is that several districts have built successful programs within their current budgets. As I will discuss in the chapters on the common beliefs and practices of successful schools (chapters 23 and 24), what Brazosport, Blue Valley, Aldine, and others have done is get a great deal from relatively small expenditures. The bad news is the obvious — broadly extending school days, weeks, or years, for every child will cost a lot more.

There are some creative ways to fill the void. Long Beach has an extensive volunteer tutoring program. Foundations and nongovernmental organizations may provide some money.

But longer days and years likely will require new local and state support. There are, however, two already-existing federal sources. One is a program called "21st Century Community Learning Centers," which provides over $1 billion a year in grants to offer "students . . . additional time to engage in activities that directly improve their knowledge of core academic subjects and improve their academic achievement."[34] The Obama administration has proposed extending the program as part of Elementary and Secondary Education Act reauthorization,[35] but if it is going to play a significant role in supporting before- or after-school learning, it will have to be much larger than currently contemplated.

Second, the issue of tutoring brings up one troublesome part of No Child Left Behind. Section 1116 (Supplemental Education Services) provides that if a Title I school has failed adequate yearly progress for two consecutive years, any struggling child in that school can thereafter obtain tutoring from designated providers. The premise is that outside organizations, including large for-profit companies, can provide educational assistance that the struggling schools cannot. In fact, any school or district that is failing cannot even be designated as a provider of tutoring services, unless it receives a waiver from the Department of Education.[36]

The statute is simply crosswise to what has happened to education in the years since it was passed. In districts where there is a commitment to individualized instruction based on constant assessment, a well-designed intervention program should be an integration of the classroom assessment, teacher-collaborative evaluation of the results, and whatever intervention occurs. The statute's idea that tutoring and schools should not be connected makes no sense unless the district demonstrates it is incapable of carrying out the program as intended.[37]

WHAT WE NEED TO DO

In order to make sure a district does "not lose sight" of any student, the most fundamental change required is a change in attitude. Ted Sizer's version of the prescription: "Design each youngster's educational program around his or her particular needs and potential. Know each child well. Accept diversity. Indeed, rejoice in it. Make standardization a policy of last resort."[38]

Those outside a district's hierarchy cannot be expected to provide the details of the strategy. But what they can do is ask probing questions that should reveal whether those in charge are doing what they are supposed to do:

- How has the curriculum been constructed? Is there heavy reliance on scripting or single textbooks, or is there use of computerized materials to adapt coursework or enhance teaching and collaboration?
- If there is use of computerized materials, have administrators and teachers been given enough training to use it well, or, are the mate-

rials treated as "add-ons" that do not mesh well with more traditional instruction?

- Do teachers collaborate on selecting supplemental materials, so that there is both the desired diversity and an assurance of quality in what is offered?
- Does the district encourage principals and teachers to innovate around computerized materials while ensuring that new ideas are tested over time against real benchmarks?
- Is the curriculum constructed around age-centered grades (e.g., fifth grade), or is the curriculum more of a continuous curve, like Jerry Weast's in Montgomery County? In any event, what is the district's strategy to deal with kids who have fallen behind? Do they have enough flexible curriculum and classroom organization that they can deal with kids who are not at grade level without requiring they repeat a grade?
- Is there a dummy's set of courses for kids deemed less capable, or is the goal that all students are expected to master the same material?
- Is there a robust career technical education program, and are its students being given the same academic courses as college-bound students?
- How much class time is occupied with teacher lectures, and how much with other forms of learning?
- How are student classroom assignments made? Is there still tracking? If so, how is it administered?
- Are districts providing a range of potential education experiences for their children? Neighborhood schools should not be the "poor cousins," which can exploit a captive audience, and other schools, including charters, magnets, career academies, and joint college programs, should all be part of what is on offer to every child. That means not only that such schools exist, but also they are genuinely accessible to every child in the district.
- If all the elements of not losing sight of a child are in place, should class size or school size be reduced? Would that expense, which is not small, help facilitate all the other changes?
- Is there an assessment system? If it is not the old-fashioned Watauga County or Andover way of doing things, is there a robust database that can generate and disseminate assessment data? How is it used? Do teachers know what to do with it? Is there a system of interventions or enrichments in place to help kids after the assessments are analyzed?

In addition to the questions, parents should press for longer days and longer years. There is no way to provide the kind of individualized learning discussed here without more time in school.

Finally, Congress needs to rewrite NCLB to give districts full financial support to make individualized education happen, whether it is through an expansion of 21st Century Community Learning Centers, the E-Rate Program to build out Internet connectivity and computerization in the schools, Supplemental Educational Services—or simply an increase in Title I. Whatever districts knew (or did not know) years ago, we now understand how to organize schools to provide real assistance to every child. The law and the facts should be on the same page.

NOTES

1. An organization called the National Forum on Assessment, which includes several education and civil rights organizations, issued a call in 1995 to rethink assessments by focusing on formative, rather than summative, purposes for them. *Principles and Indicators for Student Assessment Systems* (Cambridge, MA: Fair Test, 1995). The work is often cited by the opponents of high-stakes testing mandated by NCLB.

2. W. James Popham, *Unlearned Lessons: Six Stumbling Blocks to Our Schools' Success* (Cambridge, MA: Harvard Education Press, 2009), 35.

3. Brian Pick, the director of academic strategy and instruction in Washington, DC, told me that his district had decided to use mClass:Dibels for K–2 reading assessments. The handheld devices allow for a quick review of student work and offer immediate suggestions to help those who are struggling. An explanation of the product can be found at www.wirelessgeneration.com/solutions/mclass-dibels.html.

4. *eSchoolNews*, "Technology Takes Formative Assessment to a Whole New Level," Aug. 4, 2010 (retrieved from www.eschoolnews.com/2010/08/04/technology-takes-formative-assessment-to-a-whole-new-level on Aug. 9, 2010). For examples of what assessment software can do, see www.edusoft.com/corporate/products_state.html which describes the capability of Houghton Mifflin's Edusoft products, and www.amered.com/aeig_moreinfo_awl_assessment.php, which describes the A+nywhere Learning System.

5. *New York Times*, "More Professors Give Out Hand-Held Devices to Monitor Students and Engage Them," Nov. 12, 2010, A12.

6. Margaret Heritage, *Formative Assessment and Next-Generation Assessment Systems: Are We Losing an Opportunity?* (Washington, DC: Council of Chief State School Officers, 2010).

7. Scholastic, Inc., and Bill and Melinda Gates Foundation, *Primary Sources: America's Teachers on America's Schools* (Seattle: Gates Foundation, 2010), 27.

8. EdSource, *Gaining Ground in the Middle Grades: Why Some Schools Do Better* (Mountain View, CA: EdSource, 2010), 9.

9. Douglas Reeves, *High Performance in High Poverty Schools: 90/90/90 and Beyond,* (Boulder, CO: Center for Performance Assessment, 2003), 3. See also Milbrey W. McLaughlin and Joan E. Talbert, *Building School-Based Teacher Learning Communities* (New York: Teachers College Press, 2006), 121.

10. Carol Ann Tomlinson, *The Differentiated School* (Alexandria, VA: ASCD, 2008), 9.

11. Margaret Heritage, "Formative Assessment: What Do Teachers Need to Know and Do," *Phi Delta Kappan* 89, no. 2 (Oct. 2007): 140–45; McLaughlin and Talbert, *Building School-Based Teacher Learning Communities*, 121–22; Paul Black and Dylan William, "Inside the Black Box: Raising Standards through Classroom Assessment," *Phi Delta Kappan* 80, no. 2 (Oct. 1998): 139–48.

12. In 2009, Holliday became commissioner of education in Kentucky.

13. Dawn Creason, *Using Baldrige to Improve Teaching and Learning* (Milwaukee, WI: American Society for Quality, 2008), 3 (retrieved from www.asq.org).

14. *New York Times*, "In Middle School, Charting Their Course to College and Beyond," Feb. 28, 2010 (retrieved from www.nytimes.com/2010/03/01,education/01schools.html on March 1, 2010).

15. Margaret Heritage, *Formative Assessment and Next-Generation Assessment Systems: Are We Losing an Opportunity?* (Washington, DC: Council of Chief State School Officers, 2010).

16. W. James Popham, *Unlearned Lessons: Six Stumbling Blocks to Our Schools' Success* (Cambridge, MA: Harvard Education Press, 2009), 136–37; Michael Fullan, *Leading in a Culture of Change* (San Francisco: Jossey-Bass, 2001), 117.

17. Caroline Wylie and Christine Lyon, "What Schools and Districts Need to Know to Support Teachers' Use of Formative Assessment," *Teachers College Record*, Aug. 3, 2009 (retrieved from www.tcrecord.org, ID Number: 15734).

18. See, for example, National High School Center, National Center on Response to Intervention, Center on Instruction, *Tiered Interventions in High School: Using Preliminary "Lessons Learned" to Guide Ongoing Discussion* (Washington, DC: American Institutes for Research, 2010).

19. For example, a doctrine and set of strategies, called Response to Intervention, which was originally developed to help special needs children with reading, has been gradually adapted to broader use, but RTI will need much greater elaboration to meet all the potential needs of districts using mini-assessments widely.

20. *Education Week*, "Duncan Unveils Details on Race to the Top Aid," June 15, 2009 (retrieved from www.edweek.org.ew.articles/2009/06/15/36duncan.h28.html on June 18, 2009).

21. Smarter Balanced Assessment Consortium (SBAC), www.k12.wa.us/smarter; Partnership for the Assessment of Readiness for College and Careers (PARCC), *Race to the Top Assessment Proposal Summary*, www.achieve.org.

22. As of 2008, twenty-one states had developed formative assessments. Editorial Projects in Education, "Quality Counts," *Education Week*, Jan. 2008, 37.

23. Although it is only one piece of anecdotal evidence, an interesting article appeared in the *New York Times* in September 2010, which suggests kids may not be as daunted as the Brazosport teachers suggested. The author, Elisabeth Rosenthal, described her children's experience with formative testing in elementary school while they were living in Beijing. She wrote, "When testing is commonplace and the teachers are supportive—as my children's were, for the most part—the tests felt like so many puzzles; not so much a judgment on your being, but an interesting challenge." Elisabeth Rosenthal, "Taking Tests the Chinese Way," *New York Times Week in Review*, Sept. 12, 2010, 1, 2.

24. Frederick Hess, Andrew Rotherham, "NCLB and the Competitiveness Agenda: Happy Collaboration or a Collision Course?," *Phi Delta Kappan* 88, no. 5 (Jan. 2007): 350; Larry Cuban, "The Perennial Reform: Fixing School Time," *Phi Delta Kappan* 89, no. 4 (Dec. 2008), 240–49.

25. Deborah Meier's Central Park East was also open until 5 p.m. and on Saturdays. Deborah Meier, *The Power of Their Ideas: Lessons for America from a Small School in Harlem* (Boston, MA: Beacon, 1995), 56.

26. *USA Today*, "Kids Reap Benefit of Long School Year," June 10, 2009, 5. There is some evidence that the longer day has resulted in higher test scores. *Education Week*, "Study Eyes Effect of Extra Learning Time on Scores," Dec. 7, 2009 (retrieved from www.edweek.org/ew/articles/2009/12/09/14time.h29.html on Dec. 8, 2009).

27. *Philanthropy News Digest*, "National Center on Time & Learning Receives $1.5 Million Grant from Broad Foundation," Feb. 24, 2010 (retrieved from http://foundationcenter.org/pnd/news/story_print.jthml on Feb. 24, 2010).

28. Troen and Boles, *Who's Teaching Your Children?*, 160–63.

29. Associated Press, "More School: Obama Would Curtail Summer Vacation," Sept. 27, 2009 (retrieved from www.google.come/hostednews/aparticle/ALeqM5ia76R77zq5_ZYc77h178ePWRNJwQD9VLOCG0 on Oct. 12, 2009); *Washington Post*, "Now Voices of Power: Arne Duncan," April 1, 2009 (retrieved from www.

washingtonpost.com/wp-srv/politics/documents/transcript_vop_duncan.html   on April 1, 2009).

30. The longer day and the longer year meet a mix of educational and social needs. They afford schools enough time to provide both whole class and more individualized instruction. The longer day also answers the problem of child care that many families, particularly the poor, face. If children could stay at school until the end of the adult workday, parents do not have to arrange for someone to look after younger children or find jobs that would allow them to be home by midafternoon.

31. Lee Jenkins, *Permission to Forget* (Milwaukee, WI: ASQ Quality Press, 2005), 2.

32. Richard Allington and Anne McGill-Franzen, "Why Summers Matter in the Rich/Poor Achievement Gap," *Teachers College Record*, Aug. 24, 2009 (ID No. 15757, retrieved from www.tcrecord.org/PrintContent.asp?ContentID=15757 on Oct. 19, 2009); Ron Fairchild and Jeff Smink, "Is Summer School the Key to Reform?," *Education Week*, May 12, 2010, 40.

33. Steven M. Urdegar, *School Improvement Zone Final Evaluation Report* (Miami: Miami-Dade County Public Schools Office of Program Evaluation, May, 2009), 112.

34. *Fiscal Year 2011 Budget Summary—February 1, 2010*, "Section III. A. Elementary and Secondary Education" ("21st Century Community Learning Centers") (retrieved from www2.ed.gov/about/overview/budget/budget11/summary/edlite-section3a# overview, found on March 2, 2010).

35. U.S. Department of Education, *A Blueprint for Reform* (Washington, DC: U.S. Department of Education, 2010), 32.

36. 34 C.F.R. Sec. 200.47(b)(1)iv)(A),(B); See, for example, *Federal Register*, May 15, 2009, 22909–131.

37. See, for example, *Mission Loc@l*, "No Faith in No Child Left Behind Tutoring," April 27, 2009 (retrieved from http://missionlocal.org/2009/04/no-faith-in-no-child-left-behind-tutoring/on March 2, 2010).

38. Theodore R. Sizer, *The Red Pencil* (New Haven, CT: Yale University Press, 2004), 115.

TWENTY-ONE

Parents: One Half of a Confused Partnership

As I said in the beginning of this discussion of "customers," schools want parents to be "just right," neither underinvolved nor overinvolved. Of course, most parents are not "just right," and, just as with students, schools do not want to recognize the real world and act accordingly.

Underinvolvement relates to not losing sight of students, so let's deal with it first, since it directly relates to the last few chapters.

THE IMPORTANCE OF STUDENT "HEADSPACE"

Jaime Escalante was the Los Angeles high school math teacher whose extraordinary success in teaching math to Latino students was the subject of the movie *Stand and Deliver*. When he died in 2010, the news was reported on national television. NBC's anchor, Brian Williams, told his viewers that Escalante's principal accomplishment was that "he motivated his students to learn math." He was exactly right. Motivation is the most undervalued asset in education.

High-performing students have parents or other mentors who instill the right beliefs, insist the kids take their education seriously, and provide material and emotional support in their day-to-day living.[1] Simply put: Behind every successful student (with rare exception) is somebody who cares.[2]

What about everyone else, especially students who are failing?[3] The National Center for Education Statistics surveyed teachers about serious problems in their schools. Lack of parental involvement was the second most cited problem—at 21.6 percent of all teachers. The most-cited problem was "students come unprepared to learn," which may well be closely related.[4]

Those findings suggest students' headspace—their sense of self-worth, personal optimism or pessimism, and confidence in the future—heavily influences their performance in school. It is therefore troubling how little institutional commitment to the social and emotional development of students and parental involvement exists even in some high-performing districts.

SCHOOLS' ATTITUDES TOWARD STUDENT MOTIVATION IN THE REAL WORLD

Schools have two choices when it comes to unmotivated students: Get parents involved or do it themselves (or arrange for someone else to do it for them). If schools are going to be accountable for student achievement, and if that achievement is dependent on student motivation, they have no other option.

Now, here is where a major disconnect occurs. There is widespread agreement on the importance of parents and parental involvement. Yet for all the talk, schools by and large spend little money, allot scarce time, and make only fitful efforts to engage parents or get student motivation right.

They see motivation as the parents' obligation, not theirs. They were taught in teachers college that it is how the world should work, and in comfortable, middle-class districts, it often does (at least for most kids). But when parents don't step up and student motivation disappears, school leaders approach the subject begrudgingly, seeming to try to wish away the fact that their parents are not pulling their weight. But wishing it away does not make it so.

No one disputes the value of parents as motivators. Chris Steinhauser of Long Beach characterized them as "equal partners" in the education process. Joel Klein in New York was even more emphatic: "A caring adult is key." All the superintendents concur,[5] as do education experts.[6]

Some districts follow through on the rhetoric. According to Chris Steinhauser, Long Beach has 9,000 parent volunteers for a student body of 90,000, all of which has been built up over many years by an extensive effort of schools and parents to recruit others. They also have 2,000 volunteers from Cal State Long Beach, which requires students to perform 120 hours of service learning. Community organizations and churches take on important projects, like making sure parents fill out scholarship applications. If, after all of that, the parents remain outside, the district understands it has the responsibility to motivate the student.

Brett Springston in Brownsville characterized his parent organization as "huge." Every Brownsville school has a parent liaison and a parent center. Springston was a recent arrival in Brownsville when I spoke to him. He acknowledged that many districts do not want to involve parents because of fear of confrontation, but he was pleasantly surprised that Brownsville had gotten comfortable with parents—and vice versa. That amazed and delighted him, especially because the district was almost entirely Hispanic and filled with the kind of recent immigrants most districts can never draw into partnership.

Oh yes, both Long Beach and Brownsville are Broad winners.

But then there is other side of the coin. During my discussions with superintendents, I was struck by how little attention the issue actually received. Much of the focus on parents, in fact, had only tangential impact on student motivation. Rather, it centered on governance questions, like the parent-teacher organization, or building community support for bond issues.

That focus is consistent with the kind of parental involvement that federal law requires districts to support as a condition of their Title I funding. Section 1118 of No Child Left Behind obliges districts to have "parental involvement plans" and to seek parental advice in how those plans and other policies at Title I schools should be crafted.[7]

Although Secretary of Education Duncan has promised to ensure the provision is included in any revision of the Elementary and Secondary Education Act (ESEA),[8] it is not enough. It does not push hard for broader plans to involve uninvolved parents, and even if it did, it does not require districts to put up enough money to make any such effort a success. Section 1118 requires that districts spend only 1 percent of their Title I allotment on parent involvement, and that amount is rarely supplemented by other monies, which districts prefer to spend elsewhere. Even good districts like Long Beach generally spend less than 0.5 percent of their operating budgets on parent support.[9] Jack Dale, the superintendent in Fairfax County, which is a wealthy district that nonetheless has a large number of poor and minority students, admitted in a bit of carefully modulated budget speak that "the parent area is under-resourced."

The results are what you would expect. Karen Seashore Louis, a noted education professor at the University of Minnesota and an expert on parent and community involvement, told me that in a survey of 145 schools, her team found few exemplary parent programs. There were good things in some places, she told me, but no systemic, exemplary effort, and case studies of eighteen randomly chosen districts showed limited systemic efforts to engage parents and community members. That, sadly, often obscured the tremendous voluntary effort of some teachers to help kids informally.

Because of the lack of resources, almost all the districts I visited had a similar, if narrow, involvement strategy: attract diffident parents by inviting them to school events that are not threatening or demanding, such as plays or awards, where they can come and go without saying a word if they want. Alternatively, Martine Guerrier, who runs New York City's parent outreach, told me her district believes that if parents know what is happening in school, they will come to care about it—and participate. Based on that idea, the city launched a variety of initiatives, including a parent call center, forums for parents to learn about schools, parent academies, and events, like school year kickoffs, designed to draw in parents. The strategy did work to get parents to take on leadership roles and to feel more comfortable about contacting teachers, but the district could not tell if it increased the involvement of uninvolved parents.

There are a small number of districts I visited with more aggressive outreach. Philadelphia is one of the few to encourage teachers and staff to go into the community in the ways they did prior to the last fifty years of turmoil in inner cities. The district has five outreach specialists (albeit for 163,000 students). To extend their reach, the district has established "partnerships" with 169 churches to encourage their parishioners to participate. Karren Dunkeley, Philadelphia's deputy chief administrator for parent, family and community involvement, believes that her staff brings in people. So does Paul Vallas in New Orleans. He does not have outreach specialists in the Recovery District, but he does have Title I coordinators in all his schools that are tasked with building up parent participation.

Dunkeley and Vallas represent a minority view. According to Joyce Epstein, an expert in parent and community involvement who teaches at Johns Hopkins, in many schools the coordinator becomes principally an ombudsman to deal with parent inquiries and complaints. The amount of time spent reaching out to uninvolved parents is insufficient for the task at hand. Which is too bad, in Epstein's view, because outreach can work if districts understand how to do it. They just rarely take the time or spend the money necessary.[10]

However, getting a parent's attention is only the first step in the process. Merely getting a parent involved is not much help unless the parent understands how to enhance her children's emotional development or support their learning. The dominant way districts try to convey that information is through a parent academy or parent classes. In Plano, for example, Doug Otto has sessions to provide parents with either basic parenting skills or direction about how they might help their children with their education. Every superintendent or parent coordinator with whom I spoke thought their academy improved student performance.[11]

The problem is that their success is dependent on initial outreach. If that does not work, nor will the academies. For example, in Miami-Dade's Zone experiment between 2004 and 2008, there was a major attempt to build parent academies. Michael Zaldua, assistant principal of Miami Central High, told me that even though the quality of the classes was good, few people came. The failure may have been in the original outreach. Zaldua characterized it as "mass marketing," meaning lots of fliers and e-mail notices, but not much by way of personal invitations or individual outreach that would have been more meaningful and welcoming to the African American, Haitian, and Cuban parents whom the district sought to engage.

Elsewhere, the problems may be different but equally off-putting to uninvolved parents. Contrary to Zaldua's experience, academies or classes are often not school centered. Philadelphia, for example, has a sleek parent center, but it is in the central office on North Broad Street, far from most schools in the district.[12] Nor are the classes able to promise that parents will meet with their child's teachers. The classes and classroom teachers rarely coordinate. The level of "partnership" created simply by attending the academies is weak at best.

Washington's chief of family and public engagement, Peggy O'Brien, ruefully summed up the problem. She acknowledged to me that, despite the hard work the Rhee administration was doing in DC, "no district has figured out parents."

THE DIFFERENCE BETWEEN WHAT SCHOOLS SAY AND DO ABOUT STUDENT MOTIVATION

Which brings us to the real problem: What if, after all the school's efforts at parent and community involvement, the student still needs a supporter, confidante, and mentor?

Schools often think they are addressing the problem by stressing to teachers the importance of showing respect for, and valuing, their students.[13] As I noted earlier, it is fundamental to Green Dot's strategy at Locke High in Los Angeles.

In high-performing districts, teachers often go one step beyond simple respect. In a "no excuses" district with a challenging curriculum, a teacher who stands up in front of a class and says, "I know you can do this . . ." is sending a message that, over time, will instill confidence. One Washington principal explained that she shook students' hands and staged "Read, baby, read" pep rallies every morning "to boost . . . children's confidence so they believe they can achieve."[14] It is as if she were channeling Jaime Escalante. It may be a key reason districts like Washington have finally started to turn around.

But respect and teachers' exhortations go only so far. Obviously, neither is a real substitute for a parent or mentor. To the extent schools do mentor, their institutional commitments to student motivation focus on a limited group of additional strategies.

Turning to the larger community is one possible solution. Lisa Walker, who is an expert in the area at the University of Chicago's Chapin Hall, thinks teachers are not the answer for absent parents. Teachers are not trained as mentors. They are not given time to be mentors. They are pushed to focus on instruction in an era of accountability.[15] She strongly advocates community involvement as the right alternative.

The strategy can work; witness Long Beach. But there is a problem with outside groups: reliability, consistency, and longevity.[16] One recent report reached the conclusion that three community programs using outside mentors in school-based settings seemed to have no impact on student achievement. They were neither long enough nor sustained enough to work.[17] That seems to be the norm, not Long Beach.[18]

High school anti-dropout programs are another option, but they are efforts to lock the barn door after the horse has escaped.[19] Instead of helping kids develop emotionally from age four or five, the schools wait until they are disaffected lost causes at age fourteen. Then the schools refer these kids to counselors, who are hardly supporters or mentors. They are "troubleshooters" who see kids because they have become habitual truants or because they are, or are about to be, criminals.

A relatively small number of districts have done better by adopting programs specifically designed to create positive student motivation toward school and life. These are mostly structured learning programs that try to build closer relationships between students and teachers, and between students themselves. The best, like AVID (Advancement via Individual Determination), focus the kids on going to college, push them toward challenging academic courses, and, in a structured way, constantly feed them the message that they are capable of doing the work necessary to make them successful.[20] Every one of the superintendents with whom I spoke who uses the programs believes they make a real difference.

However, there are limits. Relatively few students wind up participating in the programs, and they often do not start until after elementary school, which is where the right attitudes and habits of mind should be formed.[21] More importantly, such programs feel like "add-ons" to the districts' agendas. They seem to think of them as a special form of assistance for a few kids who can draw particular benefit from them, not something to use with the larger school population.

There are more and better options.

DEVELOPING THE WHOLE CHILD: WHY SOME CATHOLIC SCHOOLS, CHARTERS, AND EVEN TRADITIONAL PUBLIC SCHOOLS GET IT RIGHT

What follows is a description of what some Catholic, charter, and even traditional public schools are actually doing to promote student motivation and increase parent involvement. I have chosen five schools that seem to have done it *exceptionally* right.[22] Here is a summary of what they can teach us:

- The schools are committed to the emotional development of every child in their charge. Programs are not limited to, or even focused on, kids in trouble.
- The schools want parental involvement. However, programs do not hinge on parents. If the parents do not offer help, the schools just find a way, alone or with the community, to do it themselves.
- The schools do not wait for parents to come to them. They go out and get them. They also have the details of a partnership in mind. They make clear what they want parents to do and how their partnership will work over time.
- Mentoring is a central part of every teacher's duties. Also, the kids often draw additional emotional support and assistance from school-created peer groups.
- In most programs, the teachers have not received much special training about how to deal with kids. That does not seem to cause a problem. These faculties like working with kids, and their interest and enthusiasm, however untrained it may be, makes a big difference to the students they help.

Lawrence, Massachusetts, Public Schools

Lawrence is an old mill town. When Wilfredo Laboy arrived in 2000, the district's performance was miserable, and the parents, many of whom were poor Dominican immigrants, often uninvolved.

Laboy believes in whole system reform, and one important piece is dealing with student motivation. His goal has been to connect every child, kindergarten through twelfth grade, to an adult. Almost every teacher and principal is involved.[23] If a child arrives in kindergarten, she is assigned to a teacher or staffer not just for the year, but for the entire time in that elementary school.[24] The adults meet with their twelve to sixteen kids every day, a student-adult relationship that is separate and distinct from the classroom teacher relationship.

Laboy understands that not all of those twelve to sixteen kids are going to need the same level of help. Some of the kids will have supportive parents and good attitudes. For them, the teachers and administrators serve as coordinators to ensure the parents know what is happening at school and how they can help. However, for those students whose parents are not involved, Laboy told his staff:

> You need to find a way to get these parents involved. Until then, these kids are yours. You instill confidence in them. You make them understand the importance of education. You help them as best you can with their physical needs and growing up issues. Work with your principal to involve the community if we cannot provide for them from our own resources. Every child needs an adult, and you are it.

He also made clear to principals that they had a special role in bringing in parents. Principals invited parents for "a second cup of coffee" to talk about their kids. One measure of their performance was how many parents were truly involved with their kids and the schools.

The effort has paid off. In 2000, eighteen parents had come to "parents' night." In 2008, the number was 1,100. Although the district's standardized test results remain well below average, they have continued to improve. In 2006, 24 percent of third graders were proficient in English language arts and 19 percent in math. In 2009, the figures were 34 percent and 37 percent, respectively. Over the same period, tenth graders' proficiency in English language arts had gone from 28 percent to 46 percent, and in math from 21 percent to 30 percent.[25]

The program obviously costs money, but less than one might imagine. Lawrence's student/teacher ratio is actually higher than the state average (15:1 versus 14:1). While the total amount spent was hard to calculate, Laboy estimated it was somewhere in the range of 1 percent to 2 percent of his budget. Luckily, he had extra financial assistance from the commonwealth, amounting to a few hundred dollars per student, which was money that most districts did not have. Student motivation was, in his view, a worthwhile investment.[26]

St. Ignatius Loyola Academy, Baltimore

At St. Ignatius Loyola Academy, a Jesuit middle school in downtown Baltimore, students arrive at 7:30 a.m. for breakfast. Each child is part of a designated small group of eight to ten kids called an "advisory."[27] Each advisory eats with its teacher advisor, who is going to be its mentor for the three years the students stay at St. Ignatius.[28]

The teacher advisors are often young. They are also mostly white, even though the middle school's boys are mostly African American. At breakfast, the kids talk about what they did the night before. Some may have had a problem with homework; some have had trouble with parents. Each student is also required from time to time to stand up and speak to the assembled group. It is noisy but orderly. The teachers listen and offer advice. They promise to help with problems.

After breakfast, the students spend a period in their advisories doing chores, handling some part of chapel, or spending some one-on-one time with the advisor. The rest of the day is spent in small classes, where the students get plenty of attention from teachers. School lasts nine hours, except in July, when it is cut to six.

St. Ignatius is one of approximately sixty-four Nativity Miguel Schools, a network of mostly Jesuit schools, which began in New York City in 1971.[29] St. Ignatius's goal is to prepare students, many of who were struggling in Baltimore City public elementary schools, for a high-powered private or Catholic high school.

The faculty is focused on getting kids motivated. Sylvia Gundy, the school's counselor and social worker and one of the few African Americans on the faculty, explained that many of the parents do little to expose their children to life beyond their poor neighborhoods. In her view, the children do not know much about the outside world, so they live in fear of it. Whether it is showing them career possibilities or high schools and colleges they might eventually attend, the teachers' goal is to get the kids to believe in themselves and in their opportunities.

Teresa Scott, who teaches the parental coaching class, says the school believes it is important to engage the parents and make them feel their opinions count. Many of those mothers and fathers simply do not know how to be involved, or do not have clear expectations for their children. She and Gundy run classes on parenting, nutrition, and other subjects. Scott is constantly sending notes home to praise kids and compliment parents if the child does well. However, if the parents sign that their child has done his homework and none is forthcoming, she holds them responsible.

Although Chris Wilson, the boyish-looking principal, says that the advisors are not trying to be substitute parents, they will do it if required. And they will push parents when they have to. According to Wilson, the teachers "quickly see for which kids it matters if they [the advisors] call home." If it matters, they know the parents care. They and the teacher are partners. If not, the advisors understand the larger role they have to play.

Most of St. Ignatius's teachers have not received special training in dealing with their kids. Gundy, who is a psychologist by training, helps students who have real problems. According to her, the key to connecting with the kids is not advanced training. It is the teacher's commitment. The racial or class differences melt if the kids and parents trust the teacher. At St. Ignatius, they do.

Servite High School, Anaheim, California

A good friend of mine, Pete Bowen, whom I hired to be the Los Angeles Unified School District's ethics officer, is now the president of a Catholic high school, Servite, in Anaheim, California. Each June, the school requires its incoming ninth graders to attend a three-day-long "freshman formation weekend." In 2008, the new class was broken into sixteen teams of seventeen students, called priories. The members of the priories do not know one another before the weekend; the school's goal is for them to learn to rely on each other to get through the next four years.

The weekend focuses on the school's commitment to three dimensions of development: academic skill, teamwork, and leadership. The members of each priory are taught to lead when their skills are best and follow when others' are. They do team exercises, like rappelling, in order to teach them to trust one another. They have to write a poem or song and perform it in front of the group. If it is hard, they can get help from their new buddies. They are taught to see the humanity in their fellow priory members and other classmates. They reflect on it and write down their thoughts in journals. As Bowen said, "It is dweeb and jock working together rather than making fun of each other."[30] The kids learn to rely on each other's skills to get through.[31]

For the next four years, the priories continue. A period is reserved each day for the priories to work together in school or out in the community, where they beg food for the homeless or solicit money to pay the rent for poor families. They write evaluations of each other, and they take responsibility for each other's behavior. If one priory member sees another doing drugs, for example, he tries to get him into treatment.

Each priory has a teacher advisor. That teacher advisor in turn works with the parents of his priory's members. The school's goal is not only for the parents to be involved on behalf of their own kids, but also to take responsibility for each other's kids.[32]

Servite is the only Catholic high school in Orange County with increasing enrollment. In five years, it has gone from 760 students to just under 1,000. Although over half its students are minority and 30 percent receive financial aid, the school sends almost every member of the graduating class to a four-year college.[33]

Knowledge Is Power Program (KIPP)

When Mike Feinberg and Dave Levin began the first KIPP school in Houston in 1995, they went into poor neighborhoods in the city recruiting students. They talked to parents. They explained why KIPP was different. It was going to be intense, with longer days and longer school years, high expectations and a demanding curriculum with lots of homework. However, it was about more than academic skills. Part of the mission, they explained, was to inculcate in students the personal traits necessary to be successful in life. The two parts together are the reason for KIPP's slogan: "Work hard, be nice."[34]

The tradition of reaching out to the community continues. Lydia Glassie, who is the director of KIPP to College for KIPP Bay Area Schools (California), which focuses on getting KIPP middle school graduates through their high schools and into college, told me that when she was at San Francisco Bay KIPP, she did what Feinberg and Levin had done before her. She spent lots of time walking around public housing and along the working-class retail section of Mission Street, handing out fliers and talking to passers-by to get them to visit the school. After that first visit, and before they could sign up their child, the parents had to come back in order to go over KIPP's commitment to excellence and sign what has come to be called "the contract," but which is really simply a nonbinding pledge that outlines the responsibilities of the parents, students, and teachers.

Ever since Feinberg and Levin first walked around Houston, KIPP has made the parents sign a "contract." It is now a short, one-sided piece of paper that summarizes what both KIPP teachers and the parents will do for the kids, and what the kids will do for themselves. The teachers, for example, promise to "make ourselves available to students and parents, and address any concerns they might have." The parents promise, among other things, to make sure the student will come to school by 7:25 a.m. and stay until 5 p.m., plus come on Saturdays and during the summer. And they promise to check children's homework every night.

Notwithstanding the parents' contractual promises, KIPP will deal with parents who are not supportive. Glassie believes, for example, that every mother, even an addict, wants the best for her child. She just may not know how to do it. And KIPP will step in if the parent drops the ball. If a student needs glasses, KIPP tries to help. If she has trouble waking up, they will get her an alarm clock.

There is plenty of opportunity for interaction. School is open from 7:15 a.m. to 5 p.m., and, with athletics, the kids may stay at school until 8 p.m. There are classes on Saturday and in the summer. The students receive two hours of homework every night, and KIPP teachers are available by phone until 9 p.m. to help them, or talk to their parents.

Teachers and principals know kids and families. Although KIPP does not yet have the extensive databases and intensive mini-assessment structure of a Blue Valley, the relationship between teachers and students is, according to Steve Mancini, the director of public relations, "pretty intensive." There is close mentoring, with the expectation that the teachers and students build up tight bonds. It is why KIPP follows its students through college.

The teachers take mentoring seriously. They focus kids on college, which is a paramount goal for KIPP students. However, there are conversations about personal traits as well. Being polite is not a trivial matter. If someone says something rude, it is a big deal to KIPP teachers. The students are taught responsibility for each other, much like at Servite. If there is graffiti in the bathroom, everyone is called together immediately to discuss the breaking of the school's values.

The schools also make a point of getting together for an hour every week for awards for academic and character achievement, and to share each other's improvements, like listening to a student read a poem she just wrote. KIPP calls it "team and family," because of its emphasis on the idea that no one gives up on anyone else. Teachers especially get the message: They cannot be isolated in their classrooms. "Your kids" are not just those in classroom, but everyone in the school.

KIPP teachers and administrators are pushed to listen to parents. The KIPP national organization puts schools through an assessment called "healthy schools" to find out what parents think and whether they believe they are being heard. The reviewers see if the contract is being carried out.

Glassie assured me that KIPP believes that it can succeed if there is a really motivated parent, or a really motivated child. Either will do.

The Harlem Children's Zone, New York, New York

The ultimate strategy to deal with student motivation and parent participation is the Harlem Children's Zone. It is an intense effort to flood ninety-seven square blocks in Harlem with social services and charter schools. The Zone's founder, Geoffrey Canada, now has a national profile after his efforts have been repeatedly applauded by President Obama,[35] and his strategy has won approval of the Department of Education's "What Works Clearinghouse."[36] President Obama seems so impressed that, as part of his proposal for revision of ESEA, the administration wants federal funds to support other programs that will follow the path the Zone has carved out.

Rasuli Lewis, the program director of the Zone's Practitioners' Institute and Canada's classmate at Bowdoin College, explained that 65 percent to 75 percent of the kids in the Zone need to participate in order for the Zone to be effective. Canada's premise is that kids in the ghetto have ten times the opportunity to fail as they do to have fun. By blanketing the neighborhood, most of what the Zone's kids hear, see, and do is positive and constructive.

The Zone's strategy goes straight at parent participation and student motivation. There is a "Baby College" where parents-to-be are taught parenting skills, followed by early childhood day care.[37] At age three, the children can join the Journey program, which is designed to provide early learning as well as day care. Later, the Zone enrolls as many kids as they can in the "Harlem Gems," an all-day pre-kindergarten for four-year-olds.

At each step, the Zone is teaching the parents more and more about parenting and how to help their children master the same early learning that better-heeled middle-class toddlers receive. At the same time, the schools expose children to aspects of life and learning that they are not likely to get from even the best-intentioned, but cash-strapped, parents. And when there is a need for more traditional social work or other assistance, like eyeglasses, the Zone provides help.

There are two Promise Academies, a charter elementary and a charter middle school. By law, their enrollment must be open to all children, not just those who have gone through the Zone's preschool programs. As a result, some Zone kids wind up in other schools, where they can continue to get Zone support.

Lewis told me the kids who go through the Baby College, Journey, and Harlem Gems often need less support than do kids who don't. On entering the Promise Academies, 100 percent of them are working at or above grade level. They do better, on average, than the other students in the schools.

The Academies are serious educational institutions. They have longer days and longer school years. Canada has built extensive computer databases, and from them tries to individualize student learning. Parental participation, though, remains important. If Academy parents are not supportive, they have social workers who reach out to bring them into the process. There is even a program for parents who were once involved in the Zone, moved away, and then moved back to the neighborhood. As Lewis said, "Everything is based on relationships."

Like many of the other successful schools, the Zone follows the students even after they leave the middle school Academy. Canada's goal is for every child to go to college and then return to help in the rebuilding of Harlem. The Zone model is not simply about educating a child, but creating an adult whose own children eventually go through the same cycle.

MONEY NEED NOT BE THE PROBLEM

There is no question that a commitment to student motivation will cost money. However, as Lawrence demonstrates, it need not be an extraordinary amount. If reformers are aggressive, they can probably find much of what they need in already-authorized categorical programs.

For example, many states have funds for violence prevention, pregnancy prevention, or gang prevention. And the federal government has a small amount of money for the same purposes. It also has one big pot of money, the grants for special education, where 20 percent of the total can be used for "prevention," rather than the provision of services to those who have been identified with a special need.[38] If the strings attached to those dollars can be loosened, a portion of the funds could be used to mentor all kids, so that some of them do not wind up needing the precise services for which the grants are intended.

The only possible new funding that might help out is the Obama administration's initiative to support Harlem Zone–like programs, but one wonders how much money they will get. The administration wanted $210 million for 2011, but the election of conservatives to Congress in 2010 has made that unlikely.

Merely saying "more money" is rarely the right answer to any education issue. However, there may be no choice here. Even if that money comes as part of a new "categorical" program (or a rewritten old one) of the sort denounced elsewhere in this book, it is worth it.

WHAT WE NEED TO DO

Parental involvement is a test case for the value of continuous improvement. Superintendents need to assess their commitment to parental involvement by setting some benchmarks and seeing how well they do. For example, how many parents come to parents' night? Or how many parents sign a child's homework? Or how many kids simply tell their teachers that their parents are either too busy or just don't care? And there is the real litmus test: If the district is willing to try mentoring for an extended period, say two years, does it move the needle on student performance or dropout rates?

If there is a willingness to become more involved in the social and emotional development of students, the five examples demonstrate that there are many ways to do it. However, there has to be an honest commitment to the process. No one is better than a teenager at spotting an adult who is not sincerely interested in her problems. And no individual teacher is going to be willing to make the effort unless the schools themselves reorganize how they operate to build opportunities for meaningful mentoring.

All of this effort will require money. While current state and federal funds may not be enough, rewriting the laws on crime or drug prevention funding and on special education to permit the use of some of the money to support these programs is a good start.

NOTES

1. This list of parent responsibilities is not intended as a total description of everything a parent may profitably do to help children. Moreover, there is interesting research on the changing scope of parents' roles as children grow up. See, for example, Nancy E. Hill and Diana F. Tyson, "Parental Involvement in Middle School: A Meta-Analytic Assessment of the Strategies That Promote Achievement," *Developmental Psychology* 45, no. 3 (2009): 740–63. It is, however, beyond the scope of this chapter.

2. John M. Bridgeland, Robert Balfanz, Laura A. Moore, and Rebecca S. Friant, *Raising Their Voices* (Washington, DC: Civic Enterprises, 2010), 24.

3. A 2009 report from Scholastic and the Bill and Melinda Gates Foundation surveyed teachers on the "single most likely reason some students in their classes won't leave high school prepared to succeed at a 2- or 4-year college." Lack of academic preparation came in first at 38 percent, but what follows is far more important for this discussion: 34 percent said lack of student motivation and 27 percent said lack of encouragement from family and friends. In other words, 62 percent of teachers think what we are about to discuss—student headspace—is the key problem for high school students failing in college. Scholastic, Inc., and Bill and Melinda Gates Foundation, *Primary Sources: America's Teachers on America's Schools* (Redmond, WA: Bill and Melinda Gates Foundation, 2010), 47.

4. NCES, table 71 (Digest of Education Statistics)—Teachers' perceptions about serious problems in their schools, by control and level of school: Selected years, 1987–88 through 2003–04 (retrieved from http://nces.ed.gov/programs/digest/d08/tables/dto8_071.asp).

5. Deborah Meier, founder of Central Park East, was a passionate believer in schools' need to reach out to parents in order to bridge cultural gaps that inevitably form when the teachers do not come from the same community or class as the students they teach. Deborah Meier, *The Power of Their Ideas* (Boston, MA: Beacon Press, 2002), 52.

6. See, for example, Anthony S. Bryk, "Organizing Schools for Improvement," *Phi Delta Kappan* 91, no. 7 (April 2010): 23–30.

7. See U.S. Department of Education, *Parental Involvement: Title I, Part A: Non-regulatory Guidance* (Washington, DC: U.S. Department of Education, 2004); Northwest Regional Educational Laboratory, *Parental Involvement under the New Title I and Title III* (Portland, OR: NWREL, 2002).

8. *Education Week*, "Want Turnaround Money? Involve Parents, Duncan Proposes," July 14, 2010 (retrieved from www.blogs.edweek.org./edweek.coampaign-k-12/201/07want_turnaround_money.html on July 16, 2010).

9. Chris Steinhauser in Long Beach told me the district spends $1.5 million annually on parent support and learning. That represents less than 0.2 percent of his operating budget. In fairness, that kind of formal accounting will not include the informal efforts schools and teachers make to reach out to students and parents. Nor does it capture the amount of time principals and teachers will spend every year answering parents' calls or meeting with them, particularly when it is not part of a formal "parent-teacher conference night." However, it is indicative of the importance (or lack of it) that schools place on parent outreach.

10. See, for example, Joyce L. Epstein and Associates, *School, Family, and Community Partnerships* (Thousand Oaks, CA: Corwin Press, 2009); Sondra Christenson, *Schools and Families* (New York: Guilford Press, 2001). There are many others with thoughtful advice, but these two will give you extremely intelligent, wide-ranging strategies and ideas for involvement.

11. Karin Chenoweth, *How It's Being Done* (Cambridge, MA: Harvard Education Press, 2009), 48.

12. Associated Press, "In Philadelphia, Reaching Kids by Teaching Parents," Oct. 12, 2009 (retrieved from http://edweek.org/ew/articles/2009/10/10/305926pex-changeeducation_ap.html on Oct. 12, 2009).

13. See, for example, Jon Saphier, Mary Ann Haley-Speca, and Robert Gower, *The Skillful Teacher*, 6th ed. (Acton, MA: Research for Better Teaching, Inc., 2008), 317–27.

14. WAMU, "School Turnaround" (transcript of Oct. 1, 2010, show "Metro Connection") (retrieved from http://wamu.org/programs.mc/10/10/trans-01-9-37678.php on Oct. 6, 2010).

15. Lisa Walker and Cheryl Smithgall, *Underperforming Schools and the Education of Vulnerable Children and Youth* (Chicago: Chapin Hall/University of Chicago Issue Brief, 2009), 7.

16. Mark Wheeler, Thomas Keller, and David L. DuBois, "Review of Three Recent Randomized Trials of School-Based Mentoring," *Social Policy Report* 24, no. 3 (2010): 14.

17. Wheeler, Keller, and DuBois, "Review of Three Recent Randomized Trials of School-Based Mentoring," 14.

18. The size of the school seeking community involvement may make a difference. Small schools that have been successful have often been distinguished by their ability to involve the larger community in finding mentors or providing material help to kids. David Merkowitz, *Ready for College* (Washington, DC: Strategic Communications, 2003), 6. That makes the success of a large district like Long Beach all the more distinctive.

19. See, for example, Camilla A. Lehr, David R. Johnson, Christine D. Bremer, Anna Cosio, and Megan Thompson, *Essential Tools* (Minneapolis: University of Minnesota Press, 2004).

20. See www.avid.org; *Glendale News Press*, "Becoming AVID Learners," Oct. 4, 2010 (retrieved from www.glandalenewspress.com/news/tn-gnp-1005-classroom,0,5103925,print.story on Oct. 6, 2010).

21. According to its website, AVID has graduated 65,300 students from high school since its formation in 1990. That is approximately 3,265 per year, or roughly 0.1 percent of the total nationwide high school graduating class (www.census.gov/Press-Release/www/releases/archives/facts_for_features_special_editions/012084.html).

22. These schools are certainly not the only ones who have taken on the obligation to deal with student emotional development and motivation. ASCD annually gives the Whole Child Vision in Action Award for schools that have quality programs that address the issue. For information on what other schools are doing, see http://ascd.org/programs/The-Whole-Child/Past-Vision-in-Action-Recipients.aspx#2010.

23. One notable feature is the involvement of teachers. One question is whether this role might be handled by expanding the role traditionally filled by counselors. Karen Seashore Louis and Molly F. Gordon, *Aligning Student Support with Achievement Goals* (Thousand Oaks, CA: Corwin Press, 2006).

24. Assigning one teacher for the six years gives parents a single point of contact not just for one year, but also for the entire time their child is in school. Specialists in parent programs advocate a single point of contact. See, for example, Anne T. Henderson and Karen L. Mapp, "Building the Parent-Teachers Relationship," *Education Week Teachers' Magazine*, May 5, 2008.

25. See www.greatschools.org/cgi-bin/ma/district-profile/235#students.

26. Lawrence may have a more extensive operation than others, but it is not alone. Paul Vallas has tried to institute the same kind of mentoring program in the Recovery School District in New Orleans. Every high school teacher is assigned ten ninth graders to mentor through twelfth grade. They are to get together with mentees at least once a week. For those kids with uninvolved parents, the mentors become the parent, dealing not just with school issues, but nutrition, housing, and other problems the kids face.

Similarly, Leo Casey, who is the vice president for high school curriculum for New York's United Federation of Teachers, explained that the two charters the UFT runs in New York City have advisory periods every day, where teachers sit down with ten to twelve students to discuss what is happening in their lives. He assured me that the union had no problem with including such mentoring in a teacher's duties, provided it is done right. In his view, that meant adequate time for the work, appropriate guidance, and, of course, adjusting compensation.

Other researchers have also found similar advisory systems in other public schools. Karin Chenoweth, *How It's Being Done* (Cambridge, MA: Harvard Education Press, 2009), 204; Linda Darling-Hammond, Jacqueline Ancess, and Susanna Wichterle Ort, "Reinventing High School: Outcomes of the Coalition Campus Schools Project," *American Educational Research Journal* 39, no. 3 (2002): 655 (all the New York small schools developed as part of the project had advisories).

27. Many small schools, whether or not Catholic, have advisories in which all students participate. Deborah Meier's students at Central Park East spent an hour a day in advisory. Deborah Meier, *The Power of Their Ideas* (Boston, MA: Beacon Press, 2002), 54; Granger High School (WA), one of the public schools Karin Chenoweth praised in *It's Being Done*, holds half-hour advisories every day for groups of eighteen to twenty kids. Karin Chenoweth, *It's Being Done* (Cambridge, MA: Harvard Education Press, 2007), 119; David Merkowitz, *Ready for College* (Redmond, WA: Bill and Melinda Gates Foundation, 2003), 3.

28. Anthony Bryk, an education scholar who has studied Catholic schools extensively, characterizes them as "communal." Anthony S. Bryk, Valerie E. Lee, and Peter B. Holland, *Catholic Schools and the Common Good* (Cambridge, MA: Harvard University Press, 1993), 127, 298.

29. L. Mickey Fenzel, *Improving Urban Middle Schools: Lessons from the Nativity Schools* (Albany, NY: SUNY Press, 2009). The network is a collaboration between the Jesuits, which started the Nativity schools, and the Christian Brothers, which launched the San Miguel school program in 1993. They joined forces in 2006. See also the 2008

Thomas B. Fordham Report, "Who Will Save America's Urban Catholic Schools?" (Washington, DC: Thomas B. Fordham Institute, 2008).

30. Bryk, Lee, and Holland, *Catholic Schools and the Common Good*, 315.

31. In a study of what worked in schools involved in Comprehensive School Reform, a program funded through 2008 as part of No Child Left Behind's effort to turn around failing schools, one key part of what worked was the development of cultures in the classroom that encouraged student autonomy. Amanda R. Bozack, Ruby Vega, Mary McCaslin, and Thomas L. Good, "Teacher Support of Student Autonomy in Comprehensive School Reform," *Teachers College Record* 110, no. 11 (Nov. 2008): 2389–407. That is consistent with not only Servite, but also Professor Coleman.

32. Other schools also have found that with increasing parent involvement, parents begin to see school as a community where their mission is to help all students, not just their own. Mark R. Warren, Soo Hong, Carolyn Leung Rubin, and Phitsamay Sychitkokhong Uy, "Beyond the Bake Sale: A Community-Based Relational Approach to Parent Engagement in Schools," *Teachers College Record* 111, no. 9 (Sept. 2009): 2232.

33. Servite is not the only school that follows the grouping strategy. Iredell County also has transition camps after eighth grade that pair students with advisors who follow them throughout high school.

34. There is an extensive history of KIPP and its strategies that uses the slogan as its title. Jay Mathews, *Work Hard, Be Nice* (Chapel Hill, NC: Algonquin Books of Chapel Hill, 2009). See also, David Whitman, *Sweating the Small Stuff* (Washington, DC: Thomas B. Fordham Institute, 2008), 152–91.

35. Paul Tough, *Whatever It Takes* (Boston, MA: Houghton Mifflin, 2008).

36. *Education Week*, "Harlem Children's Zone Study Gets 'What Works' OK," March 31, 2010 (retrieved from www.edweek.org/edweek/inside-school-research-2010/03/harlem_childrens_zone_study_pa.html on March 31, 2010). A recent National Bureau of Economic Research Study concluded that children at the Promise Academy had closed or eliminated the achievement gap in math and English language arts. However, it could not conclude that the community investments alone had brought about the results. Will Dobbie, Roland G. Fryer, *Are High Quality Schools Enough to Close the Achievement Gap? Evidence from a Social Experiment in Harlem*, Working Paper no. 15473 (Cambridge, MA: National Bureau of Economic Research, 2009).

37. The Children's Zone's approach has been advocated in the literature. See, for example, *Educating Everybody's Children*, 2nd ed., ed. Robert E. Cole (Alexandria, VA: ASCD, 2008), 54.

38. Scholastic, the American Association of School Administrators, and the UCLA Center for Mental Health in the Schools have developed a program called "Rebuilding Learning," which is training school districts to take the infrastructure of counselors and others built around these prevention programs and turn them into a broader strategy designed to deal with every child's barriers to learning. See http://rebuildingforlearning.scholastic.com.

TWENTY-TWO

Parents: Long-Ignored Customers and Owners

PARENTS AS CONSUMERS

Making parents effective partners is going to be easier if teachers and administrators treat them properly as consumers.

But schools rarely treat parents to good customer service. "Overly involved" parents create as many problems, in the eyes of school administrators and teachers, as do the underinvolved ones.

The result is customer service with an attitude.

A Rarity: The Right Kind of Customer Service

As I traveled around the country, I repeatedly asked if anyone had done any customer service training. Simple answer: a few "yes" but mostly "no." Peggy O'Brien, Washington's director of family and public engagement, told me that customer service training is now part of DC's principals' academy. However, such direct responses were rare. The less effective alternative is a program like New York's, which has an extensive network of school parent coordinators who are specifically charged with handling parent concerns. Although a positive step, that seems like simply hiring one person to clean up after someone else made a mess. Better not to have the mess in the first place.

In LA, I had tried a more direct approach. I first offered to arrange customer service training for school staff, but found few takers. Then I found money in the budget for a parent "hotline" where parents could call in to make complaints or ask questions about parent and student rights. I thought the hotline might be a way to cut off problems before they festered. You might think the schools would have thought the hotline was a great idea since it might take some of the burden off their plate. Evidently not. Parents were not told. Posters were not posted. The staff I had delegated to handle the calls was bored silly with inactivity on most days. You would have thought all was rosy out there in LA's schools—until the next lawsuit came in.

I also asked about hotlines during my travels. Philadelphia has one, but most districts saw no need. Parents were welcome to call the principal.

Getting to the Truth: Discussion and Disclosure

Often at the prodding of state legislatures and the federal government, there have been significant improvements in some aspects of customer service in recent years.

No Child Left Behind (NCLB) sets a baseline for customer service. As noted above, there has to be meaningful consultation with, and annual evaluation by, parents of plans to involve them in schools. The law further requires significant disclosures of information. Parents must be told the student achievement results for their children's school. The notice must explain their options if the school has failed to make its adequate yearly progress. The schools must also describe what they are doing to improve failing schools and offer parents the opportunity to receive information about teachers' qualifications.

States have often imposed even broader disclosure obligations on districts. The additional information is frequently useful. Depending on the state, the information may include graduation rates, dropout rates, standardized test results for years or subjects not covered by NCLB, and, as will be discussed in a moment, parent and/or student ratings of school quality.

But parents can demand more in individual school districts—informally or by exercising their rights to public records under state law. Appendix II contains a wide-ranging "Disclosure Document" that covers many of the topics in this book. Each of the items listed refers to a fact critical to an element of a high-performing school. For example, the answer to the question about when teachers are hired gives a basis to decide if schools recruit early enough to get good candidates and have enough time to give them appropriate induction training during the summer.

It is not intended as a "report card," with a letter grade, like an A, a shorthand summary of school quality. Rather, the Disclosure Document intends to provide real benchmarks. If the numbers are bad, parents can put a child in another school, or they can use the information as leverage to demand that the school improve its performance. Think of it as parent-driven total quality management.

All of this material is helpful. However, they are not the only places where parents can get real feedback—or exercise their consumer rights.

The Internet

The biggest aid to parents as customers may be the Internet. Teachers in many schools now post homework assignments, descriptions of curriculum, and classroom events on the Internet. For parents with Internet access, it is now possible to have a much clearer, and more "real time," picture of what is going on in school.

Schools and districts have also developed extensive websites that are filled with information about student activities and school and district policies. The challenge is whether the sites are more than superficial summaries of event calendars and announcements. The key "tell-tale" is whether the sites have blogs associated with them, where opinions could be shared and issues discussed. In the interactive Web 2.0 era, those discussions create community and accountability.

The challenge of the Internet is that it is not ubiquitous. Many parents, particularly the poor, still are not connected. Some districts are solving that problem with direct action: Plano and Broward County, for example, give a used district computer to parents who have attended parent academy classes but who do not have one. Unfortunately, others, like New York, have to settle for handing out free e-mail addresses. Helpful, but not a great fix.

The Ratings Race

Various states have policies that allow parents to balance out some of the district website self-promotion. Texas, for example, requires that schools ask parents to "rate" their performance, and that such ratings be posted on the Internet for everyone to see.[1] The Council of Chief State School Officers has its own site, School Matters, that invites parent comments, and there are privately financed sites, like Great Schools, as well. Moreover, in some places, the parent ratings are incorporated into state evaluations of district performance. In turn, principals and superintendents are evaluated in part based on parent satisfaction.

Various states have policies that allow parents to balance out some of the district website self-promotion. Texas, for example, requires that schools ask parents to "rate" their performance, and that such ratings be posted on the Internet for everyone to see.[2] The Council of Chief State School Officers has its own site, School Matters, that invites parent comments, and there are privately financed sites, like Great Schools, as well. Moreover, in some places, the parent ratings are incorporated into state evaluations of district performance. In turn, principals and superintendents are evaluated in part based on parent satisfaction.

The pressure for good ratings is likely to lead to continued improvement in customer service. Here is another case of "what gets measured, gets done." Every Texas superintendent with whom I spoke was conscious of those report cards. They wanted good marks from parents so they were being as responsive as they could.

Choice Is a Pressure Point—and an Outlet

One development that may help customer service is the increasing amount of choice students and parents are acquiring over which schools to attend. Is it to be a charter, magnet, small theme school, or the one down the block?

Parents then can vote "with their feet," signing up for what appeals to them, but going elsewhere if the message is not to their liking. Even if not all parents take advantage of this option, the pressure may make all schools pay more attention to parents and their right to good customer service. It is the logic of the "school choice" movement. Inject competition into school placement, and schools will do what they have to do to get students to attend.

PARENTS AS OWNERS

School districts are public institutions. In essence, parents and other tax-payers are the "owners." In fact, one fundamental premise of this book is that the change it describes can best be brought about when the owners tell those who work for them what they want the enterprise to do.

The general trend in education is to devolve power from central of-fices to schools. That will lead, eventually, to a system where even tradi-tional public schools wind up looking and acting a great deal like char-ters, which means the schools will be entirely (or almost entirely) self-governing. They will have boards of trustees, and, if the laws and prac-tices are structured appropriately, parents can have virtually complete authority over what happens.

One bridge between the short term and the long term is a new Califor-nia law (now being considered elsewhere as well) that allows the major-ity of the parents at a school to petition a district to turn a public school into a charter.[3] While it is too early to tell what changes the law will bring, it may well hasten the transformation of schools that will create more parent councils, and perhaps more parent control.

However, that is the future. What about participation in district poli-tics where so many of the decisions are made today?

Parents Participating in District Governance

The more pressing problem right now may be the lack of participation in district politics.

Participation at the level of the individual school is high. Measured in terms of attendance at "parent nights" or parent-teacher association meetings, a vast majority of parents are at least somewhat involved. (See chapter 3.) That participation does not extend to the district level, which is a significant problem since that is where most school policy is now set.

The alternative means of accountability is to place responsibility in some distant authority, like the state's education department, which may eventually act by taking over a failing school or putting a district, like Lawrence, in receivership. However, these are extreme measures. It is simply not healthy for accountability to kick in only when there has been total system failure.

Part of the low local participation level can be ascribed to the shift of decision making to the federal and state governments, but the shift does not explain the entire decline in interest.

One large cause is how school boards conduct themselves. Outsiders are simply not welcome, and frozen out when they show up to participate. As discussed in chapter 4, boards need to focus on the big picture. Not only is that important so that a superintendent can manage, but also, once a board descends into the minutiae, ordinary folks are just shut out. They do not know the facts. They do not know the rules. They may not even understand why they should care unless it is about their child or their school.

The simplest answer to increased participation is to drag school boards back to the big picture and to discussions that make sense to ordinary people.

This entire book is premised on the hope that parents and taxpayers will in fact participate, be heard, and be prepared to hold school boards and mayors accountable. Getting school boards to act so that the participation is meaningful is fundamental.

WHAT WE NEED TO DO

Parents need to demand real consumer information. They need a school report card from their districts, and they need to make sure that the district provides timely and current information about their kids, the instructional program, school activities, and district issues.

Finally, parents need to demand that districts provide them real opportunities to participate. Specifically, parents must demand from the board that:

- Customer service is taken seriously.
- Information about classes, homework, activities, and other important events is posted on websites or otherwise sent home, and that parents without computers are assisted in becoming connected on the Web.

- Policy making is transparent, with relevant information posted well in advance of board meetings.
- The board revisits a district's goals and major policies every year or two.
- The board avoids minutiae and concentrates on big-picture issues.
- The district creates classes or provides educational materials posted on district websites that help parents and taxpayers understand the process and applicable laws.
- The district collects and disseminates benchmarks that measure whether the district has fulfilled its promises (like the disclosure document in appendix II).
- The superintendent files a "state of the district" message well in advance of any discussions setting forth his or her position about whether each of the policy goals has been met.

Parents and taxpayers are now armed with knowledge and a process that makes possible having their voices heard.

NOTES

1. Title I of NCLB requires schools to provide "report cards" to parents. They focus on student achievement on standardized tests; there is no federal requirement for the inclusion of parent ratings.

2. Title I of NCLB requires schools to provide "report cards" to parents. They focus on student achievement on standardized tests; there is no federal requirement for the inclusion of parent ratings.

3. *New York Times*, "At California School, Parents Force an Overhaul," Dec. 7, 2010 (retrieved from www.nytimes.com/2010/12/18/education/08teacher.html on Dec. 8, 2010).

Part V

The Template: The Things High-Performing Schools Have in Common

It is more important to ask the right four questions (from chapter 1) than for everyone to come to the same answers. Nonetheless, despite their differences in size, ethnic makeup, and wealth, most of the high-performing districts I visited had much in common. That fact is immensely important. The resulting template of common beliefs and practices may not be the only way forward, but it is clearly one path ahead. No one should be told that "it can't work here." Yes, it can.

TWENTY-THREE

Six Beliefs

Beliefs, those ideas and attitudes circling in people's heads, are hard to frame, let alone distill. The six listed here may not be sufficient to make a particular district successful, but they are most likely necessary. One thing is certain: They do not look or feel like the beliefs of the mass-production era.

BELIEF 1: EVERY CHILD CAN — AND WILL — LEARN

Several interviewees, like Green Dot's Marco Petruzzi, said, "You must have a high-performance culture with clear expectations and consequences."

Easy to say; hard to do. How can you tell when it's the real thing?

Every one of the high-performing or turnaround districts held principals to a set of goals, one of which was that test scores would rise, or, in the case of high-performing districts, be maintained. There were no waivers or exceptions. These districts have all rejected James Coleman's conclusion that socioeconomic status is going to be more influential in determining a student's fate than is the education that child receives. Their attitude contrasts with comments a reader still regularly sees on education blogs: "Schools," someone writes, "cannot be expected to fix all of society's ills," which is offered as an excuse, or explanation, for opposing some accountability measure. I never heard the equivalent in a high-performing or successful turnaround school. *Nobody there ever said, "We are doing the best we can."*

That commitment also underlay the assumption that all students could tackle demanding curricula. Expectations matter. Because the material represented real, substantive learning (rather than "dummies'

247

courses"), it was the district's implicit way of saying to every one of its teachers that it trusted students could master the material—and that they, the teachers, could teach it. That, in turn, pushed teachers to say to students, in effect: "I know you can do it." No excuses.

A more obvious sign of the commitment may be what does *not* happen. When Nick Fischer got to Fall River, the high school was counseling many struggling, working-class students to drop out even before graduation. He put a stop to the practice. Instead, he opened an evening school for sixteen- and seventeen-year-olds who had to work. In 2009, Fall River had the biggest reduction in dropouts in Massachusetts.

People do not acquiesce in problems or rationalize failure. They find solutions.

BELIEF 2: EVERY CHILD WILL GRADUATE, AND EVERY CHILD WILL EITHER GO TO COLLEGE OR BE WELL PREPARED FOR A CAREER

Once again, the great test is not saying the words.

It is about having the will to make it happen. Are district leaders and staff really focused around the goal, and are they willing to make the effort necessary for such an ambitious objective?

The clearest focus may be Jerry Weast's strategy in Montgomery County, reflected in a curriculum that starts with advanced placement (AP) classes and works back to pre-kindergarten. That sends a signal about the district's ultimate goal for every student. Similarly, the availability of advanced AP or International Baccalaureate classes in high schools throughout a district is an indication that college-level work is expected, which demonstrates to students that teachers and administrators believe they are in fact college-capable.

The other part, intensity, may be best tested by seeing whether a district pays attention to the little things that schools have to do to make college-going a reality. Terry Holliday in Iredell County required that his cabinet discuss the case of every child who had dropped out of high school. The point here is not just that the district was organized to try to recover every dropout. What was key was Holliday's demonstration of his commitment that there simply were not going to be dropouts on his watch.

BELIEF 3: THE DISTRICT WILL MAKE A DISTINCT AND UNIQUE CONTRIBUTION TO THE COMMUNITY, TO EDUCATION, OR BOTH

Every one of the districts that were doing well had pride. They had framed a mission to which faculty and staff subscribed.

In the small, high-performing districts, it was a mixture of pride of place and pride in performance. In Great Neck, Roslyn, and Watauga County, despite their geographic and income differences, the message was much the same. We did it for the community, they all say. We educated our children well.

The Harlem Children's Zone is the grand experiment, with the sweeping goal of sending thousands of children off to college and then bringing them back to create the next Harlem Renaissance.

In many ways, Pearl River may be the best demonstration of vision and mission. When it started its transition, it was a blue-collar town with no community emphasis on college-going or any other sign of high performance. Then its board decided that they would turn things around. Over time, their reputation grew and enthusiastic teachers signed on, even though salaries are merely average. More families with a focus on education moved in precisely because the schools were exemplary. Now, Pearl River thrives on its spirit of innovation *and* the esteem in which it is held by townspeople.

The private schools and charters that succeed all have extremely clear senses of mission. The Knowledge Is Power Program and Green Dot believe that their distinct styles will give low-income children far superior educations and a way out of the ghetto. The Catholic schools share what is truly a "mission," grounded in religious teaching about the moral obligation to minister to the whole child and prepare him or her for life.

Finally, there are those institutions that believe they are, or want to be, "the best." It is easy to see why Phillips Andover, with its large endowment and long history, believes it is the best, but there are districts that share the same attitude. When I asked Jack Dale, the Fairfax County superintendent, about continuous improvement in the district, he responded by saying that their goal was not continuous improvement; it was about consistently being "the best."

There is one other thing that is common to these districts' visions and missions. Being respectful and caring of students is important. It is the only way to convince children to believe in themselves and to have the confidence they will be able to go to college or start a career. That is, for example, exactly how Petruzzi explained Green Dot's strategy in taking over LA's Locke High School, and how all the staff at St. Ignatius prefaced their description of their student advisories.

BELIEF 4: ACADEMIC PREPARATION IS THE FOCUS AND HAS PRIORITY OVER ALL OTHERS

Every one of these districts has made clear to its principals that they are going to live or die on student achievement. Tom Payzant said that his success in Boston was attributable in large part to his "laser-like focus on instructional improvement." All the other elements of a successful reform package have to be in the service of that one.

Nowhere was that more apparent than in football-mad Texas. I visited four districts in the state. Not one of those superintendents suggested that a principal could save his job by having the football team win the state championship. It is all about results on the Texas standardized tests and being able to show up well on the Texas school report card.

Where this focus has its greatest impact is on budgeting and resource allocation. There are constant pressures to put money in all sorts of projects in a school system. It is only when there is widespread agreement that academic achievement is the first priority that the district can organize its spending and use of teacher time successfully. Every one of those districts has found that money within their current level of operations. Iredell County may be the best proof: With his focus on mission and data, Terry Holliday got the district to be in the top 10 percent for performance in North Carolina, while being in the bottom 10 percent in cost.

Two districts highlight the importance of this commitment to academics. As I described earlier, in Montgomery County and Brazosport, the school boards voted to put extra money into minority schools in order to close the achievement gap. Those were extraordinarily courageous votes. While Montgomery County has a reputation for being politically liberal, one cannot discount the pressure on school officials from high-income white parents to keep the schools serving their children well funded. The fact that the Brazosport school board, located deep in the heart of conservative, southern Texas, made the same commitment, speaks for itself. Without the dual commitments that every child can learn and that the prime focus was on academics, neither place would have been able to gather enough support to make or sustain those decisions.

BELIEF 5: ADMINISTRATORS AND TEACHERS TRUST EACH OTHER

The word "trust" came up over and over again in the interviews. That is the end result of teachers, administrators, and the superintendent all seeing each other as working together.

In the "old days," teachers worked in isolation. They did not trust other teachers and saw no reason to share. They might like the principal but did not want to be overexposed, lest it result in pressure to do things differently. And central offices were generally put down as lacking any sense of how things really were in the field.

The distance between the central office and front-line teachers in the big city districts may be one of the greatest challenges to reforming them. For example, there is constant pressure to break up LA Unified, largely fueled by teachers' belief that "333 South Beaudry," which is where the central office is located, has neither any common sense nor their best interests at heart.

While no other big city probably has such a profound gap, they all share the problem. Talking to Joel Klein one-on-one should make clear his genuine commitment to good schools and quality teachers. However, even after several years in office, the tension between Klein and the union was significant (to the end of Klein's tenure in 2010), and many New York teachers seem ready to demonize the central office as much as would their counterparts in Los Angeles. As we shall see in chapter 25, just such a lack of trust was one of the problems that doomed Miami-Dade's highly touted "Zone" experiment.

Carl Cohn and Chris Steinhauser cited trust as a key difference between their operations in Long Beach and Los Angeles or New York. Their central office is small. Much of the decision making has been pushed out to the schools. Teachers and principals are counted on to develop new strategies. The central office sees itself as supporting them, rather than the other way around. That reflects trust. Teachers reciprocate.

Trust makes working out all sorts of problems easier. It makes teachers willing to be evaluated in a Peer Assistance and Review (PAR) program. And it makes it easier to deal with other tough issues as well. Montgomery County, which has a PAR, is a good case in point. During the 2009 recession, the administration and union sat down and, in order to avoid layoffs, agreed to an $89 million revision in the union contract to save jobs and programs.

BELIEF 6: CONTINUOUS, RIGOROUS IMPROVEMENT BASED ON RESPONSES TO DATA IS FUNDAMENTAL TO ALL ASPECTS OF A DISTRICT'S OPERATION

Today we have two new, fashionable phrases in education: "continuous improvement" and "data-driven decision making." The words seem self-explanatory, but they herald a big departure from the historic way educators have done business.

First, it requires that schools set a vision and goals, which in itself is a departure from the old days. Then there has to be some benchmark ("metric" in bureaucratic speak) to determine if there is progress toward the goals, and to which people are going to hold themselves accountable by being willing to act on the results.

The belief system required has a few key characteristics. One is simply the willingness to hold oneself accountable. The related trait is that one will be candid and not simply try to spin one's way out of trouble. And the final fundamental part of the equation is flexibility of thinking. Even if one is willing to accept the verdict represented by some measurement, one has to be able to think through the options to come up with something better.

Districts have historically been unwilling, or unable, to do any of these things. A commitment to real continuous improvement is nothing short of turning education upside-down.

TWENTY-FOUR

Eight Practices

The second part of the template of improvement is a set of specific practices that follow from the beliefs. Unlike the beliefs, there may be some room for variation here. Some places, for example Phillips Andover, have done well without big computer data platforms, which I list as Practice 5. However, they have other ways of not losing sight of a child, as I described earlier. In other words, the goal does not change, even if the means do.

PRACTICE 1: TAKE CURRICULUM SERIOUSLY

In the prior chapter, we discussed the belief system around curriculum. However, there is a tangible part as well. For example, when I visited Aldine, the 2009 Broad winner, Assistant Superintendent Priscilla Ridgeway attributed its success to broad faculty support for what the district calls "managed instruction," which spells out clearly for teachers what content is to be taught and when, for every grade level across every school.[1] Although they generally do not require all teachers to follow the same steps in instruction, they have identified what they consider good pedagogy and work with teachers to build it into their practices.

The result is curriculum that is coherent and connected. What happens in fifth grade math logically follows what happens in fourth, or, as Jerry Weast does it: Everything builds to ensuring a student can get at least a 3 on an advance placement exam. They have thought about scaffolding, pacing, and mapping—which means that they rely heavily on the next practice: collaboration. Old-style loose coupling would simply destroy that kind of well-constructed curriculum.

At the same time, they have avoided making the curriculum as rigid as in the old days. In addition to a core of content knowledge and skills, there are means to tailor material or projects to interest students and meet their individual needs. In particular, the districts have adopted supplementary curricula to help struggling students or to offer enriched learning for those running far ahead. In short, the districts take curriculum seriously.

PRACTICE 2: ENHANCE COLLABORATION

The ideal of collaboration, which is so essential to training, professional development, and not losing sight of the child, plays out quite clearly in each of these districts. Every one had schools that were collaborative. They set aside time for teachers to meet every week. In transforming districts, it was not just a function of more time for meetings. The purpose changed as well.

The meetings review student progress. Many use data from recent formative assessments.[2] The object is to decide what to do with those who need help, or who are far enough ahead that they need additional stimulus to maintain their interest. The collaboration then carries through in teaching strategies. Block scheduling, team teaching, and group interventions can be successful only when everyone is working together.

The other subject is professional development. With some significant exceptions, such as in Washington, the districts encourage teachers to form learning communities and identify where they need professional development. No superintendent has abandoned directing what he or she thinks is necessary training, but they recognize the value of allowing teachers to collaborate on what they themselves identify as relevant.

The districts worked hard to allow for the scheduling of as much collaborative time as possible. For example, in Blue Valley and Iredell County, electives like band or art were scheduled at fixed times so all of a grade's primary teachers might be able to meet together. The point is that the districts believed enough in collaboration to make the effort, and at times spend some money, to make them happen. Superintendents like Doug Otto often commented that the amount of time should probably be larger, but that they were constrained by money or contracts. Unfortunately, no district provided more than four hours per week, and most were in the one- to two-hour range.

PRACTICE 3: EXPAND PROFESSIONAL DEVELOPMENT

Every one of these successful superintendents emphasized the impor-tance of well-trained administrators and teachers. That translated into at least three observable differences with traditional schools.

First, even relatively small districts like Portsmouth created their own principal academies. David Stuckwisch, Portsmouth's no-nonsense superintendent, upon arrival, was faced with twenty of his twenty-three schools lacking accreditation. He knew he lacked qualified middle man-agement, and he did not think that the typical training programs were going to produce the graduates he needed. He approached Regent Uni-versity, created a program, and pushed potential administrators through it. Twenty-one of his schools are now accredited.

Second, superintendents recognized the need to train new teachers better. As a preliminary step, places like Chicago and New York have created models of what constituted good teachers and good teaching based on the work of people like Charlotte Danielson. That gives the districts some common understanding of what they want these new teachers to do. Also, every one of the superintendents stressed the need for principals to be education leaders who spend more time observing teachers in classrooms.

After that, the strategies varied. Only one district had a pre-school induction period for new traditionally trained teachers in the summer that lasted more than two weeks, although, as noted earlier, many thought a longer period, with something like a "boot camp," was a good idea. Most districts had some mentoring for new teachers and additional coursework, but the extent varied. Many districts have master teachers, especially for math and reading in elementary school, who support all faculty, although much of their time might be spent with the new re-cruits. Administrators also encourage teacher meetings and informal teacher exchanges to bring new teachers along, sometimes as a substitute for mentoring and sometimes as a supplement to it.

Finally, many districts tried to draw teachers into taking responsibility for much of their professional development by letting them set at least part of the improvement agenda. With data, it is often easy for teachers to see that they themselves, or some of their peers, need more help.[3] Simi-larly, the Peer Assistance and Review assessments generate improvement plans for teachers in trouble. In smooth-running operations like Blue Val-ley, the professional development is not simply about rescuing flounder-ing faculty. The teachers seize the opportunity because they believe they can work jointly on improving their practice. Nonetheless, there have been clear exceptions, like Washington and San Diego, where the Rhee and Bersin administrations simply were not confident that the teachers were sufficiently supportive of new teaching methods to give them some role in deciding what should be on the training agenda.

PRACTICE 4: GIVE TEACHERS MULTIPLE ROLES

Professional learning communities require teachers to take on different roles.

Moreover, superintendents almost universally claim that one of their goals is to keep more good teachers in the classroom (as distinguished from becoming administrators), which means offering them more options in what they might do and more pay for doing it. The result is the diversification of teachers' roles, like making them mentors, or math or reading specialists. Most districts are paying a supplement to these teachers, although the amounts are often small, rarely exceeding $4,000 a year on top of a regular teacher's salary.

What was surprisingly good news was that for relatively small amounts of money, most districts seemed to be able to find enough capable people to take these jobs.

PRACTICE 5: BUILD ROBUST DATA PLATFORMS

Watauga County, Phillips Andover, KIPP, and St. Ignatius may have lacked robust data systems that tracked all sorts of information about students and school operations, but the other schools and districts had such systems or were far along in the process of building them.

Every district with a data platform is in the process of expanding it, making it more flexible, and adapting it to classroom conditions. For example, the quicker a student can take mini-assessments and the faster they can be scored, the less intrusive the process is on the rest of the learning day. Districts with enough money or community support have been giving away laptops, smart phones, and now even iPads, to students or parents who do not have them. Many of the districts are fully committed to wi-fi access in every classroom in the district.

Without a robust district-wide data platform, the next two practices can't happen.

PRACTICE 6: ASSURE REGULAR FORMATIVE ASSESSMENTS

Some districts I visited, like Baltimore, still rely on formative assessments given once every six to nine weeks to determine whether students are keeping up. The more prevalent model during the road trips was one where student learning is assessed once every week or biweekly, with some districts, like Aldine, adjusting frequency according to staff ability to facilitate effective interventions.

This type of formative assessment truly changes the nature of teaching. The job is now much harder and far more intellectually challenging than the one-curriculum, one-pedagogy, one-teacher paradigm of the old days. When considered in that light, there should be no surprise at Gerald Anderson's story about the demise of frequent mini-assessments in Brazosport following his departure in 2000.

The teachers' insistence on rolling them back raises an important issue: Does their use constitute too much testing? So far as I can tell from talking to superintendents and reviewing the literature, there is little factual basis for opposing frequent mini-assessments. However, some, like the Miami-Dade teachers and principals (but not senior administrators) I interviewed, complained bitterly that the weekly or biweekly assessments in the Zone were highly burdensome and without benefit. Even though frequency was one cited objection, when you read further in the next chapter, you may conclude, as I have, that frequency was not the principal reason the mini-assessments were a problem in Miami-Dade. Rather, the assessments were resented for the administrative paperwork they created and dismissed because of the central office's strict requirements for how they could be interpreted and used.

PRACTICE 7: INSTITUTE AGGRESSIVE ENRICHMENTS AND INTERVENTIONS

Among those districts that were already high performing, like Blue Valley and Iredell County, there is a robust program to intervene to help struggling students, and most also provide enrichments for those who are far ahead.[4] In other districts, like New York, the central office shared the goal, had committed to developing a strong assessment and intervention scheme, but had for any number of reasons, including money, not yet been able to put it all in place.

There are three principal strategies. The first two are only useful for elementary and middle schools. The simplest is for reading and math specialists to "pull out" kids who need help during regular classroom time, or, as in Pearl River, during a specifically designated period when no new learning will occur. Alternatively, the schools have "blocks" of time designated for math or reading. They are often longer than typical periods, sometimes ninety minutes to two hours in length. Kids switch around during the periods, depending on how well they have mastered the material.

The third strategy is usable at any grade level. Schools provide help time before or after school, on Saturdays, or in the summer. In New Orleans, Recovery District Schools reserve two hours, generally 2:30 p.m.

to 4:30 p.m., for some type of individualized instruction or activity for all students. Other schools use the same strategy, except that for them attendance is solely for those who need the help. KIPP and St. Ignatius, which have regular, longer days, simply build the interventions and enrichments into their schedules.

The after-school period bumps up against two problems. One is that some principals and superintendents worry about younger children's stamina. They try to avoid interventions that lengthen the school day. The other is that high schools face problems with sixteen- to eighteen-year-olds who either want to, or have to, work. Those after-school sessions are likely to conflict with their jobs. As noted above, Nick Fischer created a special after-hours high school in Fall River that met these students' needs.

One solution is the increased use of computer recovery programs where time and place might be less important. We are not there yet. No superintendent reported an intervention strategy for kids still in school (as distinguished from those who had dropped out) that relied solely on computer programs, although there are Internet-based programs, like Florida's Virtual Academy, which are essentially totally digitally based. Most educators, however, are not yet convinced; they still want students in school some part of the time, to get immediate, personal help and have some oversight.

Few superintendents mentioned tutoring by private providers, as contemplated in No Child Left Behind. In the districts described in this book, the interventions are driven by mini-assessments and the considered judgments of teachers and administrators. The superintendents have a good case that help from within is likely superior to that which a private tutor can provide. Their success suggests the tutoring provisions in No Child Left Behind should be restructured.

Finally, the strategies and content of the interventions varied. One technique is in widespread use. Response to Intervention, which originally focused on reading problems for special needs children, is now used as a structure for helping other students, starting with groups and eventually working down to one-on-one tutoring.

Beyond that, experts have different views about what the interventions should look like.

Some, like New York City, were still working hard in 2009 to develop their own material and strategy. Conversely, teachers in the Miami-Dade Zone were given explicit instructions about how to respond, and Philadelphia has online analysis available to guide teachers' interventions. What all that tells us is that a body of knowledge is being built to guide teachers. Unlike past failures with curriculum innovation in the 1970s and 1980s, the discipline of continuous improvement and data may genuinely improve how we help struggling students.

PRACTICE 8: GUARANTEE SAFE AND CIVIL SCHOOLS

One of the more extraordinary aspects of the discussions with superintendents and other administrators was how little time was spent on the issue of safety. Fifteen to twenty years ago, it would have been a constant preoccupation for many district leaders. To put it in proper perspective, rather than think of the issue as less important, think of it as something good districts have learned how to handle better.

Green Dot's strategy when it took over LA's violence-ridden Locke High School may capture the strategy best. According to Petruzzi, Green Dot has focused on creating "a respectful atmosphere in all interactions," which includes having every adult in the school getting to know students on a personal level. The idea is to convince kids not to be violent in the first place instead of emphasizing how to control situations when they are. For KIPP, the same strategy is the "Be Nice" part of their "Work Hard, Be Nice," slogan. However framed, the push is to emphasize respect and civility as a school priority.

* * *

With the exception of safe and civil schools, all these practices are closely linked together. One is not going to have quality assessments or effective interventions without collaboration, lots of training, specialist teachers, and those robust computer databases. One cannot pick and choose here. The details may vary; the need to do them all together does not.

NOTES

1. *Education Week*, "Tight Focus on Instruction Wins Texas District Prize," Oct. 7, 2009, 1.

2. Watauga County, the Catholic schools, and Phillips Andover had no such data, but they found other ways to keep track of students.

3. Michael Fullan has written that peer interaction works when "(1) the larger values of the organization and those of individuals and groups mesh; (2) when information and knowledge about effective practices are widely and openly shared; and (3) when monitoring mechanisms are in place to detect and address ineffective actions. . . ." Michael Fullan, *The Six Secrets of Change* (San Francisco: Jossey-Bass, 2008), 45.

4. Other researchers confirm the importance of these quick interventions in high-performing schools. Karin Chenoweth, *How It's Being Done* (Cambridge, MA: Harvard Education Press, 2009), 198.

TWENTY-FIVE

A Case Study in What It Takes to Fail

Miami-Dade County's "Zone" (not to be confused with Geoffrey Canada's Harlem Children's Zone) experiment is a great test case to see whether, by putting together many of these positive characteristics, a district is guaranteed success. It is not.

Superintendent Rudy Crew came to Miami-Dade in 2004. The State of Florida was pressing the county to improve its dismal schools. Crew immediately put into effect his Zone experiment in 39 of the district's 380 schools.

The Zone looked as if it should have been a winner. The schools received new principals, all of whom had been trained at Harvard and were supported by mentors on their return. The faculties at the Zone schools were fired; they could reapply to the principals if they wanted to stay on. Others were enticed to sign up because pay for all teachers in the Zone was increased. School days were one period longer, and the school year was lengthened. There was weekly or biweekly assessment and a strategy of intervention to help failing students. Teachers received a heavy dose of professional development. The union was willing to work with the district.

All of this made Miami-Dade County a 2008 Broad Prize finalist. But it did not work. The Zone was canceled in 2008, and Crew was fired. The ostensible reason was a lack of money, but the 2009 final report on the Zone confirmed what people had always thought. Test scores at Zone schools were no better than at other Miami-Dade schools. It had not been worth the effort.[1]

Teachers and administrators offered several explanations. There was general agreement that Crew had been rushed to start the Zone because of pressure from the state. He had not had time to get teachers to buy in to the approach. He may not have cared, however, because the teachers

261

and administrators found him inspiring to listen to but aloof and dictatorial in his management style. It was all "top down" and no "bottom up."

The new principals were of mixed quality. There was a feeling that ethnic politics and friendship had played a role in who had gotten the jobs. A few seemed to understand how to build collaboration in the schools, but the teachers perceived that many felt so much pressure from the central office that they would not share leadership with the teachers, most of whom they did not know. The principals turned over quickly.[2]

The central office did not speak with one voice. Teachers and principals criticized district leadership as being divided between the Old Guard and the people who were running the Zone. The principals targeted the old-style managers to whom they reported. These people were criticized for insisting on doing it "their way," even though they were not fully supportive of the Zone or of principals' own efforts to meet the goal of improved scores.

The decision to clean out faculty had serious repercussions. The principals did not hire back even well-regarded teachers. Shawn Denight had been one of those terminated from Edison High. Even though he had been a Florida Teacher of the Year, he could not return. The turmoil in having schools with large numbers of new teachers as well as new principals made building effective organizations difficult.

The new teachers were in fact too new. Denight, Stephanie King, and Christine Kirchner, all of whom did some training for the Zone, worried that the new teachers were not interested in using what they were being taught. They had not bought in to the Zone concept. On top of that, no one was going to help them once they were back in the schools.

A more troublesome problem was the Zone strategy regarding pedagogy. Elementary and middle school teachers were given scripted lessons they were expected to follow. The older, more experienced teachers like Gwen Trice, who was at Crowder Elementary in the heavily African American section called Liberty City, balked. She realized she could not follow the script verbatim and complete the curriculum. That made life at school untenable because administrators were told explicitly that their job was to make sure that teachers did as they had been told. (Shades of Fred Bateman!) There was, as a result, a great deal of pressure and not much collaboration.

The Zone schools did weekly or biweekly assessments, but they were not deemed effective. The teachers were ordered to spend vast amounts of time recording results. On top of that, they were expected to follow specific directions about what interventions they were to provide for children who were failing. That demeaned their professionalism, even though the strategy should have been premised on promoting it. Their judgment was damning: Assessments took away from teaching rather than adding a powerful tool to make it better.

The extra periods and extra days seemed a waste to the teachers. Many kids, especially in high school, cut the last period. The summer sessions were "just more of the same" and did not offer students anything different from what they were receiving during the regular year. Not surprisingly, there was a fair amount of truancy during the summer school period.

The Zone tried to enhance parent outreach, but confused parent classes with actual outreach. They put on more parent classes and sent information home. But no one put a human face on the invitation, even though such personal relationships were important in the communities that were targeted. Trice, for example, was told not to go to students' homes after visiting several, as had been her practice for many years. As noted earlier, few parents actually showed up.

Here are at least some of the principal lessons to be learned. There was a distinct lack of trust between teachers and the administration. That, in turn, led to a completely top-down effort, with no attempt to push decision making out to the schools and then to the teachers. If good teachers thought extra periods and extra days were a waste of time, there was something fundamentally wrong with either the Zone's implementation or at least the way in which it was communicated to those who had to carry it out. Finally, the decision to reconstitute all these schools by firing teachers, even good ones, created ill will and consternation.

The ultimate lesson learned is to remember you are dealing with people. It is not just what you want to do, but how you do it, that counts.

NOTES

1. Steven M. Urdegar, *School Improvement Zone—Final Evaluation Report* (Miami: Miami-Dade County Public Schools, Office of Program Evaluation, 2009).

2. Michael Fullan has observed that it does no good to train principals for the new order and then refuse to give them the authority required to carry it out. Michael Fullan, *Transformational Leadership* (San Francisco: Jossey-Bass, 2006), 94. That seems, at least in part, to have been precisely the problem in Miami-Dade.

TWENTY-SIX

The Things Not Done

This chapter is reserved for those things only a few districts did.

One has already been covered at length: a school's institutional commitment to ensuring student attitudes and motivation and parental involvement. There are two more:

OUTSOURCING

By now, it should be clear that school districts do not have a lot of managerial depth.

When I was Los Angeles Unified School District's general counsel, one of the most frustrating parts of the job was supporting senior staff's effort to negotiate contracts, run the bus service, maintain the warehouse, or deal with real estate (which might be collectively called "non-core" functions). The people we had in charge were not up to the job, and, although we tried to do better over time, we were confronted with low pay scales, arcane rules, and a state prohibition on outsourcing much of the work to others. We were not alone in our frustration.

Of all the districts I visited, only Washington, DC, New York, and New Orleans have outsourced a significant number of non-core functions. In Washington, DC, either the district government or private industry provides food service, transit, facilities, and information technology. In New York City, Joel Klein has created support organizations that are designed to take over some or all of the noneducational functions that the district or a school would have had to perform. Eight of the organizations are privately run; four remain within the Department of Education. At the school level, the principals have help from people who are in effect business managers, whose task is to oversee the support organizations' service (which is a benefit in itself even if someone within the district still manages the service).[1] In New Orleans, Vallas is committed to using private contractors wherever possible.[2]

All of these superintendents recognize two values in outsourcing: It likely saves money, and, more importantly, it conserves whatever management capability their districts possess for the really important function: education.

Some other districts rely on another unit of government, like a park and recreation department, or a private contractor, like a food service contractor or bus operator, for a single service or two.[3] A small number have business managers who relieve principals of some of their traditional management duties. In other words, there is some outsourcing, but not enough.

Only Larry Bowers, the chief operating officer in Montgomery County, doubted he could get the same kind of responsiveness from an outside source. No one else fundamentally opposed the conclusion that Rhee, Klein, and Vallas share about the value of concentrating on education and outsourcing non-core functions.

In some states, whether or not they agree or disagree is irrelevant. The states have bans on outsourcing. However, such bans are not universal, and where outsourcing is an option (or where the ban can be repealed), it is worth serious consideration.

ETHICS

School districts do not take seriously the need for ethical behavior among staff.

Superintendents or senior administrators in seven districts (Lawrence, Fall River, Portsmouth, New York, Washington, DC, New Orleans, and Montgomery County) acknowledged they either still had problems with corruption or favoritism, or had just fixed them within the past few years. Ethics is not a problem from another era. It is a real issue today.

Only three districts I visited have a code of ethics. That is a serious omission. John Simmons, one of the innovative charter school leaders in Chicago, thinks the key values in a school are honesty, openness, trust, respect, and cooperation. By my count, the first four are what ethics is all about, and collectively, they lead to the fifth.

Throughout my service in Los Angeles, as well as in a surprising number of interviews, superintendents, senior staff, and teachers have all doubted they could trust the honesty and fairness of someone making an important decision in a school. Teachers did not trust principals, principals did not trust union representatives, school board members did not trust each other, and everyone was willing to entertain really dark suspicions about the superintendent.

When this kind of distrust pervades a district, collaboration and team spirit, all central to a high-functioning school, are simply impossible.[4]

Because of scandals that had occurred prior to my arrival at LAUSD, the board had passed a requirement that my office create an ethics code, which all employees were eventually going to be required to sign. The project met fierce resistance from the unions and earned only tepid support from most administrators. They all viewed the ethics code as a piece of political theater.

Their dismissal of the idea of a code then seemed inexplicable when they complained, as they regularly would, about people playing favorites, or cutting corners, or getting kickbacks. There is no way to reconcile the whining and the hostility to the code unless one wants to argue that articulating a code and making people sign it makes no difference on behavior.

If teachers are to collaborate with administrators, and administrators are going to begin serious evaluations of faculty, there has to be a commitment to ethics. If no one believes anyone else is acting in good faith, and making decisions on merit, the entire structure that I have described for the last many chapters is almost certainly going to fail, as it did in Miami-Dade. Ethics codes are pieces of paper. They cannot be confused with actually being ethical. But they do represent the institution's commitment to the ideal, and that is at least one way to encourage that it will happen.

NOTES

1. Vivian Troen and Katherine C. Boles, *Who's Teaching Your Children?* (New Haven, CT: Yale University Press, 2003), 156.
2. Elsewhere, I found other instances where there was at least limited outsourcing. Outside New York City, the State of New York has created Boards of Cooperative Educational Services (BOCES). The boards were created to take advantage of economies of scale in a variety of instructional and support functions that individual districts could not achieve. For example, BOCES provides Pearl River with information technology services.
3. In 2010, Detroit sold off its bus fleet to deal with its growing deficit. *Detroit Free Press*, "PDS to Sell Off Its School Buses," Feb. 24, 2010 (retrieved from www.freep.com/article.2010224/NEWS01/2240421/NEWS/DPS-to-sell-off-its-school-buses on Feb. 24, 2010).
4. Sharon D. Kruse and Karen Seashore Louis, *Building Strong School Cultures* (Thousand Oaks, CA: AASA/Corwin Press, 2009), 83.

Part VI

Beyond the School District: The Role of the States and Federal Government

The sad separation of authority, responsibility, and funding will continue. It is never going to be rolled back. The states and the federal government will set the rules and provide a great deal of the money. What they now need to do is accept some of the responsibility, especially when it comes to making renewal a reality. If the states and federal government do not support the kinds of reforms described earlier, they will not happen. It is not enough for them to claim an interest in better schools. They have a real role in creating them.

TWENTY-SEVEN

The Role of the States

School districts are creatures of the states. State law authorizes them and dictates how they operate. And in many cases, the states are the principal funders of districts, especially low-income ones. What, then, should the states do to promote schools for the twenty-first century?

MONEY

Over the last fifty years, the states have taken over more and more of the funding responsibility, and they have all, to a greater or lesser degree, become more intensely involved in district decision making.

Neither the money function nor rule making is going away. The issue is whether they can be done wisely enough to contribute positively to the education children actually receive.

Funding has three issues tied together:

- Is there enough?
- Is it stable?
- Is it so tied up with strings that it is not worth receiving?

The simple, bad news is that there are no good answers to any of these questions.

For example, what is "enough" is almost impossible to answer. A court (or any reasonable person) may be able to conclude that absurdly low funding levels are "inadequate," but deciding what is in fact "adequate" is something else entirely.

The facts in the real world make clear how hard that is to do. A good case in point is the comparison between Los Angeles and Long Beach. They are neighboring school districts, with similar populations that are

271

heavily low income and Spanish speaking. Long Beach has almost 100,000 students, and Los Angeles is around seven times larger. Let's look at the numbers (from 2006 to 2007):

- Los Angeles spent more than $10,430 per student. On California's Academic Performance Index (API), 18 percent of LA's schools scored better than 800, and 23 percent scored below 650.
- Long Beach spent only $8,756 per student. But 29 percent of its schools scored above 800 on the API, and only 8 percent scored below 650.[1]

That comparison is not unique. The Center for American Progress, a liberal think tank in Washington, DC, published a study in early 2011 that compared dozens of districts and reached the same conclusion: The cost-effectiveness of districts varies widely across the country.[2] More money does not necessarily mean better results.

Similarly, stability in funding is important, but, as states have demonstrated over the last two years, it can be hard to maintain. Even states like California, which have gone so far as to pass a referendum creating a constitutional guarantee of stability, cannot deliver on the commitment when their economies crash.

Finally, for every "string" that seems like unnecessary meddling in a district's or a school's business, defenders of categorical funding can come up with at least one or two examples where some worthwhile use of funds would not likely have happened without legislative direction.

If there are no hard-and-fast prescriptions to solve the problems, are there any ideas that at least might improve the current situation? Here are three:

- To help determine adequacy, the states should think about pursuing a strategy similar to the one the Federal Health Care Financing Agency (HCFA) employs in deciding how much it should be paying for doctors and services under Medicare. An expert commission makes recommendations for each region of the country for most types of care and major procedures. Congress can override the recommendations, but at least there is some expert basis for the legislative discussion about what is reasonable. Similarly, parents and taxpayers can push their legislators to follow—or ignore—the recommendations, which is at least an improvement in the way many states conduct budget deliberations today.
- To enhance stability, states can follow either or both of the following strategies: One is to create a large rainy day fund, an idea that is widely talked about and rarely seriously implemented. The other strategy is to try to avoid wide swings in state revenue. California's Proposition 13 is the poster child. By limiting increases in the property tax, the state eventually wound up relying heavily on income

and capital gains taxes, both of which fluctuate far more wildly in response to economic changes. If funding stability is the goal, reducing tax volatility is important.

- For categoricals, the best rule may be to follow Jim Collins's adage about "having the right people on the bus."[3] The more you trust people, the fewer rules you will need to guarantee they will do what they are supposed to do. Conversely, the less trust, the greater the impulse to set precise rules. That dictum should carry through to school funding. The more a school or a district meets its targets for school achievement or dropout prevention (or whatever else), the less it should be subject to directions on how it spends its money.

ACCOUNTABILITY, TRAINING, AND A COMMITMENT TO A LARGER VISION

The states have a few other issues to deal with as well. We have discussed most of them at some length earlier in the book, so I will limit myself to a brief summary here.

First, the states have by and large embarrassed themselves over accountability issues. Most prominently, many states degraded the standards by which they evaluated annual student tests required by No Child Left Behind, such that the results lost much of their credibility. As a consequence, forty-two states (as of this writing) have adopted the new national standards for math and reading, which were promoted by the Obama administration. States' rights advocates can complain, as they have, about the loss of state control. But if the states are going to be irresponsibly political, they cannot expect better treatment.

State irresponsibility goes beyond standards. When state legislatures passed legislation barring the use of student achievement data as part of teacher evaluations, they were acting in response to pleas from teachers' unions. Student achievement was not at issue. Teacher job protection drove the bans. Once again, it is not surprising that the Obama administration chose to act by pressing states to repeal such laws in order to win some of the $4 billion in Race to the Top money awarded in 2010.

If the states want to lead reform, they have to inventory all their education-related legislation and decide what they should throw out. In an era where everyone preaches innovation and flexibility, the states' education codes tend to enshrine everything but.

They also need to overhaul their state departments of education. Most are simply oversize nannies, enforcing compliance with all the state's rules. They are not now prepared to promote reform or help districts do their job. Even if citizens are more active in district affairs, the departments' ineffectiveness has to change.

The states also control most of teacher education through their funding of state colleges that produce the vast majority of American teachers. State government stewardship of those institutions has been ineffective. Too much state money still goes to schools that do not produce good teachers. The states need to step up their oversight, but more importantly, they need to be willing to shift the bulk of the money to school districts, allowing them to offer or buy training that will in fact produce the teachers they need.

Finally, states decide on the rules for traditional school districts and charters. They design the playing field and define how all of them will work collectively to provide a system that offers quality education to all students. They cannot move forward piecemeal. They need a vision of how to meet the requirements of their state constitutions to provide free, public education for their children, and they have to take the politically courageous step of legislating with the long term in mind. As we shall discuss in chapter 29, they can no longer think of charters as "experimental" and traditional schools as closely controlled and the dumping ground for problems the charters do not want. They are going to have to come up with a new vision of fair competition.

NOTES

1. NCES (IES), Digest of Education Statistics, table 91—Revenues, expenditures, poverty rate and Title I allocations of public school districts enrolling more than 15,000 students: 2006–07 and fiscal year 2009 (retrieved from http://nced.ed.gov/programs/digest/d09/_091.asp); LAUSD, "LAUSD Continues Growth, Double-Digit Gains on the 2010 API and AYP Results" (news release), Sept. 13, 2010; California Department of Education, *Local Education Agency List of Schools, 2006 Base Academic Performance Index (API)* (Sacramento: California Department of Education, 2007) (retrieved from http://api.cde.gov/AcntRpt2007/2006Base_Dst.aspec?cYear=&allcds=1964725&cChoise=2006BDst).

2. Center for American Progress, *Return on Educational Investment: A District-by-District Evaluation of U.S. Educational Productivity* (Washington, DC: Center for American Progress, 2011).

3. Jim Collins, *Good to Great* (New York: HarperCollins, 2001), 41.

TWENTY-EIGHT

The Role of the Federal Government

Finally, there is the question of what should be the federal role in public education.

Because this book is being written as the reauthorization of the Elementary and Secondary Education Act (ESEA) is debated in Congress, the temptation is to engage on the level of how to make incremental changes in the current law. That is not a trivial discussion, but it is just a subissue of the larger question about what should be the federal government's role vis-à-vis the states, the districts, and the schools.

ACCOUNTABILITY, STANDARDS, AND THE NEW NO CHILD LEFT BEHIND

The reauthorization of the ESEA may present the most complicated set of federal education issues since the law was first created in 1965.

The Obama administration continues to support testing, arguing that only testing is going to ensure accountability and a continuing focus on closing the achievement gap. The goal for reauthorization is to find a credible measure of accountability while avoiding the pitfalls of the Bush-era version.

The Obama administration has tried to sidestep some of the peculiarities of NCLB testing by pushing for the use of "value added" measures, like those pioneered in Tennessee. It has offered $350 million to create new assessments to go with the new common core standards, in part to deal with "value added's" problems and in part so that it can avoid the criticism that the testing is nothing more than "fill in the box" answers that do not test writing skills or critical thinking.

The consequences of failure will also change if the administration gets its way. Instead of demanding any school that fails to meet the requirements for three years in a row face a set of increasing sanctions, the administration wants to concentrate on the lowest-performing 5 percent of Title I (or Title I eligible) schools (with lesser reforms for those who are in the next tier up).

The proposal does not, however, come to grips with all the criticisms that have been leveled at the statute. For example, if student test scores are going to be used to evaluate teachers or pay them and to make all sorts of other decisions about closing schools, then there really has to be testing in all subjects in all grades. However, I do not want to go further; most of these issues have been addressed previously, and any interested reader hopefully has some idea of what an improved testing regime should look like.

What is worth further consideration are two much larger, more philosophical questions underlying NCLB.

That question about high-stakes testing is just a part of a larger issue of how much policy should be driven from Washington. Diane Ravitch, a prominent education historian who was an assistant secretary of education in the George H. W. Bush administration, has done an about-face, concluding that testing and choice, the act's hallmarks, have been failures. She worries about the federal government's usurping not only the state's role,[1] but also that of the local district. She argues: "Good policy does try to incorporate knowledge of local conditions,"[2] which only those on scene can possibly know.

The most telling dissenter may be Jerry Weast. Here is a superintendent who has done virtually everything that the administration would want. In 2010, his district won the Baldrige Award. Yet he refused to sign up immediately for Maryland's Race to the Top application. In an op-ed in the *Baltimore Sun*, Weast worried that the application would commit the district to giving up its unique, and successful, assessment policies, and he was not about to do that.[3] Washington's "one size fits all" may not only drive change; Weast's complaint shows the federal government may also screw it up.

Even if reformers like the federal agenda, there is a real issue of whether having Washington make fundamental decisions ultimately enhances the viability of schools and districts. At the very beginning of this book, there was a discussion of the problem with separating funding, authority, and responsibility. The more aggressive Washington becomes in setting the rules, the more authority moves away from the grassroots.

There is a way to compromise between the two positions. The Obama administration has to be held to one of its promises in its *Blueprint* for the new law: "Our proposal will encourage and support local innovation,"[4] which is coupled with an assurance it intends less interference in well-run schools.[5] Parents and taxpayers should make clear they expect that commitment will be honored. No strings on money given to well-managed schools should interfere with day-to-day operations. To the extent the strings exist, they should be limited to ensuring the most basic purposes for which money has been received—such as being used solely for the benefit of low-income children, or to maintain accountability by requiring adherence to high standards and fair assessments.

Even when schools fail, there should be more room for local participation than currently contemplated by the administration. For example, the administration intends to insist on the use of one of four turnaround options to fix failing schools. That is too heavy-handed. It should not dictate what happens without first giving schools or districts the right to devise their own plan that speaks to what they perceive to be their problems and needs. For example, the law might be structured as follows:

> A district may first attempt to turn around a failing school using a plan that has been adopted by a public vote in which at least 25 percent of the district's registered voters participated, and where such a plan has been approved by the state education agency. In the event no such plan has been adopted or approved, the district shall be required to follow one of the four turnaround plans described in this legislation. If there is a district plan, the district shall have two years to demonstrate to the satisfaction of the state education agency and the U.S. Department of Education that the plan has significantly improved student learning. If not, the school or district shall adopt one of the four turnaround plans prescribed here.

MONEY

Which brings us to a final, and inevitable, subject: money.

Money (or the lack of it) causes no end of complaints. There are two worthy of mention here.

The smaller, and more obvious one, is that the federal government should pay for what it requires states and districts to do. The Individuals with Disabilities Education Act (IDEA) is a perfect example. As I noted earlier, when Congress passed the law, it promised to fund 40 percent of the cost. Actual appropriations have never gone above 17 percent. Spending obligations like IDEA further undermine the vitality and coherence of districts. The problem is especially galling when school budgets are being cut, because IDEA obligations remain the same.

The other complaint centers on the approximately $14 billion provided every year to local education agencies to support low-income schools.

As Gerald Anderson and Jerry Weast understand, it is going to take more money to give children in a heavily low-income school the same education they might receive in one with fewer poor kids. A state that simply believes in equal funding for districts does not treat its poor students fairly, and few states even get that far. What made possible the seemingly equalized per capita funding numbers for urban and suburban districts quoted in chapter 3 was in large part federal Title I funding.

However, there is a problem lurking when considering what this money is supposed to buy. Title I districts are the ones most heavily reliant on state dollars, and state dollars are not stable. And as I just discussed in the prior section, there are really no state-based solutions likely to do more than moderate the worst excesses of that budget volatility.

Budget uncertainty sucks the life out of reform. A superintendent and board trying to figure out what one has to spend when that number is a moving target until June or July is not focused on reform. We can have reform, or we can have unstable budgets in districts heavily dependent on state money.

Stability is so important to districts facing reform that the federal government should not merely continue Title I funding. It should use its ability to run unbalanced budgets to step up to taking greater responsibility for providing some budget certainty to districts with large numbers of low-income students.

In 2009, it did just that. The administration put $53 billion in the 2009 stimulus bill to protect schools from disastrous budget cuts.[6] As the recession continued, there were literally hundreds of articles in newspapers all over the nation describing how teachers faced more cuts in 2010–2011 because that support was a one-time appropriation.[7] In response, the administration got passed a further $10 billion in the summer of 2010, which it estimated saved 325,000 teachers' jobs. [8]

If we are committed to reform, we cannot treat the federal government as an occasional provider of "last resort." There has to be some continuing commitment from the federal government that school money will be stable.

At a minimum, if a district or state receives a federal grant to build out a new program or innovation, it should come with a federal commitment to maintain the effort over some significant period of years.[9] More broadly, the federal government should make the same commitment to any school or any district that has received turnaround funding. It is simply a waste of federal money to turn around the school and then see it roll back its new operating plan or cut teachers' salaries because the state cannot continue to fund the program at the level necessary to make it work.

How far this guarantee might extend is a matter of political will. The value of any guarantee, however, is unquestioned if we are going to be committed to genuine school improvement.

NOTES

1. *New York Times*, "Obama Pushes States to Shift on Education," Aug. 17, 2009 (retrieved from www.nytimes.com/2009/08/17/education.17educ.html on Aug. 16, 2009).

2. *Education Week*, "Taking Back School Reform: A Conversation between Diane Ravitch and Mike Rose," May 12, 2010 (retrieved from www.edweek.org/tm/articles/2010/05/12/roseravitchschoolreform.html on May 14, 2010).

3. Jerry D. Weast, "County Supports State's Goals but Must Safeguard the Gains It Has Made," *Baltimore Sun*, April 19, 2010 (retrieved from www.baltimoresun.com.news/opinion/oped/bs-ed-montgomery-schools-20100419,0,7166584,print.story on April 19, 2010).

4. *A Blueprint for Reform* (Washington, DC: U.S. Department of Education, 2010), 6.

5. *New York Times*, "Obama Proposes Sweeping Change in Education Law," March 14, 2010, 1.

6. *Education Week*, "Recession's Toll on K–12 Budgets Both Wide and Deep," Jan. 13, 2011 (retrieved from www.edweek.org/ew/articles/2011/01/13/16landscape.he0.html on Jan. 13, 2011).

7. See, for example, *Washington Post*, "Thousands Face Furloughs; Schools May Lose Millions," March 16, 2010, 1.

8. *Washington Post*, "President Obama Signs $26 Billion Jobs Bill to Aid State Payrolls," Aug. 11, 2010 (retrieved from www.washingtonpost.com/wp/edyn/content/article/2010/08/10/AR201081004201.html on Aug. 11, 2010).

9. One can design a system so that the federal government is obliged to come to a state's aid only when there is a genuine revenue shortfall, not a shortfall caused by a diversion of money to other purposes or by a tax cut. However, the mechanics of such a system are again beyond the scope of this book.

Postscript

The Future of the American Public School System

TWENTY-NINE

The Education System We Need—the System of Schools We Want

The template in part IV describes what an individual district or an individual school can look like right now. But how should American public education evolve in the future?

We already know the answer. If you piece together all the trends and good ideas described in preceding chapters, the picture emerges. We are on our way to moving from school systems to systems of schools. Eventually, much or all of school management will devolve to the schools themselves. Districts may still exist, but their functions will be different.

WHY CURRENT SCHOOL DISTRICTS DO NOT WORK

It should by now be apparent that the local school district is a unit of government that, in its current form, has more weaknesses than strengths:

- The size and shape of school districts make little sense. Some are tiny; some are county-wide or city-wide, and Hawaii has one district covering the entire state. Student populations range from 100 to 200 to over 1,000,000 in New York City alone. As a consequence, districts face a range of problems from being too small to be efficient to so large that the central office is unmanageably distant from both schools and parents.
- Districts have often perpetuated the disparities of wealth and race in this country. Poor districts like the Ravenswood district of East Palo Alto, California, exist next to wealthy ones like Palo Alto, with

283

the arbitrary district boundary a barrier to both reasonable integration and funding.

- Districts have been monopoly providers of education services within their jurisdictions. Historically, they set the rules, provided the
  services, and were their own oversight.
- In the past fifty years, political participation in district elections has
  dropped significantly, leaving control of districts to highly motivated groups, like unions or religious activists.
- School boards often micromanage or split into factions. In too many
  cases, they become barriers to reform or good management. Low-
  income schools are the most likely victims of board politics, particularly in districts that still have schools that predominantly serve
  different races or different socioeconomic groups.

WHAT IS DRIVING US TOWARD A
NEW TYPE OF SCHOOL DISTRICT?

There are several developments in the management of schools and districts, some of which have already been discussed, that are likely to have
a profound impact on the shape and function of school districts over
time.

The one that may ultimately have the most powerful effect is the trend
to decentralize the management of schools away from the central office to
the school itself. By placing the responsibility for improved learning
squarely on the shoulders of principals (and secondarily on faculty),
superintendents either have, or are inevitably going to have, to cede to
those principals key management decisions, like budget and hiring.

The other powerful push toward decentralization comes from charters. Although they may have first been characterized as "experimental"
ways to test out new ideas when they started in the 1990s, they are hardly
experimental anymore.

Because they were "experimental," the charters have been freed from
most of the rules that bind traditional public schools. Even though they
are now permanent fixtures, that freedom is deemed fundamental to
charters, and it is not going away.

As a result, in many ways, the competition between charters and traditional schools is unfair. One group of schools, charters, gets to design
themselves to fill a niche they see in the community, while the other
group, traditional schools, is hide-bound by hundreds of pages of state
laws and school board rules.

As charters have become permanent fixtures, they have made the
norm of public schools all functioning one way in response to an extensive set of rules seem less compelling or attractive.[1] It also does not fit
with the logic of differentiated instruction, where the existence of distinct

schools that can attract different kinds of students is a vital part of any strategy to deal with students with a range of interests and learning styles.

The disparity cannot continue, and it won't. In Los Angeles, there has been constant pressure over the past eight years from parents, teachers, and administrators, and even some school board members, to convert many of the district's schools into charters.[2] In the Recovery School District in New Orleans, Paul Vallas is far down the road to achieving exactly that vision, with two-thirds of his schools now charters.[3] Similarly, Clark County (Las Vegas) has begun converting traditional schools to "autonomous" ones that function in much the same way as Vallas's charters.[4] And in places large and small across the country, charters and traditional schools are collaborating or mimicking one another.[5] The trend is not going away; on the contrary, as the number of charters grows, the pressure will become more intense.

Current studies of charters' effectiveness are inconclusive.[6] Some do well. Some do not. Merely being a charter does not yield superior performance. Merely being a traditional public school does not guarantee inferior results. Neither should win; neither should lose. They should simply compete in order to allow the better schools to attract more and more students over time.

A related pressure is the attractiveness of small schools. Because principals and teachers understand the importance of meaningful interaction with their students—and with each other—the typical student body will likely grow smaller over time. Smaller schools are easier to start up, from requiring less space to fewer teachers. That means more potential entrants into the school market.

Parents' high level of participation in schools—in contrast to their low participation in districts—is another indication of where power and focus may flow. Parent participation at schools is robust and creates the possibility of genuine accountability. None of the districts I visited had any creative ideas how to increase parent participation in district elections or deliberations, even though some, like Pearl River, had certainly devoted real thought to the question.

Finally, there is the thorny, and seemingly unending, conundrum of school funding. For the past forty years, the courts and legislatures have tried to figure out how to equalize funding so as not to penalize students who just happen to live in poor districts, which, incidentally, likely need more money than other districts in order to deliver an equal education experience. On top of that, the property tax, even if a stable revenue source (other than in 2009–2010), has grown more burdensome.

One of the most compelling reasons for local school districts was that they collected and disbursed money from the property tax collected in their jurisdictions. Now, even wealthy districts are in revolt against such local funding. In the spring of 2010, taxpayers in a large majority of New

Jersey school districts rejected the annual school district budget because of the high increases they were going to face in their property taxes.[7] As support for the property tax declines, the need for districts to play their traditional role of financial intermediary in education declines as well.

THE SCHOOL DISTRICT OF THE FUTURE

So where does all this leave us?

If you accept most of these pressures or trends as either desirable or inevitable (meaning that, either way, they are not going to disappear), then we all might want to consider the eventual reshaping of local education in America to look something like the following:

> School districts will get out of the business of operating schools. Instead, all schools—whether charters or what used to be traditional schools operated by districts—become governed by the same set of limited rules that now govern charters.

The idea is not radical. The executive director of the American Association of School Administrators Dan Domenech has argued for precisely this change.[8] So has Columbia Teachers College professor Jeff Henig and two of his colleagues, who have described such a system as the "Portfolio Management Model" in their 2010 book, *Between Public and Private: Politics, Governance, and the New Portfolio Models for Urban School Reform.*[9]

Individual school councils and administrators get to determine their own key policy decisions like budget and staff. They might operate independently, or they might cluster to create a coordinated K–12 grouping,[10] or they might be jointly affiliated, for example, multiple KIPP or Green Dot schools in the same area.

A Level Playing Field

If choice among schools is to be meaningful, then there has to be a level playing field on which they all operate.

The criteria for admission to all schools would have to be modeled on lotteries, which charters currently use, or open enrollment plans like the ones used in Long Beach. Some provision can be made for giving neighborhood students a priority or a designated share of total seats, while allowing students from elsewhere in the district to apply for the remainder. The connection between poor schools and poor neighborhoods, which has dogged us for decades and enraged politicians and educators, left and right, must be broken.[11]

Charters would have to accept certain obligations that many experts believe they have skirted over the years.[12] The most obvious is that they would have to take responsibility for special education. Tom Hehir, Harvard's special education expert, told me he has long worried that charters have not taken on their fair share of special education children, leaving traditional public schools unfairly burdened with a disproportionate share of such students. Similarly, a 2010 study by Columbia Teachers College found New York's charters had fewer English language learners than other City schools,[13] and two studies in Los Angeles found charters actually reinforced segregation of student bodies.[14] Charters would also have to come to grips with discipline and retention policies. Now, difficult or failing children are often counseled out of charters, leaving them to be taught by traditional schools. That can no longer happen if these schools are, collectively, part of "a system."

Charters would have to accept certain obligations that many experts believe they have skirted over the years.[15] The most obvious is that they would have to take responsibility for special education. Tom Hehir, Harvard's special education expert, told me he has long worried that charters have not taken on their fair share of special education children, leaving traditional public schools unfairly burdened with a disproportionate share of such students. Similarly, a 2010 study by Columbia Teachers College found New York's charters had fewer English language learners than other City schools,[16] and two studies in Los Angeles found charters actually reinforced segregation of student bodies.[17] Charters would also have to come to grips with discipline and retention policies. Now, difficult or failing children are often counseled out of charters, leaving them to be taught by traditional schools. That can no longer happen if these schools are, collectively, part of "a system."

And then there are vouchers. Voucher schools are unlike charters. They accept students whose tuition is paid for with public money, but do not have to play by many of the rules necessary to keep competition among schools fair.[18] Their admissions policies do not require a neutral admission process, or one that has a full share of special education students. Nor do they have to retain disruptive or failing students, or bear some responsibility for their placement if those children are kicked out or fail. And not all are even held accountable through testing in the same way both traditional public schools and charters are.

An example of the problem is the impact of the Milwaukee voucher program, one of the largest in the nation, on the public schools in that city. William Andrekopoulos, the superintendent, told me that his city's voucher schools had only 3 percent special education students in 2009, while the public schools had upward of 18 percent of their students so designated.[19] There was no way, in his view, that one could compare the results of schools when that kind of imbalance existed.[20]

Were private institutions willing to accept all these obligations, it might be feasible to include them in a "system," but it would come at a price. They would lose their character. Jewish schools likely would not want to take a large number of Christians, but they would have to at least expose themselves to that possibility (e.g., a lottery admissions process) in order to be an equal participant in this kind of system. Similarly, high-performing private schools that require students to test in should not have to lower their standards. We tolerate these sorts of schools because we respect the First Amendment's rights to freely associate and to freedom of religion even though they may have monochromatic student bodies, too few special education students, or a discipline policy that looks nothing like the one in traditional public schools. But tolerating their existence in a parallel universe is different from integrating them into one that is built on public money and designed to serve public purposes.

This incompatibility has nothing to do with the issue of whether it is appropriate under the First Amendment to use public money to pay for education in church-related schools. It also does not rely on the various studies that have argued for—or against—the effectiveness of voucher schools in comparison with their public alternatives.[21] Rather, the question is how to build a competitive system of schools that collectively offer equal choices, where none of them are unfairly burdened by obligations the others do not share.

The New Role of the District Office

The school district "central office" still has a major role to play in such a system, albeit it looks different from the old one. There is no other entity in position to ensure that all the schools within its jurisdiction play by whatever the rules are, deliver high-quality instruction, and, if necessary, observe their obligations regarding integration and the equitable provision of services.

No individual school operator can be forced to take on those responsibilities. The district has to remain obliged to make sure every child has enrollment options that include a quality school in the child's neighborhood and a range of choices within reasonable distance.

The central office can also continue to operate buildings, the area transportation system, and any number of other non-core functions, like IT services. In some cases, the logic of central office operation is tied to its larger role ensuring things like equity. By controlling buildings, for example, the central office can guarantee new entrants space necessary to ensure equal options in every part of town. In other cases, like IT services, the reason may simply be that there are genuine economies of scale.

Money

The idea of a geographic education monopoly that both raises and spends funds will become passé. It is a perfect time to address all of the inequalities of intra- and interdistrict funding that have appeared throughout this book.

The first pressure we will see as decision making is decentralized may come from how money is allocated. Even if we still have districts taxing and dividing money, the process of how it is distributed cannot remain the same. The central office won't be spending the funds, and those who are, individual school principals, will now demand every dime they can get—without strings.

To resolve the problem, the district may well settle upon a per capita formula, similar to the way charter schools are now funded. That makes sense, since all schools are now effectively competitors on an increasingly level playing field. And there will undoubtedly be pressure to weight the funding to provide additional money for low-income students. No principal is going to want to have to accept potentially large numbers of such students, as she might in a lottery, without having additional money to meet their extra needs.

Any discussion of a formula quickly moves to the larger question. If districts are no longer monopoly providers of education within their jurisdictions, should they still be tax collectors?

The obvious answer is total funding from monies raised statewide. That may raise questions about whether currently wealthy districts would be willing to accept the possibility that their schools would not receive as much money as they have now. It is a thorny issue and beyond the scope of this book. Whatever the problems, the general idea of moving to statewide funding is long overdue.

Were there to be a shift to state funding, then there is little reason to maintain the current pattern of school districts. In states like New York, California, New Jersey, and Pennsylvania, which have literally thousands of districts of varying sizes, the lines could be rethought. If the property tax in Roslyn no longer funds the school district, should the district still follow the town boundaries? If it is now a regulator and perhaps a provider of some additional services, would it be more reasonable to have one district in Nassau County, or perhaps just two or three?

Conversely, if New York City is no longer the principal source of funding for the schools, might it not be more efficient to break up the city's Department of Education and create one for each borough? There might be issues about how to ensure the continued integration of the schools, but for most other purposes, reducing the size of the sprawling district makes great sense.

HOW DO WE GET THE DISTRICT OF THE FUTURE?

Other than in a few places like New Orleans, this vision of a highly decentralized school district with decision making vested in individual schools is futuristic. Even if one wanted to create such a governance scheme tomorrow, the system could not handle it. There are, however, places to get started.

The first and most likely place to begin is the continued empowerment of the individual school. There are enough models of success built around enhancing local school decision making that other districts should be willing to adopt the idea as well. The Obama administration is a strong supporter of the idea. In addition to proposing new support for charter schools in a reauthorized Elementary and Secondary Education Act, it wants to aid "autonomous" public schools, like those in Las Vegas, which are in fact schools that operate largely independently of their districts.

The support for both of these types of schools is a massive push in the direction of further decentralization. If the reauthorization contains the right language, parents and taxpayers should push their districts to apply for funds that will be test cases for decentralization—either full-blown or some partial devolution of decision making that at least tests some of the reasons why such a system might be worthwhile.

The biggest limitation on the growth of a decentralized model may be the resistance of current traditional public schools to convert to autonomous, charter-like entities. Teachers and administrators may simply not want to work in this kind of environment, or even if they are willing to try, the changes in roles and responsibilities may be more than they can accept.

The other limitation on the growth of decentralized schools may be adequate numbers of good administrators who can handle the increased demands of a decentralized school. Unlike prior reform efforts, this one has focused on the need for more skilled administrators who fit the precise needs of decentralized schools. The Obama administration proposes as part of its *Blueprint* to provide money for such training, and they want to offer it to non-university trainers, like New Leaders for New Schools, or school districts, all of which will expand the size of the pool of capable principals. It is a good first step.

Even if the end result of the current round of reform does not yield fully decentralized schools and rethought districts, it should lead to an improved result. The consistent theme of this chapter is that schools need to heed twenty-first-century management theory, which is all about pushing decisions to the front lines and empowering workers to make decisions. All of the improved training, shared decision making, and enhanced capacity to meet the needs of individual students sustain that idea, and the idea, in turn, justifies them.

* * *

As I finish this book in 2011, education is high on the national agenda. For that, we owe President Obama and Secretary of Education Arne Duncan our thanks. They have set out a vision, and whether or not others agree with it, they have raised our collective awareness.

But that is not enough.

Renewal needs every parent's, every taxpayer's, and every educator's support. And, it needs *smart* support. Merely voting for someone who says they want great schools is different from backing someone who actually knows what to do. Hopefully this book has helped you see the difference.

That means parents and taxpayers have to start by going to the meeting where the school board begins consideration of whom they will hire as the next superintendent. That, however, is only the first step. You need to stay involved. A superintendent may be good, but she is going to be much better with strong public support. Public education is not like road maintenance. You don't just pay your taxes and then let someone else handle the details. Your job is ongoing, not subject to outsourcing, and not satisfied by a comment to your neighbor over the back fence about some craziness at the board meeting the other night.

Your effort is worth it. For your benefit, for your child's, and for your country's.

NOTES

1. *The Providence Journal*, "R.I.'s Charter Schools Ponder Their Purpose as They Face Dramatic Expansion," Nov. 15, 2010 (retrieved from www.projo.com/news/content/charter_school_changes_11-15-10_ATKRSBT_v118.37b12cc.html on Nov. 29, 2010).

2. *Los Angeles Times*, "An Unplanned Revolution in L.A.'s Public Schools," Jan. 10, 2010, A1.

3. *New Orleans Times-Picayune*, "New Orleans Charter Schools Will Outnumber Traditional Schools 2 to 1 Next Year," May 5, 2010 (retrieved from www.nola.com/education/index.ssf/2010/05/new_orleans_charter_schools_wi.html on May 7, 2010).

4. The Obama administration's support for "autonomous" schools is based on the experience of Clark County (Las Vegas, Nevada), which has created several "autonomous" schools that function much like charters although they remain loosely affiliated with the school district. *Fostering Innovation and Excellence* (Washington, DC: U.S. Department of Education, 2010), 10.

5. See, for example, *Education Week*, "Regular Public Schools Start to Mimic Charters," Nov. 8, 2010 (retrieved from www.edweek.org/ew/articles/2010/11/10/11charter.h30.html on Nov. 8, 2010); *Texas Tribune*, "Charter and Public Schools Align in the Valley," Dec. 3, 2010 (retrieved from www.texasribune,org/texas-education/public-education/charter-and-public-schools-align-in-the-valley on Dec. 4, 2010).

6. See, for example, *New York Times*, "Many Charter Schools, Varied Grades," May 2, 2010, 1; *Politics Daily*, "Charter Schools: An Experiment with Mixed Results," Jan. 21, 2010 (retrieved from www.politicsdaily.com/2011/01/23/charter-schools-an-experiment-with-mixed-results on Jan. 23, 2010).

7. *Newark Star-Ledger*, "N.J. Voters Reject School Budgets in Heated Elections," April 21, 2010 (retrieved from www.nj.com/news/index.ssf/2010/04/nj_voters_reject_school_budget.html on April 22, 2010).

8. Daniel A. Domenech, "The Attraction of Charters: Waived Rules," *The School Administrator* 67, no. 5 (May 2010): 41. So has Deborah Meier. Deborah Meier, *The Power of Their Ideas: Lessons for America from a Small School in Harlem* (Boston, MA: Beacon, 1995), 115.

9. Jeffery R. Henig, Katrina K. Bulkley, and Henry M. Levin, *Between Public and Private: Politics, Governance, and the New Portfolio Models for Urban School Reform* (Cambridge, MA: Harvard Education Press, 2010).

10. Michael Fullan, *Transformational Leadership* (San Francisco: Jossey-Bass, 2006), 96.

11. Meier, *The Power of Their Ideas*, 98–99.

12. Jim Manzi, "Keeping America's Edge," *National Affairs* 2 (Winter 2010) (retrieved from www.nationalaffairs.com/publications/detail/keeping-america's-edge on Dec. 29, 2009).

13. *Education Week*, "NYC Charter Schools Are Short ELLs," May 10, 2010 (retrieved from http://blogs.edweek.org/edweek/learning-the-language/2010/05/nyc_charter_schools_are_short.html on May 11, 2010).

14. *Los Angeles Times*, "Charter Schools' Racial Divide: Two Studies Find That the Campuses Skew toward Segregated Student Bodies," Feb. 5, 2010, AA1.

15. Jim Manzi, "Keeping America's Edge," *Economic Perspectives* 32, no. 3 (2008) (retrieved from www.nationalaffairs.com/publications/detail/keeping-america's-edge on Dec. 29, 2009).

16. *Education Week*, "NYC Charter Schools Are Short ELLs," May 10, 2010 (retrieved from http://blogs.edweek.org/edweek/learning-the-language/2010/05/nyc_charter_schools_are_short.html on May 11, 2010).

17. *Los Angeles Times*, "Charter Schools' Racial Divide: Two Studies Find That the Campuses Skew toward Segregated Student Bodies," Feb. 5, 2010, AA1.

18. Meier, *The Power of Their Ideas*, 76–78.

19. *Milwaukee Journal Sentinel*, "New Data Shows Similar Academic Results between Voucher and MPS Students," April 7, 201 (retrieved from www.jsonline.com/news/education/90169302.html on May 6, 2010).

20. A recent (2010) study undercut some of Androkopolous's complaints. The academic performance of Milwaukee's vouchers and the public school system turned out similarly. *Milwaukee Journal-Sentinel*, "New Data Shows Similar Academic Results between Vouchers and MPS Students."

21. See, for example, Cecilia Elena Rouse and Lisa Barrow, "School Vouchers and Student Achievement: Recent Evidence, Remaining Questions," *Annual Review of Economics* 1 (2009) (retrieved from www.annualreviews.org on May 18, 2010); Patrick J. Wolf, *The Comprehensive Longitudinal Evaluation of the Milwaukee Parental Choice Program: Summary of Third Year Reports* (Fayetteville, AR: University of Arkansas School Choice Demonstration Project, 2010), 10; Tampabay.com, "Study Finds Vouchers Don't Make Difference," June 29, 2009 (retrieved from www.tampabay.com/newsw/education/k12/article1014461.ece on July 1, 2009); Vivian Troen and Katherine C. Boles, *Who's Teaching Your Children?* (New Haven, CT: Yale University Press, 2003), 105.

Acknowledgments

This book could not have been written without the extraordinary cooperation of the many people who sat down and talked to me about their schools and ideas. My first interview was with Doug Otto, superintendent of the Plano, Texas, Independent School District. I showed up for an hour meeting and wound up staying for almost three. The same sort of gracious welcome happened over and over again, even as superintendents, principals, and teachers struggled to deal with all their normal responsibilities on crowded school days. This collective willingness to be helpful may be best epitomized by Arne Duncan, who was superintendent in Chicago when I interviewed him. He kept a weeks' old promise to speak with me—even though he had been named secretary of education just five hours earlier.

So, to all of those listed below, I say, from the bottom of my heart, thank you:

Arlene Ackerman

Andres Alonso

Emily Alpert

Gerald Anderson

William Andrekopoulos

Donnalyn Jacque Anton

Fred Bateman

Katherine Blasik

Peter Bowen

Larry Bowers

Valentina Brown

Anne Bryant

Leo Casey

Maria Cedeno

Sundai Chari

Sandra Cokeley

Carl Cohn

Stephanie King

Chris Kirchner

Becca Bray Knight

Doris Kurtz

Wilfredo Laboy

Michael Lach

Jody Leleck

Art Levine

Rasuli Lewis

Marcia Leyles

Karen Seashore Lewis

Steve Mancini

Bob Moore

Steve Nelson

Peggy O'Brien

Maria Ott

Doug Otto

Deborah Cunningham

Karen Cushing

Jack Dale

Delores Davis

Shawn Denight

Arne Duncan

Bill Demaree

Karren Dunkley

Richard Elmore

Joyce Epstein

Nicholas Fischer

Milagros Fornell

Ron Friedman

Lydia Glassie

Eric Gordon

Pamela Grossman

Martine Guerrier

Sylvia Gundy

Paul Hegre

Tom Hehir

David Helme

Kaya Henderson

Jeffery Henig

Margaret Heritage

Rick Hess

Billie Hicklin

William Hite

Terry Holliday

Terry Horowitz

Susan Moore Johnson

Brad Jupp

Joel Klein

Janice Klein-Young

Joel Packer

Elizabeth Parks

Tom Payzant

Marco Petruzzi

Brian Pick

Nancy Que

Michelle Rhee

Amy Rhyne

Craig Richards

Priscilla Ridgeway

Amanda Rivera

John Rogers

Mike Roos

Bernard Rostker

Teresa Scott

John Simmons

James Spence

Brett Springston

Chris Steinhauser

David Stuckwisch

Jon Supovitz

Gwendolyn Trice

Tom Trigg

Adam Urbanski

Paul Vallas

Jamie Virga

Adrian Walker

Jerry Weast

David Weiner

Sam Williams

Chris Wilson

Michael Zaldua

Irma Zardoya

Appendix I: The Blueprint for Action—an Outline of What We Need to Do

ACTION POINT 1: THE LEADERSHIP OF EVERY SCHOOL AND DISTRICT NEEDS TO BE ABLE TO BUILD AND DRIVE STUDENT ACHIEVEMENT.

District Governance—The Board or Mayor and the Superintendent

- The board or mayor resolves the big policy questions and does not micromanage.
- The superintendent manages, and speaks for, the district.
- The superintendent has a plan, with a time line and metrics to measure success, which is the way the board or mayor holds the superintendent to account.
- The new superintendent has various jobs as articulator of a vision, role model, creator of a team of senior managers, education leader, manager, and, most importantly, builder of trust in both the schools and the community that the vision for the schools is right.
- *But* if the board is not united on reform, skip it until they are.

Principals

- The district actively recruits teachers whom it believes will be good principals.
- The district provides recruits with continuous training that meets its needs for education leaders who believe in continuous improvement, understand instruction, are comfortable with data, and know how to collaborate with teachers and give them authority to make decisions.
- The district places significant authority over hiring, budget, and management in the hands of principals, subject to principals demonstrating their capability.
- Districts hold principals strictly accountable based on a series of measures including student achievement, parent satisfaction, dropout rate (in high school), and other measures.

- Districts reward principals for excellent performance, which may include some form of monetary bonus.

How We Are Going to Make That Happen

- If you are a parent or taxpayer, attend school board meetings or meet with the mayor (if not individually, then as part of a group that can demand meetings) and participate in the selection of a new superintendent.
- Insist the board or mayor not micromanage. The job of reining in an out-of-control board is not left solely to the superintendent.
- Ensure the new superintendent meets with lots of people to discuss any reform plans.
- Give the new superintendent a fair hearing. No one forms opinions too quickly (even if trusted people, like teachers, oppose the reforms).
- No participation in the blame game—of either the education or community variety.
- Focus on academic achievement, even if it means reallocating money from other activities.
- Above all, everyone is patient.
- Actively seek out capable administrators among the faculty or reach out to other organizations, like New Leaders for New Schools, for quality candidates.
- Provide and then protect an explicit budget item for administrator training. Provide ongoing training for new administrators.
- Understand the "loose-tight" concept while devolving authority down to capable principals—and act on it.
- Recognize outstanding performance by principals. There are clear standards and clear rewards, which might include some form of monetary bonus.
- Promote school councils or parent satisfaction surveys (or both), but the hiring and firing of principals remains in the hands of the superintendent.

ACTION POINT 2: SCHOOL FACULTIES ARE CAPABLE OF TEACHING EVERY CHILD IN THEIR CLASSES AND ARE WILLING AND ABLE TO COLLABORATE WITH EACH OTHER AND THE ADMINISTRATION ON INSTRUCTION AND THEIR OWN PROFESSIONAL DEVELOPMENT.

- District leadership promotes teachers' fundamental beliefs in excellence, improvement, candor, and collaboration and a shared common vision with the administration.

- Districts are the central focus of teacher training, both before they begin teaching and after they join the district.
- Districts are professional learning communities with an infrastructure of people and training programs that will support teacher learning throughout their careers.
- Districts operate alternative certification programs, either alone or in concert with other districts or nonprofit organizations or universities.
- For teachers educated in traditional colleges of education, districts recruit actively only from schools with a record of creating high-performing teachers.
- Districts provide extensive and supportive induction, including much longer programs in the summer before traditional teachers start teaching.
- Districts are organized so that teachers have time, opportunity, and incentive to collaborate among themselves on their own training and professional development, and administrators should collaborate with them, with everyone taking responsibility for student achievement and teacher quality. Districts have a Peer Assistance and Review program with their teachers.
- Districts have competent human resources departments that reach out to good colleges of education in a timely fashion, process applications efficiently, and organize interviews with school teams promptly so that hiring can take place early enough in the year to allow the district to hire high-quality candidates.
- Districts have a clear idea of what constitutes good teaching, apply that standard in evaluating the effectiveness of any teacher, including decisions about tenure (if it exists) and pay for performance.
- Districts abandon the single salary schedule. There is a pay structure that rewards those who take on extra duties, like mentors or master teachers, provides incentives for science, technology, engineering, and math and special education teachers (or whoever else may be in short supply) and makes attractive the staffing of hard-to-staff schools.
- Any pay for performance system should focus on collegial awards—at least until there is more data on the impact of such systems.
- Union contractual provisions on seniority and bumping end, and the principle that governs all hiring is that a principal and a school's faculty have the fundamental right to decide with whom they want to work.
- Tenure is eliminated, although reasonable alternative job protections are available.

- Underlying everything else, a district's teachers should understand that the district really does believe every child can learn and that there are no excuses for failure.

How We Are Going to Make That Happen

- Build a system in which the middle 80 percent of teachers can excel.
- Recognize money is the most expensive way to motivate people. It is not a silver bullet. What is key is getting the system right. That may take some more money, but only after being clear on the system should you decide on how to fund it.
- Insist that the district become focused on training, including being committed to the development of an effective professional learning community.
- Insist that the district operate an alternative certification program, or at least participate jointly in one.
- Ensure that the necessary money is available and is protected even when budgets are tight.
- Demand information regarding training, including the scope of summer training, the number of mentors and frequency with which they meet with new teachers, the frequency of teacher meetings as part of the professional learning community, the number of teachers who have been in an improvement program, and the results.
- Demand the data for each teacher with regard to the achievement of his or her students. Do not ask for just results on standardized tests. Also ask for information that will give some context, like tracking the number of special education students or English language learners in the class, the turnover of students during the year, and whether the teacher has had the assistance of aides or teaches in some special setting, like team teaching.
- Support revising or eliminating the single salary schedule, seniority, bumping, and tenure. Pay special attention to hard-to-staff schools.
- Require management to identify all schools with heavy staff turnover, excessive numbers of new teachers, and low student achievement. Require plans for how they will be turned around (whether or not the federal government requires action).
- Go out of your way to thank teachers.

ACTION POINT 3: THE SYSTEM OF INSTRUCTION KEEPS EVERY CHILD IN FOCUS.

- Education is no longer an exercise in mass production; it is now the application of a significant body of knowledge about instruction to each child, much like the other professions of law or medicine.
- Curriculum is rigorous. There are no "dummy's courses," even for those following a career technical path.
- Curriculum selection does not assume that there is one program or strategy that fits every child's needs.
- Districts accept as an institutional commitment that every child has a mentor, whether it is a parent, a teacher, or a member of the community.
- Informational technology and computers are not "add-ons," but integral to instruction, which means teachers are better trained in their use and appropriate computer hardware and software are available.
- Robust databases capture large amounts of data about student progress, and such data are readily available to teachers and administrators.
- Frequent mini-assessments are regularly used to determine not only whether students have mastered material but also what can be done to help those who need assistance.
- Interventions and enrichments are offered promptly.
- Instruction for special education students and English language learners is subject to semiannual reports that include data on degree of inclusion in mainstream classes, success on accountability tests, graduation rates, and any other metrics parents deem relevant to assess the effectiveness of the programs.
- School days and school years are lengthened for all students.
- Curriculum is redesigned to emphasize continuous learning from (pre-) kindergarten through high school graduation. Grades (e.g., fifth grade) are deemphasized and schools keep track of what each student has actually mastered.

How We Are Going to Make That Happen

- Build a consensus that, as part of a district's promise that every child can learn, every child is guaranteed the same education: children needing assistance promptly receive assistance, and those far ahead are offered enrichments. Budget accordingly, even when that means providing more funds to some schools— or some students—than others.
- Make sure teachers are trained to use computers as a resource for materials, as a means of instruction, and as effective assessment tools.

- Resist the notion that frequent mini-assessments are "too much" testing, but make sure that they are part of a process where teachers use the information to diagnose learning issues and then act on them.
- Support longer school days and longer school years.
- Remain open to school structures not centered on grades (e.g., fifth grade), but rather on students' actual mastery of material.

ACTION POINT 4: PARENTS ARE TREATED WELL AS PARTNERS, CUSTOMERS, AND OWNERS.

- Schools believe parents should be treated well as partners, customers, and owners.
- Schools reach into the community, visiting parents and other organizations rather than requiring contact by parents coming to school sites.
- Schools have a firm idea of how parents need to collaborate with them on the education of their children and communicate that to parents, whether through a "contract" or some other method.
- Schools use websites and e-mails to communicate regularly with parents about homework, events at school, or individual student issues.
- Parents rate school performance, and such ratings, if not already required by law, are published by the district.
- Schools provide disclosure documents to the community that broadly review school performance.
- Districts provide customer service training for employees.
- Districts provide easily available points of contact for parents, such as a hotline.
- District boards focus on major issues rather than minutiae.
- District websites provide adequate explanation of what will happen at upcoming meetings.

How We Are Going to Make That Happen

- Encourage parents to take an active role in their schools and districts.
- Encourage active parents to recruit other parents to become involved. The district and parents create opportunities for teachers and administrators to come to neighborhoods to talk about education.
- Create blogs and other social networks to discuss school issues.
- Insist on respectful treatment and use instances of poor customer service as teachable moments to drive improvement.

- Demand transparency: school report cards and district websites that meaningfully discuss the issues.
- Develop a full agenda of issues and organize to get them adopted by the district. Reformers run for the school board to carry out their platform.

ACTION POINT 5: CREATE A SCHOOL DISTRICT THAT BELIEVES IN CONTINUOUS IMPROVEMENT AND TOTAL QUALITY MANAGEMENT.

- District leadership is trained in some form of continuous improvement.
- Benchmarks cover subjects beyond student achievement, including anything that has material impact on district costs or operations.
- Data is developed that addresses the benchmarks and is regularly analyzed by district management.
- The superintendent and senior staff regularly engage in cycles of "Plan, Do, Study, Act" in order to improve district operations.
- Senior management in charge of nonacademic functions has experience in the relevant area, so that those with construction backgrounds handle buildings, IT specialists are in charge of computers, etc. Former teachers are not routinely promoted to such positions unless they have demonstrated expertise.
- Non-core functions are considered for outsourcing. The goal is to relieve the district from managing aspects of its operation it is not likely to run well. Outsourcing may save money, but current staff should be allowed to bid to provide services.
- Districts are serious about ethical conduct, which they may choose to demonstrate by creating a code of conduct to which all employees must adhere.

How We Are Going to Make That Happen

- Ask for a management review conducted by an outside organization that will analyze the cost and effectiveness of district operations and suggest benchmarks appropriate for continuous improvement.
- Push the district to publish the results of the data collections and the subsequent discussions of how the district intends to improve results.
- Establish a group of community leaders to work with non-core staff and district leaders to ensure that any consideration of outsourcing provides them a fair opportunity for continuing employment.

- Demand that districts engage in a public process to develop a code of ethics (if one does not exist) and ensure there is a designated senior administrator or lawyer who is responsible for handling allegations of breaches of the code.

ACTION POINT 6: DISTRICTS NEED TO BE REORGANIZED INTO A SYSTEM OF SCHOOLS.

The Near Future

- States review categorical programs, eliminating as many restrictions as possible. States also commit to limit categorical funding to no more than 5 percent of state aid.
- States eliminate laws that inhibit innovation or impose counterproductive rules, like barring the use of student data in teacher evaluations.
- States create boards of experts like the Health Care Financing Agency's advisory board to provide guidance on what constitutes adequate funding for public education in the state.
- States adopt a plan to stabilize school funding. The federal government provides part of the assurance of consistent funding in times of economic downturn.
- The states and federal government recognize the importance of keeping local schools vibrant by allowing them to make as many decisions as possible, consistent with their demonstration of taking those responsibilities seriously.
- States and the federal government focus training money on school districts rather than schools of education, and states actively drive improvement in colleges of education.
- The federal government continues to provide financial support to low-income schools.
- The federal government supports research into innovations that will support innovative, flexible schools and systems of schools.

The Long Term

- States pass legislation that requires districts to establish plans to transition all traditional schools to autonomous entities with powers and obligations like charters.
- States pass enabling legislation authorizing districts to regulate school operations and to provide certain services, such as transportation or building maintenance, to schools.
- States review the current boundaries of school districts and realign them consistent with efficient discharge of their new duties.

- States revise funding formulas so that money follows individual children rather than being raised or spent according to district boundaries.

How We Are Going to Make That Happen

- Build a broad coalition including administrators, educators, and parents/taxpayers to lobby state legislatures and Congress.
- Write blogs and letters to the editor, and actively recruit people. This is a job that cannot be outsourced.
- Be patient and be smart. Resist the notion that silver bullets or demons are a reasonable substitute for system reform, no matter how long it takes.

Appendix II: A Proposed School "Disclosure Document"

Information Sought	*Answer*	*Reason—How to Evaluate—Related Chapter*
	Administrators	
The number of administrators	Total ___ Principal(s) ___ Assistant principal(s) ___ Others ___ (Describe duties of assistant principals and others) _____ _____	The administrative staff, especially the principal, has to be an education leader, manager, and primary community connection. The right number of people depends on the school size and whether functions like building maintenance are handled elsewhere. Chapter 5.
The experience of the administrators	Principal: Number of years has been a principal: ___ Assistant principals: Number of years each has been an assistant ___ Others: ___	Length of service needs to be compared with school performance. If administrators are new, they need to be given at least two years to achieve significant school improvement. If they have been around for several years of stagnating results, it is time for a change. Chapter 5.
Does the district have a program to recruit new administrators from its teacher ranks? If so, does it pay all or part of a new administrator's training?		Many teachers will not make good administrators. Successful districts find quality candidates and encourage them to train to become administrators. Chapter 5.
Does the district have a principal's academy? If so, what percentage of its needs does it expect to satisfy from the academy?		Many districts are now training their own principals. The results are often superior to traditional programs. Chapter 5.
If the training program has been in existence more than five years, how many of its graduates are currently employed as district administrators?		Some of the training programs have had mixed success. If they are not delivering the kind of administrators a district needs, they should be overhauled or terminated. Chapter 16.

Does the district have a formal mentoring program for administrators? If so, how many hours per year do mentors work with their new administrators?		Ron Friedman in Great Neck and other superintendents support new administrators during their first years on the job. In their opinion, it is a vital part of training. Chapter 5.
Do principals have tenure?		Tenure for principals makes holding them accountable for school performance difficult. Chapter 5.
	The Faculty	
The number of faculty teaching full-time, part-time, and as substitutes. The number of days actually taught by the faculty. The percentage of Monday and Friday classes taught by substitutes.	Total ⸏⸏⸏⸏ Full-time ⸏⸏ Part-time ⸏⸏ Permanent substitutes ⸏⸏ Ad hoc substitutes ⸏⸏ The number of days (by grade or subject) taught by a substitute ⸏⸏ The percentage of substitutes on: Monday ⸏⸏ Friday ⸏⸏	Too many substitutes reflect a faculty that is not likely well coordinated and collaborating, and substitutes often are not effective. Chapter 7, 16.
The number of faculty certified (or not certified) to teach the subjects they are teaching or who have bachelors' or masters' degrees in those subjects.	Total ⸏⸏ By subject: English⸏⸏ Math ⸏⸏ Science ⸏⸏ Social science ⸏⸏ Foreign language ⸏⸏	Certification may not demonstrate that teachers are capable of teaching a subject well, but the lack of certification is a good place to begin a discussion with school administration about the capability of the faculty. Chapter 12.
The experience of the faculty (number and percentage of total faculty).	Less than two years teaching ⸏⸏ Two to five years ⸏⸏ Five to ten years ⸏⸏ Over ten years ⸏⸏	A large number of new teachers suggest the school is hard to staff. New teachers need experienced colleagues to work with in order to perfect their abilities. Chapter 16.
The length of time the faculty has taught at the school (in percentages of the entire school faculty).	Less than two years ⸏⸏ Two to five years ⸏⸏ Five to ten years ⸏⸏ Over ten years ⸏⸏	High turnover is generally a bad sign, except in schools that are in the process of reconstitution or transformation. Chapter 16.

The frequency that teachers with less than two years of experience meet with mentors or master teachers.	At least: Once a week ___ Biweekly ___ Once a month ___ Less frequently ___	New teachers generally do better when meeting with mentors at least once a week. Chapter 8.
The promptness of hiring new teachers.	100% hired at least eight weeks before start of new year ___ 75% hired at least eight weeks before start of new year ___ 25% hired at least eight weeks before start of new year ___ 0% hired at least eight weeks before start of new year ___ 100% hired before start of new year ___ 75% hired before start of new year ___ Date last permanent teacher hired ___	Hiring teachers early is important for two reasons: (1) having a reasonable opportunity to get good candidates; (2) having enough time to provide meaningful instruction. Chapter 8.
Number of teachers who have taught at more than two schools in the last five years.		A telltale sign of the "dance of the lemons." Chapter 16.
Numbers and percentage of teachers granted/denied tenure in the last three years.		Granting tenure to all teachers suggests a failure to do a reasonable evaluation of skills. Chapters 12–13.
Total size of student body and student-teacher ratio.	Size ___ Ratio ___	Having a lower student-teacher ratio at least gives the school a better chance to focus on the individual needs of every child, although such a ratio alone does not guarantee improvement. Chapters 2, 19–20.
Number and description of mentors, master teachers, and facilitators working part-time or full-time at the school.		Schools should be professional learning communities, and professional learning communities require mentors, master teachers, etc. Chapters 8–14.
Total number of education support staff by job description.	Counselors ___ Nurses ___ Librarians ___ Special needs aides ___ Paraprofessionals (teacher aides) ___	Teachers cannot carry all the burdens of a school, especially dealing with the physical and emotional problems students face. Chapters 7, 16.

Description of student information contained on a database that is available to teachers or administrators.		A robust database can help keep track of students, manage special education plans, and facilitate formative assessments. Chapter 19.
Amount of meeting time provided to teachers each week (by grade or subject).		Teacher collaboration is key for professional development and tailoring instruction for students. Most schools provide no more than an hour weekly; three to four hours per week is desirable. Chapters 9, 20.
	Students	
Number of hours of school per day; number of days in the school year.		In order to provide individualized interventions and enrichments, the day needs to be longer than six hours. Many good foreign systems are in session over 200 days a year. Chapter 20.
Number of students taking advanced placement or International Baccalaureate classes; breakdown by race.		The existence of high school AP or IB courses suggests a focus on college entrance. Chapter 18.
Special programs (such as language immersion, AP, IB, "health academy") offered at the school.		If a district is committed to the proposition that every child can learn, then there has to be reasonable opportunity for students to excel. Chapter 18.
Number and percentage of students who scored at least a 3 on the AP test or passed the IB exam each of the last two years (broken down by race).		Same.
Number and percentage of career technical students taking college-track courses.		Relegating career-track students to "general education" courses consigns them to a second-rate high school education. Chapter 18.
Community programs provided on campus (tutoring, recreation, etc.).		Community-based programs for instruction and recreation are helpful; providing some or all of them on campus is a way to coordinate better with school instruction. Chapters 19–20.

Description of formative assessments (frequency, scope). An answer such as "subject to teacher's discretion" is not acceptable.		Regular formative assessments (weekly or biweekly) are valuable ways to ensure prompt provision of help or enrichments. Chapter 20.
Description of how the school helps struggling or gifted and talented students.		The prompt provision of interventions and enrichments help keep students on track. Chapter 20.
Number of students receiving interventions by grade in each of the last eight weeks.		Same.
Description of the strategy to assist special needs students. Include the number of special education teachers who regularly teach in the school by grade and subject.		Special education programs are often poorly administered. If nothing else, the proper management of such programs reduces the risk districts will have to spend more money sending students it cannot educate well to private schools. Chapter 17.
Percentage of time special needs students spend in "mainstream" classes.		The goal of IDEA is to mainstream special education students. Chapter 17.
Percentage of special needs students who graduate high school in four years.		Same.
Percentage of special needs students who prevail in administrative proceedings or litigation.		Special needs students' parents can bring administrative and court cases if not satisfied with the level of service. It is a useful measure of how well districts are doing satisfying these students' needs. Chapter 17.
Number of students in English language learner programs and average amount of time ELL students remain in such programs before being fully integrated into mainstream classes.		Achievement data needs to confirm that the mainstreaming is not premature. Chapters 17, 20.

Does the school have "tracked" classes, or are all grades and subjects "de-tracked"?	Yes ___ No ___ If not, describe the criteria by which students are separated into different classes and the differences in the curriculum used in the different classes: _____ _____	Tracking can be a form of invidious discrimination. De-tracking, however, poses real management challenges. The information is a starting point for a discussion about whether children are being unfairly sorted or just getting lost. Chapter 19.
Number of student suspensions in the prior year for violent or abusive behavior.		One indicator of whether the school is a safe environment. Chapter 16.
Number of on-campus incidents reported to police authorities in the prior year.		Same as above.
Average class size by grade or subject.		Small classes are helpful, especially in K–3, low-income schools, but the larger question is significant in times of budget shortfalls to see if the district's strategy for budget balancing focuses on changing class sizes. Chapters 19–20.
Number of computers available for use by students per class-room or computer lab (including smart phones or handheld devices).		Computerized instruction is now key to individualizing instruction, recovery, and various forms of group learning. It also is fundamental for new forms of assessment. Chapters 18–20.
Policy regarding posting of classroom information on the Internet.		An important information tool for students and parents. Chapter 22.
Policy regarding posting school information on the Internet.		An important information tool for parents. When decisions are to be made, information should be made available early enough to allow for review, and if there are various positions, all sides of a discussion should be included, not just the district's or school's own position. Chapter 22.

Existence of student advisories or other peer- or student-teacher group mentoring.	Yes ___ No ___ If so, describe: _____	Student advisories, etc., are a reflection of an institutional commitment to ensuring good student attitudes about themselves and about learning. Chapter 21.
	Parents	
Frequency of parent-teacher organization or local school council meetings (including contact information).		Meetings should be at least monthly to allow for meaningful participation. Chapter 22.
Frequency of scheduled parent-teacher conferences.		If parents are going to be real partners, there has to be frequent interaction (at least twice a year) with teachers. Chapter 22.
Existence of parent classes either at school or in the district (and description of the classes).		In order to involve many parents in their children's education, there have to be classes on school, instruction, and collaboration with schools. Chapters 21–22.
Annual expenditures for parent outreach programs (broken down by type of outreach). Mandated Title I funds should be separated from other funds used.		Most districts spend little on parent outreach. If they are a Title I district, they are mandated to spend a small amount; it should be broken out from the total number to see how much additional money is used for the purpose. Chapter 21.
Total number of parents who attend any of the following in one year: • **Parent academy** • **Parent-teacher night** • **Parent volunteer activity** • **Parent-principal or parent-superintendent meeting**		Parents often go to parent-teacher nights, but the numbers who volunteer, meet with administrators, or attend an academy is lower. Where districts are successful in involving parents in these activities, they should be applauded and, if possible, the programs expanded. Chapter 21.
The number of non-parent volunteers who participate in a school activity and the frequency or total number of hours of		Schools often say that "volunteers" in the community are supporting their work. In some communities, like Long Beach, it is true, but in many, the frequency and

their efforts.		extensiveness of the efforts are minimal. Knowing the size of the effort should help focus on what might be done to increase it, if necessary. Chapter 21.
	Accountability	
For high schools: the number and percentage of graduating seniors entering college (broken down by the number going to four-year schools and the number going to two-year schools and by race and gender).		President Obama has said all students, upon graduation, should be college or career ready. This information provides a way to evaluate that criterion. Chapter 22.
For high schools: the percentage of graduating seniors who were required to do remedial work in two-year and four-year college.		Forcing high schools to collect information about how their students did after graduation will allow for a discussion of the actual quality of the education the school provided. Chapter 22.
For high schools: percentage of special needs students who entered in ninth grade and graduated in four years.		Prompt graduation or special education students is a measure of how effective the school's special education programs have been. Many students will not make it in four years, but having the number improve year to year is a sign of an improved program. Chapters 17, 22.
For high schools: the number of students who dropped out during the year and the ninth through eleventh graders who failed to return to school for the next year.	Dropouts during the year ___ Ninth graders who did not return for tenth grade ___ Tenth-graders who did not return of eleventh grade ___ Eleventh graders who did not return for twelfth grade ___	While I have advocated every school should have an institutionalized commitment to ensuring student self-confidence and a belief in learning, any significant number of dropouts (over 10%) should make the case irrefutable. Chapter 21.
Required NCLB disclosures about student performance.		Required by statute. Useful, if limited, information about school performance. Chapter 22.
Comparison of school's performance on standardized tests (such as those required to comply		A good way to test "no excuses." Chapter 22.

with NCLB) with comparable schools in the district or state.		
Description of any corrective action taken in the past three years as a con-sequence of failure to make adequate yearly progress (or other measure).		Schools and districts should engage parents and taxpayers fully in their improvement efforts. Chapter 22.
Other required state disclosures about performance or other subjects.		Useful to add to the checklist to remind administrators about the full extent of what-ever state or federal law requires. Chapter 22.

Index

accountability, xiv, 95, 243, 251, 285; state governments and, 273

Ackerman, Arlene, 167, 168

administrators: teachers as, 53, 256; trust among, 250–251. *See also* principals; superintendents

admissions: lottery, 286, 287, 289; open enrollment, 168, 199, 286

advanced placement (AP), 196, 199, 248

Advancement via Individual Determination (AVID), 226

Alabama, 108

Aldine, 50, 99, 106, 113, 146, 161, 214, 253, 256

Alliance for Excellent Education, 77

alternative certification programs, 111–115

Alvarado, Anthony, 87

American Civil Liberties Union, 133

American Federation of Teachers (AFT), 11, 12, 135

Anderson, Gerald, 24, 37, 44, 50, 96, 160, 168, 213, 257, 277

Andrekopoulos, William, 287

Arizona, 136, 137

Arkansas, 108

artisanal education, xiii, 5, 87, 95, 212

Atlanta, 198

authority and responsibility, funding and, 18, 269

AVID (Advancement via Individual Determination), 226

Baldrige, Malcolm, 6, 211

Baldrige Award, 6, 276

Baltimore, 150, 256; St. Ignatius Loyola Academy, 143, 213, 228–229, 249, 256, 257

Baltimore Sun, 276

Bateman, Fred, 10–11, 262

Beaumont, 98

beliefs of high-performing schools, 245, 247–252; academic preparation is the focus and has priority over all others, 249–250; administrators and teachers trust each other, 250–251; continuous, rigorous improvement based on responses to data is fundamental to all aspects of a district's operation, 251–252; every child can—and will—learn, 247–248; every child will graduate, and every child will either go to college or be well prepared for a career, 248; the district will make a distinct and unique contribution to the community, to education, or both, 248–249

Bersin, Alan, 87, 255

Between Public and Private: Politics, Governance, and the New Portfolio Models for Urban School Reform (Bulkley, Henig, and Levin), 286

Big Picture Learning Company, 202

Bill and Melinda Gates Foundation, 123, 190, 203, 211

blame game, 26–27, 29, 30, 31

block time, 198, 257

blogs, 241

Bloomberg, Michael, 124

Blue Valley, 24, 54, 78, 99, 143, 144, 145, 189, 191, 210, 212, 214, 231, 254, 255, 257

Boston, 29, 37, 56, 78, 112, 149, 151, 164, 167, 249

Boston Globe, 37

Bowen, Pete, 229

Bowers, Larry, 266

Brazosport, 24, 26, 50, 214, 250; Anderson in, 24, 37, 44, 50, 96, 160,

168, 213, 257; Williams in, 44, 143
Brizard, Jan-Claude, 160
Broad Center for the Management of
  School Systems, 53
Broad Foundation, 57, 213
Broad Prize, x, 3, 57, 98, 146, 223, 253,
  261
Broad Residency Program, 57
Broad Superintendents' Academy, 57,
  62
Brooklyn, 50
Broward County, 189, 241
Brownsville, 3, 76, 99, 146, 161, 204,
  222–223
Brown v. Board of Education, 179, 180
Building Engaged Schools (Gordon), 191
bumping, 11, 47–48, 165
Bush administration, 107, 275, 276

California, 112, 166, 192, 242; funding
  in, 15, 16, 17, 18, 272, 289;
  Proposition 13 in, 272; Servite High
  School, 229–230, 231
California State University, 56, 84, 107
Canada, Geoffrey, 232, 233
career technical education, 197,
  201–202
Carnegie Foundation, 107
Carver, John, 38
Casey, Leo, 11
Catholic schools, 200, 226, 249; St.
  Ignatius Loyola Academy, 143, 213,
  228–229, 249, 256, 257; Servite High
  School, 229–230, 231
Center for American Progress, 272
Central Park East School, 181
Charlotte, 167
charter schools, 6, 47, 200, 226, 242, 249,
  274, 284–285, 286–287; Green Dot,
  54, 84, 166, 203, 225, 247, 249, 259,
  286; Knowledge Is Power Program
  (KIPP), 56, 84, 200, 213, 230–232,
  249, 256, 257, 259, 286; obligations
  of, 287
Chicago, 24, 36, 47, 49, 51, 52, 77, 87, 99,
  112, 136, 137, 160, 169, 255; Duncan
  in, 31, 36, 111; Rivera in, 86, 88, 122
church-related schools, 287–288. *See
  also* Catholic schools

City Slickers, 201
civil rights, 179, 197
Civil Rights Act of 1964, 159
Clark County, 285
class size, 202–204
Cleveland, 165
Clinton administration, 107
Coalition for Essential Schools, 181
Cohn, Carl, 32, 57, 87, 98, 169, 251
Cokeley, Sandy, 76, 88
Coleman, James S., 159, 247
collaboration, 10, 32, 60; district-
  university, 56, 107–108; enhancing,
  254; teachers and, 10, 46, 70, 71, 75,
  87, 88, 89, 96, 98, 99, 143, 147, 149,
  151, 191, 254
collective bargaining, 11, 12, 47, 120
Collins, Jim, 36, 273
Colorado, 136, 137
combat pay, 167, 168–169
Committee of Ten on Secondary School
  Studies, 177–178
community, 222, 223, 225–226, 227;
  school districts' contribution to,
  248–249; service to, 200;
  superintendents and, 29
computers. *See* Internet and computers
ConnectEd, 200, 202
Connecticut, 58, 86
consensus building, 33–34
Constitution, 15; First Amendment to,
  135, 287–288
continuous improvement, 5, 34, 35, 46,
  70–71, 75, 78, 96, 101, 234, 249,
  251–252, 258
Council of Chief State School Officers,
  33, 241
counselors, 226
Crew, Rudy, 214, 261
Crist, Charlie, 136
curriculum, 87–88, 175, 177–178,
  187–193, 195, 225, 247, 257; building
  of, 187–188; career technical
  education in, 197, 201–202; Internet
  and, 189–191, 192, 199, 203;
  scaffolding, pacing, and mapping
  in, 188, 253; taking seriously,
  253–254; textbooks in, 178, 183, 188,
  189, 191, 192

customers, 4, 4–5, 175

Dale, Jack, 46, 49, 88, 223, 249
Danielson, Charlotte, 88, 122–123, 136, 138, 255
Darling-Hammond, Linda, 97, 99, 113
data-driven decision making, 5, 46, 97, 251–252, 258
data platforms, 256
Deming, W. Edwards, 5
Denight, Shawn, 262
Denver, 147
Dewey, John, 177–178, 181
discrimination, 135
Doane College, 107
Domenech, Dan, 286
dropouts, 226, 248
DuFour, Rebecca, 96
DuFour, Richard, 96
Duncan, Arne, 31, 36, 43, 106, 107, 111, 122, 127, 213, 223, 290
Dunkeley, Karren, 224

Eaker, Robert, 96
education: artisanal, xiii, 5, 87, 95, 212; as service, 4–5; vocational, 197, 201–202. *See also* individualized education; learning disabilities and special education; mass-production eduction
Education Week, 141
Elementary and Secondary Education Act (ESEA), 214, 223, 232, 275, 290. *See also* No Child Left Behind
Eliot, Charles W., 177
enrichments and interventions, 198, 257–258
Epstein, Joyce, 224
Equality of Education Opportunity, 159
Escalante, Jaime, 221, 225
ethics, 266–267

failure, cycle of, 26–27, 29, 30, 31
Fairfax County, 46, 49, 54, 56, 88, 200, 204, 223, 249
Fall River, 25, 46, 51, 52, 214, 248, 258, 266
federal government, 18–19, 243, 269, 275–278; Bush administration, 107, 275, 276; funding and, 277–278; Individuals with Disabilities Education Act (IDEA), 17, 77, 179–180, 181, 277; Race to the Top, 100, 122, 123, 145, 168, 213, 273, 276. *See also* Elementary and Secondary Education Act; No Child Left Behind; Obama administration
Federal Teacher Incentive Fund, 146
Feinberg, Mike, 230–231
Fenty, Adrian, 126
First Amendment rights, 135, 287–288
Fischer, Nick, 25, 46, 51, 70, 147, 214, 248, 258
Florida, 54, 136, 192; Miami-Dade County, 38, 88, 200, 214, 224, 251, 257, 258, 261–263, 267; Virtual Academy, 189, 258
free speech, 135
Friedman, Ron, 58
funding, 15–18, 285, 288–289; authority and responsibility and, 18, 269; categorical, 17–18; federal government and, 277–278; principals' control over, 47; state governments and, 271–273; student motivation and, 233, 234; taxes in, 15, 16, 17, 18, 165, 272, 285, 289, 291
The Future of Management (Hamel), 4

Gardner, Howard, 180, 181, 191, 200
Gates, Bill, 204
Gates Foundation, 123, 190, 203, 211
Georgia, 107, 112; funding in, 15
gifted students, 199, 200
Gladwell, Malcolm, 182–183
Glassie, Lydia, 230, 231, 232
Gordon, Eric, 165
Gordon, Gary, 191
Gorman, Peter, 167
government: outsourcing and, 266. *See also* federal government; state governments
grade system, 178, 183, 195–196
graduate schools, 47, 53, 55, 56; improving, 58–61
Gray, Vincent, 126
Great Neck, 58, 84, 249

Green Dot, 54, 84, 166, 203, 225, 247, 249, 259, 286
Guerrier, Martine, 223
Gundy, Sylvia, 229

Haertel, Edward, 125
Hamel, Gary, 3
Hanushek, Eric, 151
hard-to-staff schools, 17, 70, 74, 114, 126, 133, 137, 146, 149, 150, 163–170; recommendations for, 170; recruiting teachers for, 163–165, 166; salaries and, 167–169
Harlem Children's Zone, 213, 232–233, 249
Harvard University, 60, 87, 106
Hawaii, 283
headspace: of students, 6, 183, 196, 221–222; of teachers, 6, 78, 141, 144
Hegre, Paul, 98, 125
Hehir, Tom, 287
Helme, David, 53
Henderson, Kaya, 86–87, 99, 147, 166–167
Henig, Jeff, 286
Heritage, Margaret, 210
Hess, Rick, 107
Hicklin, Billie, 210
high school dropouts, 226, 248
Hite, William, 147
Holliday, Terry, 25, 56, 57, 59, 211, 212, 248, 250
Horace's Compromise (Sizer), 178–179
Houston, 148
Houston Chronicle, 97
human relations, 9–13
human resources departments, 164

I LEAD Academy, 56
IMPACT, 126
individualized education, 180–181, 183, 187, 191, 209, 213; cost of, 214–215; enrichments and interventions, 198, 257–258
Individuals with Disabilities Education Act (IDEA), 17, 77, 179–180, 181, 277
Institute for the Study of Knowledge Management in Education, 181
intelligences, multiple, 180, 191

International Baccalaureate (IB) classes, 199, 248
Internet and computers: in assessments, 181, 209, 210–211; data platforms, 256; in intervention strategies, 258; parents and, 241; school and district websites, 241; superintendents' use of, 30; in teaching, 189–191, 192, 199, 203
Interstate School Leaders Licensure Consortium: Standards for School Leaders, 33
interventions and enrichments, 198, 257–258
Iredell County, 25, 26, 29, 56, 211–212, 248, 250, 254, 257

Jackson, Santiago, 201
Johnson, Susan, 86, 88, 113
Jupp, Brad, 145, 147

Kansas City, 196
King, Stephanie, 88, 99, 262
Kirchner, Christine, 262
Klein, Joel, 31, 33, 36, 46, 124, 134, 135, 187, 222, 251, 265, 266
Klein-Young, Janis, 200
Knight, Becca, 53
Kurtz, Doris, 28, 35, 43, 47, 56, 76, 177, 199

Laboy, Wilfredo, 27, 29, 54, 227–228
Lach, Michael, 77
Langan, Christopher, 182
Las Vegas, 285, 290
Lawrence, 27, 227–228, 233, 243, 266
leaders, 4, 21. *See also* principals; superintendents
leadership: levels of, 36–37; teams, 27
learning communities, professional, 95–101, 134, 145–146, 147, 212, 254, 256
learning disabilities and special education, 126, 179, 287; charters and, 287; Individuals with Disabilities Education Act (IDEA) and, 17, 77, 179–180, 181, 277; teachers for, 74, 78, 149, 150
Learning Point Associates, 142

Leleck, Jody, 88, 122, 137
Levin, Dave, 230–231
Levine, Arthur, 53, 55, 60, 106
Lewis, Rasuli, 232, 233
Leyles, Marsha, 191
Linwood Middle School, 212
Littky, Dennis, 202
Locke High School, 166, 203, 225, 249, 259
Long Beach, 33, 48, 51, 98, 99, 108, 148, 161, 188, 223, 226; California State University and, 56, 84, 107; Cohn in, 32, 57, 87, 98, 169, 251; funding and budgets in, 47, 223, 271; open enrollment in, 168, 199, 286; Steinhauser in, 28, 48, 188, 222, 251; volunteers in, 214, 222
loose coupling, 10, 98
Los Angeles, 24, 26, 33, 55, 60, 85, 127, 133, 169, 250–251; charters in, 285, 287; funding in, 271; Green Dot schools in, 54, 84, 166, 203, 225, 247, 249, 259, 286; non-core functions and, 265; Romer in, ix, 31, 36, 38, 55; school-parent communication in, 239; teacher salaries in, 150; teachers removed in, 135; teachers replaced in, 165; trust and ethics in, 266, 267; vocational education in, 201
Los Angeles Times, 18, 127, 128, 135, 145
lottery admissions, 286, 287, 289
Louis, Karen Seashore, 223
Louisiana, 56, 57, 59, 107, 108; Recovery School District, 36, 87, 146, 200, 213, 224, 257, 265, 285
Lynchburg, Virginia, 10–11

MacArthur South High, 200
magnet schools, 199
managed instruction, 253
management theory, 3–6, 290; data-driven decision making, 5, 46, 97, 251–252, 258; and industrial model of teaching, 9–13; total quality management, 5, 24, 28, 34, 35. *See also* continuous improvement
Mancini, Steve, 231
Marine Corps, 85, 143
Maryland, 56, 57. *See also* Baltimore

Massachusetts, 58; Fall River, 25, 46, 51, 52, 214, 248, 266; Lawrence, 27, 227–228, 233, 243, 266
mass-production education, xiii, xiv, 4, 5, 21, 43, 46, 53, 54, 87, 95, 97, 149, 177–178, 179, 180, 192, 195; and industrial vs. professional role for teachers, 9–13, 30, 97, 188; teacher evaluation and, 119–120, 122
math, 198, 257, 273
mayors, 23, 38
McCourt, Frank, 182, 182–183, 197
McKinsey & Company, 37, 73, 141
media, 30–31
Meier, Deborah, 83, 181
Memphis, 168
mentors: for new teachers, 86–87, 89, 97, 99, 149, 151, 255; for students, 183, 221, 225–226, 227, 231, 234
Merseth, Katherine, 113
MetLife Survey, 142, 145, 160
Miami-Dade County, 38, 88, 200, 214, 224, 251, 257, 258, 261–263, 267
Michigan, 15
Milken Family Foundation, 98, 100, 146
Milwaukee, 287
Minneapolis, 98
Minnesota, 98
Mississippi, 61
Missouri, 15, 16
Montgomery County, 47, 49, 61, 88, 122, 137, 250, 251, 266; ethics and, 266; Weast in, 34, 52, 168, 196, 199, 248, 253, 276
Moore, Bob, 144
Mulgrew, Michael, 136
"multiple pathways" strategy, 202

National Association of Secondary School Principals, 181
National Board for Professional Teaching Standards (NBPTS), 12, 120, 123
National Bureau of Economic Research, 87
National Center for Education Statistics (NCES), 48, 49, 75, 86, 221
National Center on Time and Learning, 213

National Commission on Teaching and America's Future, 100
National Council for Accreditation of Teacher Education (NCATE), 107
National Council on State Legislatures, 160
National Education Association (NEA), 11, 12, 136, 169, 177
National Education Policy Center, 127
National Education Technology Plan, 190
National Staff Development Council, 97
NCLB. *See* No Child Left Behind
New Administrator Program, 56
New Britain, 28, 29, 35, 47, 56, 76, 199
New Haven, 150
New Jersey, 54, 112, 212, 289
New Leaders for New Schools (NLNS), 57, 58, 61, 62
New London, 147
New Orleans, 289; ethics and, 266; outsourcing in, 265; Recovery School District, 36, 87, 146, 200, 213, 224, 257, 265, 285
New York, 24, 26, 35, 47, 51, 83, 165, 204, 251, 255, 257, 258; bonus awards in, 148; Central Park East School, 181; charters in, 287; ethics and, 266; funding in, 289; Harlem Children's Zone, 213, 232–233, 249; Klein in, 31, 33, 36, 46, 124, 135, 187, 222, 251, 265, 266; McCourt in, 182, 182–183, 197; outsourcing in, 48, 265, 266; parent outreach in, 223, 239, 241; principals and administrator training in, 47, 49, 50, 54, 56, 57, 58; school districts in, 283; School of One program, 189; Stuyvesant High School, 182, 200; teacher training in, 106, 112; tenure in, 135–136; test data in, 124
New York Times, 212
No Child Left Behind (NCLB), 119, 123–125, 146, 160, 167, 180, 187, 191, 197, 217, 240, 258, 273, 275–277; Title I of, 215, 217, 223, 224, 276, 277–278; Title II of, 100, 107
North Brunswick, 212

North Carolina, 56, 61, 86, 141, 146, 169; Charlotte, 167; Iredell County, 25, 26, 29, 56, 211–212, 248, 250, 254, 257; Watauga County, 54, 210, 249, 256

Obama, Barack, 214, 232, 290
Obama administration, 16, 60, 100, 107, 144, 145, 168, 190, 202, 214, 233, 273, 275, 276, 290
O'Brien, Peggy, 225, 239
Ohio, 58, 107
Oklahoma, 136, 137
Open Court, 188
open enrollment, 168, 200, 286
Oppenheimer, Robert, 182
Orr, Margaret Terry, 60
Otto, Doug, 32, 37, 99, 224, 254
Ouchi, William, 47
Outliers (Gladwell), 182
outsourcing, 48, 265–266

Packer, Joel, 169
Palo Alto, 283
parents, 4, 175, 239–244; as consumers, 239–242, 243; Internet and, 241; involvement of, 221–222, 222–225, 226–233, 234, 239, 285; as owners, 242–243; participation in school politics, 18, 242–243, 284, 285; recommendations for, 243–244; student motivation and, 222–225, 226–233
Parks, Elizabeth, 78
Pathways, 56
pay for performance, xiv, 67, 119, 120, 137, 141, 142, 146–148, 149, 159, 160
Payzant, Tom, 29, 37, 47, 54, 78, 164, 249
Pearl River, 24, 26, 49, 50, 76, 89, 189, 249, 257, 285
pedagogy, 87, 88, 79, 188, 192, 195, 257
Peer Assistance and Review (PAR), 98, 137, 251, 255
Pennsylvania, 289
personalized education. *See* individualized education
Petruzzi, Marco, 203, 247, 249, 259

Philadelphia, 24, 26, 36, 87, 167, 168,
169, 204, 224, 225, 240, 258
Phillips Andover Academy, 84, 178,
209, 249, 256
Pittsburgh, 150
Plano, 24, 32, 37, 56, 99, 189, 224, 241
politics, 15–19
Portfolio Management Model, 286
Portsmouth, 29, 43, 56, 106, 146, 169,
255, 266
poor, 126, 133, 146, 159–161, 283, 285,
286; frequent moves by, 126, 183. *See
also* hard-to-staff schools
practices of high-performing schools,
245, 253–259; assure regular
formative assessments, 256–257;
build robust data platforms, 256;
enhance collaboration, 254; expand
professional development, 255; give
teachers multiple roles, 256;
guarantee safe and civil schools,
259; institute aggressive
enrichments and interventions,
257–258; take curriculum seriously,
253–254
press, 30–31
Prince George's County, 147
principals, 4, 21, 43–62, 284; authority
of, 47, 48–49; defining job of, 46;
failure of, 50–51; firing of, 44, 50–52,
61, 144, 167; licensing requirements
for, 59–60; old-style, 43–44, 53;
outsourcing and, 48, 265; providing
resources for, 47–48;
recommendations for, 61–62;
recruiting of, 52–55, 61; salaries and
bonuses of, 49–50; staff hiring and,
47–48; superintendents and, 48–49,
61; teachers and, 76, 88, 96–97, 98,
120, 122, 250; tenure of, 51; training
of, 46–47, 55–61; twenty-first-
century, 44, 55–61; working with,
44–50; workloads of, 48
private schools, 52, 183, 249, 287
Pro Comp, 145
professional learning communities,
95–101, 134, 145–146, 147, 212, 254,
256
Promise Academies, 213, 232–233

Pueblo, 181
Public Agenda, 55, 142, 160, 161

Q Comp, 98, 125

race and racism, 179, 283
Race to the Top, 100, 122, 123, 145, 168,
213, 273, 276
Ravitch, Diane, 276
reading, 198, 257, 273
reconstitution, 144, 167
Reeves, Douglas, 211
Regent University, 56
Response to Intervention, 258
responsibility and authority, funding
and, 18, 269
Reuther, Walter, 11
Rhee, Michelle, 31, 36, 76, 86, 126, 134,
225, 255, 266
Rhyne, Amy, 211–212
Richards, Craig, 52, 53, 60
Ridgeway, Priscilla, 106, 113, 253
Rivera, Amanda, 86, 89, 122
Rochester, 160
Rogers, John, 84, 209, 210
Romer, Roy, ix, 31, 36, 38, 55
Roslyn, 249
Roza, Marguerite, 150

safety, 166, 259
St. Ignatius Loyola Academy, 143, 213,
228–229, 249, 256, 258
Sanders, William, 125, 127
San Diego, 25, 29, 32, 51, 87, 169, 255
Scholastic, Inc., 190, 211
school boards, 243, 284; responsibility
attributed to, 18; superintendents
and, 23, 28, 32, 37–38
school districts, 19, 242, 274; business
processes of, 164; central offices of,
250, 288; contributions to
community and education by,
248–249; decentralization of, 242,
284, 289, 289–290; ethics and,
266–267; future of, 286–290; human
resources departments of, 164; as
monopoly providers of education,
284, 289; new type of, 284–285; "no
excuses" attitudes in, 160–161, 225;

outsourcing by, 48, 265–266; political participation in, 18, 242–243, 284, 285; reasons for current failures in, 283–284; shared vision in, 32; size and shape of, 283; smaller, superintendents in, 29–30; teacher training and, 106–107, 115; urban, superintendents in, 30–31, 35; websites of, 241

schools: choice of, 242; length of day and year, 213–214; private, 52, 183, 249, 287; safety of, 166, 259; size of, 202–204, 285; voucher, 287, 288; websites of, 241. *See also* admissions; charter schools; funding

Scott, Teresa, 229

seniority, 11, 47, 97, 133–134, 136, 137, 165

Servite High School, 229–230, 231

Shanker, Albert, 12, 120

Simmons, John, 99, 266

Singapore, 99

Sizer, Ted, 178–179, 181, 188, 195, 215

social networking, 30

socioeconomic status, 247

Southwest Airlines, 144

special education. *See* learning disabilities and special education

Springston, Scott, 76, 146, 204, 222

Stand and Deliver, 221

Stanford University, 106

state governments, 18–19, 243, 269, 271–274; accountability and, 273; funding and, 271–273; teacher education and, 274; vision needed by, 274

State University of New York, 106

Steinhauser, Chris, 28, 48, 188, 222, 251

Strategic Learning Initiatives, 99

Stuckwisch, David, 43, 56, 106, 146, 169, 255

student achievement: in pay-for-performance schemes, xiv, 67, 119, 120, 137, 141, 142, 146–148, 149; as priority, 249–250; in teacher evaluation, 123–127, 135, 136, 137, 273

student motivation: difference between what schools say and do about, 225–226; examples of schools which promote, 226–233; funding and, 233, 234; parents and, 222–225; schools' attitude toward, 222–225

students, 4, 175, 195–204; assessment of, 209–217, 256–257; avoiding losing sight of, 177–183, 215, 221, 254; career technical education for, 197, 201–202; in de-tracked classrooms, 197–201, 202; grade system and, 178, 183, 195–196; headspace of, 6, 183, 196, 221–222; matching of teachers and, 198; mentors for, 183, 221, 225–226, 227, 231, 234; multiple intelligences and, 180, 191; in old days of education, 177–179; recommendations for, 215–217; school and class size and, 202–204, 285; teachers' expectations about, 159–161, 182–183, 247–248; tracking of, 197, 199, 201, 202. *See also* curriculum; individualized education; learning disabilities and special education; poor

student-teacher transaction, 6, 13

Stuyvesant High School, 182, 200

summer learning loss, 126, 214

summer school, 85

superintendents, 4, 21, 23–39, 284, 291; community and, 29; consensus building and, 33–34; and cycle of failure and the blame game, 26–27, 29, 30, 31; as education leaders, entrepreneurial managers, and political actors, 28, 33; expectations about, 24–25; job requirements of, 27–33; leadership teams built by, 27, 32–33; parental involvement and, 234; principals and, 48–49, 61; recommendations for, 39; responsibility attributed to, 18; as role models, 27, 32; school boards and, 23, 28, 32, 37–38; selection of, 23, 24–37; skills and traits needed in, 34–37; in smaller districts, 29–30; teachers and, 29, 121–122; top-down governance favored by, 32; trust and confidence built by, 27, 28–31; in urban districts, 30–31, 35; vision communicated by, 27, 32; written plans and, 28

Supreme Court, 15; *Brown v. Board of Education*, 179, 180

TAP (System for Teacher and Student Advancement), 98, 100, 146, 148

taxes, 15, 16, 17, 18, 165, 272, 285, 289, 291

teacher education and training, 83–90, 95, 96, 105–108, 163, 254; in alternative certification programs, 111–115; boot camp idea and, 85, 255; continuous, 70, 71, 75; districts and, 106–107, 115; district-university collaboration and, 107–108; expansion of, 255; in induction period, 77, 83–90, 255; mentors and, 86–87, 89, 97, 99, 149, 151, 255; professional learning communities and, 95–101, 134, 145–146, 147, 212, 254, 256; recommendations for, 89–90, 100–101, 115; state governments and, 274; undergraduate, inadequacy of, 105–106

Teacher Man (McCourt), 182

teachers, 4, 21, 67, 69–71; accountability of, 145, 146, 147; as administrators, 53, 256; benefits and pension plans for, 141; bidding on vacancies by, 165; bumping and, 11, 47–48, 165; collaboration and, 10, 46, 70, 71, 75, 87, 88, 89, 96, 98, 99, 143, 147, 149, 151, 191, 254; continued support needed by, 88–89; continuous improvement and, 5, 70–71, 75, 78, 96; contracts of, 11–12; consensus and, 34; disciplinary proceedings against, 135; evaluation of, 119–128, 135, 136, 136–137, 273; expectations about students, 159–161, 182–183, 247–248; firing of, 120, 133–134, 135, 141, 144, 165, 167; headspace of, 6, 78, 141, 144; hiring of, 47–48, 105; incompetent, 11, 12; as industrial workers vs. professionals, 9–13, 30, 97, 188; keeping and working with, 73–79; loose coupling and, 10, 98;

love of teaching in, 142; matching of students and, 198; as mentors for new teachers, 86–87, 89, 97, 99, 149, 151, 255; motivation for, 141–152, 159, 163; multiple roles for, 256; number needed per year, 74, 134; principals and, 76, 88, 96–97, 98, 120, 122, 250; recommendations for, 78–79, 89–90, 151–152; resignations of, 164–165; seniority of, 97, 133–134, 136, 137, 165; shortages of, 73, 74–75; social status of, 73; special education, 74, 78, 126, 149, 150; STEM, 74, 78, 149, 150; summer school and, 85; superintendents and, 29, 121–122; team building and, 144–145; tiers of quality of, 69–70, 83, 128, 134; trust and, 250–251; turnover problem with, 77–78; working conditions for, 74, 75–77, 78–79, 141. *See also* curriculum; hard-to-staff schools; tenure

teacher salaries, 11, 75–76, 77, 78–79, 89, 97, 141–152; hard-to-staff schools and, 167–169; pay-for-performance, xiv, 67, 119, 120, 137, 141, 142, 146–148, 149, 159, 160; salary cost averaging, 167–168; single salary pay structure, 149, 150

teacher-student transaction, 6, 13

Teachers Union Reform Network (TURN), 12, 98

teachers' unions, 11–12, 30, 134, 135, 136, 165, 273; learning communities and, 97; media and, 30, 31; trust and, 31

Teach for America (TFA), 113, 114–115

Tennessee, 56, 276

tenure, xiv, 11, 48, 67, 70, 83, 85, 119, 120, 133–138, 141, 160; of principals, 51; recommendations for, 137–138; teacher quality and, 135, 136, 136–137

Texas, 107, 112, 169, 241, 250; textbooks in, 192. *See also* Brazosport

textbooks, 178, 183, 188, 189, 191, 192

Third Creek Elementary School, 211–212

Thomas Jefferson Science High, 200

Time, 77
Tomlinson, Carol Ann, 211
total quality management (TQM), 5, 24, 28, 34, 35; data-driven decision making, 5, 46, 97, 251–252, 258. *See also* continuous improvement
Trice, Gwen, 262, 263
trust, 27, 28–31, 47, 250–251, 266–267, 273
tutoring, 214, 215, 258
21st Century Community Learning Centers, 214

United Auto Workers, 11
United Federation of Teachers, 11
University Community Academy, 198
University of California, Los Angeles, 200, 202, 210
University of California, Santa Cruz, 56, 86
Urban Superintendents Association, 10

Vallas, Paul, 36, 87, 96, 146, 200, 224, 265, 266, 285
value-added testing, 125, 127, 275
Velasco Elementary School, 44
Vermont, 16
violence, 166, 259
vision, 143–144
vocational education, 197, 201–202

vouchers, 287, 288

Walker, Adrian, 37
Walker, Lisa, 225
Warner Avenue Elementary, 169
Washington, D.C., 26, 31, 50, 76, 86, 137, 147, 166, 225, 239, 254; ethics and, 266; outsourcing in, 265, 266; Rhee in, 31, 36, 76, 86, 225, 255, 266
Washor, Elliott, 202
Wasley, Patricia, 150
Watauga County, 54, 210, 249, 256
wealth disparities, 210. *See also* poor
Weast, Jerry, 34, 52, 168, 196, 199, 248, 253, 276, 277
websites, school and district, 241
Weiner, David, 50, 144, 204
Weingarten, Randi, 11, 12, 135
Westchester, 76
Westwood, 169
"What I Learned at the Education Barricades" (Klein), 187
whole class instruction, 198
Williams, Brian, 221
Williams, Sam, 44, 143
Wilson, Chris, 229
Wisconsin, 56, 57

Zaldua, Michael, 224–225

About the Author

Harold Kwalwasser writes and consults on education policy. He is the former general counsel of the Los Angeles Unified School District, the second largest in the United States. He was a key part of a leadership team whose focus was building a modern twenty-first-century school system. Throughout the course of a long career in both the public and private sectors, he has analyzed why organizations succeed or fail, and has been a proponent for education reform as he travels the country speaking to parents, educators, and community leaders.

CPSIA information can be obtained at www.ICGtesting.com
Printed in the USA
BVOW020622180412

287902BV00002B/2/P

9 781610 486880